D1014726

ALSO BY DIANA B. HENRIQUES

The Wizard of Lies:
Bernie Madoff and the Death of Trust

The White Sharks of Wall Street:
Thomas Mellon Evans and the Original Corporate Raiders

Fidelity's World:
The Secret Life and Public Power of the Mutual Fund Giant

The Machinery of Greed:
Public Authority Abuse and What to Do About It

A FIRST-CLASS CATASTROPHE

A FIRST-CLASS CATASTROPHE

THE ROAD TO BLACK MONDAY,
THE WORST DAY IN WALL STREET HISTORY

DIANA B. HENRIQUES

A NEW YORK TIMES BOOK | HENRY HOLT AND COMPANY | NEW YORK

Publishers since 1866
175 Fifth Avenue
New York, New York 10010
www.henryholt.com

Henry Holt® and ® are registered trademarks of
Macmillan Publishing Group, LLC.

Library of Congress Cataloging-in-Publication Data

Names: Henriques, Diana B., author.
Title: A first-class catastrophe : the road to Black Monday, the worst day in
  Wall Street history / Diana B. Henriques.
Description: First edition. | New York : Henry Holt and Company, [2017]
  | Includes bibliographical references and index.
Identifiers: LCCN 2017002890| ISBN 9781627791649 (hardcover)
  | ISBN 9781627791656 (electronic book)
Subjects: LCSH: Stock Market Crash, 1987. | Financial crises—United
  States—History—20th century. | Stock exchanges—United
  States—History—20th century. | Finance—United States—History
  —20th century.
Classification: LCC HG4551 .H425 2017 | DDC 332.64/273—dc23
LC record available at https://lccn.loc.gov/2017002890

ISBN: 9781627791649

Our books may be purchased in bulk for promotional, educational, or business use. Please
contact your local bookseller or the Macmillan Corporate and Premium Sales Department at
(800) 221-7945, extension 5442, or by e-mail at MacmillanSpecialMarkets@macmillan.com.

Designed by Kelly S. Too

Printed in the United States of America

3 5 7 9 10 8 6 4 2

For Floyd Norris

admired colleague, trusted mentor, cherished friend

CONTENTS

CAST OF CHARACTERS

WASHINGTON

BANK REGULATORS AND WHITE HOUSE OFFICIALS

Howard H. Baker Jr., White House chief of staff (1987–88)

James A. Baker III, White House chief of staff (1981–85) and secretary of the Treasury (1985–88)

Nicholas F. Brady, chairman of the Presidential Task Force on Market Mechanisms (1987–88) and secretary of the Treasury (1988–93)

C. Todd Conover, comptroller of the currency, an independent official within the Treasury Department (1981–85)

E. Gerald Corrigan, vice president of the Federal Reserve Bank of New York and special assistant to New York Fed President Paul Volcker (1976–80), president of the Federal Reserve Bank of Minneapolis (1980–84), and president of the Federal Reserve Bank of New York (1985–93)

Alan Greenspan, chairman of the Federal Reserve System from August 1987 to January 2006

William M. Isaac, chairman of the Federal Deposit Insurance Corporation (1981–85)

Donald T. Regan, secretary of the Treasury (1981–85) and White House chief of staff (1985–87)

Paul A. Volcker, president of the Federal Reserve Bank of New York (1975–79) and chairman of the Federal Reserve System (1979–87)

STOCK MARKET REGULATORS

Richard G. Ketchum, director of market regulation at the U.S. Securities and Exchange Commission (1983–91)

David S. Ruder, chairman of the SEC (1987–89) and former dean of the Northwestern University School of Law

John S. R. Shad, chairman of the SEC (1981–87) and the former vice chairman of E.F. Hutton and Co.

Harold M. Williams, chairman of the SEC (1977–81)

FUTURES MARKET REGULATORS

Wendy Gramm, chairman of the Commodity Futures Trading Commission (1988–93)

Kalo A. Hineman, acting chairman of the CFTC (1987–88)

Philip Johnson, chairman of the CFTC (1981–83) and longtime legal counsel to the Chicago Board of Trade

Susan M. Phillips, a CFTC commissioner (1981–83) and chairman of the CFTC (1983–87)

James M. Stone, chairman of the CFTC (1979–81) and a CFTC commissioner (1981–83)

WALL STREET

W. Gordon Binns Jr., investment manager for the General Motors pension fund (1981–94)

Robert J. Birnbaum, president of the American Stock Exchange (1977–85) and president of the New York Stock Exchange (1985–88)

Roland M. Machold, director of the New Jersey Division of Investment and manager of the state's pension funds (1976–98)

John J. Phelan Jr., vice chairman of the NYSE (1975–80), NYSE president (1980–84), and NYSE chairman and CEO (1984–91)

CHICAGO

William J. Brodsky, executive vice president and chief operating officer of the Chicago Mercantile Exchange (1982–85), and president of the Merc (1985–96)

Leo Melamed, chairman of the Chicago Mercantile Exchange (1969–73, 1976–77), special counsel to the Merc (1977–85), and chairman of the Merc executive committee (1985–91)

Richard L. Sandor, chief economist and vice president of the Chicago Board of Trade (1972–75), and a former business school professor at the University of California at Berkeley

BERKELEY

Hayne E. Leland, a Harvard-educated economist who joined the business school faculty at the University of California at Berkeley in 1974

John O'Brien, a founding partner, with Leland and Mark Rubinstein, of Leland O'Brien Rubinstein Associates and its chief executive (1981–97)

Mark Rubinstein, an options pricing theorist and finance professor who joined the business school faculty at the University of California at Berkeley in 1972

R. Steven Wunsch, a vice president at Kidder Peabody in the 1980s, specializing in derivatives, and an informal adviser to LOR Associates

AUTHOR'S NOTE

It is difficult to convey to a modern audience the emotional impact of the stock market's gyrations in the 1980s, or indeed in any distant decade, because the most popular measures of market value have grown so much in the intervening years.

For example, on the worst day of the 1929 crash, the Dow Jones Industrial Average lost about 38 points, an insignificant move in modern markets. But on that day, the Dow had opened at just under 300 points, so that 38-point drop represented an unprecedented 12.8 percent decline. That record stood until the crash of 1987.

Similarly, the Dow's daily point swings in this story may sound unremarkable at a time when the index is calculated in five digits. At this writing in early 2017, the Dow has surpassed 20,000 points, but for much of the early 1980s, the index hovered between 1,000 and 1,500 points. To feel the modern punch of the market's gyrations in those years, double the long-ago Dow points and add a zero—thus, a loss of just 50 points back in early 1981 would be roughly equal to a 1,000-point drop in early 2017. For Dow point changes for the years after January 1987, when the index hit 2,000 points for the first time, just add a zero to the older figure—thus, a 100-point drop in late 1987 loomed as large as a 1,000-point drop today. This rule of thumb, while not precise, will give some sense of how people in the 1980s perceived the market's historic moves. Of course, the percentage changes can provide a more exact comparison.

Time also has blurred the scale of monetary sums cited in this story. To get a general sense of the modern magnitude of those figures, triple the dollar amounts before 1985 and, thanks to declining inflation, double the dollar amounts after 1985.

A FIRST-CLASS CATASTROPHE

PROLOGUE

On that historic autumn Monday, it seemed possible that the entire American financial system would crack apart. The next day, it seemed certain that it would.

The storm had not come out of a cloudless sky. There had been years of heedless expansion, months of growing anxiety, weeks of looming trouble and fading options. Then, Monday dawned—a day so terrifying that those uneasy months and weeks seemed placid by comparison.

Global markets teetered. High-speed computer trading, driven by mathematical models, outran the pace of mere humans. Poorly understood derivatives set off depth charges everywhere, revealing hidden links that bound together the banks, insurers, giant investors, and big brokerage firms that populated Wall Street. Those connections stretched across all the regulatory borders that rival government agencies defended so fiercely. At the edge of the cliff, some questionably legal steps saved a key firm from collapse, a failure that would have tipped a crisis into a catastrophe.

For many, this chronology instantly calls to mind the financial meltdown that erupted on Monday, September 15, 2008, with the collapse of the Lehman Brothers brokerage firm. The day after "Lehman Monday," the U.S. Treasury Department and the Federal Reserve were fighting frantically to rescue the massive insurance firm AIG, which neither agency officially regulated but which was linked to other giant firms around the world through a set of financial derivatives called "credit default swaps." Those events triggered widespread panic that eclipsed almost anything the markets had seen since 1929.

Almost anything. Because the events just described, the events at the core of this story, did not happen in the harrowing weeks of September 2008. They happened on October 19, 1987, a day almost immediately dubbed "Black Monday."

On that single day, the Dow Jones Industrial Average, the pulse rate of the most prominent stock market in the world, fell a heart-stopping 22.6 percent, still the largest one-day decline in Wall Street history. That was the equivalent of an urgent midafternoon news flash today screaming, "DOW FALLS NEARLY 5,000 POINTS!"

A one-day decline of 22.6 percent is almost unthinkable for us now. It was *truly* unthinkable for the men and women of 1987. We can look back on their experience, but when they looked back, they saw nothing that remotely resembled Black Monday—not during the Great Depression, not when America went to war, not even after a presidential assassination. Until 1987, a very bad day in the stock market meant a decline of 4 or 5 percent. A horrible day meant a drop of 10 or 11 percent, a figure exceeded only during the historic crash of 1929. Then, on Black Monday, the unthinkable suddenly became the unforgettable, a market crash so steep and so fast it seemed that the entire financial system would simply shake apart like an airplane plunging to earth.

On that day, the new toys of Wall Street, derivatives and computer-assisted trading, fed a justifiable fear that an overdue market downturn would become an uncontrollable meltdown. The avalanche of selling briefly halted a key Chicago market and came within minutes of officially shutting down the New York Stock Exchange. Hong Kong closed its markets for a week. Tokyo and London, financial centers almost on a par with New York, were battered. Aftershocks hit days, weeks, and even months later. It took two years for the market to climb back to its 1987 peak.

Black Monday was the product of profound but poorly understood changes in the shape of the marketplace over the previous decade.

Wall Street (shorthand for the nation's entire financial industry) had become a place striving to get both bigger and broader, seeking profit in as many diverse markets as possible. Meanwhile, Wall Street's clients had undergone a staggering mutation: they were exponentially larger and more demanding, and they became far more homogenized, subscribing confidently to academic theories that led giant herds of investors to pursue the same strategies at the same time with vast amounts of money.

As a result of these two structural changes, government regulators in Washington faced a new world where, time and again, a financial crisis would suddenly become contagious. Thanks to giant diversified firms and giant diversifying investors, a failure in one regulator's market could spread like a wind-borne plague and infect those overseen by other regulators. After years of these outbreaks, Black Monday was the contagious crisis that the system nearly didn't survive.

AS DRAMATIC AND unprecedented as it was, Black Monday would become the Cassandra of market crashes—a vivid warning about critical and permanent changes in the financial landscape, but a warning that has been persistently ignored for decades.

As the events of 1987 receded into the past, its lessons were lost. Myth quickly replaced memory, and Black Monday, if it was remembered at all, was recalled as the crash without consequences. By the end of the decade, a broken market appeared to have magically repaired itself and then marched into a rich, less-regulated future. The subsequent prosperity, which rarely faltered through the 1990s, seemed to be proof that nothing really important had happened on that October day.

Yet, when the mythology is stripped away, it is not at all surprising that Black Monday and the 2008 crisis sound so much alike. All the key fault lines that trembled in 2008—breakneck automation, poorly understood financial products fueled by vast amounts of borrowed money, fragmented regulation, gigantic herdlike investors—were first exposed as hazards in 1987.

It is not an overstatement to say that Black Monday was the first modern market crash, the first to spotlight these fundamentally new risks. Most previous crashes, including 1929, essentially resembled one another, from the Dutch tulip bulb mania in the late 1600s, to the collapse of London's South Sea Company in the early eighteenth century, to the "air pocket" drop that shook the U.S. stock market in late May 1962. Black Monday was a new kind of crisis, involving new players and new financial products never before involved in a stock market crash.

Today's most dangerous crises, the ones that threaten the very survival of the financial system, are not modern-dress reenactments of the "tulip mania" bubble in old Amsterdam. They are warp-speed flash-backs to Black Monday.

TO CALL THE events that unfold in this book "the stock market crash of 1987" is a misnomer. The crash wasn't limited to the stock market, and it didn't erupt suddenly on Monday, October 19. To fully understand the causes and consequences of that devastating day, we have to begin the story nearly eight years earlier, in the first months of 1980, when Jimmy Carter was in the White House, powerful computer-driven investment strategies were a mystery to most of Wall Street, and politicians and bureaucrats had an unshakable faith in rigid regulatory borders.

As the curtain rises on this tale, there is a palpable sense that uncontrolled market panics have been relegated to history's dustbin. There had been a deep, drawn-out bear market in the mid-1970s, but the nation had not seen a sudden cataclysmic crash since 1929, and most of the people who had experienced that crash as adults were retired or dead. The market regulatory structure that had emerged from the rubble of 1929, with the Securities and Exchange Commission as its cornerstone, had stood solid and unshaken for almost fifty years. Familiar and respected, it seemed an immutable part of the political landscape.

In 1980, each separate colony of finance, whether it dealt with farm commodities or corporate stocks or life insurance or bank deposits, expected to deal with problems on its own turf in its own way, without regard to its neighbors. Financial storms were isolated events—if a major company failed, the stock market coped; if a bank got into trouble, the Federal Deposit Insurance Corporation stepped in; if an insurer faltered, some state regulator would take action. None of these events seemed to pose a threat to the financial system as a whole; indeed, they were barely felt in the neighboring precincts of the marketplace.

That vision of reality was already a dangerous delusion by 1980. Indeed, if October 1987 was a runaway train, its victims should have seen it coming. In a roiling escalation of unfamiliar crises that began in 1980, the financial system experienced a shoot-out in the commodities market that ricocheted off several banks and brokerage firms, a high-speed cash hemorrhage at one of the nation's largest banks, outbreaks of fraud in the bond market that triggered panicky runs on a host of other banks, a computer mishap that nearly brought the Treasury bond market to a standstill, and a worsening epidemic of closing bell nosedives that traumatized the stock market.

In short, the nation's malfunctioning financial machinery had been jolting toward disaster since the dawn of the decade. By rights, that disaster, when it finally came, should have been called "the Crash of the Eighties."

And the journey toward that crash began with two eccentric oilmen from Texas who had developed an unlimited appetite for silver.

PART ONE

VANISHING BORDERS

SILVER THURSDAY

He was a towering six foot seven, his round, balding head perpetually wreathed in cigar smoke. Paul A. Volcker, the chairman of the Federal Reserve System, was formidable even when he was cheerful. On Wednesday afternoon, March 26, 1980, he was furious.

Volcker, in office for barely seven months, had been pulled out of a meeting by a frantic message from Harry Jacobs, the chairman of Bache Halsey Stuart Shields, the second-largest brokerage firm on Wall Street. The Fed had almost no authority over brokerage firms, but Jacobs said he thought "it was in the national interest" that he alert Volcker to a crisis in the silver market—a market over which the Fed also had virtually no authority.

Jacobs's news was alarming. Silver prices were plummeting, and two of the firm's biggest customers, a pair of billionaire brothers in Texas named William Herbert and Nelson Bunker Hunt, had told him the previous evening that they could not cover a $100 million debit in their Bache accounts, which they had used to amass millions of ounces of actual silver and paper claims on millions more. If silver prices fell further and the Hunts did indeed default on their debt to the firm, the silver they had pledged as collateral was no longer worth enough to cover their obligations. Bache was confronting a ruinous loss, possibly a threat to its financial survival. Jacobs suspected the Hunts also owed money to other major banks and Wall Street firms and may well have pledged more of their silver hoard as collateral.

Volcker immediately wanted to know which banks had made loans to the Hunts. He didn't regulate Wall Street brokers or silver speculators, but he emphatically did regulate much of the nation's banking system. There, at least, his authority to act was clear.

Indeed, Volcker had been responding to fire alarms in the banking system for weeks, as banks and savings and loans struggled with rising interest rates—themselves a consequence of Volcker's attack on the raging inflation that had sapped the economy for nearly a decade. Confidence in America's banks was as fragile as blown glass, and the last thing Volcker needed was a "bolt from the blue" like this. Yet, here was the head of Wall Street's number-two firm warning him that some big banks were financing what sounded like wildly speculative silver trading by a couple of Texas plutocrats.

Within minutes, Volcker had reached out to Harold Williams, the urbane and seasoned chairman of the Securities and Exchange Commission, the primary U.S. government regulator of Bache and its fellow brokerage firms. Williams was at a conference in Colonial Williamsburg; he ducked into a side room, spoke with Volcker about Bache, and then phoned to tell his staffers to check immediately on the rest of Wall Street's exposure to the silver speculators. Williams then hurried back to Washington. A senior Treasury Department official and the comptroller of the currency (another bank regulator) were also alerted to the potential crisis. Both headed for the Fed's headquarters on Constitution Avenue. Together, perhaps they could cover all the financial corners of this unfamiliar crisis.

To do that, the group needed a regulator with some authority over the silver markets. Volcker called the office of James M. Stone, who had been tapped less than a year earlier by President Jimmy Carter to be the chairman of the Commodity Futures Trading Commission, a young federal agency that regulated the market where most of this silver speculation had gone on.

At age thirty-two, Jim Stone—a cousin of the notable filmmaker Oliver Stone—had already studied at the London School of Economics and earned a doctorate in economics from Harvard. His doctoral thesis had been published as a prescient book predicting how computers would revolutionize Wall Street trading, first by doing the paperwork but ultimately by sweeping away the traditional stock exchanges entirely. Stone was a slight, brilliant, and determined young man, but his view that regulation played a positive role in the markets made him deeply unpopular in the industry he regulated and put him at odds with his more laissez-faire CFTC colleagues. One grumpy board member at a leading Chicago commodity exchange privately dismissed him as a "little twerp." Almost everyone in political circles (except Volcker, apparently) knew that young Dr. Stone had become so isolated at the CFTC that he could barely get support for approving the minutes of the last meeting.

When Volcker got Stone on the phone, his question was similar to the one he had asked Harold Williams at the SEC: how big a stake did the Hunt brothers have in his market?

"I can't tell you that. It's confidential," Stone said.

The politely delivered answer stopped Volcker cold; he was momentarily speechless. Then he let loose.

Volcker conceded later that he "did not react very well" to Stone's refusal to share the vital information, even after the CFTC chairman explained that a law passed in 1978 barred his agency from revealing customer trading positions, even to other regulators. Stone simply did not have the authority to comply with the Fed chairman's request.

Stone, like Volcker, instantly saw that the silver crisis was a danger to the financial system because of the hidden web of loans that linked the banks and the brokerage firms to the Hunts and to one another. He promptly headed for Volcker's office. Sometime later, the SEC's Harold Williams arrived. Aides shuttled in and out, working the telephones, checking silver prices, and pressing bankers and brokerage finance officers for straight answers.

By 6 p.m., as twilight filled the deep, high windows of Volcker's office, the ad hoc group had finally established that at least a half-dozen major Wall Street firms, including Merrill Lynch and Paine Webber, had set up trading accounts for the Hunts and that a number of major banks had been lending money to those firms, or directly to the Hunts, since at least the previous summer, transactions secured by a growing pile of rapidly depreciating silver.

Eight months earlier, on August 1, 1979, silver was trading below $10 an ounce. Prices rose through Labor Day, past Thanksgiving, and into the Christmas holidays. At $20 an ounce, silver had broken out of its traditional ratio to gold. At $30 an ounce, the sky-high price prompted newlyweds to sell their sterling flatware before burglars could steal it. Printers and film manufacturers, which used silver as a raw material, started laying off workers and feared bankruptcy. Through it all, the Hunts kept buying, largely with borrowed money.

Then, on January 17, 1980, silver prices paused at $50 an ounce and started to slide. At that point, the Hunts' hoard was worth $6.6 billion. After that date, prices dropped sharply; they had fallen to $10.80 on Tuesday, March 25, the day before Harry Jacobs at Bache called Volcker. At that price, the Hunts owed far more than their silver would fetch in the cash market, and their lenders were pressing for more collateral of some kind.

It was on that Tuesday evening that the brothers told Jacobs they were unable to pay anything more. The next day, they shared the same unwelcome news with their other brokers. Crisis had arrived, and panic might quickly follow if a big bank or brokerage firm failed as a result of the Hunts' default.

That's where Paul Volcker stepped into the story. After their Wednesday war room conference, held together more by personality and mutual respect than by any clear lines of authority, Volcker and his fellow regulators sweated out Thursday's trading day. Stone, in defiance of the CFTC's legislative restrictions, had finally given his fellow regulators an estimate of how much money the Hunts owed in his market: $800 million. That figure, which turned out to be an understatement, was so staggering it prompted the shocked bank regulators immediately to order examiners to visit various vaults to be sure that the Hunt brothers hadn't pledged the same silver to multiple lenders.

By Thursday, the rest of Wall Street had gotten wind of the silver crisis, and the stock market had a wild day. The Dow Jones Industrial Average fell by as much 3.5 percent before stabilizing, as traders reacted

brothers, secured largely by the family oil company. The l
allow them to pay their staggering debts on Wall Street.

Monday morning, with the bankers still working on the fin
im Stone of the CFTC took a seat at a huge, microphone-studded
ence table in a House of Representatives hearing room on Capitol
lso summoned to the hearing were Harold Williams of the SEC
enior Treasury official involved in the crisis.

subcommittee chairman was a veteran New York Democrat
Benjamin Rosenthal, and he was as angry as Volcker had been
ys earlier. "We are deeply concerned that the activities of a hand-
commodity speculators could have such a profound effect on our
's financial markets," he said in his opening remarks.

at was especially new and scary was that the crisis involved comes markets, banks, brokerage houses, the stock market, and even
business, the source of the Hunt brothers' wealth. Rosenthal
ded to know if there had been sufficient coordination among the
the SEC, the Treasury, the Office of the Comptroller of the Cur-
and the Federal Reserve.

worrisome response: Maybe not. But the improvised effort (and
ky rebound in silver prices) had prevented a series of domino
ts, and the regulators promised to do better if they ever faced a
ly messy crisis again.

ly in the hearing, Stone was asked for details about the Hunts'
oldings.

annot discuss position information," Stone replied, in a frustrated
f his answer to Volcker. "That is forbidden by Congress."

re knowledgeable about the ban than Volcker had been, Rosenthal
d back, "You are forbidden to make it public. It is not forbidden
it to Congress."

is *not* forbidden to give it to Congress," Stone conceded, a bit
rdly. "Our commission has voted—with myself in the minority,
t add—to do that only upon subpoena."

senthal held tense, hurried consultations with staff aides. The
was not under the control of Rosenthal's subcommittee; the com-
n was supervised by the House and Senate agriculture committees,
e of its importance to the producers and users of farm commodities

to rumors that the Hunts and some of theii
stocks to raise desperately needed cash.

Of course, it is true that every share of
bought—by someone, at some price. When fa
than to buy, prices have to drop sharply befoi
a few shares. The term *heavy selling*, then, mea
only at increasingly lower prices—not that e
one is buying.

With that caveat, "heavy selling" is what h;
ket reacted to fears of a default by the Hunt l
veteran said that Thursday's trading reminde
sponse to President John F. Kennedy's assassir
official called the leadership at the New York Stc
that day to assess how it was faring in the storr
and on Wall Street was that the Hunts' faili
would mean that those creditors would def
spreading the contagion.

Infusions of cash by the owners of the mos
houses prevented an immediate disaster, bu
one really knew where all the fault lines ran
had before the next aftershock. The silver cri
the country, and "Silver Thursday" entered \
bad days.

By Friday, March 28, the price of silver ha
crisis seemed to have eased, but the Hunts stil
of money. By Sunday afternoon, March 30, it \
able to pay it unless someone lent them the
crazy dilemma, but one where Volcker's autl
chairman looked at the widening cracks in th
dation. He considered the pressure that ano
interest rates would put on the banking indu;
ure would impair the Fed's fight against inflat
stood watchfully on the sidelines as a team of
attending an industry convention in Boca R
through Sunday night over the terms of a nev

Hunt
would

Or
print,
confe)
Hill. :
and a

Th
name
five d;
ful of
natior

W
modit
the oi
dema;
CFTC
rency,

Th
the lu
defau
simila

Ea
silver

"I
echo

M
snapf
to giv

"I
awkw
I mig

R
CFTC
missi
becai

such as wheat, pork bellies, and soybeans. "We're going to deal with that as a separate issue," Rosenthal said. It was apparent that the chain of command in Congress was as tangled as it was among regulators.

A few moments later, Rosenthal observed that Stone had voted against many of the CFTC decisions in the silver matter. "The majority of the commission seems to be going down one road and you seem to be going down another road," he said.

"There are certainly differences in philosophy," Stone answered. "My philosophy tends to hold that where these markets affect the financial fabric of the United States, more regulation is needed. That is the case even if these markets do not in themselves pose substantial dangers." He added, "I do not think that is the majority view of the commission."

Indeed, the majority of the CFTC had done little to forestall the unfolding silver crisis except to "jawbone" the exchanges where the Hunts were trading, urging them to use their "self-regulatory" power to do something.

"The market, in a very real sense, cured itself," one CFTC commissioner proudly testified. He and another commissioner stoutly denied that this uproar in their markets posed any threat to the nation's financial health.

Then it was Harold Williams's turn as a witness.

The SEC chairman was asked about concerns he had expressed at previous hearings about the "efficacy" of the CFTC. "I would say we have more concern today than we did last Tuesday—significantly more," he answered.

From then on, as Stone sat silently at the table, the SEC chairman and, later, the deputy Treasury secretary who worked on the silver crisis rehashed the jurisdictional warfare that had beset the CFTC from the moment it was born. It was a discussion that would become numbingly familiar in the years to come.

THE CREATION OF the Commodity Futures Trading Commission in 1974 was initially resisted by the exchanges it was supposed to regulate, especially the two largest futures markets, the Chicago Board of Trade and the Chicago Mercantile Exchange. Those exchanges, whose informal motto was "Free markets for free men," were each more than one hundred years old, and they had long resented any meddling in their own regulation of their trading floors. They had bowed to the CFTC only because they had played a sizable role in drafting the statute that created it, a law that would confound judges and frustrate other regulatory agencies for decades.

At the time of the silver crisis, most Americans had no idea what the "futures markets" centered in Chicago actually did.

Here's what they did, and still do: they allow buyers and sellers of all sorts of things to protect themselves from damaging price changes. Here's what else they do: they give the traders who stand between those buyers and sellers a chance to profit from those same price swings. The financial instruments that shift the price risk (to those who are willing to bear it, from those who aren't) are called futures contracts. In Chicago, they are universally known just as "futures," as in "they bought silver futures" or "he trades wheat futures."

In 1980, when market news in the newspapers and on television focused almost exclusively on blue-chip stocks, futures seemed dauntingly complex. To some degree, the Chicago markets had encouraged the idea that futures were far too complicated for the average regulatory and congressional brain to comprehend. In reality, nobody needs to master how futures contracts work to understand the role they play in this story, but some basic details will help to explain why the futures markets exist. Futures are simply standardized contracts to buy or sell a fixed amount of something, at a fixed price per unit, on a fixed date in the future. Traditionally, that "something" had been something you could eat, such as corn, wheat, or pork bellies, or something you could at least touch, such as oil or silver. Businesses that produce those things and businesses that use them as raw materials rely on the futures markets to protect against adverse price swings.

For example, here's how a wheat farmer could use futures to lock in a price for the crop he has just planted: Imagine the farmer expects to harvest 5,000 bushels of wheat and, to stay in business, he must get $3.50 a bushel for his crop, for a total income of $17,500. To guarantee that he gets that payday, he can sell a futures contract covering 5,000 bushels of wheat to be delivered in six months at a price of $3.50 a bushel.

(The buyer of the contract could be a cereal company that wants to lock in the price it will have to pay for the next wheat harvest.) By selling the contract, the farmer makes $17,500—the same amount he needs to get at harvest. If the price of wheat then falls to $3 a bushel, his crop will fetch only $15,000. However, the farmer can now buy the futures contract back for just $15,000, closing out his position at a profit of $2,500. So his total income is $17,500—that is, $15,000 for his crop and a $2,500 profit on his futures trade. In effect, he got $3.50 a bushel, just as he'd hoped, even though wheat prices fell. The same arithmetic works in reverse: if wheat prices had gone up to $4 a bushel, the farmer would have gotten $20,000 for his crop and lost $2,500 on his futures trade— which still works out to $3.50 per bushel. (Yes, in the latter case he'd have gotten more money if he hadn't hedged, but he opted to lock in a necessary profit rather than gamble between a windfall and a ruinous loss.)

The utility of futures contracts to farmers and cereal companies is obvious. However, the driving fact about those contracts is that they can be traded like baseball cards. That fact was the lifeblood of the giant Chicago futures exchanges, and about a dozen smaller futures exchanges around the country.

And the vast majority of futures contracts *are* traded: they are bought and sold, in pursuit of profit, by traders who have no intention of delivering or collecting the underlying commodity. Traders who sell futures contracts to grain companies, or buy them from farmers, are called speculators. Their goal is to profit from the same constantly fluctuating prices those hedgers want to avoid.

There is a long and ignorant tradition in America, especially in Congress, of blessing hedgers but denouncing speculators, who are blamed when consumers face higher prices for bread or gasoline, or when farmers cannot profit from their harvests. The fact is that you simply cannot run a marketplace without both hedgers and speculators. Speculators expand the community of traders ready to deal with the market's hedgers, and they are willing to trade when wild price fluctuations might send the timid hedgers to the sidelines.

That is another essential fact to remember about commodity markets: luckily for the hedgers, speculators in those markets thrive on fluctuating prices. They relish price volatility—the wilder the roller-coaster ride, the more money they can make. Stock market investors might prefer small, steady price ticks—upward, preferably, but nothing too dramatic either way. But calm seas are unwelcome among futures traders. Stormy markets are their reason for being. If markets were quiet and predictable, nobody would bother to hedge and nobody could make any money speculating.

This tolerance for volatility was hardwired into the minds of the speculators who, by and large, were the people running the Chicago markets that the CFTC was struggling to regulate.

THE FUTURES CONTRACTS that really worried the SEC's Harold Williams and his fellow financial regulators had nothing to do with tangible commodities such as wheat or corn or even silver. These regulators were worried about "financial futures," newly designed contracts based on the shifting prices of intangible assets in the world's financial markets.

The Treasury and the Fed were fretting about futures based on government bonds; the SEC was concerned about futures based on mortgage-backed securities and (still on the drawing board) futures based on major stock market barometers such as the Value Line index or the Dow Jones Industrial Average. The basis for all these fears was that these new futures contracts would somehow damage the markets that had long set the prices of stocks and bonds—the cash markets. Regulators of those cash markets feared that the speculative, freewheeling futures market would gradually usurp the power to set prices. That, in turn, could distort the way capital flowed through the stock market to finance the American economy. America's ability to sell the Treasury bonds that covered its budget deficits could be affected. The Fed's power to influence interest rates, which influenced inflation, could wane.

In the fight over financial futures, Jim Stone was clearly the odd man out at the CFTC. Just days before the silver crisis, he was dressed down at a public meeting by another commissioner merely for questioning whether futures based on the Value Line index, proposed by the Kansas City Board of Trade, would serve any useful economic purpose.

"Why not a futures contract for people who buy lottery tickets in New Hampshire?" Stone asked at the meeting. He couldn't see what possible purpose a "stock index futures contract" could have except to gamble on the stock market without having to put up as much cash as it would take to place the same bet on the New York Stock Exchange.

That was for the market to decide, Stone's challenger insisted. He went on to deplore the agency's "inexcusable delay" in acting on the Value Line proposal, blaming it on "fear of the Fed, the Treasury and the SEC."

There were other stock index futures proposals being developed, along with a host of other innovative futures contracts based on everything from bank certificates of deposit to "Eurodollars," American currency held in overseas accounts. Other commissioners saw these new products as a boon to the Chicago markets, but Stone profoundly disagreed—and, unlike his colleagues, he was willing to listen to the concerns expressed by other regulators. Still, he was only one vote, and a Democratic vote, at that. In 1980 his tenure as chairman was only as firm as President Carter's grip on the White House.

— 2 —

BRIGHT IDEAS

Silver Thursday was still a week away when Ronald Reagan, starting to surge in the Republican presidential primaries, visited the New York Stock Exchange on March 19, 1980. With the casual grace of a leading man, Reagan strode toward the exchange entrance at 11 Wall Street, his tan trench coat draped over his shoulders, his dark hair coiffed and shiny. His personal glamour overshadowed the rumpled, unpretentious man who had arranged the campaign visit: John S. R. Shad, the vice chairman of E.F. Hutton and Co.

John Shad, at age fifty-seven, was a portly, affable-looking man with glasses, outsize earlobes, a sagging jawline, and a receding hairline. He had first met Reagan two years earlier, when a fellow Hutton executive invited Shad to the Bohemian Grove, a secretive summer retreat for powerful and wealthy men, located in the redwood forests north of San Francisco. Shad had recently lost a bitter battle for the chairman's spot at the firm and had settled into an uneasy accommodation with the new leadership. He was a smart man, full of intellectual curiosity. A navy veteran, he had earned an MBA from Harvard on the GI Bill, and more or less for the mental exercise, he and his wife Pat had earned law degrees together at New York University while he worked his way up at Hutton.

When Reagan announced his presidential bid, Shad agreed to head up his New York campaign, and this high-profile visit to the NYSE was one result. After a tour of the crowded, paper-strewn trading floor, they took elevators up to the exchange's luncheon club, a wood-trimmed haven staffed by white-coated waiters who relished stock tips more than the traditional kind. Never comfortable in front of a microphone, Shad mumbled the obligatory introduction: "Ladies and gentlemen, I present to you the next president of the United States."

Later that summer, Shad arranged for Reagan to meet privately with some of New York's business elite, and campaign donations followed. As one of Reagan's earliest Wall Street supporters, Shad could hope for some role in a Reagan administration, which would lessen some of the sting from losing out on the Hutton chairmanship. His ambition came with certain costs; his Wall Street paycheck was ten times what he would make in Washington, and his complex investment portfolio would have to be unwound. Still, he remained interested in public service.

Reagan won the Republican nomination and was pitted against the incumbent president, Jimmy Carter, whose reelection hopes were shadowed by the intractable inflation that had plagued him and his two predecessors and by his own failed efforts to free the Americans held hostage for months in revolutionary Iran. Negotiations for the hostages' release were dragging on fruitlessly. On the inflation front, however, Carter had already taken a key step toward victory by tapping Paul Volcker as the new Fed chairman, the steward of the nation's monetary policy. Unfortunately, Volcker's progress against inflation had come at the expense of the economy, leaving Carter to run for reelection during a slump that gave ammunition to his adversary.

When Volcker was sworn in as Fed chairman in August 1979, most adults had grown up in an era when inflation was normally about 3 percent a year. By that measure, inflation had not been "normal" since 1966. A month after Volcker took office, inflation reached an annual rate of 12.2 percent, despite fairly anemic business activity. The time-tested medicine for high inflation was to raise interest rates, but higher rates were poison to a stagnant economy. Volcker believed the corrosive effect of inflation was a bigger long-term threat to working families than the fallout from high interest rates, and Carter supported him. The Fed let interest rates rise sharply, the bond market fell into turmoil, the stock market was leery, and the economy slumped—just as the 1980 presidential campaign began.

Wall Street was deeply worried, and Carter wasn't saying much that was reassuring.

Reagan was. His sunny optimism sweetened his more draconian attacks on government bureaucracy. Regulatory constraints on business, ranging from antipollution rules at the Environmental Protection Agency to corporate bribery investigations by the SEC, were a prominent target in his speeches. Reagan's goal of cutting taxes and red tape was immensely popular in the business community. As Carter had already acknowledged, the federal government had enacted a lot of unnecessary rules in the early postwar years, when American businesses and banks faced little foreign competition—rules that were now a burden in an increasingly global business environment. One Reagan supporter suggested that his campaign invite major business lobbying groups to submit their ten most ill-conceived regulations for inclusion "on a 'hit list' much like the FBI's 10 Most Wanted List."

If the leaders at the Chicago futures exchanges had been surveyed in that effort, just about everything the CFTC did would have wound up on the list. Their most immediate complaint was Jim Stone's dug-in opposition to the new financial futures pending before the commission. Financial futures promised to become a gold mine for the Chicago futures exchanges, and innovators there, who believed these new products also would be a real benefit to American businesses, were impatient to get their new ideas to market.

AT THE HEAD of the army of frustrated Chicago traders stood a brilliant force of nature named Leo Melamed.

Born Leo Melamdovich in Poland in 1932, Melamed was a human dynamo with coal-black hair, dark hooded eyes, a broad, expressive face, and a gift for debate that hinted at the courtroom lawyer he once planned to be. After the Nazis invaded Poland in 1939, Melamed and his parents, both Yiddish educators, fled eastward across Siberia. In 1941, when he was nine years old, his family finally wound up in Chicago, by way of

Japan. As a young man, Melamed charmed his way through a local college and then entered law school. Sometime around 1953, while looking for part-time work as a law student, he stumbled upon the Chicago Mercantile Exchange, where traders in loose, colorful jackets struck deals at the top of their lungs as clerks scurried around plucking up the scattering paperwork. Barely twenty years old, Leo Melamed was drawn to the vital energy of the Merc trading floor and never left.

Melamed liked loud suits and louder sports cars, and he was rarely seen without a cigarette dangling from his lips or fingers. He got his law degree in 1955 and split his time between law and futures trading until 1966, when he began trading full-time. The next year, at age thirty-five, he became the youngest trader ever elected to the Merc's board of governors—the first step in a career of imaginative and sometimes controversial leadership that would last a half century and reshape the futures industry.

When Melamed joined its board, the Merc was the number-two futures exchange in Chicago, by a long distance. For decades, the grandeur of first place had belonged to the Chicago Board of Trade, housed in a soaring Art Deco skyscraper in the heart of Chicago's financial district. Its neighbors were the aggressive Continental Illinois bank and the powerful Federal Reserve Bank of Chicago, located in matching Greek temples on the flanking corners.

Melamed was determined to improve his scrappy second-place market, whose only big contract was on pork bellies. Working first from a perch on the board's new products committee and, as of 1969, from his seat as chairman, he tossed a host of new futures contracts into the trading pits to see what would prosper. Some ideas (futures on shrimp, turkeys, and apples) flopped. Others (futures on hogs, cattle, and lumber) were successful, and trading volume grew.

In 1972, Melamed led the Merc in the introduction of the first widely successful financial futures, based on the colorful and unfamiliar foreign currencies Americans encountered when they traveled abroad. By his account, he first got the idea in the late 1960s, from a fellow trader who "was the first in our crowd who had attempted to dabble in currency. He found it nearly impossible." The big banks wouldn't take his small orders. Not long afterward, the same complaint was raised in the *Wall Street Journal* by the economist Milton Friedman, an expert on monetary policy at the University of Chicago.

Under treaties signed after World War II, major Western currencies were pegged to the American dollar, and the dollar was pegged to gold. By the late 1960s, that system was breaking down. Friedman, the star of an economics faculty already known for the free-market tilt of its research, had argued for years that exchange rates should be set by traders, not by treaties. If that ever happened, though, the world would need a way to hedge the risks of fluctuating exchange rates. Melamed put the Merc staff to work on developing futures contracts pegged to foreign currencies.

The Merc's board approved his idea early in 1970. A few months later, to Melamed's horror, a tiny article in the *New York Times* reported that a struggling futures exchange in Manhattan, the International Commercial Exchange (ICE), had already developed foreign currency futures. Trading opened in New York on April 23, 1970.

"My heart sank," Melamed recalled. He and a colleague flew to New York to take a look. When they got to the exchange's home at 2 Broadway, they found the trading floor and slipped inside.

"It was deserted. There was no trading," Melamed reported. To his great relief, these new contracts were too small to be of interest to large-scale hedgers and speculators, the primary players in the foreign exchange markets.

By August 15, 1971, when President Richard Nixon announced the end of the postwar currency regime, Melamed was ready with a contract that commercial hedgers and speculators could easily use. But first he had to inform his Washington regulator about the new product. In 1971 that regulator was the Commodity Exchange Authority, a tiny Depression-era agency located in the basement of the Agriculture Department building. The authority was not well versed in the foreign currency markets, to say the least, and it had no clear jurisdiction over the new contracts anyway. "Fortunately for us," Melamed later remarked, "at the time . . . there were a bunch of free market folks in very high government places."

On December 18, 1971, Western political leaders unveiled the new international currency regime. At a press conference a week later, Melamed unveiled the International Monetary Market, a Merc affiliate that would trade futures on British pounds, Canadian dollars, West German marks, Italian lire, Japanese yen, Mexican pesos, and Swiss francs.

The new market opened on May 16, 1972. Both history and Leo Melamed ignored the tiny currency futures exchange in Manhattan. As far as either was concerned, the era of publicly traded financial derivatives had dawned—in Chicago.

THE CHICAGO BOARD of Trade, the Merc's hometown rival, joined the Merc on the financial futures bandwagon in 1975, thanks to Richard L. Sandor, a young economics professor on sabbatical from the business school at the University of California at Berkeley. A diminutive powerhouse with boundless enthusiasm for practical innovation, he was part of the first wave of brilliant émigrés from academia to settle in the realm of finance.

Sandor, a New Yorker, had arrived on the Berkeley campus in 1966 after earning a doctorate in economics from the University of Minnesota. Perhaps no campus in America was as firmly linked to the placard-toting, slogan-shouting stereotypes of the unruly 1960s as Berkeley. The university's hillside campus had given birth to the Free Speech Movement, an influential protest against campus curbs on political activism, and Berkeley became a key organizing point for national antiwar marches and civil rights confrontations.

By the 1970s, there was another buzz on campus, and it was occurring at the business school. Berkeley's business school may not have had the wealth and prestige of Harvard's or the free-market ferocity of the University of Chicago's, but it was still at the forefront of a revolution in financial engineering.

Less than fifty miles south of Berkeley, what would later be called Silicon Valley was producing computers that could analyze huge collections of numbers, such as the daily prices on America's stock markets. The scholars at Berkeley and elsewhere who used such data to draw conclusions about the movements of the stock market became known as "quantitative" theorists, or "quants." They were already using mathematical ideas to guide investment strategies, and some moved beyond that to ideas that would reshape entire markets. One Berkeley faculty member laid out a theoretical sketch for a fully computerized stock market—in 1962, a decade before the most primitive automated markets took shape in the real world. In 1970, Richard Sandor designed a fully automated futures market that would make Leo Melamed's world in Chicago obsolete. In the early 1970s, a faculty celebrity named Barr Rosenberg had come up with new computer modeling tools to help big investors select the best mix of stocks for their portfolios—and, in the process, built an international reputation and a multimillion-dollar consulting business.

These ideas challenged traditional investment managers, who firmly believed that the way to build a portfolio was to study individual stocks issued by specific companies. In the 1950s, scholarly skeptics of this "stock-picking" concept had painstakingly collected stock prices going back decades; in the 1960s, they analyzed those prices on primitive computers and reached a shocking conclusion: random collections of stocks, chosen by literally throwing darts at the stock tables in the *Wall Street Journal*, generally outperformed handpicked portfolios. This so-called "random walk" method of investing was an idea that, in a few years, would radically transform the way giant institutions deployed their money in the market.

Another group of "quant" scholars, loosely centered on the University of Chicago, looked at the same historical data about stock prices and reached a slightly different but equally world-changing conclusion about Wall Street. These scholars saw the stock market as a computer (vastly faster and more efficient than any at their disposal) that could absorb all the relevant information about every stock and generate the appropriate price for that stock at any moment of the day.

It was a vision of the stock market as a beehive, where information known to some was instantly communicated to all. In this beehive, prices were the product of all the rational and well-informed decisions made by all the rational and well-informed traders in the marketplace at that moment. As these theorists saw it, *everyone* was smarter than anyone.

This notion about how the stock market worked became known as the "efficient market hypothesis," and it would be hard to pick an academic theory that has had a greater impact on American markets. Those who subscribed to the efficient market hypothesis believed that markets should be left alone to practice their beehive brilliance without government interference. After all, if *everyone* was smarter than anyone, *everyone* was certainly smarter than Uncle Sam. That notion, too, would shape the financial landscape far into the future.

In the San Francisco Bay area of the early 1970s, lightbulbs of financial innovation were burning bright everywhere, not just at Berkeley. A remarkable team of computer geeks and misfit bankers, working in a small unit at Wells Fargo Bank in San Francisco, had seized on the "random walk" concept and were trying to build portfolios for their pension fund clients that would behave as much as possible like the overall market. Their endeavor, called "indexing," outraged the traditional stock-picking analysts at the bank—and helped nurture the giant institutional investors who would rise to prominence in the next decade. Dubbed Wells Fargo Investment Advisors, this innovative team was road-testing index funds long before the Vanguard mutual fund family introduced the concept to the retail market in 1975. It also pioneered the statistical tools for measuring pension fund performance, a commonplace concept now that was unavailable to corporate treasurers five decades ago.

The seeds of vast and potentially disruptive power were planted in these two innovations. Indexing gave rise to giant funds that were all likely to shift their assets in the same direction at the same time, because they were recalibrating their portfolios to track the same market index. Their clients' ability to measure how closely they tracked that index meant money managers would be wary of deviating from the herd—and might be inspired to look for even better results if they could, to attract more big pension funds as clients. The tools they developed to seek those extra bits of profit would be as disruptive as the index funds themselves.

Careful scholars always acknowledged that each of their theoretical models was a stripped-down, simplified version of reality, and wasn't meant to replicate the messiness and noise of the real world. Unfortunately, their caveats did not travel anywhere near as far as their theories.

By the time those theories were starting to spread to Wall Street and Washington, they already were being skeptically examined by some in academia.

Well before 1980, some bright thinkers were poking holes in the efficient market hypothesis. One hole was the paradox about market knowledge. In theory, prices in an efficient market would instantly reflect any new knowledge, so nobody could get "an edge" by finding hidden gems or overlooked bargains. And knowledge about individual companies was expensive to acquire—in those pre-Internet days, it typically meant plane fare and long-distance telephone bills, plus some leased computer time. If the market was so efficient that investors couldn't profit from their hard-earned knowledge, why would they bother to gather that knowledge in the first place? Yet they did.

Other skeptics raised even more fundamental questions: Were human beings really the cool, rational investors envisioned by the efficient market theory? Or were they, in fact, prone to panicky overreactions, herd instincts, stubborn misperceptions, and magical thinking? Anyone who observed how actual investors behaved during a crisis probably would not describe that behavior as cool or rational. Slowly, these skeptics began to find academic followers, and the course of research began to shift toward what would be called behavioral economics.

Well into the twenty-first century, however, academic warnings about flaws in the efficient market hypothesis would be largely ignored by legislators, politicians, and financial policymakers. The notion that "markets cure themselves" without government interference had firmly taken root in Washington in the 1970s, and it would spread like kudzu over the policy-making landscape for decades.

AT BERKELEY, RICHARD Sandor's visionary idea for an electronic futures market languished when the traders who commissioned the research opted for a more traditional market instead. He then designed the Berkeley business school's first course on futures trading and invited a host of important industry figures to speak to his classes. One of his guest lecturers was Warren Lebeck, a senior executive at the Chicago Board of Trade. Their relationship blossomed, and in 1972 Sandor took

a sabbatical from Berkeley to become the Board of Trade's chief economist. Lebeck and Sandor soon devised the world's second major financial futures contract—a contract based on the interest rates on the
mortgage-backed notes that Wall Street called "Ginnie Maes," a nick-
name inspired by the initials of the issuer, the Government National
Mortgage Association.

The nation's banks and savings and loans owned millions of home
mortgages and should have been desperately looking for a way to
hedge themselves against the threat of gyrating interest rates. They
weren't—because in 1972 they could not imagine an era in which interest rates would fluctuate enough to require hedging. Sandor made the
rounds of S&Ls and commercial banks in Manhattan, warning that
the stable rates of the recent past were "a historical anomaly" that would
likely vanish under the weight of large government deficits. One executive heard him out and then simply asked, "What are you smoking?"

However, it turned out that mortgage lenders in California were
interested in the new contract, and the Chicago Board of Trade forged
ahead. By 1975, Sandor's Ginnie Mae futures contract was ready. Unlike
the Merc's foreign currency contracts introduced three years earlier,
Sandor's brainchild had to be cleared by Chicago's new regulator, the
Commodity Futures Trading Commission, which had just opened its
doors in Washington.

CHICAGO VS. NEW YORK

For a moment in 1973, the Nixon administration considered putting the futures markets under the jurisdiction of the Securities and Exchange Commission, which had been the nation's primary market regulator for forty years.

Had that been done, it would have prevented decades of bureaucratic warfare, but the chairman of the SEC at the time fatefully declined. Instead, the CFTC was created and put under the supervision of the congressional agriculture committees, which had overseen its tiny predecessor, the Commodity Exchange Authority.

Some of the wealth generated by the futures market had been spent to cultivate the Farm Belt's powerful congressional delegation, which meant that the Chicago exchanges played a muscular role in drafting the 1974 law that created their new regulator. The Chicago Board of Trade, with Richard Sandor's new Ginnie Mae futures in mind, told its lawyer, Philip Johnson, to make sure that the bill defined "futures contracts" as broadly as possible and gave the new agency exclusive jurisdiction over them.

Phil Johnson, a small, elegant man with peachy skin and bright eyes, had begun his Chicago legal career in the mid-1960s as an antitrust lawyer at Kirkland and Ellis. Along the way, he developed a passing fluency in the language of the futures market, so when the law firm's partner assigned to the Chicago Board of Trade retired, Johnson was drafted to replace him.

And in the 1974 wrangling over the CFTC's creation, Phil Johnson more than earned his keep.

The old law that set up the Commodity Exchange Authority limited its reach to futures contracts based on a list of specific tangible products. Wheat was on the list, for example, but silver and foreign currencies weren't. The first impulse of those designing the new regulatory agency was predictable.

"Someone suggested that we just add 'securities' to the list," Johnson recalled, but he felt that would have been "a red flag" to the SEC and its backers in Congress. Instead, he proposed that the new agency be given jurisdiction over the futures exchanges themselves, not just over the specific contracts that traded there.

Johnson also helped draft a clause that would ward off the SEC in countless future battles: the new CFTC, by regulating the futures exchanges, would have jurisdiction over *all* exchange-traded futures contracts, no matter what they were based on, and those contracts could be based on all "goods and articles except onions" but also on "all services, rights and interests." (Because of an onion futures trading scandal on the Merc years earlier, federal law prohibited futures contracts based on onions, a bizarre restriction that continues to this day.) Thus the new CFTC would regulate all futures contracts, even those based on mortgage securities and foreign currencies, unless Congress explicitly took such jurisdiction away.

The result was that Chicago created the regulatory agency it wanted, or at least one it could tolerate: a small agency that would monitor a vast market on short rations, a commission further weakened by the fact that it had to beg Congress every few years to renew its very existence through a "reauthorization" bill.

One of the new agency's first acts was to approve the Chicago Board of Trade's request to start trading Ginnie Mae futures. Ginnie Mae certificates were clearly "securities," and the new contract drew immediate howls from the SEC, the first quarrel in a long, bitter jurisdictional argument.

In 1975, a CFTC lawyer and Phil Johnson, representing the Chicago Board of Trade, were summoned to a meeting with Harvey Pitt, the SEC's strong-minded young general counsel. When they arrived at Pitt's large office, they found it packed with SEC lawyers perched on radiator covers and the backs of armchairs, leaning against the walls, even sitting on the floor. Pitt's message was firm and clear: if Ginnie Mae futures started trading in Chicago, the SEC would go to court.

The CFTC's counterargument was simple: The law that had created the CFTC gave it exclusive jurisdiction over futures contracts based on *anything* except onions. And the Chicago Board of Trade's new product was indisputably a futures contract; that it was based on an SEC-regulated mortgage security didn't matter.

The SEC argued that the law that had created the SEC in 1934 gave *it* jurisdiction over securities trading, and Ginnie Mae mortgage certificates were clearly securities! How on earth could the CFTC trump that?

The dispute remained unresolved until July 1975, when the Chicago Board of Trade started trading Ginnie Mae futures—leaving the SEC fuming and unpersuaded, but with no option but an unseemly lawsuit against a fellow regulator. Ultimately, the SEC decided not to fight it out in the courts—and an early chance to avoid fragmented supervision of two closely linked markets was lost.

FACED WITH THE Chicago Board of Trade's coup in developing the first interest rate futures, Leo Melamed was determined to keep the Chicago Mercantile Exchange at the head of the financial futures parade. In May 1976 he received CFTC approval for futures pegged to the interest rates on short-term Treasury bills. In response, the Chicago Board of Trade promptly launched a futures contract pegged to ten-year Treasury bonds. It would prove to be the more popular contract.

Soon, the financial futures trading pits of Chicago became almost as busy as the pits trading pork bellies, wheat, and soybeans. Almost anyone who wanted to hedge interest rate risks—and more people did, as rates became more volatile—had to do business with Chicago.

In 1978 the CFTC had to seek reauthorization from Congress to continue in operation. Before a vote, Congress asked the General Accounting Office to review how the new agency was doing. The result was a report card that nobody would want to take home to the parents, one that identified weaknesses that would be evident during the silver crisis in 1980 and that would linger throughout the decade to follow.

The GAO's conclusions: The CFTC was beset by weak management and high staff turnover. It had not pushed futures exchanges to set rules that were fairly and vigorously enforced, which meant that self-regulation by the exchanges "is not yet a reality." And CFTC regulation was not filling the gap. The commission's market surveillance program, the only way it could spot manipulative or collusive trading, was hampered by a lack of accurate price data from the cash markets for commodities. The agency was "understaffed, overextended, and lacking in the ability to enforce compliance effectively" in some of the markets it regulated, the report said.

The new agency had dealt so ineptly with its many regulatory burdens, the GAO concluded, that Congress ought to shift authority over most financial futures (notably, those based on stocks and bonds) to the more seasoned regulators at the SEC.

The Farm Belt members of Congress, grateful for Chicago's support and skeptical of the SEC's grasp of futures markets, fought back fiercely and warded off any shift in jurisdiction. Thus, yet another opportunity to streamline market regulation was lost. Looking to make a stronger argument at the next reauthorization hearings, set for 1982, the Fed joined with the SEC and the Treasury to conduct a formal joint agency study of the economic impact of the new products, which were just beginning to be called "derivatives."

With that review under way, two things happened that lit the fuse for a regulatory showdown.

First, a delay in the sale of new Treasury bills in March 1979 put sudden and unexpected pressure on the Merc's Treasury bill futures contracts. The Fed and the Treasury had been alarmed: was someone trying to push futures prices up by getting control of a substantial share of the market's supply of Treasury bills, as the Hunts would later do with silver? Those Treasury contracts had expired without a crisis, but a similar incident occurred early in 1980, this time on Paul Volcker's watch. He had been sufficiently shaken to urge the CFTC to impose a moratorium on new financial futures until the joint agency study was done.

At the time, the Chicago Merc had four contracts based on short-term Treasury bills, contracts expiring in March, June, September, and December. The Board of Trade had four contracts based on Treasury notes, which had longer maturities than Treasury bills and also expired in those months. The Treasury and the Fed wanted the CFTC to impose a moratorium on any additional contracts of that sort. Archival documents show that the Merc and the Board of Trade were aware of the pressure the CFTC was facing, especially from Volcker.

Then, a second development persuaded Melamed that Chicago had no choice but to defy its regulators, regardless of the political consequences.

For years, Chicago had endured New York's contempt for the commodities markets, expressed largely by simply ignoring them and treating them as irrelevant to the "real" Wall Street. Then, in the summer of 1980, the New York Stock Exchange paid Chicago the sincerest compliment: it imitated Chicago and opened its own financial futures market. It then asked the CFTC to let the new exchange trade Treasury futures expiring in February, May, August, and November—different months from the Chicago products, but still a competitive threat. To Chicago's chagrin, the CFTC did not reject New York's application.

That was where these twin rivalries—Chicago vs. New York, and Chicago vs. the CFTC—stood in early July 1980.

Both the Merc and the Chicago Board of Trade instantly announced that they were adding those additional four months to their existing Treasury contracts. The CFTC asked them, and then told them, to hold off. The agency was on somewhat shaky ground, given its willingness to let the NYSE get into the act. Still, it delivered an ultimatum: the Merc must announce by 5:30 p.m. on July 7 that it was withdrawing its new products.

The day following the ultimatum, the Merc's board of directors voted unanimously to ignore the CFTC's order. The Chicago Board of Trade followed suit. The new contracts opened for trading on July 11.

It was a remarkable act of rebellion and another insult to the CFTC—one that gave its rival regulators fresh reasons to be skeptical of its ability to supervise the financial futures market.

Paul Volcker found the whole episode "troubling," and believed that the Fed or the Treasury should have "veto power" over any new futures contracts on Treasury securities, and perhaps on foreign currencies, too. He also thought the SEC should be able to veto futures contracts that were based on stocks and stock indexes.

In response, the Chicago exchanges claimed that their new contracts were "grandfathered" under the CFTC's original approval of their Treasury contracts for the other months. They refused to back down.

Coming just months after the silver crisis, the fight drew media attention, and the CFTC sought to reassert its authority. It promptly adopted rules unambiguously requiring the exchanges to receive permission whenever new contracts were added. Yet when the dispute came before a federal judge months later, he sided with the exchanges. All that remained were the sour headlines and the worrisome impression in Washington that, once again, rough and rowdy Chicago had gotten the best of its young regulator.

The CFTC wasn't really Chicago's primary target in this skirmish, of course. Its real foe was the New York Stock Exchange.

"WHATEVER CHICAGO CAN do, we can do better," boasted the mayor of New York, Ed Koch, his impish grin firmly in place and his balding head reflecting the spotlights. The crowd cheered and hooted as the puns and clichés piled up.

"We have seen the futures and they are ours," said the state's slightly more decorous governor, Hugh Carey. The governor paused for the boisterous approval from the crowd, and added, "You're never going to sell New York short!"

It was August 7, 1980, the first day of trading on the New York Futures Exchange—known as the NYFE, pronounced "knife." The newly built trading floor was encircled by huge banks of electronic monitors showing flickering trade data. Printers and Teletype machines filled niches at the side of the floor. Jacketed traders, whose oversize name tags identified their firms, milled cheerfully among the celebrities in tailored suits.

Beaming in the opening-day crowd was the proud father of the new futures exchange, John J. Phelan Jr.

The forty-nine-year-old Phelan had been president and chief operating officer of the New York Stock Exchange for barely a month. A tall, solid man with dark slicked-down hair and a cleft chin, Phelan had an Irish wit that softened the commanding bark he had adopted as a marine in Korea—he still wore his watch military-style, with its face on the underside of his wrist.

Phelan had deep roots in the stock exchange culture. His father had served two terms on the NYSE governing board in the 1960s and had spent a lifetime on the exchange floor, most of those years as a "specialist."

Specialists had the exclusive right to oversee trading in specific stocks, and in return they received a tiny slice of each trade. Their lucrative monopoly carried with it the obligation of making sure there was a ready market for those stocks whenever the exchange was open for business. The stock exchange was essentially a vast auction house where stocks were continually put up on the block for bids; in that sense, the specialists were the auctioneers, the key drivers of the auction machinery. Unlike at Sotheby's or Christie's, these auctioneers could raise their own paddles to bid, and indeed were expected to do so if public bidding flagged or faltered.

"The market is a great equalizer," the junior Phelan once observed. "If you really think you're smart, you should trade the market for a while."

The family story that anchored John Phelan's career was similar to the stories of other men in leadership roles at the exchange, whether their heritage was Jewish, Irish, Polish, Italian, or Anglo-Saxon. The senior John J. Phelan had been a proud and generous Irish Catholic; he enjoyed membership in the Friendly Sons of St. Patrick, one of the oldest fraternal societies serving the city's Irish American community, and he was inducted into the Knights of Malta. He started work in his mid-teens, experienced the crash of 1929, and survived the Great Depression. In 1931, still in his mid-twenties, he bought a two-story Dutch Colonial home in the Long Island suburb of Garden City. His only son and namesake was born that same year and grew up in the home his parents would occupy for thirty-five years.

By the 1970s, the Phelan firm handled trading in about fifty stocks, including prestigious companies such as Kaiser Aluminum—proof of its good reputation on the trading floor. Beginning when he was sixteen, John Jr. spent summers working on the trading floor with his father, complaining that "the pay was low, the trip [from home] was terrible, and the job was awful." He told his dad, "There must be a better way to make money." After high school, he put in two years at Adelphi University, but he dropped out in 1951 and enlisted in the U.S. Marines. He returned from Korea in 1954, signed up for night classes at Adelphi, and went to work for the family firm. For the next decade, he and his father worked side by side in the world they both knew best—the trading floor, the Irish societies, the Catholic charities. When John Phelan Sr. died at age sixty-one in 1966, his funeral service was a pontifical requiem mass at St. Patrick's Cathedral in Manhattan.

Tradition, linking generations of fathers and sons, was the lifeblood of the NYSE trading floor. The NYSE traced its roots to two dozen stock traders who in 1792 drew up rules to govern the trading they regularly conducted, first under a fabled buttonwood tree and then in a nearby coffeehouse. As the young country grew, the NYSE, familiarly known as the "Big Board," emerged as its premier stock market, first among a host of smaller city exchanges scattered from Boston to San Francisco. Since 1903, the NYSE's working day had begun with the insistent clang of a bell rung on a handsome stone balcony at one end of the trading floor. The exchange drew about a half million tourists each year, and its iconic marble-columned building at the corner of Wall and Broad Streets in Lower Manhattan was declared a historic national landmark in 1978.

A year after that, as an active but unpaid vice chairman of the NYSE board and head of a new committee on technology, John Phelan started remodeling. The work wouldn't change the market's magnificent Greek

Revival façade, but Phelan sincerely hoped it would radically change what happened inside the building—because he knew, firsthand, how very close the exchange had come to falling apart a decade earlier.

TO ITS RIVALS in Chicago, the Big Board may have looked impregnable and powerful, but that image was the product of exceptional secrecy and deft public relations. In truth, the mighty NYSE had barely survived a financial crisis that climaxed in 1970.

That crisis was born in the "back offices" of Wall Street, where clerks carried out the unexciting but critical functions of documenting trades and then delivering money to the sellers and stock certificates to the buyers. For most firms at that time, the "back office" was a pencil-and-paper operation augmented by a few battered typewriters and Teletype machines and plagued by low wages and high turnover.

The long fuse for this crisis was lit by the market rally that began in 1949, lasted for more than a decade, stalled briefly in early 1962, and then continued almost nonstop into the late 1960s. Brokerage firms advertised heavily and hired more salesmen in more branch offices. Wall Street grew sleek, rich, and careless. By 1968, the pace of trading had become feverish; new trading volume records were set every few weeks.

As the number of trades rose, orders were lost, stock certificates were lost, cash and checks were lost. One visitor behind the scenes reported that "stacks and stacks of stock certificates with pieces of paper clipped or stapled to them lie on tabletop after tabletop." The back offices of Wall Street were being buried by the paperwork generated by this remarkable bull market, and the resulting errors were costing firms a lot of money.

After reaching a record high in December 1968, the Dow dropped relentlessly, falling 36 percent by May 1970. The volume of orders followed the Dow downward, easing the back-office backlog but cutting Wall Street's revenues and its partners' profits. This ebbing tide showed that many firms no longer had enough capital to continue trading. Hundreds of member firms were in danger of bankruptcy, including six of the ten largest firms. In 1970, about 16,500 Wall Street workers lost their jobs, and brokerage firms shut down hundreds of branch offices across the country. Arguably, 1970 was the darkest year the NYSE had experienced since the Great Depression.

Typically, in bad markets, small, shaky partnerships close their doors or quietly merge themselves into stronger firms. Unfortunately, by the summer of 1970, even big firms with iconic names were in desperate trouble.

The leaders of an NYSE committee dealing with the crisis feared that the collapse of a major firm, with its resulting customer losses, would kick off a "run" on other firms that would bankrupt the exchange. If investors panicked and closed their accounts, weaker members would go under. If that happened, stronger members would likely resign from the NYSE rather than pay to cover the failed firms' losses. The Big Board would be left with the tab.

One committee member later recalled, "Everybody seemed to come to a decision that we just couldn't let a major firm go bankrupt . . . that if we did let one go under, there would be a panic." Tens of millions of dollars were raised to rescue firms or indemnify wary merger partners— and the danger slowly receded.

Somehow, the crisis was largely hushed up. One veteran of the experience noted later that the public had no idea how close to destruction the NYSE actually came.

Yet the crisis was no secret to John Phelan. He had been a floor official at the exchange since 1967 and helped muster membership votes in support of the crisis committee. In 1971 he was elected to his first term on the exchange's board, which brought him even closer to the harrowing rescue missions, and he was elected vice chairman in 1975. Over the next few years, his influence grew, and in 1979 his colleagues begged him to stay on for an unusual second term as vice chairman.

It was a time of almost constant turmoil for the NYSE. Just as this desperate financial crisis was playing out, regulators in Washington became increasingly determined to radically change the way the NYSE did business.

SINCE FRANKLIN ROOSEVELT'S New Deal of the 1930s, populist politicians had seen the NYSE as a privileged and greedy club that was scornful of "the little guy," and they weren't far wrong. In the late 1960s its clubby traditions gave rise to abusive trading that went unchecked and unpunished by exchange officials. The paper crunch further angered the SEC, although the agency bore some of the blame after letting firms neglect their back-office infrastructure.

Market regulators began to demand that the NYSE erase the fixed commission rates it had enforced for 180 years—"price-fixing," muttered lawyers with the Justice Department. Regulators also urged the NYSE to repeal a rule that required member firms to trade Big Board stocks only on the exchange floor—"restraint of trade," grumbled the government's antitrust experts. That rule gave rise to an over-the-counter market for Big Board stocks, conducted by firms that were not Big Board members. This informal market was serving primarily big professional investors, who sometimes got better prices than small investors could get on the Big Board. "Healthy competition," said advocates of unfettered markets. "Unfair to small investors!" said populist lawmakers suspicious of Wall Street.

The Big Board found few friends in Washington willing to defend its cherished traditions or to argue that this deep, centralized marketplace, where fully 90 percent of America's daily stock trading was conducted, was a national asset worth preserving.

The NYSE's image problem in Washington had far-reaching consequences. In 1975 a testy Congress ordered the SEC to foster a "national market system" linked electronically, to diminish the Big Board's monopolistic power. The same year, the NYSE bowed to years of pressure and eliminated fixed commissions, a step that brought a fresh string of Wall Street bankruptcies and vastly increased the bargaining power and trading activity of giant institutional investors, especially the pension funds and mutual funds responsible for a growing share of NYSE trading volume. These giant investors wanted cheaper, faster ways to trade shares and were not going to take "tradition" as an excuse. Congress seemed to be fully in their corner.

The financial bloodbath of 1970, a brutal bear market in 1973–74, the slashing of commission revenue in 1975, and continued nibbling by competitors decimated the leadership ranks on Wall Street. By 1980 the NYSE executive offices were populated by hardened, pragmatic survivors. Anyone incapable of adapting quickly to radical change or inclined to cling too tightly to tradition had been driven out.

In June 1980, John Phelan, emphatically a pragmatic survivor, became the first paid president of the exchange, working closely with William M. "Mil" Batten, the retired CEO of J.C. Penney who had served as chairman since 1976. Batten became the friendly face of the exchange on Main Street and in Washington, while relying on Phelan to lead the exchange's modernization effort. Batten could see that Phelan was the man to get the job done.

Both knew what the Big Board was up against. "Nobody wants to change anything until it's raining disaster, and then they all start running around," Phelan said. He had no intention of idly waiting for some disastrous downpour.

One of Phelan's projects was to take a page from Chicago's playbook. In 1979 he leased space in a nearby office building for a new futures market. The NYSE's lawyers quietly assured the CFTC that the new exchange would have an experienced supervisory staff and robust trading rules. The NYFE then applied to the CFTC for permission to trade a roster of new contracts, including Treasury futures—and ignited the regulatory showdown in Chicago.

WHEN PHELAN BECAME the stock exchange's president, its vast central trading floor was a village of beautifully crafted wooden trading posts: U-shaped structures, each with dozens of slots and niches and tiny brass-trimmed drawers. The kiosks were arranged in pairs to form room-size ovals, and they were tailored perfectly for the face-to-face trading of the previous century.

Phelan replaced these traditional posts with fourteen sleek new laminated versions. Filing slots and tiny drawers were out; electronic screens and more telephones were in. Thin arching rods, like spider legs, sprouted from the top edges of each structure and held computer monitors out over the trading floor. To some of the old-timers, the new trading posts looked like alien spaceships.

It was the most sweeping renovation in the history of the exchange, though some people on Wall Street still considered the NYSE to be antiquated compared to its younger, more automated stock-trading rivals—chiefly the increasingly competitive Nasdaq market.

Nasdaq proclaimed itself to be the "Stock Market of Tomorrow—Today." Its traders were not clustered around kiosks on an Edwardian-era trading floor in Lower Manhattan. They were at firms across the country, following stock price movements on flickering television-size computer monitors stacked on their desks. Huge mainframe computers and massive telephone cables in remote office parks linked their monitors to other dealers and to some institutional customers. The fledgling Apple Computer company was one of its high-tech listings; other young, flashy technology companies were flocking to be listed there as well. Nasdaq's traders were certain their market would soon supplant the older exchanges.

Phelan emphatically disagreed, almost as a matter of faith. He believed that face-to-face trading, the specialist-led "auction market" of the NYSE, was the best way to arrive at a fair price and maintain an orderly market. Within that vision, though, he was determined to move the Big Board along the technology curve as quickly as he could, to preserve its primacy as America's stock market.

Phelan's dream of modernizing the NYSE was constrained by the reality that greeted him, literally, on the trading floor each day: namely, the men (and a few women) who traded stocks there, amid the ghosts of those who had done the same job a century before. Phelan's makeover would speed up the collection of orders and the processing of paperwork, but all those automated tributaries, growing larger and moving faster every day, still flowed into one big reservoir: a trading floor populated entirely by human beings.

Even in the Nasdaq market, the shiny new computer monitors only reported current prices. To make a trade, dealers still had to pick up the telephone and call another human being. For all the space-age claims, these were still human markets, moving at the speed of life.

As Phelan watched the ribbon cutting at the New York Futures Exchange in August 1980, Mayor Koch unwittingly hit a nerve when he joked, "I don't know how you all make money in this venture, but I hope you make lots of it." The exchange wasn't quite sure it would make money with this new venture, either. The rebellious exchanges fighting for their franchise in Chicago had an enormous advantage over the infant NYFE, despite the prestige of its famous parent.

John Phelan merely smiled at the mayor's joke, and shook a few more hands. The future had to start somewhere, and this was as good a place as any.

— 4 —

SHIFTING GEARS

The Election Day weather in Washington on November 4, 1980, was as unsettled as the national mood, with clouds, gusty winds, some rain, and even a few rumbles of thunder.

At the CFTC chairman's office on K Street, Jim Stone was catching up on his paperwork. He planned to watch the election returns with a friend that evening, but by 4 p.m., they could see where the votes were flowing. They decided to meet at a nearby bar. As the two nursed their drinks, television reporters chatted about what looked like a Republican landslide, despite low voter turnout. Ronald Reagan won 489 electoral votes, to 49 for Jimmy Carter. Even Stone's staunchly Democratic home state of Massachusetts had landed in the Republican column.

Although Jim Stone's appointment as a CFTC commissioner did not expire until the summer of 1983, the CFTC chairmanship was a political plum bestowed by the White House and tradition demanded that the chairman tender his resignation to the new president. There were issues pending before the commission that Stone cared deeply about—those half-dozen proposals for futures based on the stock market, for example—and he wondered whether "principled dissent" was the next chapter in his Washington career. After all, he was the only commissioner likely to challenge Chicago's experiments with financial futures.

Across town at the SEC, Harold Williams was equally uncertain about what the election would mean for him. His SEC had already trimmed the regulatory burdens on small businesses, as Reagan advocated, but it was unlikely the new president would leave a Carter appointee in such a prominent position.

In Chicago, Leo Melamed and his friends at the Merc and the Chicago Board of Trade were jubilant at the election results. Reagan's long coattails had given the Republican Party control of the Senate, and thus control over future confirmation hearings. Surely there would be a more conciliatory chairman at the SEC who wouldn't try to grab jurisdiction over financial futures. Even better, there would be a new chairman at the CFTC, someone more acceptable to Chicago than the "little twerp" Jim Stone. In a preelection executive session at Chicago's exclusive Mid-America Club, the Chicago Board of Trade's directors had already drafted a wish list of twenty-one possible contenders. The last name on their list was Philip Johnson, their longtime attorney, who had helped craft the most potent phrases in the 1974 law that created the CFTC.

"If the industry supports a candidate, under Reagan we stand a chance to get the pick," one director reasoned—adding that they should "strike quickly." Could the two bitterly competitive exchanges in Chicago come together behind a consensus choice?

In Manhattan, the longtime E.F. Hutton executive John Shad could look with satisfaction on his own contribution to the Reagan landslide. The fund-raising event he had arranged at the NYSE in March was one of the most lucrative the candidate held that month. Shad's quiet hopes for a Washington appointment might actually materialize—if he had the stomach for the confirmation process. He made almost $500,000 a year as vice chairman of E.F. Hutton, and he was one of the firm's largest shareholders—selling his Hutton stock would cost him about $2.5 million in capital gains taxes. Still, if the White House called, could he really decline to serve?

E.F. Hutton's stock had hit a new high on the New York Stock Exchange on Monday, November 3, the last trading day before Election Day. Trading was light that day, only about 36 million shares, and John Phelan had little to worry him as the market observed its traditional

Election Day holiday—the last time it would do so, as it turned out. However, daily trading volume was routinely running as much as 50 percent ahead of the previous year. Could the order-processing systems at the Big Board handle the load, or would Phelan soon face the kind of crunch that had crippled the Street a dozen years earlier?

That question, at least, was quickly answered. The day after the election, there was a huge market rally. A tidal wave of buy orders began with the opening bell. By 11 a.m., the ticker was running a half hour behind. By lunchtime, a crowd had gathered by the floor entrance to crane and squirm for a look at the monitors showing the hourly trading volume, cheering each advance. By the final bell, a new record had been set: 84.1 million shares had changed hands.

Despite the ticker tape delay, Phelan was relieved. "The Street seems to be processing it very well," he told a visiting reporter. Perhaps the back-office paper crunch at Wall Street firms really could be consigned to history. The exchange was coping well, too, he added: "It's a busy day, but not hectic."

"HECTIC" WOULD ARRIVE soon enough—on a snowy day in early January 1981, courtesy of a grandstanding investment guru named Joseph E. Granville.

Joe Granville, like John Shad, had built his reputation at E.F. Hutton. He was a technical analyst who sifted through trading statistics for clues to future market movements. The *Granville Market Letter* was mailed out every Saturday to at least eleven thousand subscribers, who shared it with uncounted thousands more. When Granville spoke, his subscribers not only listened, they obeyed.

The first newsletter of the new year arrived in mailboxes and brokerage offices on Monday, January 5. Like all of Granville's directives since the spring of 1980, it encouraged investors to buy aggressively. On January 6 the Dow closed above 1,000 for the second time since Reagan's election, and forecasts were generally bright. Sometime that evening, however, Granville had an abrupt change of heart. The small staff at his headquarters outside Daytona Beach, Florida, worked into the night making telephone calls and sending telexes to the much smaller list of clients who paid a fat extra fee for constant updates on his advice. His message to those elite followers: "Sell everything."

And at the opening bell on January 7, they did. With many more sellers than buyers, it took a while before some major stocks could even start trading. The Dow ended down almost 24 points, a steep drop of more than 2.5 percent. The daily trading volume was almost 93 million shares, eclipsing the record set on the day after Reagan's election.

The Big Board could not possibly have handled this wild, herdlike selling without the new technology Phelan had recently put in place. The day would have been wilder still if the Granville cult had included giant institutional investors, selling shares by the millions just because some investment theory said they should. Still, the day offered a glimpse of what a modern selling stampede might look like.

ON JANUARY 20, 1981, Ronald Reagan was sworn in as the fortieth president of the United States. At the traditional champagne luncheon with congressional leaders, he announced that the fifty-two American hostages held in Iran for more than fourteen months were flying home. The sense of new beginnings carried through to the inaugural balls that evening—the president, at ease in his formal wear, and his wife, Nancy, elegant in a white beaded one-shoulder gown, took a few twirls on the dance floor at ten of them.

Reagan's various transition teams had scouted out budget savings and bureaucratic reforms at each federal agency and had privately filed their reports. The Cabinet nominations had been made—they included a secretary of transportation who planned to trim aid for mass transit, a secretary of the interior who favored broader commercial exploitation of federal lands, and a secretary of energy who had publicly said he wanted the job so he could "close the Energy Department down."

The new secretary of the Treasury was someone with financial experience: Donald T. Regan, the tough-talking longtime chief executive of Merrill Lynch, who had served with John Phelan on the board of the New York Stock Exchange. John Shad, who may have hoped for that job, was still under consideration for a sub-Cabinet post, and Chicago was still quietly lobbying for influence over the CFTC choice.

IN CHICAGO, ON the day after Reagan's inauguration, the dean of the Northwestern University School of Law, David S. Ruder, settled into his seat on a plane bound for Southern California. A well-regarded legal scholar, he had been invited to speak at the annual Securities Law Institute conference at the Hotel del Coronado, the red-roofed, white-washed Victorian resort on San Diego Bay.

Ruder was a tall, cherubic extrovert with thinning hair, a passion for financial history, and a bottomless capacity for committee work. He also knew nearly every prominent regulatory lawyer in Washington. Decades of volunteer work across the legal profession had left him with a fat address book and a lot of friends, some of whom would be at the conference.

Soon after he arrived, he learned that many of his colleagues were disturbed by a *Wall Street Journal* report on the confidential blueprint that one of Reagan's transition teams had drafted for the Securities and Exchange Commission. Reading the story, Ruder quickly came to share their concerns.

The SEC transition team was urging that the agency's budget shrink by more than 35 percent over three years: an immediate 17 percent cut and smaller cuts in the following two years, requiring a 40 percent reduction in its staff. The powerful enforcement division would be largely shut down, its work farmed out to regional offices. The report insisted that this was not "a 'bare bones' proposal and that the mission of the agency was still to be fully implemented."

Under the plan, however, that mission would be different. The report called for "less government intervention in the free-market activities of the securities industry" and "significant deregulation" of Wall Street. "In the past, there had been too aggressive an approach towards regulating an area which can be and is corrected by market forces," it noted, echoing the theory of an efficient, rational marketplace in need of little supervision.

The report did acknowledge that the SEC "has begun to eliminate certain of its more burdensome regulatory requirements in recent years," but apparently the agency had not gone far enough or fast enough. The Reagan team wanted government regulations weighed for their economic impact on business, not just for whatever good they might do for the general public. The authors of the transition team report were tired of a Washington regulatory culture run by lawyers, and they felt it was time to put some businessmen and economists in power at the SEC.

Unsurprisingly, the report urged that Harold Williams be replaced as chairman by the end of February, if possible. It also warned that "in virtually every area, the leadership of the various divisions is unsatisfactory either because of philosophic incompatibilities or [a lack of] competence." Therefore, the new chairman should make "sweeping changes in senior staff promptly."

Ruder had stayed in close touch with the SEC for more than a decade through securities law conferences and bar association work. He occasionally had disagreed with some of the agency's legal conclusions, but he did believe in financial regulation—fair, evenhanded regulation that was strong enough to curb the worst impulses of a greedy breed. He simply did not believe that markets would, or could, regulate themselves. He was worried about what a new SEC chairman would do in light of the transition report.

David Ruder was not alone in his dismay. By lunch, consternation had spread through the Del Coronado like food poisoning. Some Washington lawyers had phoned their offices to secure their own copies of the report; hotel fax machines were disgorging pale pages from the document, which were being shared over coffee at linen-draped tables.

The chairman of the conference was A. A. "Al" Sommer Jr., a distinguished securities lawyer and former SEC commissioner. With the hallways and conference rooms abuzz, he convened a meeting of about two dozen lawyers in his hotel suite, a group that included former SEC commissioners and senior staffers of all political stripes. After much discussion, it was decided that those so inclined would write the White House and share their concerns.

When Al Sommer returned to his law office in Washington the following Monday, he crafted a passionate four-page letter to the new White House counsel, Edwin Meese III, saying that he spoke for many of the lawyers at the San Diego conclave. While some belt-tightening was no doubt possible, he wrote, cutbacks on the scale suggested by the transition report would shrink the SEC's staff to its size in 1962—when the nation's population was 20 percent smaller and the NYSE traded fewer than 4 million shares a day.

And the call for "a virtual clean sweep" of the senior staff would be "disastrous," Sommer warned. The report's "blanket judgment" on the ideology and competence of the division directors was "patently erroneous." Firing all of them "can only have a devastating effect on morale," he added.

At the SEC's offices on North Capitol Street, the transition report had been a jolt—the courteous visits from members of the transition team in mid-November had not prepared the staff for such a harsh prescription. Most veteran staffers felt that the draconian recommendations would never be implemented; the SEC was not without its defenders in Congress. Nevertheless, given the array of iconoclasts already populating the Reagan Cabinet, no one could feel entirely certain of how the SEC would fare under the new administration.

With gallows humor, senior staffers would inquire of one another, "So, which are you—philosophically incompatible or incompetent?"

THREE WEEKS BEFORE Reagan's inauguration, on December 31, 1980, Harold Williams had submitted his letter of resignation to the president-elect, expressing his intention to leave by March 1. First, though, there was a bit of unfinished business: a request by the Chicago Board Options Exchange, the nation's premier marketplace for options trading, to start trading options on Ginnie Mae mortgage securities.

The key difference between futures and options is that futures are two-way obligations and options aren't. Like a futures contract, an option contract allows its purchaser to buy or sell a fixed amount of something, at a fixed point in the future, for a specific price. True to its name, and unlike a futures contract, an option does not require its purchaser to do anything. However, the investor who sold that option—or "wrote" it, in market parlance—is obligated by its terms; if the option buyer decides to exercise the option to sell or buy, the option writer *must* take the other side of the trade, even if it means a big loss. In exchange for taking on that risky duty, the option writer collects a fee from the option buyer, called a "premium."

In 1980, options were a bit more familiar to affluent Americans than futures contracts were because stock options had started to be included in executive pay packages. Those stock options were fairly simple. If you were given an option to buy 1,000 shares of IBM for $40 a share, and IBM rose to $60 a share, you could exercise your option, buy the shares for $40 each, and immediately sell them for a profit of $20 a share. If the price of IBM fell to $20, you obviously would not exercise the option. Speculators who didn't get free stock options in their pay packages could buy or sell publicly traded stock options that worked much the same way.

Substitute Ginnie Mae mortgage certificates for those shares of stock, and you've got the proposal that the Chicago Board Options Exchange had submitted for approval by the SEC, which regulated the options market.

In 1975, as Williams knew, the SEC had been outraged by the Chicago Board of Trade's proposal to trade Ginnie Mae futures contracts, approved by the CFTC. The SEC had given up on that earlier jurisdictional battle, but this one was different. The SEC had been the Chicago Board Options Exchange's regulator since the exchange opened in 1973.

Now, with enthusiastic support from the mortgage and banking industry, the CBOE was proposing to trade Ginnie Mae options. Options were cheaper to buy than futures and gave speculators more bang for their bets, so the proposal was clearly a competitive threat to the futures market.

The shoe of innovation was now on the other foot. The Chicago Board of Trade, determined to protect its monopoly on Ginnie Mae derivatives, had sent a long letter to the SEC raising legal objections to the CBOE's creative proposal. Nevertheless, on February 26, two days before Williams was to step down, the SEC voted to approve trading in Ginnie Mae options.

The furious leaders of the Chicago Board of Trade headed to federal court to argue that the SEC's action was illegal. To the SEC's chagrin, the court temporarily barred the introduction of Ginnie Mae options until the matter could be sorted out.

Two days before the SEC's options vote, the White House had

announced that John Shad was the president's choice to replace Harold Williams. The SEC's lawyers had no idea whether Shad would agree that the SEC should regulate Ginnie Mae options. If Shad did decide to fight, the CFTC's small troop of lawyers would not be led into battle by Jim Stone. On March 3 the White House announced its choice for the CFTC chairman's post: Philip Johnson, the supremely effective outside counsel for the Chicago Board of Trade.

Leo Melamed and his colleagues had gotten their wish—one columnist observed that Chicago "has been unable to conceal its glee." Melamed would later claim that Johnson was chosen "principally as a result of my strong lobbying efforts," adding, "I was tired of political appointees who knew nothing about our markets." Johnson insisted he was his own man, not Chicago's puppet. Still, it would be hard to imagine anyone whom Chicago would rather have in its corner for the fight over Ginnie Mae options.

But first Shad and Johnson needed to be confirmed in their new jobs by the Republican-controlled Senate. In private meetings with senators, Shad apparently indicated that, as SEC chief, he would ignore the controversial Reagan transition report. The topic barely came up at his confirmation hearing, which lasted all of seventy-five minutes. Instead, he was asked about his extensive stock holdings, complimented on his willingness to make the financial sacrifice the SEC post represented, and finally quizzed lightheartedly about the conflicts with Chicago.

"What is your view on jurisdiction over futures and options trading as far as federal regulatory agencies are concerned?" asked Senator Paul Sarbanes, a Democrat from Maryland.

"Between the SEC and the Commodity Futures Trading Commission?" Shad inquired.

"That is the one that leaps to mind, obviously," the senator said. The room erupted in laughter.

Shad said he would need to research the issue. "But it seems to me that if you are charged with regulating the cash market, you should have some responsibility for the derivative market," he added. "One is a function of the other." His answer no doubt reassured the SEC's legal staff.

Things did not move so smoothly for Phil Johnson. His lack of visible partisan loyalty prior to his nomination offended some powerful

Republican senators, who delayed the vote on confirming him to the CFTC job.

Meanwhile, Reagan had announced that he was cutting $47 billion from the federal budget previously submitted by Jimmy Carter. The SEC's budget was reduced, not as severely as many other federal programs were, but enough to make its lean rations even leaner.

For the SEC and CFTC, austerity had arrived, and its visit would last for years. Indeed, austerity would be a far more effective "deregulator" than either John Shad or Phil Johnson.

5

A DEAL IN D.C.

John Shad was sworn in on May 6, 1981, as the twenty-second chairman of the Securities and Exchange Commission. Phil Johnson wasn't confirmed as the new chairman of the CFTC until June 8, but when he finally got settled in, one of his first official acts was to arrange to have lunch with his counterpart at the SEC.

The Monocle restaurant in Washington had the ambience of a neighborhood pub, but the neighborhood it served was Capitol Hill. Occasionally, the phone near the tavern's door would ring to summon lunching lawmakers for an important vote. On an afternoon in the early summer of 1981, Phil Johnson and John Shad slid into a booth in the back of the restaurant.

Both men were newcomers to public service. Both agreed with President Reagan that American business was smarter and contributed more to the common good than government did. And both knew that they needed to craft a peace treaty in the turf war over financial derivatives before the courts or Congress imposed an outcome that neither agency could stomach.

So here they were, scanning the tall, stiff menus at the Monocle and sending the waiter on his way with their orders.

Wouldn't it be better, Shad said, if the two of them worked out these jurisdictional disputes without "making a major issue of it"? He added, "I really think that it would be desirable if we could do this quietly."

Johnson agreed. What would it take, for example, to resolve the dispute over Ginnie Mae options? And what would persuade Shad to accept other CFTC-approved derivatives—especially the stock index futures that Chicago wanted so badly?

Well, stock index futures worried Shad. He could not ignore what had happened the year before, when the crisis over the Hunt brothers' futures contracts destabilized the cash market for silver. What if that happened in the stock market? Why couldn't the contracts just be settled with an exchange of money, Shad suggested, eliminating the need for traders to buy and sell all the underlying stocks?

Johnson must have smiled to himself. What Shad wanted was something called "cash settlement"—and it was precisely what he had hoped to persuade Shad to accept when they sat down to lunch.

The commodity markets had long been wary of settling futures contracts with cash; they saw physical delivery as the force that kept futures markets tethered to reality. The price of *wheat futures* would necessarily converge with the price of *wheat* because sometimes—rarely, but sometimes—a trader would have to make or take delivery of actual wheat at the going price at some grain elevator.

Yet there was an important difference between traditional commodity futures and financial futures: The price of wheat futures effectively became the price of wheat, because wheat didn't really trade anywhere else. Stocks did—every day, the publicly accepted prices of the stocks in the Dow Jones Industrial Average were determined not in a trading pit in Chicago but on the trading floor of the New York Stock Exchange.

What if the stock market produced one value for the Dow and the futures pits produced another? Without physical delivery, the price of a Dow futures contract could fall under or float above the real-world price of the Dow stocks on the NYSE. What would happen then? In the summer of 1981 the answer to that fateful question wasn't clear—indeed, it wasn't even considered.

As it happened, the financial engineers in the futures markets had already figured out that cash settlement was the only way stock index futures could work for traders in their pits, and Johnson and his fellow CFTC commissioners were inclined to agree.

The scene might have been funny if the consequences had not been so profound. Here, over lunch, John Shad was urging Phil Johnson to do exactly what Johnson already wanted to do. And to get Johnson to do that, Shad was prepared to make major (and arguably unnecessary) concessions—ceding jurisdiction over stock index futures contracts to the CFTC and forgoing any meaningful control over the design and approval of those contracts.

"Both of them thought the turf fight between their staffs was unseemly," according to one well-informed account. To Shad, it seemed like "two kids sorting marbles. You take the red ones and I'll take the green ones."

Johnson and Shad returned to their offices and gave new marching orders to their surprised staffers, proud that the logjam of pending applications for new financial derivatives could finally be broken.

ONE DAY DURING that same summer of 1981, the executive who ran AT&T's giant employee pension fund entered the tall, icy-white marble lobby of the General Motors building on Fifth Avenue in Manhattan and took an elevator to the twenty-fifth floor, a wood-paneled setting with thick hall carpets and brass doorknobs. The visitor, David P. Feldman, found the right suite and told the receptionist he was there for lunch with Gordon Binns, the new head of General Motors' $12 billion employee pension fund.

Binns greeted his visitor with a faint Virginia drawl. He was instantly likable, projecting both Southern courtliness and unpretentious warmth. As Binns arranged for sandwiches to be delivered, Feldman took a seat at a small conference table by a window with a view of Central Park. Binns grabbed a pen and a fresh legal pad, settled down across from Feldman, and started asking questions.

How did Feldman measure the performance of money managers who used very different investment strategies? Did he rely much on bank trust departments? Had he looked into the "quantitative" investment strategies coming out of academia? What did he think about index funds?

Two hours later, Binns had pages of notes—and Feldman had a new friend in the increasingly powerful community of pension fund managers.

Walter Gordon Binns Jr., was born a few months before the 1929 stock market crash and grew up in Richmond, Virginia. A gifted student, he majored in economics and earned a Phi Beta Kappa key at the College of William and Mary, but he didn't linger in the South. In August 1949, a month after his twentieth birthday, he graduated and immediately headed north to Harvard, where he earned a master's degree in government. He later added an MBA from New York University. After service in the U.S. Army, he joined General Motors in 1954 and started rising through the ranks in its finance department. Somewhere along the way, he started drinking heavily—and somewhere a bit further along the way, he stopped. A cheerful teetotaler for the rest of his life, he faithfully sought out Alcoholics Anonymous meetings in cities around the world as he traveled.

By 1980, he was assistant treasurer at the giant automaker, familiar with every aspect of the GM pension fund's operations. He knew General Motors had added some common stocks to its pension portfolio years before. That portfolio was managed by seven major banks; its performance had been anemic, to put it kindly. The pension fund stood dead last among nineteen comparable corporations, based on recent rankings, and GM's new chairman, Roger B. Smith, wasn't happy about that.

To fix it, Smith turned to Binns, who suddenly needed to learn everything he could about selecting and monitoring the money managers who could produce the gains Smith was demanding. Dave Feldman of AT&T would not be the last pension fund executive Binns would invite to lunch as he explored ways to steer his pension fund deeper into the stock market.

In the summer of 1981, that looked like a smarter move than staying in the "safe harbor" of the bond market, the traditional mooring for many conservative pension funds. Interest rates were high and still climbing, as the Fed fought inflation. High interest rates reduced the value of older bonds that paid a much lower rate of interest, and some traditional pension fund portfolios were packed with those old bonds, losing value with each upward tick in interest rates.

Other pension fund managers had weighed anchor and sailed out of the bond market years earlier. One of them was Roland M. Machold, the director of the New Jersey Division of Investment and the hands-on manager of that state's employee pension fund.

When Machold first arrived as the investment division's deputy director in 1975, the state pension fund held about $5 billion but owned only fifty stocks—mostly "bondlike" utility stocks paying high dividends but rarely gaining in value. That had to change—and under Machold, it did.

Roland Morris Machold was a product of Philadelphia society and old Wall Street. His father was a partner in the prestigious Philadelphia investment banking firm of Drexel and Company; Machold went to Yale, as his father had, and then to the Harvard Business School. After graduating in 1963, he took a job at Morgan Stanley, which had only about a hundred employees and served only blue-chip corporate clients.

Over the next decade, Wall Street changed. Cherished clients started shopping for better deals; gentlemen's agreements were shockingly broken. Trading desks got bigger and louder. Investment bankers seemed more ruthless. The hours were long, and the work grew less congenial.

Machold was tired of taking the last train home to Princeton, New Jersey, where he and his wife were raising a young family, so in 1975 he resigned from Morgan Stanley, with no strong sense of what to do next.

The answer came on a very cold Sunday morning at the historic Quaker meeting house, a tiny one-story stone building a bit south of Princeton that had been in use since before the Revolutionary War. Machold was that month's designated leader of the contemplative Quaker service, which meant he was responsible for tending the fire in the wood-burning stove, the building's only source of heat, and for bringing worship to a close at an appropriate moment by stirring in his seat and greeting the person beside him. That morning, the fire wasn't cooperating. As Machold fretted silently about how to get up and stoke it without prematurely terminating the service, a genial older man near the door caught his eye, then slipped out to his car and returned with tightly crumpled pages of that Sunday's *New York Times* to feed the fire.

When the service ended, Machold went over to thank his rescuer, who introduced himself as Richard Stoddard, the longtime director of the New Jersey Division of Investment. Prodded by Stoddard, Machold shared a bit of his own career history and admitted that he was at a crossroads.

Stoddard, too, was at a crossroads. He was on the brink of the state government's mandatory retirement age but had not been able to find a successor at the salary available. Perhaps Machold would consider applying for the job?

He did, and was promptly hired. He reported for work at a stately but slightly shabby mansion left over from Trenton's prosperous past. Windows were framed by chintz curtains on the inside and ivy on the outside. One former bedroom held a tiny market news ticker and five or six small desks pushed together to form the division's "trading desk." The employee directory read like the United Nations phone book; many employees had grown up in immigrant families and found work with the state government, perhaps after getting a degree from a local college. It was definitely not Morgan Stanley, but Machold loved it.

In December 1976, Stoddard retired after a dozen years of service; in those twelve years, the pension fund had grown from $1.4 billion to $5 billion. While still deputy director, Machold had encouraged Stoddard to raise the percentage of the fund's assets invested in common stock to about 20 percent, from just 10 percent when he arrived. As director, he pushed that figure higher. He hired a retired Prudential executive to actively manage the bond portfolio. The fund's performance got better, and Machold began to be noticed in the pension community. By 1981, despite a less-than-roaring stock market and a turbulent bond market, the fund had grown to $8.3 billion.

Machold and Binns were members of a growing army that would reshape the financial landscape in the 1980s. Since 1974, the nation's pension funds had increased their stock holdings almost 20 percent a year; as of 1980, their combined portfolios exceeded a quarter of a trillion dollars and were still growing. They were rapidly becoming the eight-hundred-pound clients that Wall Street could not ignore—titans whose concentrated financial power was unprecedented in the American market.

DESPITE HIS COMMITMENT to streamlining the NYSE's operations, John Phelan's vision of the exchange was unapologetically traditional: he believed the stock market existed primarily to serve individual inves-tors, in sharp contrast to the bank-dominated stock markets of Europe and Japan. In Phelan's view, individual investors tended to be long-term investors and were the ballast when a storm hit. His staff regularly mon-itored the proportion of Big Board trading that was done by individu-als, as opposed to institutional investors. He took pains to emphasize publicly that, on his trading floor, small investors were on an equal foot-ing with these emerging giants.

The major Wall Street brokerage firms that owned seats on the exchange did not share Phelan's vision. They were growing less inter-ested in individual investors and instead coveted clients such as Roland Machold, who directly managed billions of dollars and always had fresh money to invest, and Gordon Binns, who hired a host of managers to move hundreds of millions of dollars around the market. These institu-tional investors were hungry for new ideas, extra research services, faster responses. To serve them, Wall Street was harnessing its trading desks to new back-office computers, which were collecting institutional orders and driving them into the stock market on a scale and at a pace that humans had never seen before and could not match.

For the brokerage firms, this transformation was essential if they were to compete for these institutional clients—not just pension funds, but also giant mutual funds, vast college and charitable endowments, and big foundations, all newly interested in adding stocks to their once-stodgy portfolios of bonds or mortgages.

The emergence of these titans as stock market investors did not seem to trouble market regulators, who apparently took comfort in outdated studies showing that institutional investors did not disrupt the market because they tended to pursue a variety of different investment strategies.

Regulators did not focus on what would happen if that ever changed and Wall Street's biggest clients started moving in lockstep.

By 1981, that shift had already begun. Institutional investors were putting more and more money into the hands of "index fund" managers. Based on academic theories about how rational markets worked, these giant portfolios, an ocean of money tens of billions of dollars deep, replicated, on a smaller scale, the entire blue-chip market represented by broad market measures of value, such as the Standard & Poor's 500 index. Even some individual investors were starting to seek out mutual funds using this approach.

These index funds, although still a relatively small factor in the overall market for common stocks, tended to buy and sell the same stocks at the same time. The most vivid example of this herd instinct came when one company was dropped from an index and a new one was added. Vast amounts of the former would be sold; vast amounts of the latter would be bought. Once a stock was in a popular index, big index funds had no choice but to buy it.

Could this trend turn into Joe Granville's "Sell everything" day on overdrive? John Phelan wanted to guard against this, so he worked to increase the NYSE's ability to handle big surges in trading volume. His goal was to install computer systems capable of handling 150 million shares a day.

Reared in an era dominated by "the little guy," Phelan could see that most of the newcomers to his market were likely to be giants—funds holding tens of billions of dollars steered by smart, profit-oriented people such as Gordon Binns and Roland Machold, who needed to make money so they could keep the retirement promises that had been made to millions of American workers.

In the shadows beyond, new private pools of cash, known as "hedged funds," were attracting money from the most affluent speculators in the world and steering it into the U.S. stock market. As an institutional investor, Gordon Binns had heard about them and was intrigued, as some were producing spectacular returns. Roland Machold occasionally got a wrongheaded sales pitch from such a fund—as a state pension fund director, working under a very conservative investment council, he wasn't interested.

None of these men, least of all John Phelan at the NYSE, could be certain what these private funds were doing, or how big they were, or what their investment strategies might be, or which markets they were playing in—options, futures, stocks, Treasury bonds, bank CDs, mortgages? These funds were not required to register with any regulatory body, much less report their portfolio holdings. In the turf wars of Washington, these were the forgotten provinces. Nobody was fighting for the right to regulate them.

THE TRUCE IN the war between the CFTC and the SEC was announced on December 7, 1981. In a conference room at the Capitol, John Shad and Phil Johnson sat at a table in front of a dark velvet curtain as an SEC spokesman explained the deal. The CFTC would no longer oppose the bid by the Chicago Board Options Exchange to trade Ginnie Mae options (though the Chicago Board of Trade would continue its fight), and the SEC would no longer challenge the CFTC's plans to approve futures contracts based on the stock market.

Beyond that, it was a hodgepodge. The CFTC would continue to regulate all futures contracts, whether they were based on pork bellies or stock market indexes. The SEC would continue to regulate stocks and single-stock options, and would regulate options on government securities and stock indexes, if those ever came into being. Shad insisted that any stock index futures contract approved by the CFTC should be based on a well-established, broad-based index. Johnson agreed that the SEC would be consulted before the CFTC approved new index futures products, but insisted that his agency was free to ignore any SEC objections.

Under the "Shad-Johnson Accord," an already complex regulatory scheme morphed into a Rube Goldberg contraption that would plague the nation for decades. The simple question "Who regulates options?" could only be answered, "It depends." However, the answer to the question "Who regulates stock index futures contracts?" was finally clear, and it was the CFTC.

Shad and Johnson had made their deal and had gotten government out of the way of the financial innovation sweeping the marketplace—

innovation that would tie the futures market and the stock market together tighter than either man could have imagined.

Unfortunately, Shad and Johnson were not traders, and their accord ignored the facts of daily life that traders confronted in the stock market: Stocks didn't trade constantly throughout the day, without interruption or limitation. Sometimes, for various reasons, trading in a particular stock had to be halted. There were rules forbidding you from buying or selling a stock at all, if your trades were based on confidential inside information, or if you were betting that a declining stock would keep dropping. None of these rules applied to the markets where stock index futures contracts were going to be traded—markets that expected to rely on constantly fresh stock prices from New York as the basis for their own trading.

Moreover, the two markets ran on entirely different settlement schedules. If you made a profit on your stock index futures trade, you got your cash overnight; if you made a profit trading stocks, you got your cash in five days. If you needed profits from your stock sales to cover your futures position, you had better have a friendly banker or a big bank account to tide you over.

These rules and practices had been in place in the stock market for decades, and there was no requirement in the Shad-Johnson Accord that they be harmonized or changed. After all, Chicago wanted to piggyback on John Phelan's market, not vice versa. For Chicago to demand that the stock market change its rules to suit the futures traders would have been like a hitchhiker jumping into a car for a lift and promptly changing the radio station—or, worse, grabbing the wheel. The NYSE was the long-established cash market for stocks; Shad and Johnson apparently expected that stock index futures would merely piggyback on that cash market without affecting it. Consequently, they did not think to ensure that the design of these new stock-based futures contracts accommodated the stock market's rules and habits. That omission would come back to haunt both markets.

For Chicago, though, the new pact was a godsend. The legal battle over stock index futures was over, and Chicago had won—well, officially, the CFTC had won, but it amounted to the same thing.

Now the Merc and the Chicago Board of Trade, and all their lesser brethren, were free to start trading the futures contract they believed every institutional investor, the emerging behemoths of the decade's markets, would want to trade.

PHELAN WASN'T THE only one preoccupied with the rise of titan investors and the changing demographics of Wall Street. Some prescient bank regulators were worried, too. One of them was a ruddy-faced, grizzly-size New Yorker named Jerry Corrigan, a young protégé of Paul Volcker at the Federal Reserve Bank of New York who had remained a close aide and ally when Volcker moved to Washington in 1979.

Like Phelan, Jerry Corrigan was an Irishman. Both liked a good drink, a good party, and a good story. Also like Phelan, Corrigan had a first-class mind that could grasp complicated problems and get them solved, usually without alienating everyone in the neighborhood.

E. Gerald Corrigan was born in the blue-collar town of Waterbury, Connecticut. In 1967, after a Jesuit education and a doctorate in economics from Fordham, he was offered a research job at the New York Fed, housed in a massive Florentine-style palace three blocks from the New York Stock Exchange. The research department, he recalled, was populated "by economist types, all from Ivy League schools or Stanford or Berkeley. And then there was me." Within eighteen months, he was the chief of domestic research.

Sometime around 1972, the second-ranking officer at the bank summoned him to the executive offices on the tenth floor. Corrigan was alarmed. "Unless you were a close relative of God, you never saw the tenth floor," he said. Moreover, it was summer, and he had chosen a pretty loud cotton blazer as the day's attire. *This isn't so good*, he thought. His reputation outweighed his wardrobe, though, and at the end of that interview, he found himself the new corporate secretary of the Federal Reserve Bank of New York, working directly with its board of governors. That is where Paul Volcker found him two years later when Volcker became president of the New York Fed.

"I don't know what happened," Corrigan later recalled, "but for unknown reasons, he and I hit it off like Ike and Mike."

Like Phelan at the NYSE, Corrigan had to wrestle early on with the challenge of modernizing a tradition-bound system—in his case, the New York Fed's accounting department which worked around the clock, under the command of a man who had worked there for thirty years. After studying what needed to be done, Corrigan told the veteran accounting director that he was going to automate the department's general ledger.

"No, you're not," the older man said calmly. "You can automate it after I retire, but for now, we'll leave my control mechanisms in place."

Corrigan was taken aback, afraid he'd missed something in his research. "Forgive my ignorance, but what control systems are those?"

The older gentleman explained that the final cash-flow tally each day was "entered into the ledger with fountain pen ink, so it can't be changed." The culture of the bank was such that Corrigan actually did have to postpone the automation for a year and a half, until the fountain pen champion had retired.

That inauspicious project—Corrigan later recalled that Volcker "laughed for a half hour" when he heard the story—launched his career as Volcker's troubleshooter. In August 1979, when Volcker was tapped by President Carter to be Fed chairman, he summoned Corrigan to his office and said, "Pack your bags. You're going to be my special assistant in Washington."

Corrigan had been at Volcker's elbow when Harry Jacobs at Bache called in the spring of 1980 to alert him to the silver crisis. Days later, he had been Volcker's eyes, ears, and telephone operator in Boca Raton as anxious bankers negotiated a new loan for the Hunt brothers.

By then, Corrigan already was getting worried about how rapidly Wall Street was changing. Banks were regulated by the Fed and the Office of the Comptroller of the Currency and the FDIC; insurance companies were regulated by officials in the fifty states; and mutual funds and brokerage firms were regulated by the SEC—and these were all becoming more deeply entwined with one another. Financial futures trading, under the oversight of the same overmatched regulators who presided over the silver crisis, would forge new and very worrisome links among all those markets.

6

STOCK FUTURES, BOND FAILURES

On February 26, 1982, a cold gray day in Washington, Phil Johnson arrived early at the Russell Senate Office Building, a massive stone trapezoid across from the Capitol. The building was a few blocks from the Monocle, the restaurant where he and John Shad had opened their peace talks the previous summer. In a few minutes, Johnson would be explaining that deal to a Senate agriculture subcommittee weighing whether to renew the CFTC's lease on life.

He would be the first to testify, so he settled in immediately at the witness table. Behind him, in the second row of seats set aside for spectators, was Jim Stone, who was still a member of the commission.

When Senator Richard Lugar of Indiana, the subcommittee chairman, opened the hearing, Johnson graciously made note of Stone's presence, calling him "a very valuable asset to the commission."

Three days earlier, Stone had sent a remarkable letter to the full Senate Agriculture Committee detailing his worries about how the borders between securities and commodities had "rapidly eroded." He noted that three of the largest commodity firms regulated by the CFTC had recently merged with Wall Street firms regulated by the SEC. The NYSE, under the SEC's wing, had a new futures exchange, regulated by the CFTC. And ten days earlier, on February 16, the CFTC had approved the first futures contract based on a stock market index: the Kansas City Board of Trade's new Value Line futures contract.

Stone had cast the only vote against the new contract, whose debut he saw as "final proof that the lines have been blurred."

The Value Line approval was a tribute to Johnson's deft diplomacy in Washington. Paul Volcker had serious concerns about stock index futures, particularly on the issue of margins. These concerns boiled down to how much skin a speculator should have in the game. Using stock index futures, an investor could control a block of stock with far less cash than would be needed to control the same stake on the NYSE. That kind of lopsided leverage didn't sit right with Volcker, especially in the aftermath of the silver crisis. Johnson had met repeatedly with the Fed chairman, trying to persuade him that margins in the futures market were adequate to prevent excessive speculation. Volcker finally agreed not to openly oppose the new contract, but he still had misgivings.

Now applications for at least sixteen new stock-based futures contracts were pending before the CFTC, including a bid from John Phelan's New York Futures Exchange to trade futures based on the NYSE Composite index. "Should this trend continue, the arguments for maintaining two separate regulatory agencies, and two distinct philosophies, will dissolve," Stone observed in his letter. "If the industries become one, the CFTC and the SEC should consolidate as well."

At the reauthorization hearing, Phil Johnson just wanted the lawmakers to bless and quickly codify the deal he had worked out with Shad. If Congress did not act, the courts no doubt would; the CFTC and the SEC were awaiting a ruling in the Chicago Board of Trade's lawsuit to block the SEC's approval of Ginnie Mae options trading.

A few moments into the sparsely attended hearing, Senator Lugar was interrupted politely by Senator S. I. "Sam" Hayakawa of California, whose modest manner veiled a brilliant mind. With a nod from Lugar, Hayakawa turned his gaze to Johnson: "I understand that trading has been approved for stock index futures by the CFTC. This appears to be an instrument through which speculators on the stock market could hedge their bets on the futures market."

Johnson nodded. "That is right," he replied.

Hayakawa seemed perplexed. "I do not understand the economic purpose of this contract," he said. Indeed, he continued, stock index futures seemed to be "thousands of miles away from agriculture. I must say, Mr. Chairman, this disturbs me very much."

Not long afterward, Senator Robert Dole of Kansas also spoke up about stock index futures. "What we are authorizing is, in effect, legalized gambling," he said, disapprovingly.

FORTUNATELY FOR PHIL Johnson, neither Dole nor Hayakawa had been at the Kansas City Board of Trade two days earlier, when the Value Line index futures started trading. In the crowd was Joe Granville, the flamboyant market guru who had triggered a small stampede on the Big Board in January 1981. "It's like a new game in Las Vegas," he said with evident delight. "Now, instead of betting on a stock, you can bet [on] the entire market. It will tell me how the people feel about the future of the market." This was not a view that would have reassured Senator Dole.

About two thousand contracts were traded that day, and the gold rush was on. Barely a week later, a CFTC economist told a futures industry gathering that the commission was reviewing fifty-seven applications for new stock index futures and futures-related options products.

In the futures market, the first exchange to develop a new contract tended to own the lion's share of trading in that contract going forward. So, there was some chagrin in Chicago that Kansas City had beaten them into the history books with the first stock index futures contract.

It wasn't for lack of trying, and no one tried harder than Richard Sandor, the former Berkeley professor who was now the chairman of the New Products Committee at the Chicago Board of Trade. He had been working on a stock index futures contract since at least 1978.

After some initial setbacks, Sandor and his team decided to pursue a futures contract based on the Dow Jones Industrial Average, arguably the most widely published stock market barometer in the world. Sandor flew to New York to pitch Dow Jones executives on the idea, offering the company between $1 million and $2 million a year for the use of its name. Dow Jones, the publisher of the *Wall Street Journal* and *Barron's* magazine, wasn't interested.

Sandor wasn't daunted. Back in Chicago, he made a fresh pitch to officials at the Board of Trade—one that opened, oddly, with a thumbnail history of aspirin. Aspirin had once been a brand owned by Bayer for its version of acetylsalicylic acid, but the company had not defended its trademark, and *aspirin* gradually became a generic term. Sandor argued that *Dow*, like *aspirin*, had become a generic term, free for anyone to use.

The exchange gave his theory a try. Two days after the Value Line index's debut, the Chicago Board of Trade sought CFTC approval for the CBT Index, a Dow clone. Dow Jones sued, the lawsuit inched along for months, and the Board of Trade ultimately lost.

Meanwhile, Leo Melamed at the Chicago Merc had gone in a different direction, eyeing the Standard & Poor's 500 index. It was nowhere near as familiar to retail investors as the Dow, but the Merc's research showed that big equity-portfolio managers—the kind of people Gordon Binns was hiring to manage the stocks in GM's pension fund—almost uniformly used that index as the benchmark for their performance. Melamed felt they were the natural hedgers for a stock index futures contract, so he put the Merc's chips on the S&P 500.

And whereas Dow Jones had rebuffed the Chicago Board of Trade, Standard & Poor's, a division of the McGraw-Hill publishing company, was at least willing to talk to the Merc. Over dinner with S&P executives, Melamed explained that he wanted an exclusive deal and said he was willing to pay S&P a dime for every contract traded, up to a maximum of 10,000 contracts a day. So far as Melamed knew, that greatly exceeded the maximum daily trading volume of any futures contract in history. A deal was struck, and the Merc entered the stock index sweepstakes two months behind Kansas City.

On April 21, Melamed watched proudly as a scrum of traders poured into a pit at the Merc to start trading the new S&P 500 futures contract, quickly dubbed the "spooz" (which rhymes with "booze"). The first day's volume easily exceeded 10,000 contracts. Spooz trading would falter a bit in the next four months, as the stock market suffered the last wounds of a bear market, but Melamed was certain that, when the next bull market found its legs, the new product would become one of the most successful futures contracts ever.

ON MARCH 24, 1982, as the Merc was preparing for the spooz debut, a bombshell from Chicago's federal appeals court hit Washington.

The Seventh Circuit Court of Appeals had heard oral arguments the previous November on the Chicago Board of Trade's challenge to the SEC's approval of Ginnie Mae options. Since then, the SEC general counsel's office had been watching and waiting. Their lawyers in Chicago got the call from the court and quickly retrieved the decision. When it was read to the SEC lawyers in Washington, they were appalled.

The Board of Trade's legal theory had been remarkable: it claimed that Ginnie Mae certificates had been magically converted into commodities the minute the futures contracts based on them started trading in Chicago. Thanks to this alchemy, an option on a Ginnie Mae certificate was an option on a commodity, not an option on a security—and commodity options, like commodity futures, fell squarely under the exclusive jurisdiction of the CFTC. The argument had raised a host of alarming questions for other regulators: Had Treasury bills also become commodities the minute the Merc started trading Treasury bill futures? If someone started trading a futures contract on IBM stock, would that suddenly turn the stock into a commodity? Was the CFTC's jurisdiction limited only by Chicago's imagination?

Giving a literal reading to the remarkably elastic CFTC statute, and ignoring the terms of the Shad-Johnson Accord, the judges ruled that the SEC had no authority to approve the Ginnie Mae options contracts. As the court saw it, the law's language meant that "literally anything other than onions could become a 'commodity' and thereby subject to CFTC regulation simply by its futures being traded on some exchange."

Indeed, the appellate court found that the expansive law that created the CFTC might even be interpreted as denying the SEC any authority at all over the stock options market. In a challenge to lawmakers, the court wrote, "Given the possible expansion of 'commodity' to include even corporate securities on which options have traditionally been regulated by the SEC, the CFTC exclusive jurisdiction clause must have some limits." Apparently, the judges felt it was the job of Congress, not the courts, to define those limits.

The ruling ignited a frenzy of alarmed protests. Even Phil Johnson at the CFTC was surprised at its reach. He was still awaiting formal reauthorization of his agency, and this was exactly the kind of thing that could inflame the SEC's allies in Congress and undo all his careful diplomacy.

Congressman John Dingell, a Michigan Democrat with strong New Deal sympathies, quickly called for hearings on amendments that would affirm the SEC's authority over the stock options market. Dingell also questioned the entire realm of financial futures, especially stock index futures. The amendments would pass easily. Dingell's profound uneasiness over stock index futures would not.

WHILE THERE WERE obviously disputes over the SEC's jurisdiction over stock index futures and Ginnie Mae options, it was absolutely certain that the SEC did not have jurisdiction over the market for U.S. Treasury bonds. Nobody did, in any practical sense. It was one of the hidden canyons in the financial landscape where a brushfire could erupt and spread to other markets almost without warning.

When the SEC was created in the 1930s, the relatively small market for U.S. government securities had been explicitly placed outside its regulatory fences. That remained true, although the government now depended on an immensely larger Treasury market to borrow money to cover a growing federal deficit.

In that market, tens of billions of dollars in Treasury securities changed hands daily among corporate treasurers, traders at giant banks, senior vice presidents at local savings and loans, and government finance officers in city, county, and state agencies around the country. Although the titans had arrived, the Treasury bond market was still governed by gentlemen's agreements and quaint notions of accounting.

The Federal Reserve had a small bit of power over this market— although "influence" would be more accurate than "power."

The New York Fed, where Paul Volcker had once presided, designated three dozen major Wall Street institutions as "primary dealers," which gave them the coveted right to submit bids when the Treasury auctioned off new securities. In exchange, these primary dealers volunteered to give the New York Fed regular updates on their financial health.

Of course, almost all the primary dealers also fell under some formal regulatory regime. The big national banks were monitored by the Office of the Comptroller of the Currency and the FDIC, and their holding companies were overseen by the Fed. The big Wall Street brokerage firms were regulated by the SEC.

However, if a financial firm put its Treasury bond trading desk into a separate business unit, that unit was regulated by no one. And that's what Drysdale Securities did.

Drysdale was a small New York brokerage house whose roots went back to a firm that had joined the New York Stock Exchange in 1890. In early 1982, Drysdale had set up Drysdale Government Securities, a separate unit controlled by the firm's star bond trader, David Heuwetter. Heuwetter had recently used some peculiar features of Treasury market accounting, and very little cash, to build up risky trading positions of at least $5 billion, a staggering amount for a firm Drysdale's size. The assumption, of course, was that Heuwetter's borrowing and trading strategy would be profitable—and so long as interest rates kept rising, pushing down bond prices in the process, that was a pretty good bet. Within the firm, the trader was "rumored to be using a secret and sophisticated computer-based trading strategy."

Drysdale Securities was a member of the NYSE, and this risky bond business did not escape the attention of John Phelan's staff. The Big Board insisted that Drysdale either insulate itself from Heuwetter's adventures or shut the operation down. The result was the spin-off in early 1982.

The spin-off alone might have been enough to worry some of Drysdale's trading partners. However, a lot of Drysdale's trades were conducted through Chase Manhattan Bank, the Rockefeller family's bank and the third largest in the country; a lesser amount was handled by two smaller but still substantial institutions.

Business practices in the immense market where older Treasury securities were traded were so casual that it was not clear—to the marketplace, at least—whether Chase and the other banks were acting simply as Drysdale's agents in the trades or were serving as clearinghouses, guaranteeing the trades in some way. Many people lending their bonds to Drysdale apparently thought they were doing business with Chase; some bond lenders in the savings and loan community or in county finance offices in the hinterland might never have heard of Drysdale.

None of these feckless traditions—which one senior banker later conceded were "not rational"—seemed to worry anyone in this huge unregulated market until Monday, May 17, 1982. That was the day Heuwetter was supposed to send Chase Manhattan a payment of $160 million, to cover the interest due on some of Drysdale's borrowed bonds. Chase would then forward the cash to the bonds' various owners. Unfortunately, the previous evening, Heuwetter had called his banker at home to ask if Chase would lend him the money to make the next day's interest payment. He would be unable to pay it otherwise.

Frantic calls were made; word quickly reached Willard C. Butcher, Chase's CEO. Bank lawyers assured Butcher that Chase had merely been an agent for Drysdale and was not legally obligated to cover the default, so Chase declined to extend the loan to the beleaguered bond trader.

Of course, that $160 million would surely be missed by the firms to whom it was owed; the default might actually put some of the smaller firms in peril. So, on Monday morning, Butcher quite responsibly reached out to the one government agency with at least a sliver of authority over the situation: the New York Fed. A group of senior staffers there met with him at 2:30 p.m. and listened as he explained the situation. He proposed calling a meeting with all the major firms involved, at which Chase would suggest they jointly cover Drysdale's default to protect the smaller firms at risk.

The New York Fed officials promptly notified Paul Volcker, who immediately summoned his one-man SWAT team, Jerry Corrigan. They both knew the Treasury market would quickly get wind of the Drysdale problem—too many firms were affected to keep it quiet, and Treasury prices were already falling sharply. What if other dealers began to fear that they would not be paid on their deals because their counterparties had not been paid by Drysdale? That could disable the market, an important source of daily working cash for countless entities in business and government. If Drysdale wound up in bankruptcy, billions of dollars in bonds could be tied up for months, even years.

Although the Federal Reserve had no clear authority in this crisis, Volcker agreed that the New York Fed should convene the meeting Chase had requested, just to learn more about what was going on. Then he tried to focus on getting ready for the next morning's meeting of the nation's key monetary policy panel, the Federal Open Market Committee (FOMC), which he chaired. Corrigan made plans to travel to New York.

Around 6 p.m. Monday evening, senior executives from seven major Wall Street firms filed into the New York Fed's fortress-like headquarters in Lower Manhattan. With Chase executives at his elbow, a Fed official carefully explained that the Fed was concerned about the "potential market consequences of the problem," but was not endorsing any plan that Chase might present.

Chase's suggestion that the banks jointly cover the Drysdale default sat on the table like a stale fruitcake. As far as these major dealers were concerned, this was Chase's problem because it had handled Drysdale's trades. Sure of his legal position, Butcher urged the dealers to sleep on the idea and reconvene at 7 o'clock the next morning at his bank's headquarters, a few blocks away.

At the Fed in Washington, alerts were going out to Treasury officials, the comptroller of the currency, and SEC staffers to warn them of possible domino effects from Drysdale's default. The SEC had some authority over Drysdale Securities, but it was soon clear that the brokerage firm was not the entity involved in this mess. The comptroller of the currency supervised Chase Manhattan Bank, but that agency's chief concern was for Chase's bottom line, its "safety and soundness," not its moral obligations to the market. Treasury officials could do little but worry about the next auction of two-year Treasury notes, less than two days away. If Drysdale's default was still hanging over the market, it could drive up the interest rate that taxpayers would have to pay on those notes.

Once again, as in the silver crisis two years earlier, Corrigan found himself in a world without tidy regulatory borders—a world where everyone seemed to be groping frantically in the dark for a lever that would prevent an explosion.

THE MEETING AT Chase Manhattan's headquarters on Tuesday morning did not go well. By one account, thirty angry brokers and bankers crowded into the conference room, having heard via Wall Street's supremely efficient grapevine that Chase was not going to cover the default.

The Treasury market continued to wobble, as word spread that Drysdale also had defaulted on interest payments owed to two other banks. Remarkably, more than thirty-six hours after Drysdale announced its default, Jerry Corrigan could not say for certain how big this problem was or how many other banks and bond dealers might be affected.

The rest of the day, Corrigan and other Fed officials wrangled with officials from Chase and the two other banks left holding Drysdale's empty bag. The decision was entirely theirs, Corrigan told them, but he thought "a decision to pay interest would have a calming effect."

Back in Washington, Corrigan's boss was complaining out loud about the Drysdale debacle. He had called the day's Federal Open Market Committee meeting to order at 9:15 a.m., but explained that he would be ducking in and out during the day to take urgent calls from New York.

"We have a rather abnormal development in the market, to say the least," he told the startled committee members, explaining that a government securities firm "can't meet its bills."

"Is this a dealer?" asked one of the Fed governors, referring to the big primary dealers designated by the New York Fed.

"It's not a recognized dealer," Volcker replied. "It is a fringe operator who apparently operated in very large size" using money raised "with some kind of rinky-dink scheme."

His concern was evident. "Chase Manhattan is in the middle of this, as the middleman." People on the other side of the firm's trades "claim that Chase is liable and Chase claims it is not, so we have a mess there. Losses are well in excess of $100 million just on that set of transactions, and we don't know what else is involved. We're trying to find out."

He outlined the stabilizing steps the Fed could take in the market-place, if his worst fears materialized and a bankruptcy judge froze the assets of other dealers who had left securities in Drysdale's hands.

Most of Drysdale's lenders were "major security houses in New York—there is a group of seven or eight of them, they're all well-known firms," Volcker said. "They should be able to withstand the loss if things ever settle, so far as we know about the loss," he said. "But that doesn't mean it won't send ripples of very deep concern all through the market."

He paused and looked around the room, a circle of anxious faces.

"Any comments, or questions that I won't be able to answer?"

There was one, from Lawrence K. Roos, the president of the Federal Reserve Bank of St. Louis: "Paul, as the Federal Reserve, what is our responsibility in a situation like this? Just to keep order?"

"Our general responsibility is to the economy most broadly, Larry," Volcker replied. "The problem in this case, as in all cases, is that the guy who is responsible is only the smallest part of the problem. If all of the financing arrangements in the government securities market are disrupted, we have a major problem."

The president of the Federal Reserve Bank of San Francisco, John J. Balles, then spoke up: "Just looking at the other side: is there any risk of our being accused of a bailout of private dealers, or whatever?"

"Yes," Volcker answered abruptly. "There is no way to avoid that." He added after a moment, "That is the nature of being a lender of last resort."

THE NEXT MORNING, the two other banks involved in the Drysdale default announced that they would cover the interest owed on the bonds. Fifteen minutes before noon on Wednesday, Chase announced that it, too, would pay the interest due on the Drysdale bonds. The call was made to Volcker: Success. Persuasion and maybe a little moral pressure from the Fed had resolved a crisis that no one had clear regulatory authority to handle—a crisis that no one had seen coming, and a crisis that no one had even been able to measure accurately in the time available.

With the silver crisis, Corrigan had seen the financial fault lines stretch in a new direction, toward the Chicago commodity markets.

Now a crack in an arcane corner of the Treasury market, regulated by no one, had shaken several major banks, regulated by the Fed and the comptroller of the currency, and some Wall Street firms regulated by the SEC.

America in 1982 had become a place where an adventurous Treasury bond speculator—or, for that matter, two silver speculators in Texas—could create an earthquake that could shake any corner, or every corner, of the nation's financial landscape.

PART TWO

TITANS AND WIZARDS

7

A PLAGUE FROM OKLAHOMA

Just before the July Fourth weekend in 1982, a banker sat in a conference room at Continental Illinois National Bank in Chicago and stared in disbelief at the federal bank examiner seated across from him.

The examiner was tapping a stack of documents, the paperwork for a loan that Continental Illinois had bought from Penn Square Bank, an aggressive "oil patch" lender in Oklahoma City. The examiner was saying the loan was bad—there wasn't enough collateral behind it, and Continental Illinois would have to write it off.

No, the banker protested. That loan was backed by the unlimited guarantee of a wealthy individual affiliated with the drilling venture that was being financed.

"No, all you have is smaller limited guarantees," the examiner said; the guarantees did not fully cover the loan.

The banker was shaken. Partly on his watch, Continental had paid nearly $1 billion to buy loans from Penn Square Bank. He had been personally reassured about the questioned loan's terms by Penn Square's top oil and gas banker, an exuberant young man he considered a close friend.

The examiner had already moved on to the next set of documents, raising fresh questions about other loans.

As soon as the banker could, he hurried to his office. He knew that bank examiners were at the Oklahoma bank, too; news coverage was suggesting that there were some problems there. His friend, his primary contact at Penn Square, had insisted the bank was just experiencing normal growing pains after a hot spurt of success. Federal regulators just wanted Penn Square to find $30 million in fresh capital—and his friend had assured him that new investors were being recruited.

Increasingly anxious, the Chicago banker telephoned his friend at home in Oklahoma City. "You've got to go to your office, or have someone go to your office, and get the examiners to unseal your files," the Chicago banker told him urgently. "You've got to send me the unlimited guarantee that you got to back up that loan."

"I'm sorry," his friend replied. "I never got it."

Without that unlimited guarantee, the loan was not worth what Continental Illinois had paid for it, if it was worth anything at all. Was the examiner right about all the other Penn Square loans stacked up on the table in the Continental Illinois conference room?

The examiner was right about most of them—enough to destroy the banker's career and enough to profoundly shake the market's confidence in Continental Illinois itself.

And that would be enough to shake the financial foundations of Chicago.

IT WOULD BE hard to overstate how much the explosive ingenuity of Chicago's futures markets had been underwritten by Chicago's major banks: First National Bank of Chicago, Harris Bank and Trust, and especially Continental Illinois.

In 1971, when Leo Melamed was drumming up support for his new foreign currency futures market, he feared that the giant national banks would see the Merc as competition for their own foreign currency business and shun the new product. And many did: one New York banker warned Melamed that foreign currency futures would serve no purpose "other than to cater to people slightly more sophisticated than those who go to the track."

But Chicago's bankers were cut from the same innovative cloth as its traders. They quickly rallied to support the new foreign currency exchange. By recommending currency futures to their institutional customers and adding their executives' names to the Merc's list of advisers, they gave the venture worldwide credibility.

The global ambitions of Continental Illinois were a match even for those of the Merc. By the summer of 1982, the bank had grown into the sixth largest in the country, and it ranked first in commercial and industrial loans. In 1978 the respected *Dun's Review* had published a glowing profile of Continental Illinois's chief executive, Roger E. Anderson, and called the bank "one of the five best managed companies" in the United States.

There were problems, of course—enormous ones that confronted the entire banking industry. Interest rates on new loans were sky-high, which meant that high-quality companies weren't eager to borrow. Meanwhile, Federal Reserve regulations capped the amount of interest that banks and savings and loans could pay to their small-scale depositors, prompting many people to pull their cash out of banks to get the higher rates offered by money market mutual funds. The Fed was reluctant to lift the interest rate cap, for fear it would doom the already shaky savings and loan industry, where institutions were failing at the rate of about five every week.

Bankers such as Roger Anderson at Continental Illinois believed the best way to survive this storm was to get bigger and broader—to push into every new market that regulators would open to them, while expanding traditional lending operations as far as the market would bear. Some markets, notably the brokerage and securities underwriting business, remained largely closed to them, but they were beating on the doors.

Clearly, a legislative fix was needed, and Congress was ineffectively mulling over what it should do when the summer of 1982 went spectacularly sour.

The problems at Penn Square quickly became public, thanks to an alert reporter for *American Banker*, the bible of the banking industry. The crisis at the bank was a shock to its depositors, but they may have been the only ones who were surprised. Rival bankers in the oil patch had watched skeptically as Penn Square ballooned from "a sleepy, $30 million-asset suburban retail bank" in the mid-1970s to a $500 million bank whose loan portfolio was stuffed with risky oil and gas loans.

The bank's troubles had also been detected by at least one of its regulators. For more than two years, examiners from the Dallas outpost of the Office of the Comptroller of the Currency had been discreetly prodding the bank to tighten its loan standards and curb its prodigious growth. The bank's top managers had made earnest promises and temporary improvements. Meanwhile, they kept selling their loans upstream to a handful of big banks, including Continental Illinois.

Examiners had arrived to give Penn Square a checkup in April 1982. After spending a week or two poring through drawers of half-completed or unreliable loan documents, they knew they were facing a full-blown disaster. Writing off the troubled loans they had already looked at would wipe out the bank's capital, and there were still many more file cabinets to open. On May 11 they sent a warning to Washington.

The warning eventually reached their boss, C. Todd Conover, a California banking industry consultant tapped by President Reagan to run the Office of the Comptroller of the Currency, an independent agency within the Treasury Department that was the official regulator of roughly twelve thousand nationally chartered banks, including Penn Square.

On June 23, Conover issued the order that gave Penn Square a week to find $30 million in new capital. He alerted one of his two fellow bank regulators, William M. Isaac, the chairman of the FDIC, which had insured Penn Square's deposits. The next day, Conover called the third regulator involved, Paul Volcker at the Fed, to tell him that Penn Square would likely need some kind of emergency loan in the next few days. And on June 30, after a week of crisis, an FDIC team swooped in to take charge in Oklahoma City, and the Fed extended a $20 million loan to brace the bank for the fatal run that regulators had feared, and had just barely headed off.

In 1982, federal deposit insurance was capped at $100,000. Tempted by Penn Square's high CD rates, many customers, including about 170 banks and other financial institutions, had put much more money into their Penn Square accounts than the FDIC insurance would cover. In fact, the total of uninsured deposits was roughly $250 million, which would constitute the largest loss by bank depositors since the Great Depression.

It was an acid test for Bill Isaac, who had been appointed to the FDIC board by Jimmy Carter and elevated to the chairmanship by Ronald Reagan. As Isaac saw it, unless the troubled bank could somehow find a new owner or merge into an existing bank, the FDIC would have to do a "payoff." In a payoff, depositors get paid up to the FDIC insurance limit, and the bank is slowly wound down. Depositors whose accounts exceed the FDIC limit get IOUs for the rest of their money. Those chits are paid from whatever can be salvaged from the failed bank's loan portfolio. Creditors, who in this case would include Continental Illinois and the other upstream banks, get any crumbs left over.

For Paul Volcker, word that almost two hundred financial institutions could be damaged by the Oklahoma bank's collapse was terrible news arriving at the worst possible moment.

Volcker's team was already on high alert; the Mexican government faced a substantial bank loan payment in August, and other Latin American debtor nations were looking shakier every day. Another small government securities firm in Los Angeles had faltered in early June in the aftermath of the Drysdale crisis, and credit concerns were still unsettling the Treasury markets. Now they had to contend with a bank failure that might cast fresh doubts on the creditworthiness of all major banks.

The fragile banking system had been a worry at the Fed for several years, but in the tenth month of a steep and deep recession, those concerns had escalated. The jumbo size that banks hoped would make them safer also made their problems more of a threat to the overall financial system. It used to be that only a handful of giant banks posed such risks, but Penn Square showed that a small, obscure bank could be just as dangerous to financial stability. New fault lines had been formed because banks increasingly sold their local loans to other banks far afield. Only a map of those transactions, a document impossible to construct, would reveal which banks might be damaged when bad loans blew up.

So, when Paul Volcker heard about Penn Square, he firmly opposed the FDIC's plan to do a payoff and argued for a workout that would prevent any losses to depositors or upstream creditors.

Initially, Conover agreed with Volcker—after all, that was how a troubled bank was routinely rescued—but neither of them could prevail with Isaac, who argued convincingly that no sane bank would agree to merge with Penn Square when no one yet knew the scale of its liabilities, except that they reached into the billions. For the same reason, the FDIC could not just take over the bank itself and operate it. So, although the FDIC had never done a payoff for "any bank even remotely approaching this size," to Isaac it looked like the only option.

GIVEN ALL THAT, it is not surprising that Volcker was cranky on Wednesday afternoon, June 30, 1982, when he gaveled the twelve-member Federal Open Market Committee to order.

The main item on the agenda was Mexico, which was on the verge of its own financial crisis because it owed its bankers $20 billion and was having trouble repaying its debts.

A failure by Mexico to repay its bank loans would be a body blow to the U.S. banking industry. The five largest banks in the country would lose between one-third and three-quarters of their capital to a Mexican default. The next five largest banks, including Continental Illinois, would lose between a quarter and half their capital. And that was just *Mexico*. There were a lot of shaky debtor nations in line behind it. Volcker got committee approval for the confidential emergency financial package that the Fed, the Treasury, and the International Monetary Fund were drafting for Mexico and recessed the meeting until the following day.

When the committee gathered the next morning, Volcker shared the saga of Penn Square.

"In general terms we have a potentially serious banking problem," he began, "arising out of a bank in Oklahoma that is teetering, or more than teetering."

The bank itself wasn't "all that significant," he said. No one would have picked it as a systemic threat to the financial system. Still, its reckless lending to the oil industry reflected "a psychology, I suppose, that anybody who digs a hole in the ground now, or even promises to dig a hole in the ground, has a bonanza—because the price of oil was going to go up forever. And the price of oil suddenly *doesn't* go up forever, and all these loans look awful."

How many other loans on the books of America's banks were solid only if prices continued to climb at a feverish pace? How many had been made solely because no one imagined that Volcker could actually defeat the inflation that had afflicted the nation for a decade?

Over the July Fourth weekend, Volcker convened officials from the FDIC and from the comptroller's office to discuss the Penn Square situation, and the group decided that Treasury secretary Donald Regan should be consulted. When Regan arrived, casually dressed, he took a seat on the sofa and listened to the opposing arguments.

Volcker and Conover thought there was a big risk of chaos in the financial markets if the Oklahoma bank were shut down on the FDIC's terms. Bill Isaac made his case for market discipline, for taking a stand on Penn Square to show that there was not an unlimited safety net for reckless banks. It is not clear if Regan sided with Isaac, as one account suggested, or if Conover thought he had and left Volcker outvoted. In any case, in the early evening of Monday, July 5, the order was given for the FDIC to begin a payoff operation at Penn Square.

A ferocious crisis of confidence, sent special delivery from Oklahoma City, had been dropped on Continental Illinois's doorstep. And it wouldn't stop there.

When the New York Stock Exchange opened on July 6, Continental's share price fell almost 10 percent on the news from Oklahoma. Losses on its Penn Square loans put Continental almost $61 million in the red when it closed the books on the second quarter of 1982.

Within weeks, senior executives at the bank admitted that they had known about problems with some of their Penn Square loans as early as the previous fall, but they insisted they had no reason to doubt the overall soundness of the Oklahoma bank. Ominously, a major credit rating agency cut the bank's rating.

The virus was spreading beyond Chicago. On the West Coast, Seattle First National Bank, known as Seafirst, had purchased more than $400 million in poorly documented oil loans from Penn Square. A week after the FDIC acted, Seafirst laid off four hundred employees and warned investors it would incur substantial losses. On the East Coast, Chase Manhattan, still smarting from the Drysdale mess of a month earlier, soon reported its own embarrassing losses on Penn Square loans. In the Midwest, Michigan National Bank owned $190 million in loans purchased from the Oklahoma bank. Penn Square losses had led one savings and loan to be declared insolvent, while another was severely impaired and several more had been hurt badly. More than 130 federally chartered credit unions had uninsured deposits with the failed bank and would have to wait for the FDIC to find additional assets before they could fully recover their cash.

On July 15, Volcker told FOMC members during a conference call that there was "nervousness in the market about financial institutions in general" in the wake of the Penn Square crisis. "Enormous numbers of rumors are being generated, which get reported to me regularly," he added.

Preston Martin, a former thrift industry regulator who had recently been appointed to the Fed board, agreed. He had heard market people "talking about what bank is going to fail next." He concluded, as did Volcker, that to tighten their grip on inflation at that moment would indicate to everyone "that we are not taking seriously the downside risk inherent in an unstable, illiquid market."

It bothered the "inflation hawks" on the committee to stand pat, but they all agreed the situation was just too fragile for them to do anything else.

THE NEXT MORNING, a little after 10 o'clock, Congressman Benjamin Rosenthal, the New York Democrat who had led the fierce silver hearings two years earlier, banged his gavel to open the first House hearings on the Penn Square crisis.

"The Penn Square Bank failure is a dramatic reminder of the need for an effective bank regulatory system," Rosenthal said. "Many millions of dollars will be lost by depositors and other financial institutions because of this failure, in spite of Federal supervision and in spite of Federal deposit insurance coverage."

Rosenthal pressed to learn how one set of bank regulators, those in the comptroller's office, could have known about Penn Square's problems for more than two years without alerting other financial regulators. The answer, of course, was that sharing details with other financial regulators would virtually guarantee the bank runs they were trying to prevent.

Then Rosenthal called Comptroller Todd Conover and FDIC chairman Bill Isaac to testify.

Isaac's candor seemed to soothe Rosenthal. The Penn Square outcome wasn't optimal, the FDIC chief conceded frankly. Ideally, a troubled bank can be sold to a healthier one, with some FDIC assistance, and all customer deposits are thereby protected. Unfortunately, in this case, Penn Square's lending practices were so dubious that it was impossible to arrange a merger.

Isaac had a knack for preempting Rosenthal's attacks. "Many people are asking: 'How could this have happened? Why did this bank fail and how did so many other financial institutions get involved? Is this failure evidence of other problems in the financial system?'" His questions were, indeed, what Rosenthal was asking.

"The short answer is that, at best, this bank engaged in shoddy, speculative banking practices," Isaac answered. "Its problems were the result of loans which should never have been made."

He felt certain, he said, that while there might be a few other sinkholes like Penn Square in the financial landscape, they "will be few and far between."

As for Continental Illinois and the other giant banks hurt by Penn Square's collapse, they could withstand their likely losses, he said. "If one can identify a silver lining behind the dark cloud of the Penn Square affair," Isaac said, with far more optimism than was warranted, "we should expect that all financial institutions will be more prudent in the future."

And if one could identify a lesson, a target for reform, behind those same storm clouds, he continued, it was that something needed to be done about the nation's fragmented approach to regulating its banks. What purpose did it serve for five regulatory agencies to oversee America's deposit-taking institutions? Why were there three separate deposit insurance funds—one for national banks, another for savings and loans, and a third for credit unions? And was it possible to provide more public disclosure about the condition and business practices of insured institutions?

"I firmly believe that significant reforms in our regulatory apparatus are needed," Isaac concluded. "It is my sincere hope that the experiences of the last two weeks will provide the impetus to move forward on these issues."

EVERY FRESH CRINGE of anxiety in the banking system during that long, shaky summer of 1982 was also felt on the floor of the New York Stock Exchange.

The Dow Jones Industrial Average, which had popped above the historic 1,000-point line twice in the month immediately after Reagan's election, had spent the summer hovering around the 800-point mark.

About the only good news during the hard times of 1981 and 1982 was that Paul Volcker's bitter anti-inflation medicine seemed to be working. Inflation had plummeted from north of 12 percent to below 6 percent, and it looked to be heading even lower, which made bond investors a little less worried and stocks a little more attractive.

Even so, on Thursday, August 12, 1982, the stock market sank for the eighth day in a row. The Dow closed at 776.92 points, more than 5 percent below its level when the month began. About 50 million shares were traded, up a bit from the previous day but nothing to get excited about. The bear market was more than a year and a half old. What could you expect?

8

BULLS AND BANKS

A little before 9 o'clock in the morning on Wednesday, August 25, 1982, word went out to the New York Stock Exchange, the Dow Jones newswire, and the corporate world at large: Bendix, a diversified manufacturing corporation based near Detroit, was launching an uninvited takeover bid for Martin Marietta Corporation, a defense industry giant based in Bethesda, Maryland. One of the wildest corporate battles in modern market history had begun, an opening salvo in the takeover wars that would define the 1980s—and would distract lawmakers and regulators from the vastly more important structural changes occurring in the financial marketplace.

The stock market had frequently been a battleground for control of American corporations—during the great railroad wars of the nineteenth century, the smaller postwar corporate raids of the late 1950s, and the shopping sprees of the so-called conglomerate kings a decade later. In all those battles, the New York Stock Exchange had hewn to its traditional standards: every share of stock in a corporation was good for one proxy vote on the company's future. That had long been the rule on the Big Board—one share, one vote—but it had been years since shareholder votes had been used in the wild, disruptive ways that Bendix and Martin Marietta had used them.

SEC chairman John Shad had built his career at E.F. Hutton handling corporate mergers and acquisitions, courteous deals that "were prudently financed and made sound business sense." He believed the SEC had no business telling shareholders how to vote their shares, or telling corporations what they could do with their cash—or their borrowing power. As members of Congress grew increasingly agitated over hostile takeovers that threatened major corporations back home, Shad braced himself for the political heat.

But the Bendix battle whispered something else to those who listened carefully: the really big money on Wall Street was stirring, flexing its muscles, testing its power. Size mattered: the bigger you were, the more risks you could take, and the more money you could make. With Washington pulling back on enforcing the nation's antitrust laws, institutions that couldn't grow internally could get the wealth and power they wanted by using the takeover game to scoop up their rivals.

Pension fund managers such as Roland Machold in New Jersey and Gordon Binns at GM were giant shareholders, with stakes in hundreds of American corporations, any one of which could become a takeover target tomorrow. Suddenly, shares of stock weren't just investments that could outpace inflation; they were ballots that would help determine the future for a major corporation and tens of thousands of American workers. Until the Bendix battle, casting those ballots didn't seem like a very important chore—Binns routinely delegated proxy decisions to the money managers he hired, and Machold referred the task to an in-house committee.

Now it was clear to everyone that the giant institutional investors, who had been steadily adding to their stock holdings since the late 1970s, could be a decisive force in the takeover wars. And both sides, corporate officers and aggressive "raiders," were eager to enlist them to vote as a bloc for one side or the other.

WITH THE BENDIX circus helping to fuel it, the stock market shot up like a rocket in early October. The market's continuing advance, which pushed the Dow to 965.97 points on Thursday, October 7, was the top story on the front page of the *New York Times* the next morning—the rally was news, of course, precisely because no one could be sure it would last.

The deluge of orders that hit the New York Stock Exchange at the opening bell that day set a record, 43.6 million shares in the first hour, and slowed the exchange's public ticker down by almost forty minutes. Each hour, the trading volume grew and the intensity of the celebration grew with it. By the final hour, traders were waving at news photographers in the visitors' gallery, flinging scraps of paper into the air and blowing police whistles like happy children. The closing bell brought a roar that filled the cavernous space above the trading floor.

It was a new record: 147.1 million shares, almost three times larger than the daily trading volume at the Dow's nadir in August. That evening, according to the *Times*, the lines in front of Merrill Lynch's stock price video screens in Grand Central Terminal "were longer than those in front of the commuter information boards."

The heavy opening had been a bit of a strain for John Phelan's upgraded order-processing machinery, but the ticker had caught up before the closing bell. If Phelan had felt any anxiety during the morning's crush, it had evaporated by the time he spoke with reporters that evening.

"We've built models and tested them up to about 300 million shares and 250,000 transactions," he exulted. "That's twice the volume today, and five times the number of transactions."

Phelan's pride was evident: if the bull was back, the Big Board was ready.

THE RALLY WAS still going strong a dozen days later, on October 19, when Jerry Corrigan stepped up to address the annual conference of the American Bankers Association in Atlanta. Corrigan was now serving as the president of the Federal Reserve Bank of Minneapolis, but he still had Volcker's ear, and thus his words were given extra attention. He was in Atlanta to talk about financial deregulation—and he wasn't singing the tune the American banking industry wanted to hear.

In recent years, banks had persuaded Congress and their own regulators to approve new products that looked remarkably like the money market mutual funds that were regulated by the SEC. Brokerage firms were getting regulatory permission to buy banks outright, saying they just wanted to provide a few helpful services to investors. Sears, a retailer of clothing and household goods, had recently opened its first "financial supermarket," offering insurance services from its Allstate subsidiary, real estate services from its Coldwell Banker subsidiary, and brokerage services from its Dean Witter Reynolds subsidiary. Prudential Insurance, which was regulated by insurance commissioners in each state, already owned Prudential-Bache Securities, regulated by the SEC, and was negotiating to buy a major bank in Georgia.

The new reality, as one legal scholar put it, was so chaotic that any bank "can choose the regulatory system to which it will subject itself."

The big banks could get even bigger, feasting on new lines of business previously closed to them. Financial operations were becoming more tangled, with odd couplings that regulators had never confronted before. In the face of those changes, Corrigan wanted the bankers in Atlanta to ask "hard questions about what banks are, and what we want them to be."

Banks took in money from depositors, made loans to borrowers, and made their money by charging borrowers more than they had to pay depositors. Taking in deposits, in Corrigan's mind, had an almost sacred aspect; putting money in a bank was an act of faith. This made banks inherently different from, say, Sears or a trucking company. "Public trust and confidence in individual banking organizations—at some point—is only as strong as is public trust in the banking system as a whole," he added.

A shoe store could open its doors, lease space in every shopping center for miles around, build up lots of inventory as styles changed, provide poor service—and fail. But shoppers would still confidently buy shoes at another store down the street.

Corrigan knew for sure that what was true for America's shoe stores was emphatically not true for America's banks.

CHICAGO'S FINANCIAL LEADERS had never been fond of Washington regulators, especially if their guidelines reined in growth, stifled innovation, or curbed profits.

Yet, in July 1982, in the immediate aftermath of Penn Square's collapse, Continental Illinois had been forced to rely on the Fed for emergency loans. As the summer lurched from crisis to crisis, Volcker grew increasingly concerned about the Chicago bank—and was baffled that CEO Roger Anderson didn't seem as worried as he was. In mid-August, while coping with Mexico's mounting problems, Volcker summoned Anderson and his entire board of directors to a meeting in Washington. It was time for some serious jawboning, while the Penn Square memories were still sharp and painful.

Staff notes of the meeting give a flavor of Volcker's remarks. He said that "it was important to deal with this credibility problem as soon as possible," because the Penn Square episode raised "important questions about the bank's management." As he saw it, the bank should show that it was serious about reform by changing its management and its lending policies, taking all the necessary write-offs, conserving its cash, and building a sounder capital base.

Anderson's responses were not preserved for the record, but a few weeks later he confidently announced that "the bank had dealt with its difficulties and could now go forward confidently, business as usual." A few upper-level retirements, a few mid-level departures (the banker who was too friendly with Penn Square among them)—and that was that.

Volcker was not fooled by these cosmetic changes. He kept trying to persuade the bank to take more meaningful steps. He visited Anderson and his board in Chicago, striding like a Visigoth giant through the bank's Roman lobby. He made the same arguments again to Anderson; he got the same responses. He argued with the directors that Anderson should be replaced; he got nowhere.

The Fed was theoretically a powerful regulator. It could have tried to force the bank to change course by threatening to deny it loans or seeking a court order to keep it from paying dividends. However, as one Fed lawyer later conceded, those steps likely would have triggered exactly the crisis they were trying to avoid.

That was the fundamental conflict Volcker faced. As he saw it, the Fed's first duty was to preserve the stability of the financial system. Its work as a bank examiner often took a back seat to bigger things, such as the global debt crisis, the pace of inflation, or the liquidity of the financial markets. Moreover, there were other regulators, lots of other regulators, supervising the nation's banks; presumably, they would address risky lending habits or reckless management if they saw problems arising.

Yet, none of these agencies seemed to know what to do about the brash, irrepressible executives at Continental Illinois, the biggest bank in Chicago and one of the shakiest banks in the country.

AMID THE HEADLINES during that unsettled summer of 1982, there was one that delighted two ambitious young economics professors at the business school at the University of California at Berkeley. It read "A Strategy for Limiting Portfolio Losses," and it sat atop an impressively long article in the June 14 issue of *Fortune* magazine.

At the foot of the article's opening page was a charming photograph of the two professors: Mark Rubinstein, a small, puckish man with a dark mustache and thick, wiry eyebrows; and Hayne Leland, tall and graceful, with a lanky frame and curling sandy hair. Casually dressed, they were sitting cross-legged on a grassy slope.

The opening words of the *Fortune* article were calculated to catch the reader's attention: "It sounds too good to be true." The story was a generally positive look at a concept the professors had developed, a way to protect a portfolio of stocks from steep losses without giving up too much of the market's future gains. The article also noted that the professors had put their ideas into practice, having founded a small firm that managed about $150 million for a half-dozen pension funds.

Just two years earlier, none of that had seemed possible.

In the early months of 1980, Hayne Leland had carved out time from his classes and research papers to make sales calls, pitching this new hedging strategy to banks and brokers in New York and Chicago. Each time, he had returned home full of optimism; each time, he waited for follow-up calls that never came.

Sometimes, there were a few guys at the meetings who knew enough statistics or math to follow his formulas. Too often, though, his idea was met with blank stares. It was so unlike the bright-eyed discussions he enjoyed at Berkeley, where the atmosphere buzzed with investment ideas that merged mathematics and markets, computers and cash, physics and finance.

Selling research ideas to Wall Street was perhaps not how Hayne Ellis Leland had expected to spend his academic career. His casual, California surfer looks belied a polished pedigree. His father's family had deep roots in the Boston area; his mother had named him for her own father, Admiral Hayne Ellis, an aide to President Wilson's secretary of the navy and later Franklin Roosevelt's chief of naval intelligence. In the 1920s, the Ellis family had owned the historic Woodley mansion in Washington, D.C., an elegant Georgian-style brick pile that was used as a summer White House by four U.S. presidents. Leland's mother and her parents had moved easily in the best circles of Washington society.

Leland was born in Boston in 1941 but grew up in Seattle. He returned east for four years of prep school at Phillips Exeter Academy, and then followed the family tradition by entering Harvard, where he majored in economics and was tapped for several elite clubs. After graduating magna cum laude in 1964, he married the debutante daughter of a titled French family, in a ceremony at the American Cathedral in Paris. He spent a stimulating year working on a master's degree at the London School of Economics and then returned to Harvard, where he earned his doctorate in economics in 1968.

Leland joined the economics faculty at Stanford, but the department there was not a good fit; the research he found most intriguing was being done in the business school. He did not get tenure in economics at Stanford, and academic politics precluded him from getting tenure on the business school faculty. So, in 1974, he moved to the University of California at Berkeley.

The Berkeley business school was buzzing with theoretical innovations that had a distinctly practical tone. Each working paper had the same caveat mimeographed on its cover: "Papers are preliminary in nature; their purpose is to stimulate discussion and comment." And they did—at annual conferences and faculty dinner parties and professional gatherings and sidewalk conversations, year in and year out. That atmosphere was catnip to Leland after the constraints he felt at Stanford.

On a September morning in 1976, Leland was convinced he had found an idea that could be valuable to those people who managed investments in the real world—a notion that came to him when, during some sleepless hours, he turned his mind to something his brother had recently said.

His brother, an investment adviser, had bemoaned the fact that there was no way to insure a stock portfolio against market losses, the way you could insure your home against fire. It couldn't work exactly like insurance, of course. What sane insurance company would write policies that could all produce claims at the same moment? A stock market decline wasn't like an isolated house fire. If one policyholder experienced big market losses, all the other policyholders would probably have big losses, too.

Maybe there was some other way. In his dark Berkeley bedroom, Hayne Leland was struck by an idea. He immediately got up, went to his study, and settled down to work, to see if his insight would make sense on paper.

There already were financial products that, if used correctly, could work almost like insurance policies: stock options, which allowed their owners to buy ("call") a stock or sell ("put") a stock at a fixed point in the future for a specific price. Stock options had been around for years, and most corporate executives understood how they worked. It was obvious to Leland that if you had only one stock in your portfolio, you could use stock options to protect yourself against future losses. If your stock's price had recently climbed from $20 to $40, you could buy a put option that would allow you (but not require you) to sell the shares to someone else for $40 at some point in the future. If the stock fell back to $20, or even lower, the option would still let you sell it for $40 a share, avoiding any loss and locking in your earlier gains. Without giving up the chance to ride the investment up to, say, $60 a share, you still protected your $20 profit—in effect, you "insured" yourself against a decline in the stock price.

Call options on individual stocks, which allowed you to *buy* shares at some point in the future at a fixed price, had been actively traded since 1973 in a formal marketplace, the Chicago Board Options Exchange. However, in 1976, put options for individual stocks, which allowed you to *sell* shares at a specific price sometime in the future, were available only on a limited basis and generally had to be negotiated piecemeal in an informal "over-the-counter" marketplace.

Leland could see that he needed a way to apply the logic of a put option to an entire portfolio of stocks. That kind of broad-based option didn't exist, but the sudden inspiration that got him out of bed that night was the notion that he could create a "synthetic put option" by using a shifting combination of stocks and cash. He tried to sketch out the mathematics before grabbing a few hours of sleep.

The next morning, he realized he needed someone who knew more about the mechanics and theory of options than he did. Specifically, he needed Mark Rubinstein, his trusted friend and colleague on the business school faculty.

Rubinstein was a rumpled man whose formidable intellect was clothed in almost childlike curiosity. He got his high school education at the Lakeside School in Seattle, the "haven for math freaks" that would also educate Bill Gates, the cofounder of Microsoft. Rubinstein had been two years behind Leland in Harvard's undergraduate economics department, and had gone on to earn his master's from Stanford and his doctorate from the University of California at Los Angeles. He developed an early passion for computer programming languages, which appealed to his innate sense of mathematical order.

Rubinstein was not only more familiar with options theory than Leland was, but he had even done some actual options trading on the Pacific Stock Exchange in San Francisco. He lost money as a trader but gained invaluable experience.

Rubinstein was intellectually delighted with Leland's concept, chuckling and expressing surprise that he had "never thought of that myself." The two young professors immediately decided to form a consulting firm to market their strategy to professional investors, once they got it perfected.

Leland wasn't sure that Rubinstein, who seemed amused by the whole enterprise, had really considered what they might be on to—how big it could be. One day, as they walked past the motley shops on Telegraph Avenue on their way back to campus, he turned to Rubinstein and said, "You realize, there could be an enormous market for this."

Rubinstein looked a little blank, and shrugged.

"Pension funds!" Leland said.

In a flash, the penny dropped. "Pension funds," Rubinstein replied. He got it.

Given the press of family and work, the two young professors spent several years ironing out the wrinkles and testing their concept on a small scale in the market. It was a great success. By 1979, they were ready to introduce their idea for "portfolio insurance" to the world.

NEITHER HAYNE LELAND nor Mark Rubinstein had any experience with Wall Street marketing, though they did have an endorsement from Barr Rosenberg, the Berkeley faculty star whose consulting firm was one of the emerging giants in the young field of "quantitative" investment strategies. Rosenberg's blessing opened doors at a number of major banks and trust departments, but nothing came of it.

Then, in the spring of 1980, Leland finally got a call about his portfolio insurance idea—but it wasn't from a prospective client. It was from a prospective partner.

The caller was a soft-spoken Midwesterner named John W. O'Brien, who worked for one of the top pension consulting firms in the country, A.G. Becker in Chicago. Leland had met O'Brien a few months earlier, at the small Berkeley conference where the portfolio insurance idea made its debut, and he had been struck by O'Brien's perceptive questions.

O'Brien, an engaging man in his early forties with curly auburn hair and a ruddy smile set off by a neat beard, had already had a remarkable career in finance. A graduate of MIT and the Harvard Business School and a former air force officer, O'Brien had started on Wall Street in 1969, when he joined an obscure but venerable firm, Jas. H. Oliphant and Company. O'Brien helped Oliphant develop and sell so-called beta books, which showed how sensitive specific stocks were to the overall market's fluctuations.

In 1972, he and some colleagues left to form O'Brien Associates, a trailblazing financial analysis firm with offices on Wilshire Boulevard in Los Angeles. Its innovations included new tools to measure portfolio performance, software to help a pension fund create a model of its assets and liabilities, and a novel market index, much broader than the S&P 500, called the O'Brien 5000. In 1975, worried that the firm's business model would not survive the end of Wall Street's fixed-commission regime, O'Brien unwisely sold the business to a partner, who changed its name to Wilshire Associates and eventually became a billionaire.

John O'Brien then joined A.G. Becker, greatly expanding the quantitative tools it offered to its pension fund clients, and he was routinely scouting for new ideas at academic conferences around the country. Inevitably, he wound up at Berkeley—at the precise moment that Leland and Rubinstein rolled out their portfolio insurance idea.

With his quantitative background, O'Brien easily followed the math. After years on Wall Street, he knew that the concept would be attractive to large pension fund managers who were increasing their stock portfolios but were wary of increasing their risks. Best of all, he was a gifted communicator who could easily translate the professors' idea into language that corporate pension fund executives could understand.

Within a year of that initial phone call, the three men had established a three-way partnership, which they called Leland O'Brien Rubinstein Associates, or LOR. Their business plan called for Leland and Rubinstein to continue teaching full-time at the business school, while John O'Brien, the new firm's CEO, worked from Los Angeles, closer to his home in the beachfront town of Pacific Palisades.

Armed with an address book stuffed with high-level contacts at pension funds and trust departments, O'Brien found a spare office in a one-man law firm in Century City, on the west side of Los Angeles. The new firm's address sounded impressive: 1900 Avenue of the Stars. In fact, the small tenth-floor suite housed O'Brien, the accommodating lawyer, a computer, some telephones, and two part-time secretaries, one of them O'Brien's wife.

A short time after setting up shop, O'Brien landed the firm's first client, an investment manager with whom he had worked at A.G. Becker. It was a tiny account by Wall Street standards, just $500,000, but it was a start. Then, on one remarkable Friday, the phone in John O'Brien's little office rang three times with three new clients signing up to "insure" a total of $50 million: the pension funds of Honeywell Corporation, the Gates Corporation, and the Automobile Club of Southern California.

The Honeywell pension fund, like the General Motors fund overseen by Gordon Binns, used more than a half-dozen different money managers, and they were not especially eager to let LOR tinker with their portfolios. One manager agreed to try LOR's portfolio insurance concept, and reported favorably on it. Soon, Honeywell was entrusting $200 million to LOR's strategy.

In March 1982, LOR placed a dramatic advertisement in *Pensions & Investment Age*, an influential industry publication. The ad explained that the firm's strategy "has the effect of insuring an equity portfolio against loss—*a guaranteed equity investment.*" LOR had started referring to its product as "dynamic asset allocation," and the ad claimed that a dollar invested according to the strategy in 1971 would have grown to $2.61 ten years later, compared to $1.89 from an investment in the S&P 500 and $2.18 from Treasury bills.

Michael Clowes, a founding editor of the pension industry publication, offered a blessedly simple explanation of the new strategy: "Leland and Rubinstein had developed a computer program that would tell a pension fund, or the fund's money manager, to sell stocks and increase cash in a carefully measured way as stock prices fell. By the time the stock prices had declined the maximum amount the pension fund could tolerate, the fund would be all cash. For example, if the fund was willing to accept a 5 percent loss of capital on its equity portfolio, the program would begin to sell stocks as prices began to decline, and the portfolio would be all cash by the time its value had declined by 5 percent. As stock prices began to recover, the program would control the purchase of stocks until the portfolio was again fully invested."

It seemed like a persuasive argument. Yet many money managers still resisted letting the brainy professors from Berkeley take the wheel with their portfolios. O'Brien, one of the most engaging salesmen ever to pick up a telephone, kept making calls, running ads, and conducting seminars.

One such seminar was held in Manhattan in late 1982, at the splendid Hotel Pierre on Fifth Avenue and Sixty-First Street. In the audience was a young mustachioed man named Bruce I. Jacobs, who had earned a doctorate from the Wharton School and had recently left a teaching position there to join the asset management group at Prudential Insurance.

When Jacobs heard about the LOR strategy, he immediately spotted a flaw. The strategy assumed that when it was time to sell stocks and move into cash, those stocks could be readily sold. Was that realistic? "From a macro perspective," he wrote in a prescient memo to clients in January 1983, "if a large number of investors utilized the portfolio insulation technique, price movements would tend to snowball." Rising prices would trigger more buying, and that would drive prices up further; falling prices would trigger more selling, with the opposite effect.

Jacobs had hit on the aspect of portfolio insurance that troubled the market's traditional traders, people who shared John Phelan's instincts and history at the New York Stock Exchange. They believed in the old rule of "buy low, sell high." With portfolio insurance, you were deliberately supposed to do the opposite—buy when prices were rising and sell when they were falling. It just felt wrong.

Indeed, the portfolio insurer's success depended on a lot of other people believing the strategy was, in fact, wrong. The LOR concept assumed there would always be a large population of wealthy, unflappable bargain hunters who would persist in buying low and selling high, investors who would step into a falling market to buy all the shares the portfolio insurers would be selling.

Those opportunistic bargain hunters certainly would not come from the rapidly growing community of index funds, who bought only those shares that helped their portfolio track some index such as the S&P 500. Firmly believing markets were rational and efficient, index fund investors weren't going to be looking for bargains when LOR's clients needed to sell. Indeed, as stock prices fell, the index funds might well be selling, too, to cover redemptions from nervous retail investors.

Indeed, if the "Chicago School" was right—if markets were rational and efficient, and current prices reflected all the information known to all rational investors—how could such bargain hunters survive? In a truly efficient market, they would soon go broke. And if that happened, it was not clear who would buy stock from LOR's clients in a falling market.

Fortunately for LOR, there were still some pension fund managers, such as Roland Machold at New Jersey's state retirement fund, who believed in buying bargains, when the price was right. How much longer would that be true?

After enjoying the fine Hotel Pierre coffee and listening to the LOR sales pitch, Bruce Jacobs didn't dwell on the "snowball" problem. There was so little money in the accounts that were using portfolio insurance that it seemed more an academic concern than a real hazard. According to the June 14 *Fortune* article on Rubinstein and Leland, LOR was guiding investments totaling $150 million—almost a rounding error for multibillion-dollar investors such as Prudential and General Motors.

It might have been just an academic concern, but the "snowball" scenario was a puzzle, and a warning.

9

CHICAGO RISING

Thursday, June 16, 1983, was the fiftieth anniversary of the Glass-Steagall Act, the landmark Depression-era law that was intended to firmly separate the nation's banking industry from the risky world of Wall Street. To mark the occasion, Congressman Timothy E. Wirth of Colorado opened a hearing that afternoon to examine how porous the Glass-Steagall wall had become and what, if anything, should be done about it.

Wirth was specifically incensed by the FDIC's approach to the issue. In a handful of cases since 1969, the FDIC's lawyers had quietly determined that the Glass-Steagall Act applied only to banks in the Federal Reserve System. By 1983, many state-chartered banks were not Fed system members but nevertheless were buying federal deposit insurance from the FDIC. These banks were eager to exploit this apparent Glass-Steagall loophole. The FDIC believed it was simply setting sensible rules for any FDIC-insured state banks that wanted to expand into new businesses, an expansion the FDIC saw as legal and probably inevitable.

Wirth emphatically disagreed. "This, it seems to us, is a legislative issue, not one to be left to an obscure regulatory institution," he said as he opened the hearing. "I find it absolutely astounding that this proposal has been made without congressional input."

His witnesses that day included SEC chairman John Shad and another SEC commissioner, Bevis Longstreth.

Longstreth, lean and crisp despite the muggy weather, was almost the mirror opposite of the portly SEC chairman. He was a New York Democrat and had been appointed to the SEC in 1981 by President Reagan, who by law could put no more than three Republicans on the five-member commission.

Earlier in 1983, Longstreth had been involved in an embarrassing split within the SEC over Shad's proposed budget for the coming fiscal year. Shad had submitted budgets in 1981 and 1982 that called for no increase in staffing, even though those years had seen a dramatic rise in the SEC's workload. Now Shad's budget request in 1983 called for a 6 percent cut in staffing. Congressman Wirth, who opposed the cuts, had asked Shad's colleagues on the commission for their views. Longstreth and his three fellow commissioners, in a private response to the congressman, said they thought staffing should in fact be increased by 4 percent. Wirth had promptly released the exchange of letters to the media.

However, on the topic of the Glass-Steagall Act, John Shad and Timothy Wirth were almost allies. Shad had frequently argued, in congressional testimony and public speeches, that the banking industry's forays into traditional Wall Street activities should be curbed until the regulatory borders could be more clearly drawn and rule books written.

The landscape Shad described was certainly in an uproar. Although the nation's banks were overseen by an entire village of state and federal regulators, none of those overseers had any jurisdiction over the securities markets. The major securities firms competed with giant banks in the commodity markets, regulated by the CFTC, and in the Treasury markets, which were barely regulated at all. Increasingly, they also competed with banks in the rapidly growing private market for over-the-counter "swaps," a new type of derivative contract that the futures exchanges wanted the CFTC to regulate in the face of resistance from both banks and brokerage firms.

At the time, most members of oversight panels such as the Wirth subcommittee seemed to have no idea what swaps were or how they worked. Swaps are simply contracts by which two parties agree to exchange two future streams of cash that each is entitled to receive. In the case of interest rate swaps, the fastest-growing category in the mid-1980s, the streams of cash being "swapped" are the future interest payments on loans. Say Bank A is due to get fixed interest payments on a $100 million loan over the next ten years. On an identical loan, Bank B is due to collect variable interest payments, which will fluctuate with the market. Assume that Bank A is worried that interest rates will rise, which would leave it stuck with fixed payments lower than it might otherwise get. Bank B, on the other hand, is convinced interest rates will fall and wants to lock in a higher rate before that happens. A swap transaction allows each party to get what it wants. They simply swap the future stream of interest payments on the two loans. (Of course, they cannot both be right about interest rates, so one of the banks may be due for a big loss on its swap strategy.)

As the swaps market matured, major banks and brokerage firms started taking each side of these swaps, acting almost like clearinghouses, collecting payments from one and making payments to the other, and pocketing a bit of profit in the process. Of course, like clearinghouses, they were also taking on future liabilities—they would have to keep making payments even if one party to the swap defaulted. The wiser bankers and brokers tried to hedge those swap risks with exchange-traded interest rate futures, which sent a fresh fault line into the futures markets. But the futures markets arguably would be far more liquid if all these swaps were traded in their pits, instead of in a private institutional marketplace.

Although these arcane derivatives had not sprung up overnight, there still was no coherent regulatory structure for them, and John Shad believed that time was running out for Congress to act.

"Just since [last] August, we have witnessed the strongest bull market in history, rising trading volume in new financial futures and options, and unprecedented movement of capital," Shad testified. "In sum, the marketplace is thundering over, under, and around Glass-Steagall."

The result was an increasingly uneven playing field. Shad noted that the FDIC's proposal would allow the 8,800 FDIC-insured banks outside the Federal Reserve System to underwrite securities, while the

5,600 banks in the Fed system could not. Banks inside the system would inevitably be tempted to shift to state charters. Clearly, the FDIC's policy was a loophole big enough to accommodate the entire banking industry.

A partial solution, Shad argued, was for Congress to adopt a Treasury Department proposal that would allow banks to enter riskier Wall Street businesses, but only through holding companies. The holding companies could set up separate units for their securities business, regulated by Wall Street's traditional regulators. Similarly, Wall Street brokers would be allowed to participate in the banking business, but only through similar separate entities overseen by bank regulators.

When offered five minutes to share his views with the subcommittee, Bevis Longstreth agreed with Shad that radical shifts in the financial landscape "have reduced Glass-Steagall to a rubble." However, he strongly doubted whether a few legislative fixes would help.

"Market discipline, which is much in vogue these days, can only assure soundness in an environment where institutions are permitted to fail," he said. But the simple truth was that financial institutions could no longer be allowed to fail—the links among them were "simply too extensive to prevent one failure from triggering another." Therefore, "market discipline" alone was an utterly inadequate regulatory tool in a financial environment where one firm's failure could put the whole system at risk.

What was needed, Longstreth said, was "a new safety net," one broad enough to cover the entire financial system but "flexible enough to enable the forces of full disclosure and market discipline to do their share—which, I submit, is not the whole job."

Longstreth pointed out that the time available for regulators to respond to a threat was shrinking, given "the velocity at which money travels" and the unexpected links among institutions. "It's like an accident on the freeway where everyone is going sixty miles an hour, and they are almost bumper to bumper," he said. "The results are going to be different at that speed than they would be at five miles an hour."

There was simply no established, coherent system for dealing with a high-speed, high-impact financial crisis. Whenever there was a crisis, the financial system held together "because there was someone there

like Paul Volcker, who had been through this before," Longstreth concluded. "But it is all in his head—it is not in any statute."

IT REMAINED UNCERTAIN how long Paul Volcker would remain the primary tool in the nation's financial crisis response kit.

His term as chairman of the Federal Reserve would expire in August
1983; it was the middle of June, and still President Reagan had not
indicated whether Volcker would be reappointed. Newspaper articles
reported that there were two Republican candidates being considered for
the job—Preston Martin, already on the Federal Reserve Board, and
Alan Greenspan, who ran an economic consulting firm in New York and
had been the chairman of the Council of Economic Advisers in the Ford
administration. Wall Street was nervous, and it showed; the Dow gyrated
on every rumor, and even Treasury secretary Don Regan conceded that
the market favored Volcker "by an overwhelming majority."

In early June, Volcker had met with Reagan in the private quarters
at the White House and told him that, if reappointed, he expected to
step down after about a year and half. Reagan did not respond then,
but at 11 a.m. on Saturday, June 18, Volcker received a telephone call
from the president, who told him that he was being reappointed for a
second four-year term. An hour later, Reagan opened his weekly radio
address with what he jokingly called a "news flash."

"I'm not wearing a hat or clutching a phone" like a fedora-topped
reporter with a hot story, the president said, "but before getting into
today's broadcast, I'd like to make an important announcement." With
an informality that was a sharp break with tradition, he told Wall Street
and the world that he was reappointing Paul Volcker to the Federal
Reserve chairmanship.

The nation's primary financial crisis response system, Paul Volcker's
brain, was securely in place for a bit longer. It would be needed sooner
than anyone expected.

"THE HOUSE THAT Leo built."

That may have been how most of Chicago's financial community thought of the new Chicago Mercantile Exchange Center, which opened for business on the Monday after Thanksgiving 1983. The Merc's tireless and creative leader, Leo Melamed, had played a pivotal role in turning a struggling market for pork bellies into the roaring hive of prosperous financial innovation that underwrote the new structure.

The $57 million building had a million square feet of office space and a forty-thousand-square-foot trading floor, the largest column-free trading floor in the world, hardwired with about fourteen thousand miles of telephone cable. A soaring forty-story office tower rose on the south side of the gigantic rectangle of the trading complex; a twin would eventually stand on the north side.

It would be almost as accurate to call the new CME Center "the house that the spooz pit built."

Since its debut on April 21, 1982, the Standard & Poor's 500 futures contract had fulfilled all Leo Melamed's hopes. The spooz had the hottest launch in the history of the futures market, with more than 27,000 contracts traded before the end of April. All but two of the remaining months of 1982 set records.

It was becoming an unequal fight. Flaws in the design of the Value Line futures contract traded in Kansas City were starting to surface, and its trading volume remained thin. On the New York Futures Exchange, the NYSE Composite index futures contract was generating more interest than other NYFE products, but it, too, was having trouble finding its market. Meanwhile, the spooz trading volume was regularly four and five times higher than that of the other active stock index contracts.

By the fall of 1983, the S&P pits were loud and crowded. "Most commodities have moments of calm—but not the S&P," Melamed had told a reporter in August. "You literally have to close out your position if you want to get a cup of coffee or smoke a cigarette."

The growing volume of spooz trading was riding the back of the bull market in New York. By June 1983, the Dow stood 50 percent higher than it had a year earlier, a record-setting gain. After treading water in the early summer, it stroked steadily ahead from August until October, when it began to flag. Anyone eager to speculate on its future course could do so on a shoestring by buying or selling S&P 500 index futures on the Merc, and a growing horde of investors did. "The world's index futures and options enable investors to play the stock market without owning a share," one account noted.

By the middle of 1983, nearly a dozen pension funds and almost half of the three hundred largest banks doing business in the United States were using the futures market to hedge interest rate risk and stock market positions. Giant insurance companies had found their way to the futures pits, too. At least ten states, including New York, had amended their insurance laws to allow the use of derivatives. Reliance on interest rate futures traded in Chicago had quickly become almost common-place for bond portfolio managers in the insurance industry. Wall Street banks and brokerage firms were rapidly ramping up their private marketing of swaps, and more of them were hedging their risks with offsetting positions in the futures markets. It was not surprising, then, that financial futures made up more than a third of *all* futures market trading in 1983, and that the spooz pit generated more than 20 percent of the total trading volume on the Merc.

That success only increased Chicago's appetite for new financial futures. By June 1983 regulators had approved twenty-five new stock index futures, options on stock index futures, and options directly on stock market indexes, in addition to the first interest rate options, which competed with the popular futures contracts based on Treasury securities.

Three months earlier, in March, the Chicago Board Options Exchange had added its own new wrinkle by introducing its own stock market index option, which it initially called the "CBOE 100 option." In July, it was rechristened the Standard & Poor's 100 option, with the symbol OEX. Like the spooz, the OEX had a stellar debut and never looked back, quickly becoming the most deeply traded option in the market. On the heels of that success, the CBOE introduced an option directly on the S&P 500 index, ostensibly a competitor for the Merc's own option based on the spooz futures.

The flood of complicated new financial derivatives was so swift and full that Wall Street's primary lobbying group, the Securities Industry Association, had unsuccessfully appealed to regulators in June for a moratorium on new products, just to give Wall Street firms time to train their sales staff and adjust their paperwork procedures. And even if regulators grasped all the complexities and risks of these new derivatives—an arguable assumption in 1983, and for years to come—lawmakers in Congress were rapidly falling behind the financial innovation curve.

10

ARBITRAGE AND ACCOMMODATION

Among the VIPs who attended the opening ceremonies at the CME Center in Chicago was a bright brunette in her late thirties named Susan M. Phillips. A formidable but softly tailored woman with a disarming smile, Phillips was a former college educator with a doctorate in economics. She had served on the CFTC since 1981. Just ten days earlier, President Reagan had tapped her as the first woman to head the agency—or any federal financial regulatory agency—a job she had been doing de facto for the previous six months.

Phil Johnson had stepped down in May, pulled back into private law practice by the lucrative opportunities his government experience had generated. Less than a year later, he joined the New York firm of Skadden, Arps, Slate, Meagher and Flom, where he specialized in the legal issues surrounding the derivatives he had helped bring to life.

Susan Phillips's formal elevation to the CFTC chairmanship had been a high-profile event in the White House, with all the consequent ruffles and flourishes. President Reagan was in rare form, calling the new appointee by her first name and detailing her academic accomplishments with admiration.

His assessment of the CFTC had been equally glowing. "This commission is one of my favorites," he said, "because it proves that government can do a good job without soaking up taxpayers' money or over-regulating the marketplace," and because it "does its job without hindering industry growth and innovation."

As the president spoke, his "favorite" regulatory agency was squaring off for a new battle with its old adversary, the SEC. As usual, the dispute arose over innovations in Chicago. This time the bone of contention was the Chicago Merc's request that the CFTC approve stock index futures based on specific industries. The Merc wanted to trade futures contracts pegged to the S&P's energy index, high-tech index, utilities index, and financial industry index. The SEC opposed those new products. Under the 1982 law formalizing the Shad-Johnson agreement, the SEC had the right to go to court if the CFTC ignored its concerns.

Susan Phillips was trying to negotiate with John Shad over this new conflict. As required by the Shad-Johnson deal, she had sent the SEC staff detailed information about the four proposed contracts. Senior staffers at the two agencies had wrangled all through October and November. When she returned to Washington after the Merc's lavish celebration, John Shad's response was waiting for her.

Unsurprisingly, Shad raised the same objections his staff had been making to CFTC staffers for weeks. First, he complained that the single-industry indexes were too narrow. Under the deal Shad had struck with Phil Johnson, stock index futures could be tied only to broad-based market indexes. Second, since there was no prohibition against trading on inside information in the futures market, Shad feared someone could use any narrow-based index to "unfairly profit from inside information" about stocks in that index—if, for example, two oil giants were secretly considering a merger. Moreover, Shad said he couldn't find any statutory support at all for a futures contract based on a single-industry index, no matter how many stocks were in it.

Nonetheless, on January 11, 1984, the CFTC approved the Merc's proposed S&P Energy Index futures contract.

By law, the SEC's only recourse was to challenge the CFTC's action in court, but John Shad was no more enthusiastic about suing a fellow regulator than he had been two and a half years earlier, when he accepted Phil Johnson's lunch invitation. He still wanted to negotiate a peaceful outcome. But once Shad made it clear that he wasn't willing to go to court, he had little leverage in the subsequent negotiations.

He gave ground on every point in dispute and bowed to the CFTC's philosophy: let the new products start trading and then deal with any problems that may arise down the road. The new "guidelines" laying out the requirements for narrow industry stock index futures, worked out in private negotiations between the two agencies, were announced to the futures market and to Congress.

Neither the markets nor Congress were happy with the deal.

NO ONE IN Berkeley who had known Steve Wunsch in his youth would have recognized the clean-cut young man who was introduced to John O'Brien sometime in mid-1983. By that time, Wunsch was a derivatives expert working for Kidder Peabody, whose West Coast sales staff was seeking some of LOR's stock-trading business. A decade or more earlier, when his long, thick brown hair was held down with a sweatband and his smile was nearly hidden by an untamed beard, Wunsch had been tooling around the country with free-spirited friends, scaling sheer rock faces with an ease that astonished his fellow climbers. One of them was a senior executive at Kidder Peabody, who eventually hired him.

Wunsch was something of a legend among climbers. There was even a vertical stretch of rock back east named for him, in honor of a gravity-defying ascent he'd made years earlier. He laughed at the jokes people made of his name—"No Free Wunsch" was a favorite. By 1983, what fascinated the former daredevil from Kidder was what John O'Brien and his Berkeley partners were doing in the market.

Or, more precisely, what they were *not* doing.

"Why aren't you using S&P 500 futures contracts for your portfolio transactions?" he asked, during one of his early meetings with O'Brien.

O'Brien could have been forgiven for just ignoring Wunsch. Kidder Peabody was pushing its own competing portfolio insurance product, although without much success. But it was really hard not to like Steve Wunsch, so O'Brien listened.

O'Brien was no longer working from a tiny shared office suite in Century City. LOR had moved up in the world, into a new office on

Wilshire Boulevard. The firm had a small suite to itself—a half-dozen spacious cubicles, a small conference room, a private office for O'Brien, and first-rate personal computers on some of the desks. The suite was on the thirteenth floor of the First Interstate Bank building, one of the tallest buildings in California and an impressive corporate home if you weren't superstitious. First Interstate had taken a stake in LOR, which led to the new location. The gilded Biltmore Hotel, three blocks away, gave Hayne Leland and Mark Rubinstein a comfortable spot to stay during their frequent visits to the office.

O'Brien was learning that imitation was not only flattering, but profitable. In late 1983, LOR had licensed its portfolio insurance concept as the basis for Aetna's "Guaranteed Equity Management," or GEM, strategy. One of the things that made the GEM strategy "so remarkable," one ad for the product noted, was the "impeccable" credentials of Leland O'Brien Rubinstein Associates: "They provide dynamic asset allocation services and nothing but. Currently, they are serving 20 other portfolios totaling over $600 million."

Remarkable, but true: in the short time since the flattering *Fortune* magazine article in the spring of 1982, the total assets protected by portfolio insurance—by LOR directly and by its licensees—had grown from $150 million to $600 million. Direct fees and licensing royalties were generating income for LOR—hence, the upgraded office suite on Wilshire Boulevard.

The mechanics of implementing portfolio insurance remained somewhat cumbersome, relying on the sale of stocks as the market declined and their repurchase as prices rebounded. Portfolio managers working for the firm's big pension clients still were not enthusiastic about that much trading, and traditionalists still resisted the strategy. O'Brien remembered a contentious conversation with an academic consultant at the First National Bank of Chicago. "It's too much trading!" he told O'Brien. "That's just crazy."

Whether or not it was crazy to trade all that stock, it was certainly unnecessary, Steve Wunsch now told O'Brien. He said that Kidder Peabody's look-alike strategy for "insuring" portfolios was different. "We don't trade the stocks, we use the futures," he explained.

Of course, O'Brien knew about the introduction of the S&P 500 stock index futures on the Chicago Mercantile Exchange in the spring of 1982, but the contract really hadn't gained much trading depth until the bull market got rolling that fall. Now, with more than a year's experience, the raucous traders in the spooz pits at the Merc were handling a robust volume of orders every day.

Would a portfolio hedge based on the S&P 500 adequately serve pension fund clients whose portfolios did not precisely match those specific five hundred stocks? O'Brien got on the phone to Berkeley.

Mark Rubinstein was intrigued enough to check out the idea. What would work best, he knew, would be a put option on a broad stock market index. Such an option would give LOR the right to sell an entire portfolio of stocks at a specific price in the future, if it wanted to. Thus, LOR could put a floor under any losses the whole portfolio incurred in a stock market decline.

By late 1983, there actually were two such options trading on the Chicago Board Options Exchange: one based on the S&P 500, which wasn't yet traded actively enough to be useful, and the far more popular one, the OEX, based on the S&P 100. Unfortunately, there were CBOE limits on how many options any one investor could hold at one time, and LOR was already "insuring" accounts too large to fit easily within those limits.

According to Wunsch, the Chicago Merc was far more accommodating about investors taking large positions in the spooz pits, as long as they were hedging and not just speculating.

Hayne Leland saw immediately that using futures contracts would sharply reduce the trading costs of their hedging strategy. The catch, of course, was that "we're not ensuring each portfolio, each customized portfolio," he cautioned. "But as long as our clients are satisfied with general market protection, we *could* use them."

So, the answer, ultimately, would be based not on mathematics, but on marketing. What would LOR's clients say? Initially they were relieved; the new approach was cheaper and less disruptive for their various money managers. Soon, many pension fund clients began to feel they could safely hold a larger stake in the booming stock market than they used to, thanks to the protection of this streamlined version of portfolio insurance.

So, O'Brien was certainly grateful to young Steve Wunsch. And since Kidder's trading desk was prospering from the trading commissions generated by LOR and its major licensees, Wunsch's bosses in New York did not object to his close ties to the California firm. His conversation with O'Brien was sparking all sorts of ideas in his own mind about how LOR could make its product better, and how it could fit more easily into the market.

ONE RAPIDLY GROWING new strategy, which also relied on the S&P 500 futures contract at the Merc, could be important to the expansion of portfolio insurance—indeed, as Steve Wunsch realized, it could provide ballast to the market when LOR's clients had to make their required purchases and sales. It was called "index arbitrage."

Here's how it worked.

Each second of the trading day, the price of each stock in the S&P 500 index was fluctuating on the stock market. The value of the index, therefore, was constantly changing. Since the S&P 500 futures contract on the Merc was supposed to track that index faithfully, *its* value was also constantly changing.

In a tidy, rational, highly efficient marketplace, the two values would always move in tandem. In the messy real world, however, that did not always happen. Sometimes—because of temporary trading halts on the NYSE, eruptions of speculative demand on the Merc, passing emotional qualms, whatever—the value of the stocks in the S&P 500 index and the price of the spooz futures would diverge, sometimes by a substantial amount. If the futures price fell below the stock market prices, traders would say the spooz was trading "at a discount." If the futures price was higher than the cash price, the spooz was said to be trading "at a premium."

When John Shad and Phil Johnson negotiated their peace pact over stock index futures two years earlier, they had not imagined that the price of the futures contract in Chicago ever would diverge widely from the value of the market index in New York. But in real life, it regularly did, and whenever that happened, it presented a classic arbitrage opportunity.

Arbitrage is simply the act of buying something in one market and simultaneously selling it at a higher price in another market. If you can buy gold in London and simultaneously sell it at a much higher price in New York, that would be a profitable arbitrage opportunity. Of course, assuming it meets the same standard of purity, gold in London is identical to gold in New York.

What gave rise to index arbitrage was the ingenious realization that, while the S&P 500 futures weren't exactly identical to the S&P 500 stocks, they were close enough. If you could buy the S&P 500 futures on the Merc in Chicago for one price, and simultaneously sell all the individual S&P 500 stocks in New York at a higher price, you could collect a fast, small, but risk-free profit from that arbitrage. Some other time, there might be a chance to profit from the opposite trade—selling S&P 500 futures in Chicago and simultaneously buying the stocks in the S&P 500 index in New York. Either way, you retained a stake in the index—which made the strategy immensely attractive to index funds.

This was not a game for small fry. To nab those arbitrage profits, you needed three things: computers that could constantly monitor prices in both markets and alert you when they parted ways; a trading desk that could instantly deliver the necessary orders and get them executed for pennies a share; and enough money to buy a lot of stocks and futures contracts at one time.

Doing trades like that, day in and day out, was called index arbitrage, and it was a low-risk way for sophisticated money managers to pick up a few extra pennies of profit for an index fund that would otherwise merely match the market.

The reason that index arbitrageurs were important to LOR was that their trades would be the mirror image of the trading required for portfolio insurance. If stock prices fell to the point where stocks were cheaper than the futures, index arbitrageurs would be buying stocks—just when LOR would be selling them. Similarly, index arbitrage traders were a source of demand in the futures pits, where they could absorb sales by the portfolio insurers who relied on the S&P 500 futures for their hedging strategy.

The larger reason that index arbitrage was important to the stock market and the futures market—indeed, to the entire financial system—was that it helped bring prices in the two markets back in line when they went awry.

All arbitrage, regardless of what is being bought and sold, serves that purpose. Buying widgets in the cheaper market drives prices up there, and selling them in the more expensive market pushes prices down there—thus ensuring that widget prices eventually reach the same level in both markets. Similarly, by buying futures when they were cheap and selling stocks when they were expensive, index arbitrage traders helped bring the futures market and the stock market back into equilibrium, with futures prices accurately mirroring stock prices.

Index arbitrage remained a mysterious market force for years, generating suspicion in the stock market and confusion in the media. Many traditional regulators and investors still thought the stock market price was the "real" price for the S&P 500 index, and didn't really care if the S&P 500 futures price was at a premium or a discount to that "real" price. They were profoundly wrong to ignore this new phenomenon; index arbitrage and portfolio insurance were links in the invisible chain that, for the first time in history, was pulling the stock market and the derivatives markets inexorably together.

Yet, there remained a nagging question: Could index arbitrage grow fast enough to keep up with portfolio insurance? Would there always be investors who zigged when LOR zagged?

IF IT HAD not been so crowded, Room 1300 of the Longworth House Office Building on Capitol Hill would have been quite lovely. A fine white marble fireplace was on one dove-gray wall, and crystal chandeliers cast a warm light. The room was the home of the House Agriculture Committee, so it was not a frequent stop for SEC chairman John Shad; his congressional overseers were on the House Energy and Commerce Committee.

Nevertheless, just before 10 a.m. on a bitterly cold Wednesday, February 8, 1984, Shad settled his bulk into a chair at the witness table and looked up at a packed room. Twelve of the fifteen members of this agriculture subcommittee were there, along with the chairman and three other members of the full committee, along with five staffers.

A full-scale verbal flogging was on the agenda, and the opening courtesies could not mask the tension in the room.

Sitting beside Shad at the witness table was Susan Phillips, who was quite familiar with the room and its occupants, as the House Agriculture Committee was one of the CFTC's overseers in Congress. During her three-plus years as a CFTC commissioner, the mood in the room had typically been congenial toward the agency.

Not today. The congressmen were there to grill Phillips and Shad about how they had resolved their latest bout of jurisdictional arm wrestling—the dispute over the single-industry index futures proposed by the Chicago Mercantile Exchange.

One of the senior subcommittee members, and the first to give an opening statement, was Congressman Glenn English, a conservative Democrat from western Oklahoma. English, who favored the CFTC's claims to jurisdiction over stock index futures, had nevertheless been wary of the original Shad-Johnson compromise, which he felt left too many areas still open to dispute. So, he was not surprised that the CFTC and SEC had found themselves at loggerheads again, but he was furious at how the conflict had been resolved, and dead certain that the CFTC had gotten the worst of the deal.

"It certainly was my understanding and, I think, the understanding of the members of the committee, that any time that there was a disagreement as to areas of jurisdiction between the CFTC and the SEC, that those disputes would be settled in court, or in Congress, and not in some back room," English said. "I was very disappointed [that] at the first hint of disagreement, we found that the two commissions were meeting in a back room and reaching some kind of accord that I think really was a detriment to the CFTC."

Congressman Dan Glickman, a Democrat from Kansas, laid out the fundamental problem: "I suspect that there is a national turf fight, developing both in the halls of Congress as well as in the financial halls throughout this country, about what agency shall get jurisdiction over what kind of instruments." However, when Congress reauthorized the

CFTC in 1982, he added, "it was Congress that kept jurisdiction over those issues, and nobody else."

Congressman Ed Jones of Tennessee was a mild presence in the chairman's seat. After his colleagues' opening tirades, he welcomed Shad and Phillips and thanked them for being there.

Susan Phillips spoke first. "While the [Shad-Johnson] jurisdictional accord is now law, it is also a process," she said. "As new products are developed, the commission recognizes that it must be prepared to respond flexibly."

Then it was John Shad's turn. He said the Shad-Johnson Accord, while "a major concession by the SEC," had nevertheless set standards for new products approved by the CFTC. Chicago's single-industry futures contracts did not meet those standards, he continued, and a court fight with the CFTC seemed inevitable. Instead, "the agencies felt that it was preferable to use their joint expertise to interpret the statute, rather than to subject the futures industry to the protracted uncertainties of litigation."

Congressman English aimed his first question at Susan Phillips, and he was blunt. "Miss Phillips, I would like for you to explain to the subcommittee exactly what it is that you gave up in that backroom meeting with Mr. Shad."

After some quibbling over the question, Phillips answered it. "We do not believe that we gave up anything," she said. "In fact, we believe that we gained considerably."

English wasn't buying it. "Miss Phillips," he responded, "are you telling the subcommittee that you did not, in the name of the CFTC, give up any jurisdiction, any authority whatsoever in this agreement that you reached with the SEC?"

She answered promptly: "Yes, sir."

English turned his glare to the big, rumpled man sitting next to her. "Well, Mr. Shad, what did you give up?"

"I agree with Chairman Phillips," Shad answered.

English seemed shocked. "Well, then you must have given up everything, and she got the good end of the deal and you got the bad. Is that the way it went?" English pressed harder: "So the SEC caved in completely to the CFTC on this backroom deal, is that right?"

Shad dodged the question and said, "I think that the futures and the commodity industries gained substantially from it, because the uncertainty, and the prospect of protracted uncertainty under litigation, was eliminated." Despite further badgering, he could not explain why the resulting deal had gone almost completely the CFTC's way.

Behind his silence was a tacit admission that the SEC's role in the evolution of financial derivatives already was smaller than he'd expected, and was getting smaller still. The CFTC was in the driver's seat now, and Shad, unwilling to wage public warfare over these jurisdictional issues, could only go along for the ride—a ride that was carrying the market toward a future that made him increasingly uneasy.

11

BANKS ON THE BRINK

It is never a good day when a bank president gets a call from a reporter asking if there is any truth to a rumor that his bank is preparing to file for bankruptcy. When a second reporter calls with the same question, the banker is going to have a very bad day.

The day was Tuesday, May 8, 1984, and the bank president who fielded the two calls—and vehemently denied the rumors—was Edward S. Bottum of Continental Illinois National Bank in Chicago. His boss, unfortunately, was nowhere near Chicago. David G. Taylor, the bank's chairman and chief executive officer, was vacationing on a boat in the Bahamas.

Taylor, a Continental "lifer" whose father had worked at the bank for decades before him, had moved into the CEO's office a few months earlier, after the bank's directors finally replaced Roger Anderson, who had presided over the train wreck that was the Penn Square Bank collapse in 1982.

Penn Square's collapse had revealed serious weaknesses in the bank's internal controls and credit judgments, and it was struggling to attract the deposits it needed to remain in business. Risk-wary money market funds bailed out almost immediately, although the Chicago Board of Trade Clearing Corporation and the Chicago Mercantile Exchange remained faithful customers.

As the bank's chief funding officer during the Penn Square crisis, David Taylor had scrambled to replace the lost domestic deposits with foreign deposits and very short-term loans from other banks, cash that came in the door for as little as twenty-four hours. Continental needed roughly $8 billion in fresh cash every day just to keep its operations going, and Taylor found the money, although Continental had dropped from sixth to eighth place in the rankings of America's banks.

Six days earlier, on May 2, Taylor had met with his primary regulator, Todd Conover, the comptroller of the currency, and the meeting had been tense. In March, Continental had sold its profitable credit card operation so that it could pay its first-quarter dividend to its shareholders. Some regulators were quietly aghast that the bank would sell off a continuing stream of profits to make a one-time dividend payment. Conover wanted Taylor to accelerate the sale of the bank's bad loans before he would even consider approving a dividend for shareholders in the second quarter.

So, when a battle-weary Taylor and his wife left on a scheduled vacation the following Sunday, May 6, he prudently arranged to phone in daily. When he called from the ship on Tuesday, Ed Bottum urged him to fly back to Chicago.

That same night, Bottum got a late call at home from one of his senior executives, with alarming news from Tokyo, where it was already midday on Wednesday. A little after noon that day, the trading desks at the big Japanese banks, institutions that regularly made short-term loans to Continental, had suddenly slammed the door in the bank's face. There would be no overnight loans from Japan that day.

Those close-knit traders, glued to their newswires and telephone consoles, made multimillion-dollar trades based exclusively on trust and reputation. Perhaps the Japanese traders calculated that they wouldn't get fired for not doing business with Continental Illinois, but certainly would get fired if they lent money to the bank and couldn't get it back. That calculation put them at the front of what would become a classic bank run, rolling through the time zones from Tokyo to Chicago.

A team of reporters at the *Chicago Tribune* later pieced together what had happened, a comedy of errors with a grim final act.

On Tuesday, a reporter based in New York for the Commodity News Service filed a short, speculative story quoting "banking sources" who said that one of Japan's financial giants might buy Continental Illinois. It also said that "federal monetary authorities" planned a "special meeting on Continental Illinois's financial performance." When that story reached Tokyo, it was picked up by Jiji, a Japanese newswire service that had a deal with CNS to translate, edit, and transmit its stories in Japan. But the translation went awry, turning a "rumor" of a takeover into a "disclosure." The translation also changed "federal monetary authorities," to "currency" authorities, which may have evoked fears that this referred to the comptroller of the currency, whose involvement would suggest more serious problems.

At three minutes before 11 o'clock on Wednesday morning, Tokyo time, this blunter story went out to Jiji's clients, which included many major Japanese financial institutions. An hour later, the news service sent out a translation of the earlier story about Ed Bottum denying rumors of bankruptcy.

"According to both American and Japanese sources, the run on Continental began in earnest when traders at the Japanese banks saw the Jiji stories," the *Tribune* concluded. "The panic followed the sun." The word spread quickly to European banking centers, and just like that, "the European money that Continental needed to keep going was no longer there."

When Wednesday, May 9, arrived in Chicago, the rumors arrived with it. They were picked up by alert ears at an affiliate of the Chicago Board of Trade, which promptly pulled $50 million from one of its Continental accounts.

The run had hit home.

TWO DAYS LATER, shortly before noon on Friday, May 11, FDIC chairman Bill Isaac got an urgent call from Todd Conover.

"Can you stop whatever you're doing and come over to Volcker's office?" Conover said.

It wasn't really a request. Isaac canceled a luncheon speech and took a car immediately to the Fed's gleaming white compound on Constitution Avenue. When he reached Volcker's office, he listened as Conover briefed his two fellow regulators and a few senior staffers about the worsening situation in Chicago.

Thursday had brought little letup in the electronic withdrawals from the bank. Overnight loans were not being rolled over; maturing certificates of deposit were not being renewed. David Taylor, now back from the Bahamas, had sent telexes to two hundred foreign banks denying the rumors galloping westward from Japan, but that had only heightened the alarm. On Wednesday, Conover had taken the highly unusual step of issuing a press release to say that he did not know of any "significant changes in the bank's operations" that would support the rumors. It had no effect on the growing panic.

The bank was running out of cash.

No one needed to be told how important it was to stop this run in its tracks. There were several thousand smaller regional and local banks with uninsured deposits entrusted to Continental Illinois, and some of them might falter or fail if they lost those funds—and that would spread the panic. Depositors at other banking giants would likely see a Continental failure as the signal to move their own funds to the safety of the Treasury market, putting other banks at risk. That, too, would spread the panic.

These men might not have known it yet, but the reaction could reach even farther than they feared. David Taylor had lured back deposits from a number of money market funds over the past year, and if Continental failed, some of them might have to "break the buck"—that is, they might be unable to meet their implicit promise to always redeem their shares for a dollar. That would send the panic surging into the mutual fund industry, a market that these men did not regulate. A sudden exodus of cash from money market funds, regulated by the SEC, would have exacerbated the overall financial gridlock, because money market funds were becoming an important source of short-term credit for other banks and financial institutions, and even for some major corporations.

Volcker, Isaac, and Conover saw something that many of their overseers in Congress did not grasp: confidence in a nation's financial system is fragile, so delicate it could be cracked by the light tap of an unfounded rumor in Tokyo. A giant bank failure in Chicago would hit it like a sledgehammer. You could argue whether depositors would really grow panicky and view all banks with the same alarm, but if it did happen, you had a staggering mess on your hands, one that could derail economic activity for months, trigger business failures across the country, and leave an entire generation wary of any kind of financial risk, as had happened in the 1930s.

So, even though rescuing Continental Illinois would almost certainly trigger withering accusations that the regulators were "bailing out the big boys" while letting little banks fail on a weekly basis, there wasn't really any question about whether to do this. If a bunch of small retention ponds are leaking and there is a rapidly growing crack in the Hoover Dam, you shore up the Hoover Dam. The question was, how?

The FDIC had the authority to put $2 billion into the bank, but the magnitude of Continental's hemorrhaging was such that all three men were afraid that this gesture would not be enough to calm the panic. They decided to wait until Conover had spoken again with Continental's executives. To give him time to do that, Volcker made sure that the Federal Reserve Bank of Chicago expedited the bank's request for an emergency loan of $3.6 billion. The money would tide the bank over until the weekend—and it would buy everyone some time.

IN CHICAGO, DAVID Taylor reached out by phone to Lewis T. Preston, chairman of Morgan Guaranty Bank in New York, to seek his help in organizing an emergency line of credit from the community of giant "money center" banks. All of them had reason to ensure Continental's orderly survival, because any one of them could be next. Several had already had to jack up the rates they paid on certificates of deposit as the price of attracting funds.

Taylor and Preston spent that weekend tracking down their counterparts at fifteen of the nation's top banks. By Sunday night, it looked as if Washington's help would not be needed. Taylor sent telexes to his largest overseas depositors, reporting that sixteen of the nation's largest banks, led by Morgan Guaranty, had set up a $4.5 billion "safety net" line of credit for Continental Illinois.

It was an enormously impressive response from the private sector, and Continental announced the arrangement with great fanfare on

Monday morning, May 14. While it was not explicit, everyone seemed to know that the mighty Federal Reserve also stood ready to lend to Continental, if necessary.

To the horror of the bankers and regulators, the impact of this historic gesture was exactly zero. The global run continued throughout the day on Monday. In just nine days, the bank had lost 30 percent of its previous funding—a hemorrhage three times larger than the worst bank runs that would occur in the aftermath of the 2008 financial crisis.

David Taylor had nowhere left to turn but to Washington.

AT 10 A.M. on Tuesday, May 15, Todd Conover and Bill Isaac returned to Paul Volcker's office. Shaken by the failure of the bank consortium's effort, they agreed that the FDIC should proceed immediately to pump $2 billion into Continental, and began to work out the details. After an hour and a half, the three regulators left for the Treasury Building to answer a summons from Secretary Regan, who wanted to be briefed on the situation before he left for Europe the next day. Regan did not oppose the plan, but later suggested that the banks in the consortium be asked to contribute to the cash infusion.

After the meeting, Volcker returned to the Fed and prepared to head to New York, where he was scheduled to receive an honorary degree from Columbia University the next day.

Lewis Preston discreetly summoned the other bankers in the "safety net" consortium to a meeting at 9 o'clock Wednesday morning at a Morgan Guaranty building in Midtown Manhattan. Wary of sparking more ruinous rumors, the easily recognized Volcker slipped into the Morgan building via a loading dock that was used for armored car deliveries. He joined Isaac, Conover, and the New York Fed's president, Anthony Solomon, as an elite squadron of top bankers filed into the conference room with their aides. All told, about three dozen people were at the secret meeting, all of them deeply worried.

Volcker, who had artfully avoided sitting at the head of the table, made a few remarks from the sidelines, urging the bankers to "act quickly and decisively to demonstrate to the world at large that we [have] the ability to cope with a major problem." Bill Isaac reported on the FDIC's plan and proposed that the bankers contribute $500 million to the rescue effort, as Don Regan had suggested. There were, by one account, some "patriotic speeches" from several of the bankers about coming together for the greater good—although Volcker later recalled that Tom Theobald, a vice chairman at Citicorp, had memorably asked, "Why would I want to help a competitor?" As the negotiations stretched into the afternoon, Volcker left to collect his honorary degree—his failure to do so would certainly have fueled fresh market worries.

Bankers and regulators worked through the night until the deal was done. At 10 a.m. on Thursday, May 17, David Taylor got the word from New York that he could convene a press conference to announce the historic rescue package: a cash injection of $1.5 billion from the FDIC and $500 million from seven major banks, and a new line of credit from the original "safety net" consortium, which ultimately would include more than two dozen banks. The Fed, of course, would remain ready to serve as the lender of last resort if the need arose.

The most critical part of the package was the FDIC's assurance that the approach it would use to stabilize Continental would fully protect "all depositors and other general creditors." In other words, unlike Penn Square, Continental would not be shut down through a payoff, which would have left creditors and uninsured depositors with losses. In fact, the FDIC had handled most previous bank failures without resorting to a payoff—Penn Square had been the exception. Bill Isaac, who had resisted the more common kind of rescue deal for Penn Square, was now on board. Having just experienced a dangerously contagious bank run that imperiled what was still a solvent institution, his top priority was financial stability.

It was essential that this rescue package deliver a knockout blow to the panic besetting Continental Illinois, and a guarantee that the FDIC would find a way to avoid inflicting losses on depositors and creditors might do that. Isaac certainly hoped it would.

And, to the immense relief of Washington and Chicago, it did.

ONE WEEK AFTER the Continental Illinois rescue, as details of the cliff-hanger negotiations emerged, the foreign exchange markets grew utterly chaotic, with jittery investors selling dollars "in response to worries over the stability of the United States banking system." Perhaps foreign bankers really didn't understand how America's Rube Goldberg regulatory system worked and therefore couldn't fully trust its promises about Continental Illinois. At Volcker's direction, and for the first time in three years, the Fed secretly pumped $135 million into the market in a single day to stabilize the dollar.

Clearly, the Continental Illinois crisis was far from over.

With the FDIC and the Federal Reserve standing behind it, Continental ought to have been a magnet for depositors, given the above-market interest rates it was offering. Yet, the foreign investors who had fled in the stampede had not returned. Money market funds were still steering clear. Big institutional investors were on the sidelines. The only path toward permanent stability seemed to be a merger with another large bank, and in mid-June, David Taylor turned his full attention to finding a suitable partner.

The bank was living on borrowed time. As June slipped into July, the stock market awaited Continental's next quarterly financial statement. While continuing to sell off small subsidiaries, it announced that it was postponing its second-quarter report while negotiations with possible merger partners continued. But it soon became clear that there simply was no credible buyer for what had recently been considered the mightiest bank in Chicago, an underwriter of the nation's biggest futures markets, and one of the top ten banks in the country.

By early July, Bill Isaac at the FDIC and his counterparts at the Fed and the comptroller's office had given up on their merger hopes and devised an innovative plan to permanently stabilize Continental Illinois: the FDIC itself would invest several billion dollars in the bank and buy the bulk of its bad loans, in exchange for preferred shares that would make it the bank's largest stockholder. The unprecedented agreement was widely expected to be announced on Thursday, July 26.

Then, at the last minute, the deal was almost torn apart by yet another jurisdictional battle: Treasury secretary Regan belatedly, and publicly, balked, saying he thought certain details of the plan were "inappropriate" and "bad public policy."

What on earth was going on? Why had Regan, who had supported the Continental rescue in May, suddenly turned hostile? The question nagged at Irvine H. Sprague, a veteran Washington official who was the third member of the FDIC's board, alongside Todd Conover and Bill Isaac.

After one particularly trying meeting, Sprague asked what Treasury was trying to do. "One high Treasury official said to me: 'This is 1984; we might look at it differently another year'—a hint that the administration was seeking to distance itself from the largest bank bailout in history during a presidential election year."

Yet there was another sore point for the treasury secretary. Regan, like John Shad and Todd Conover, supported a pending bill that would allow banks to expand into new businesses, so long as they did so through separate subsidiaries of the banks' parent holding companies. The idea was that the holding company structure would protect the banks from the risks posed by those new ventures. But because of restrictive bond covenants, the only practical way to inject cash quickly into Continental was through the holding company. Sprague later speculated that Regan was "concerned that the precedent would undermine the validity" of the argument that holding companies would insulate banks from danger.

When Regan publicly attacked the rescue plan, Bill Isaac was publicly silent, but privately he "hit the ceiling," Sprague said. Sprague was fuming, too.

"Different problems required different solutions," Sprague said later. As he saw it, the FDIC and Treasury could "massage our prejudices by allowing the holding company to fail. Or we could save the bank." And by saving the bank, they could reduce the risk that a highly contagious panic would spread throughout the financial system.

Finally, the logjam broke on Wednesday evening, July 25. Cooler heads had apparently prevailed at Treasury, or perhaps at the White House. The Treasury Department pedaled firmly away from Regan's demands. "They are the banking regulators," one unidentified Treasury official told the *New York Times*, with an almost audible shrug.

At the FDIC that evening, Bill Isaac outlined the rescue package during a conference call with Volcker, Conover, and the leaders of the House and Senate banking committees. Isaac also reminded them that "no taxpayer money" would be used in the rescue plan because the FDIC was financed by premiums paid by the banking industry. Meanwhile, his staff worked through the night on the paperwork so the deal could be announced in Chicago on Thursday morning.

It was an "extraordinary intervention in the banking business," according to the *New York Times*. A new management team was put in place, with David Taylor returning to his finance position, his white-knuckle mission accomplished. At the end of September, shareholders of Continental Illinois approved the FDIC's purchase of an 80 percent stake in their bank, the price of avoiding a collapse that would have wiped them out entirely.

By then, the world had learned a little more about how precarious the whole episode had been—the Fed's need to step into the foreign currency markets in May, the huge loans Continental needed just before the rescue in July, the staggering $12 billion in deposits that had hemorrhaged from the bank since the first of the year.

Something like this wasn't supposed to happen, but it nearly did. And those who struggled to prevent it knew how easily it could happen again.

PART THREE

CONTAGION

12

MERGERS AND MUTATIONS

The frantic and fragile rescue of Continental Illinois early in the summer of 1984 had shown bank regulators just how quickly a crisis could erupt and how tough it was to stop one once it got rolling. However, the regulators who coped with that crisis at least recognized what they were dealing with: a bank run, albeit an especially fast and persistent one. Bank runs were a familiar species of trouble that had been around for about as long as there had been banks.

But when Jerry Corrigan looked at the rest of the financial landscape from his post as president of the Federal Reserve Bank of Minneapolis, he saw new hazards that regulators had never dealt with before, things that could blow up without warning almost anywhere in the financial system. All around the world, giant banks and brokerage firms were creating new hybrid derivatives that were privately negotiated, individually tailored, and rarely if ever traded. These derivatives were almost impossible to value, or even count, because they weren't clearly shown on bank balance sheets or brokerage firm filings. As private contracts, they created invisible obligations between all kinds of financial institutions, debts that could suddenly go sour and leave one party to the contract exposed to enormous losses.

Corrigan had shared his concerns at a meeting of the Federal Open

Market Committee in May 1984, just as the Chicago crisis was unfolding. These gimmicks, "interest-rate swaps and other things," were piling up in the shadows of the banking system, Corrigan told Paul Volcker and his colleagues on the committee. And they involved risks that "may not be totally understood, even by those who are playing in the markets."

He added, "And worse than that, they may not even be fully understood by *us*. Needless to say, this is not a point in time when we can afford to be blindsided."

He publicly repeated that warning in June, in a speech to bankers attending the International Monetary Conference in Philadelphia. Corrigan wasn't opposed to a future in which banks, discount brokers, and insurers could all dabble in one another's business, he said. But that was a landscape that would contain a daunting array of risks, including systemic risk, which he called "the ever-present snowball effect." With large banks and other financial firms tightly but invisibly linked to one another and to counterparts overseas, systemic risk was a growing concern.

"I have in mind such things as futures, options, options on futures, interest rate swaps," and a host of other contingent liabilities, he said. These derivatives were often structured through Wall Street brokerage firms, and they were being used heavily by giant insurance companies. And because most of them were invisible to auditors and regulators, it was impossible to gauge how many Wall Street firms and insurance companies would be in danger if a major firm on one side of a derivatives deal failed.

One of the new financial derivatives that Corrigan was uneasy about, the swap, was already one of the hottest products on the financial scene. A writer for *Euromoney* magazine had observed in late 1983 that "the swap market has turned the world's capital markets into a global Olympic Games. Every day, barriers are broken and records set."

No one could be sure how big the private swaps market actually was. Citicorp was said to have handled $7 billion in swaps in 1983. There were other estimates that, by late 1984, swaps covered a total of roughly $70 billion in debt, three times the level of just one year earlier. Insurance companies, many of which were subject to state laws limiting their use of futures and options, had become a particularly hungry market for swaps; by one estimate, insurers alone had done roughly $100 billion in swaps in 1984.

Barely a week before Corrigan's speech in Philadelphia, a vice president of a major New York bank had told the *New York Times*, "No one ever walks into my office and says, 'Hey, I just made a loan to finance a forklift.' Today all they talk about are these fancy financings that I can't understand." A Wall Street executive assessing the insurance industry's appetite for swaps had urged caution: "Insurers should consider the inherent risks involved in this unregulated market."

Unregulated? Indeed, one of the knotty problems surrounding swaps was whether they were regulated at all—and if so, by whom? The Wall Street executive who warned insurers of an "unregulated" market was repeating the common wisdom about swaps, but no one could be entirely certain that he was right.

In 1977 the CFTC's general counsel had asserted in advisory letters that some of these new derivatives seemed to resemble futures contracts closely enough to fall under the CFTC's expansive jurisdiction. The agency's lawyers initially laid out a four-prong test for these hybrids, but then, over the next two years, they said their new test was not actually the final exam, and that each product would be examined "in context."

Of course, the futures exchanges had long been clamoring for the CFTC to outlaw these over-the-counter derivatives. The rapidly developing swaps industry, a powerful collection of banks, brokerage firms, and insurance giants, insisted otherwise. The argument was far from over. As one legal scholar noted, the CFTC did not seem to have the gravitas necessary to make its position stick: "It is a relatively new agency, tiny by federal standards, something of a legislative plaything, and more than a little beholden to those it regulates for its appropriations and jurisdictional mandate."

It seems remarkable that an agency blessed with a statute as elastic as the one Congress had given the CFTC, with the support of the politically powerful exchanges it regulated, could not make a more emphatic case for regulating swaps and other over-the-counter derivatives. Were the banks and giant brokerage firms simply too powerful? Did the CFTC staff decide it already had too much on its plate? Or was the agency just wary of regulating a market that seemed to be working fine without regulation?

For whatever reason, the CFTC persistently failed to stake out and enforce a credible claim of jurisdiction, even as the market grew exponentially larger. As a result, the financial futures markets were denied a substantial reservoir of liquidity, support they would desperately need in the crises to come, and the potentially hazardous web of swap obligations that linked giant financial institutions remained invisible to regulators for decades.

That didn't seem to worry the Washington regulatory agencies or their congressional overseers as much as it worried Jerry Corrigan.

THE LATE SUMMER of 1984 found John Phelan settled into the chairman's office at the New York Stock Exchange. After four years in the number-two job, he had been promoted in the spring to chairman and chief executive, a post that combined the roles he and the retiring chairman, Mil Batten, had filled since 1980.

His first day in his new office, back on May 24, had been rocky. Sometime during the day, rumors swept the trading floor: Manufacturers Hanover, among the weaker New York City banks, was allegedly trying to raise money in London because nervous investors had shut it out of the U.S. market. Both the bank and its regulators denied the rumors, but the stock market began to sink rapidly, and the concern quickly spread to other financial markets.

It was only a week after the FDIC's rescue of Continental Illinois, and bankers and investors were acutely aware that the run on that bank had continued despite the FDIC's public assurances. The *New York Times* diagnosed the Manufacturers Hanover situation as "a serious case of the jitters," but that hardly captured the profound uneasiness that had greeted John Phelan's first day as chief executive at the Big Board.

In his four years as an exchange executive, Phelan had steadily expanded the capacity of the Designated Order Turnaround (DOT) system, an electronic network designed to expedite the handling of small orders from individual investors. Then, in 1984, Phelan bowed to the demands of the firms that served giant institutional investors—investors whose trading was becoming more important to the NYSE every day—and made a simple but fateful change in the rules. He gradually opened the DOT system's "in-box" to larger and larger orders—a step that turned this "SuperDOT" system into Wall Street's preferred tool for rapidly submitting large, complicated trades, including those generated by portfolio insurance and index arbitrage.

These large transactions, calling for buying or selling a long list of stocks at the same time, were known on the NYSE floor as "program trading." Program trading wasn't new. For more than a decade, when a mutual fund or pension fund manager wanted to acquire or dump a variety of stocks quickly, Wall Street trading desks had used a low-tech way to accommodate them. They simply sent in big multi-stock orders to the exchange floor and relied on squads of clerks to distribute them to the right trading posts as quickly as possible. Some firms had order slips that were preprinted with the list of stocks most commonly involved in their customers' trades, so their clerks could fan out and deliver them even sooner.

The specialists on the floor had learned to watch for these "buy programs" or "sell programs"—the sudden scattering of a covey of clerks bearing preprinted orders was a dead giveaway that a shopping spree or selling binge was occurring.

The same thing was happening now—in larger volume, at faster speeds, and much more frequently—but it was no longer as visible because a growing number of these program trades hit the floor electronically, via the expanded SuperDOT system. These stealth orders were unsettling to the specialists and other traders, because they conveyed no sense of scale. It was impossible to know how many giant orders were coming in, and the level of nervousness on the floor increased noticeably.

A savvy Paine Webber executive on the NYSE trading floor put together a "plain-English" primer on this new form of program trading and was inundated with requests for copies from other market professionals. His guidebook laid out the various ways pension funds and other big institutional investors were using program trading. Some just wanted to cut the time between making an investment decision and implementing it. Others were engaged in index arbitrage strategies, selling or buying the stocks in a certain index and simultaneously making the opposite trades in the futures or options markets. Some, such as Roland Machold at the New Jersey state pension fund, were using it as part of their "apartheid divestment" efforts, selling off big blocks of stock in companies with a commercial presence in South Africa. And some, such as Gordon Binns at the GM pension fund, needed program trading to implement the portfolio insurance strategies that fund was using to hedge its growing stock holdings.

To the professionals, these were separate and distinct uses of program trading, with different purposes and different consequences. But to most outsiders, and many journalists, they were all lumped together under one label. This would create a lot of confusion and miscommunication as the practice became more common, and more controversial.

BY LATE 1984, the other forces roiling the stock market were a little easier to define. A spate of controversial takeover deals had erupted, and fortunes were being made and lost on the latest rumors about the next acquisition target or the possible collapse of a pending deal.

It had become clear as early as the epic battle over the Bendix Corporation that John Phelan could not stay on the sidelines in these arguments. He felt the exchange had a duty to protect corporate shareholders, and some of the maneuvers that executives were using to protect their companies from would-be raiders struck at the heart of shareholder democracy.

Increasingly, though, takeover deals were squeezing Phelan between two of his important constituencies. The companies listed on the exchange wanted the NYSE to allow them to issue a class of stock that could outvote their common stock. With that "super-voting" stock in friendly hands, the firms would be safe from corporate raiders. But many major pension funds and other giant institutions, the fastest-growing source of trades on the NYSE, were firmly opposed to "super-voting" shares, which diminished their rights as common stockholders.

That opposition reflected structural changes in the investment community. Traditionally, disappointed institutional investors "voted with their feet," selling their shares rather than challenging management. But managers of index funds never had that option: if a company's stock was in the index their funds tracked, they had to own it. Giant pension funds such as the ones run by Machold and Binns had to be as diversified as possible, and narrowing their holdings to avoid takeover battles would increase the risks they were taking with their pensioners' assets.

Despite his belief that takeover battles generally were not an issue for regulators, SEC chairman John Shad had expressed some concern about a practice called "greenmail," in which a company would buy back a potential raider's shares at a premium price to make him go away. This higher stock price was not available to other shareholders in the marketplace—including the giant institutional investors, who felt ill-used.

Though it was not in his nature to suffer in silence, Roland Machold might have quietly simmered a bit longer in the takeover debate, but two back-to-back greenmail deals, involving the Disney Corporation and Texaco, lit his fuse. As it happened, the deals had also whetted the anger of a veteran California politician who wielded enormous influence as a trustee of his state's giant public pension funds.

The Californian, state treasurer Jesse Unruh, phoned Machold to vent his views, adding that he was reaching out to public pension fund managers in other states. "There must be a better way than sitting by and getting ripped off," Unruh fumed. Pension funds, he went on, "have been passively standing by for too long, while their shareholder interests have been stepped on."

Some fund managers held back, wary of Unruh's unabashed political activism or vulnerable to local political pressures, but not Roland Machold. By the late summer of 1984, he was making plans to attend an organizational meeting Unruh wanted to hold in Chicago that fall. The idea was to form a group that could wield enough financial power to insist that corporate managers and would-be raiders sit down and explain themselves to their giant shareholders. The organizers were thinking of calling it the Council of Institutional Investors.

The council was to be open to private-sector retirement plans as well, and a few union pension funds signed on. But Gordon Binns apparently was not comfortable with Unruh's idea. The top executives at General

Motors had already decided to create "super-voting" shares to deter raiders. How could Binns join forces with other pension funds trying to prohibit such protective strategies?

Roland Machold was not constrained by corporate politics, and he heartily supported Unruh. Together they helped build an organization that would soon demonstrate just how very large and powerful these titan investors had become.

AT A PRACTICAL level, these takeover fights had another unwelcome side effect. On a growing number of trading days, John Phelan's surveillance team at the NYSE had noticed unusually prescient trading just ahead of the headlines about a new or developing deal. The SEC's regulatory staffers in Washington were noticing the same thing, particularly on the options exchanges. John Shad was especially hostile toward insider trading and had shifted scarce resources into his enforcement division to fight it.

For the next two years, takeovers and the insider trading conspiracies they were feeding would inflame public outrage. The takeovers profoundly reshaped the civic life of countless communities across the country, often in unfortunate ways, and insider trading increased public and congressional suspicion of Wall Street.

For all the visible storm and drama of these battles and investigations, their unseen consequences were arguably of more lasting significance, because they were a nearly ruinous distraction from the structural hazards developing in the American market. The nation's financial stability was not directly threatened by hostile takeovers, but it surely was threatened by the invisible chains that now shackled together a host of disparate, blindly competitive, and increasingly automated markets. Greedy lawyers and unethical bankers did not increase the structural risks of this new marketplace, but gigantic and increasingly like-minded institutional investors did. These new risks did not arise because the regulatory system failed to police takeover practices or criminal trading activity; they arose in a regulatory community that was poorly equipped, ridiculously fragmented, technologically naïve, and fatally focused on protecting turf rather than safeguarding the overall market's internal machinery.

Nevertheless, hostile takeovers and insider trading became the primary preoccupation of regulators and lawmakers. Facing continuing pressures on its budget, the SEC found the resources to attack insider trading by, among other things, spending less on market regulation. Bank regulators worried about banks financing risky takeover deals and savings and loans buying deal-linked "junk bonds," but failed to challenge closely the bank mergers producing a breed of financial giants. Regulators across the board neglected the unregulated swaps that were flooding the markets and linking giant players together in new and invisible ways. Congress shifted its focus to headline-grabbing criminal cases against Wall Street plutocrats and largely abandoned any serious effort to address these profound market changes.

In short, amid the distractions and demands of takeover battles and criminal investigations, Washington mostly ignored the real hazards that were developing in the financial landscape. Titan investors got exponentially bigger, their investment strategies grew dangerously more similar, and their effect on daily market trading grew more pronounced. The computer power of investors on Wall Street grew at a pace that outstripped that of regulators and traditional traders. The links between stocks, bonds, options, futures, and unregulated derivatives such as swaps grew stronger, less visible, and more dangerous.

To be sure, a growing body of opinion saw the new derivatives as tools for reducing risk—and, examined deal by deal, they may have been. Aggregated across the financial landscape, they weren't. As Jerry Corrigan had pointed out to the bankers in Philadelphia, the whole world could not be hedged against the same risk at the same moment. Risk could be passed around, but it couldn't be eliminated.

SENIOR BANKERS ACROSS the country heard the bad news first, thanks to sunrise calls on Wednesday, October 3, from the bank's chairman and president. The calls alerted them to brace for a rocky day.

Still, the bankers were surprised—shocked, in fact. The calls were from the formidable First National Bank of Chicago, the eighth-largest bank in the country and the city's leading bank since the sudden eclipse of Continental Illinois that summer. The bank announced that it was writing off hundreds of millions of dollars' worth of bad loans and reporting the first quarterly loss in its long history. Wall Street analysts immediately began to worry that this was just the first in a string of immense third-quarter losses in the banking industry. Shares of almost every major bank in the country fell sharply that day.

The anxiety in the market did not deter Congressman Fernand "Fred" St. Germain, a silver-haired Democrat from Rhode Island who was chairman of the House banking committee. In September, St. Germain had held two scathing hearings questioning the rescue of Continental Illinois. The first session opened with him reading a seven-page denunciation of the toothless regulators and reckless bankers who had allowed the crisis to happen. He then spent the day interrogating a quartet of former and current senior bank examiners. The next day, he pounced on Todd Conover, the comptroller of the currency, and did not let up for five hours.

On Thursday, October 4, with First Chicago's loss the biggest financial news of the day, the St. Germain panel convened once again, with FDIC chairman Bill Isaac waiting to be interrogated. Before the hearing, he had emphatically assured reporters that First Chicago was in no danger of becoming the next bank rescue target.

St. Germain gaveled the crowded room to order and devoted most of the first hour to a staff report disputing Todd Conover's testimony in September about how many other banks might have failed if Continental had been allowed to go under. The subcommittee's staff had come up with a much smaller number than Conover had.

On the strength of that, St. Germain asserted that regulators "knew full well that the domino theory was concocted. At most—and this stretches a pessimistic scenario pretty far—maybe a half-dozen institutions would have been on the edge of a failure line."

It was a bizarre and naïve argument, given the frightening risks that had been building up in the financial system since 1980 and the panic that had engulfed the banking world during the Continental crisis in May. If a Continental failure had been immediately followed by the collapse of a dozen other banks, what would the reaction have been? Would it have been markedly less if only a half-dozen banks had failed at that moment? Who could possibly say? No one could confidently guarantee that First Chicago would not be in trouble before that day's hearing adjourned.

Unexpected scheduling conflicts forced St. Germain to postpone Bill Isaac's testimony until that afternoon. When the FDIC chief returned to the witness table, he was angry.

"Frankly, I'd like to get something off my chest," Isaac said. "I took great personal offense at what I witnessed here this morning." The attack on the regulatory estimate of how many banks were threatened by the Continental crisis called into question his "intelligence and integrity" and that of his team, he said. "The committee staff knows better," he went on. "They have met with our staff. They know what we did. They know why we did it. And what we heard this morning, frankly, was disgraceful."

In May, with a giant bank rapidly circling the drain, he had not had the luxury of pinpointing the consequences for each of the several thousand banks with money deposited there, he explained. Besides, the exact number of banks at risk had been irrelevant to his decision to rescue Continental. Regulators had acted to save the giant Chicago bank, he continued, because the overall consequences of its collapse would likely have been "catastrophic."

Isaac painted a vivid picture of what he believed would have happened if the FDIC had taken the same route with Continental Illinois as it had with Penn Square—if it had paid off the 850,000 insured depositors up to the FDIC limit, wound down the bank, and given everybody else IOUs that might be worth something when the long bankruptcy process was over.

He pointed out that the insured depositors, the lucky ones, would have had to wait several months to get their money. "No grocery money, no payroll, no money to pay your mortgage. Accounts would've been frozen for 850,000 depositors for one month, two months," he said. "Now you go to the uninsured—those people had over $30 billion worth of exposure. And that money would've been frozen in a bankruptcy proceeding for years and years and years."

About 2,300 other banks insured by the FDIC would have had $5.8 billion frozen in the event of a payoff at Continental Illinois. They, too, would have received IOUs that ultimately might have been worth seventy or eighty cents on the dollar, "but it would have taken a good long time and they would've had a piece of paper until it happened."

Then there would have been the corporate casualties, he continued grimly. Continental Illinois had been the largest domestic lender to American businesses. If the FDIC had shut it down, "we would have been in a collection mode on every one of its loans. Every one of those borrowers would have had their lines of credit cut off. You would have had corporate bankruptcies throughout the land."

Moreover, he said, "You would've shaken confidence in other major institutions . . . if we had closed down a *solvent* bank and paid off [only] insured depositors, what message would we have sent to the rest of the world trying to deal with U.S. banks?" In the midst of the crisis in May, he and his fellow bank regulators were also dealing with other distressed banks and savings and loans across the country. He asked: Would any of them have lasted twenty-four hours if Continental had failed?

Congressman Frank Annunzio, a Democrat and the only Chicago legislator on the subcommittee, ruefully suggested a silver lining to the disaster Isaac described. In the wake of those catastrophes, the lawmaker quipped, "the Democrats might have won the [upcoming] election."

"I won't touch that line," said Isaac, a loyal Republican. "All I am saying is, the ramifications could have been *catastrophic* . . . I think I'm probably about as hardline on the need for discipline in the banking system as anybody in the country, and I frankly didn't have the courage to do it."

Annunzio seemed a little ashamed of the beating Isaac was getting for the sin of rescuing Chicago's biggest bank. "I am just wondering," he said, "if you would have been sitting here today, before this committee, being *praised* if Continental had gone under?"

If the FDIC had let that happen, Isaac responded, "I think this committee probably would have been justified to consider lynching me."

The grilling continued for several more hours, but Isaac never wavered in his insistence that, in the same circumstances, he would have made exactly the same decision—to save Continental Illinois.

Neither he nor his persecutors in Congress could have known it then, but if he hadn't done so, events three years later might well have been even more destructive than they were.

13

BERKELEY RISING, BANKS FALLING

For several years, John O'Brien had been talking about portfolio insurance with executives at the Denver-based Johns-Manville Corporation, and his diligent visits finally paid off in 1984—with results that put portfolio insurance, and LOR, into the spotlight and significantly sped up the changes transforming America's financial markets.

Johns-Manville was facing a future of legal claims from people sickened by its original flagship product, asbestos insulation; those potential liabilities had led the company to file for bankruptcy protection in 1982. As its creditors wrangled, the bull market that began that August pushed the value of its pension fund higher and higher. By 1984, the pension fund's assets totaled $350 million, considerably more than was needed to cover its retirement obligations. That surplus could be used to help pay ailing workers—unless the gains were suddenly washed away by a market downturn. Many lawyers representing creditors wanted the fund to take its winnings and get out of the stock market, but the pension fund's managers said that would deny the fund any future market gains, which might produce even more money for creditors.

To O'Brien, it looked like a case study for an LOR sales pitch, but he had not been able to sell that argument to the company.

Then, sometime in early 1984, O'Brien received a phone call from the assistant treasurer at Johns-Manville. How, exactly, would LOR set up a hedging strategy to protect the pension fund's gains while still capturing some future profits, beyond the cost of the portfolio insurance? That call led to a meeting in Denver with Johns-Manville's treasurer, who asked if O'Brien would explain the strategy to the creditors committee, which would meet two weeks later.

When he arrived at the company's home office on the day of that meeting, O'Brien was shown to a conference room occupied by members of the creditors committee and representatives of J.P. Morgan, which was advising them. "You have fifteen minutes," he was told. A snowstorm was threatening; several people around the table had planes to catch and wanted to beat the bad weather.

Startled, O'Brien did the best he could in the time allowed—but his pitch was slightly different from those he had been making since 1981. Thanks to guidance from Kidder Peabody's Steve Wunsch, LOR now implemented its hedging strategy by buying and selling the S&P 500 index futures contracts on the Chicago Mercantile Exchange, not by buying and selling stocks on the New York Stock Exchange.

The use of S&P 500 index futures had become increasingly popular with pension funds, endowments, and banks. In January 1984, less than two years after the new derivatives were introduced, the SEC had agreed to let mutual funds use them "as hedges against the effects of changing market conditions." No one around the conference table could sensibly oppose the LOR proposal just because it used futures contracts instead of stock transactions.

After O'Brien finished his presentation, someone at the table said, "This sounds plausible to me."

O'Brien suspected that the J.P. Morgan adviser was "calling the tune." After a brief absence that O'Brien assumed was used to consult with the home office, the Morgan banker returned and told the committee that the LOR approach was "theoretically possible" but had never been done on this scale before. O'Brien, still in the room, was thanked for his time, and he returned to the airport to catch his own flight, back to Los Angeles.

The following Monday, the treasurer of Johns-Manville called O'Brien, reporting what initially sounded like a "good news, bad news" joke. LOR was being hired to implement its signature strategy, but it would have to share the assignment with J.P. Morgan. The bank had tried to persuade Manville to let it handle half the $350 million portfolio, the executive said. "I told Morgan that wasn't fair," the executive continued, "but they could have 20 percent of the portfolio."

O'Brien was glad LOR would be managing 80 percent of the Johns-Manville assets, but he still was "kind of miffed" that the big New York bank had horned into the deal. However, a few weeks later, a major pension industry publication reported that Johns-Manville was using portfolio insurance, advised by J.P. Morgan and Leland O'Brien Rubinstein. Suddenly, LOR was in the same sentence, in the same deal, with one of Wall Street's most prestigious firms. In a stroke, new business streamed in, and the assets being managed by LOR grew to $700 million. "What seemed like a defeat turned into a huge advantage," O'Brien acknowledged. It gave the firm, and its strategy, tremendous credibility in the community of institutional investors.

Of course, it also meant that the formidable J.P. Morgan was joining the ranks of those selling portfolio insurance to the giant pension fund market.

AS CHICAGO PREPARED to welcome the new year of 1985, Leo Melamed at the Chicago Mercantile Exchange got an extremely welcome holiday present.

For two years, he had been braced for the conclusions of an ongoing study of the new financial futures and options markets being conducted by the Federal Reserve, the CFTC, and the SEC, with assistance from the Treasury Department.

When Melamed counted noses, he feared the CFTC would be outvoted, 3 to 1, on the study's final conclusions, unless the Treasury sided with the CFTC to create a tie. The SEC was likely to be hostile toward financial futures, based on the long struggle over who would regulate them. And Paul Volcker had long been wary about financial futures and most other Chicago innovations.

When the report, an inch-and-a-half thick and weighing more than four pounds, was finally delivered to Congress in December, Melamed was exultant. Indeed, the primary conclusions could have been written by Melamed himself: The futures and options markets served "a useful economic purpose" by allowing economic risks to be shifted from "firms and individuals less willing to bear them to those more willing to do so." The new markets "appeared to have no measurable negative implications for the formation of capital" and may actually have improved market liquidity, the researchers concluded.

The new study, larded with investor surveys, complex definitions, and "rational" economic theories, did not offer any ammunition for the turf war between the CFTC and the SEC. The study noted the similarities between financial futures (regulated by the CFTC) and options (regulated by the SEC)—they served similar functions, were traded by many of the same players, and "have similar potential for causing harm if they function improperly." Therefore, it continued, "there is need for close harmonization of federal regulation of these markets."

The study's authors were confident—despite nearly a decade of contrary evidence—that the two agencies could achieve that harmony through communication and cooperation, so there was no need for new legislation to "establish an appropriate regulatory framework."

Remarkably, little attention was devoted to the fundamental changes in the architecture of the markets being caused by the widespread and rapidly growing use of futures and options by the largest and most active investors in the country. The study briefly acknowledged that arcane strategies such as portfolio insurance and index arbitrage had caused some aberrations in the market, but it suggested that "the potential for such disruptive trading" should merely be monitored.

FLURRIES OF SNOW mixed with the leftover New Year's Eve litter in Manhattan on Wednesday, January 2, 1985, Jerry Corrigan's first day as president of the Federal Reserve Bank of New York. It was a homecoming of sorts, anticipated since the announcement of Corrigan's appointment to the post in September. He now sat at the desk that used to be Paul Volcker's.

Corrigan's first task was to address the takeover deals and debt-fueled management buyouts that were outraging members of Congress.

The giant Manhattan bank holding companies, such as Citigroup, were the only players in that game that the Federal Reserve directly regulated. Corrigan knew that many of the debt-heavy deals that were raising hackles were being financed by New York banks that, frankly, should have known better.

Meanwhile, in Washington, his mentor Paul Volcker was watching a job change that could prove risky for his own tenure. Treasury secretary Donald Regan and James A. Baker III, the president's chief of staff and an architect of his reelection victory in November 1984, were switching jobs. Volcker knew that Baker was a political savant of great charm and effectiveness, but the new secretary of the Treasury would almost certainly have his eye on a possible 1988 presidential campaign by his close friend, Vice President Bush. In all likelihood, he would want to be sure that the economy didn't deliver any unpleasant election-year surprises because of high interest rates.

Baker was a practical conservative, and his primary task was to reshape a tax reform proposal drafted under Regan's supervision and get it through Congress. The job switch meant that, for the next few years, the Treasury's top job would be held by someone whose focus was intently on politics and the presidential agenda, not on the flaws in the regulatory system that were becoming more apparent with each new financial crisis.

ON VALENTINE'S DAY 1985, Roland Machold made his way from his home in Princeton to Lower Manhattan, his destination the office suite occupied by New York City comptroller Harrison J. Goldin. Goldin was also expecting Jesse Unruh, California's pension fund power broker, to join them. A tall, beefy man, Unruh hated to travel, preferring to do his organizing work by phone from Sacramento. Less than a month earlier, though, the Council of Institutional Investors had held its first formal meeting in Washington, and today the group was going into action for the first time.

Machold, Unruh, and Goldin were presiding over a daylong engagement with the key players in a takeover drama being acted out at Phillips

Petroleum. In December, the company had made a greenmail payment to deter the corporate raider T. Boone Pickens, who walked away with a $90 million profit. The company now planned to "recapitalize" itself by giving a third of its shares to its employees and offering other stock-holders (who included the pension funds run by Machold, Goldin, and Unruh) a package of new stock and bonds whose value was in dispute on Wall Street.

That recapitalization scheme prompted another corporate raider, Carl Icahn, to launch his own takeover bid for Phillips, mustering the services of the investment bank Drexel Burnham Lambert along with several Drexel clients to help him finance an $8.1 billion bid. He also had the support of the takeover speculator Ivan F. Boesky, who was unhappy with the package of securities Phillips had offered. The company's greenmail payment to Pickens had been deeply unpopular among institutional investors, and Phillips stock had been on a roller coaster ever since.

Icahn and Boesky were hoping that the big institutional investors would side with them, and Phillips executives were hoping they wouldn't. This Valentine's Day meeting was a chance for all sides to make their case to the newly formed Council of Institutional Investors—and one by one, they did.

It was better than any Broadway show, Machold thought, but it was more than theater, really. It was the debut of a new force in the takeover battles to come—public pension fund chiefs wielding shares worth tens of billions of dollars were claiming a seat at the takeover table.

The best way to see the new reality taking shape in the market is to jump forward two weeks, to a congressional hearing on a broad range of takeover issues, initially focusing on the Phillips battle. As Carl Icahn, Boone Pickens, and several Phillips executives sat simmering beside him, Jay Goldin carefully explained the new institutional council's origins and its agenda. Almost two dozen public pension fund directors, with authority over more than $100 billion, were now part of the new council, he reported. As an initial priority, they were determined to speak out against "the dangers to our beneficiaries" of the practice "often cari-catured as greenmail."

When management used company money to pay greenmail, he explained, the payment was made with assets owned by all the shareholders but it benefited only the hostile few. Someone had to speak up for all shareholders, and that's what this new council of titan investors intended to do. In the Phillips case, their opposition would eventually contribute to the defeat of the company's recapitalization plan.

"Clearly, the role we represent is likely to grow, as assets owned by pension funds increase exponentially in the American economy," Goldin said, matter-of-factly. "The leviathan that these funds represent is only beginning to be felt as a distinct and powerful economic factor."

The impact of this "leviathan" would not be limited to takeover battles. Congress couldn't say it had not been warned.

WITH EACH PASSING year, it came to seem that potentially disastrous financial explosions could occur anywhere—and how far the shock waves could spread was anybody's guess.

That was evident from the extraordinary gathering in Paul Volcker's lofty conference room on Wednesday, March 13, 1985. The leather chairs around the vast central table were occupied by members of the Ohio congressional delegation, who had brought along some anxious savings and loan executives from back home—where frightened depositors were suddenly lining up to withdraw their cash.

The unlikely fuse that triggered this crisis had been lit nine days earlier and a thousand miles away, with the failure of ESM Government Securities, a small bond trading firm in Fort Lauderdale, Florida. One of ESM's biggest trading partners was the Home State Savings Bank in Cincinnati, a large thrift that estimated about $150 million worth of its government securities were in ESM's hands when the Florida firm failed on Monday, March 4.

Like almost six dozen other thrifts in Ohio, Home State did not have federal deposit insurance. Instead, its deposits were insured by the Ohio Deposit Guarantee Fund. Although the fund sounded official—its motto was "All savings guaranteed in full"—the fund was actually a bargain-priced private insurance company with no ties to the state government.

With about $130 million in assets, it was supposed to insure $5 billion in deposits in the state that were not covered by the Federal Savings and Loan Insurance Corporation (FSLIC), the FDIC's sister agency serving the thrift industry.

Within days, the risk that ESM's collapse posed to Home State was front-page news in Cincinnati. Depositors rushed to retrieve their cash, and Home State had a bank run on its hands. The Cleveland Fed and top aides in Volcker's office in Washington quickly made emergency loans to the thrift. On March 6 the state of Ohio announced it would "safeguard" all deposits covered by the private insurance fund. Rationally speaking, that should have been the end of the panic.

Yet, as in the Continental bank crisis of a year earlier, frightened depositors paid absolutely no attention to these government assurances. The run at Home State continued through the rest of the week; by the time the thrift closed its doors on Friday evening, March 8, an estimated $154 million in cash had been withdrawn.

On Sunday, March 10, Ohio officials put Home State into receivership, unable to find a buyer for it. By the following Wednesday, long lines were forming outside other thrifts insured by the private insurance fund, even though they had no exposure to the failed firm in Florida. News coverage about the bank runs was starting to attract notice far outside Ohio.

That's why the thrift executives had flown to Washington that morning and gathered in Volcker's office.

The towering central banker had done everything he could to show his concern, but the tools Volcker had available were limited. He could extend emergency loans to help with the bank runs, but what these thrifts really needed was federal deposit insurance, and the Fed didn't sell that—the thrifts had to get it from the FSLIC. With congressional pressure, and perhaps a little rumbling from the Fed, the FSLIC chairman agreed to meet with the Ohio visitors the next day.

That meeting did not go well. The FSLIC's parent agency, the Federal Home Loan Bank Board, had been bailing frantically for years against a rising tide of red ink in the savings and loan industry. Its chairman had no interest in insuring these Ohio thrifts, much less insuring them on an expedited basis in the middle of a panic. It would take months to examine them, he said, and there was a mandatory ten-day waiting period. Besides, as he reportedly told the thrift executives during the tense session, this was a state problem.

On Friday, March 15, Ohio's governor declared a "bank holiday" for all the privately insured thrifts in the state, asking merchants to be patient with customers who had suddenly lost access to their cash. The greater Cincinnati area was hardest hit, with more than forty institutions shut down and no clue when or if they would reopen.

Bank holiday was a term that conjured up anxious Depression-era memories for older depositors, especially in the four other states where some thrifts were covered by private insurance: Maryland, Pennsylvania, Massachusetts, and North Carolina. Officials in those states began to worry in private even as they expressed confidence in public. The news was full of scenes of panicked depositors in Ohio who had camped out on cold sidewalks overnight to make withdrawals.

Early on Saturday, and into the dark hours of Sunday, senior Federal Reserve staffers, FDIC aides, and state officials convened at the Federal Reserve Bank of Cleveland, trying to cope with a crisis that began in the Treasury bond market and now had spread across more regulatory borders than the Ohio River.

The Fed and the FDIC had airlifted two hundred bank examiners to help the grudging and underfunded FSLIC handle the applications from the healthy Ohio thrifts seeking federal deposit insurance. There were efforts to find national banks to buy Home State and perhaps other thrifts as well, which would make them immediately eligible for FDIC coverage, but regulatory barriers at the state and federal level confounded the search.

On Monday, the foreign currency market delivered its verdict on the expanding mess. The dollar plunged in value against the British pound and the German mark; the price of gold soared to its highest level in weeks. Many currency traders pointed directly to the Ohio thrift crisis, citing fears that this sharp spike in fragility would tie the Fed's hands in monetary policy. On Wall Street, the concern was broader—investors were worried that the crisis would continue to be contagious. "If this drags on too much longer, there's a systemic risk in those states where there is private deposit insurance," one financial analyst said. "That's why everybody wants it over."

Paul Volcker wanted it over, too. On Tuesday, March 19, he invited the governor of Ohio to fly in for a meeting with the chairman of the FSLIC. With Volcker there, an authoritative presence without any actual authority, the FSLIC chairman assured the governor that applications from the Ohio thrifts were indeed being expedited.

That seemed to reassure Ohio depositors, but how could Volcker reassure the markets? He couldn't just step out in front of microphones and make calming statements—for the world's senior central banker even to announce a press conference in such nervous times would risk a market reaction. Fortunately, on Wednesday he was scheduled to give a speech to the National Association of Cattlemen. Speaking more to the markets than to the bemused ranchers, Volcker said that the Fed was "working with the Ohio authorities" and "will be prepared to lend to them as they are deemed to be in strong enough condition to reopen."

But the stability of the financial system relying on the Fed's promises was growing ever more uncertain.

14

WITCHING HOURS

On Thursday, March 28, 1985, almost exactly five years after Ronald Reagan visited the New York Stock Exchange as a candidate, he returned, the first sitting president to visit the Big Board.

At his side was his new chief of staff, Donald Regan, who greeted John Phelan as an old friend. As they threaded their way across the trading floor, the president shook hands and waved. Regan and Phelan edged him determinedly toward the stone balcony where Reagan would deliver his prepared remarks and ring the opening bell.

"This is a great view from up here," the president joked, once he reached the balcony. "It's kind of like being at a Saturday night tag-team wrestling match at the Garden."

He detailed how his administration had helped restore health to the stock market during his first term and promised to do more in his second term. "That's our economic program for the next four years," he concluded. "We're going to turn the bull loose!" The opening bell rang right on time, amid shouts of "Ronnie! Ronnie! Ronnie!"

Phelan escorted Reagan and his chief of staff to the gilded Edwardian boardroom on the sixth floor, where the president fielded polite questions from the guests gathered there and told a few familiar stories. Then he was on his way.

While the visit had been a credit to the team Phelan had put together, he still needed a right-hand man, someone to take on administrative duties so he could cultivate the political relationships that had paid off so handsomely that morning. In short, he needed someone who could be for him what he had been for Mil Batten.

For weeks, Phelan had been quietly courting Robert J. Birnbaum, the able president and chief operating officer of the American Stock Exchange, to take the number-two job at the NYSE. Birnbaum had joined the Amex in 1967 and had held his job there for the past eight years. He was no-nonsense in his business dealings; his unsentimental style reminded some people of a surgeon short on bedside manner.

When Phelan discussed the NYSE job with Birnbaum over lunch in his private dining room, he mentioned that he was talking with four candidates. "They're all great," Phelan said, "but we're also looking at you." He beamed expectantly.

"Well, of course you are," Birnbaum said. "Unless you were all retarded, of course you'd be looking at whoever was in my job."

Perhaps his blunt style spoke to Phelan's inner marine. In any case, a short time later, Bob Birnbaum signed on as Phelan's top lieutenant. His move sparked rumors of a merger between the NYSE and the American Stock Exchange, promptly squelched by the Amex's chairman, Arthur Levitt. The merger whispers reflected the business pressures the NYSE was facing as giant institutional investors pushed for faster, cheaper trading services and a closer alignment with the latest derivative products to support their new financial strategies.

The American Stock Exchange and a few other regional stock markets had developed healthy options markets to compete with the Chicago Board Options Exchange, but the NYSE had not been successful in such ventures. Its offspring, the New York Futures Exchange, had struggled from the moment its ribbon had been cut in 1980.

And it was harder to see a future built around the simple business of trading blue-chip stocks, face-to-face, on the NYSE floor in Lower Manhattan. Some giant investors had begun to trade around the clock, around the world; more would surely follow. And Wall Street firms already had the computer connections necessary to fill their big clients' largest stock orders "upstairs," at their own trading desks, without routing them to the floor. The NYSE's defense against this "upstairs trading" had been rules that limited such off-floor trades and efforts to maintain the deepest and most transparent market for its listed stocks, with prices reported for all to see and specialists who were willing to use their own capital to maintain an orderly market.

If the day came when big institutional customers cared more about secrecy and speed than about transparency and price, or when the NYSE's specialists could not maintain order in the midst of a herdlike stampede—what then?

John Phelan was automating whatever and wherever he could, but those investments would be wasted if the Big Board did not keep its blue-chip listings.

The takeover mania had created an existential threat to those NYSE listings. In July 1984, three prominent Big Board companies, General Motors, Dow Jones and Co., and Coastal Corporation, had created "super-voting" classes of stock to ward off corporate raiders, in violation of the NYSE's bylaws. That action should have disqualified these companies from being listed on the exchange.

If the NYSE stood its ground, raider-wary companies could move their listings to a safer market. Both the American Stock Exchange and the Nasdaq market permitted their listed companies to have multiple classes of stock.

So, Phelan did not kick the three blue chips off the Big Board. Instead, he appointed an advisory committee to study various options. In January, the committee recommended that the NYSE allow listed companies to have more than one class of stock, so long as the common shareholders approved.

The forces opposed to the NYSE changing its listing standards were formidable. Institutional shareholders, corporate raiders, regulators, and powerful members of Congress argued that "one share, one vote" was the essence of shareholder democracy and should never be abandoned. Congressional hearings were planned, and Phelan would be expected to testify.

In his heart, he believed that the existing rule against "super-voting" shares was the right one. The question was whether preserving "shareholder democracy" for giant institutional investors would end up destroying the New York Stock Exchange.

Meanwhile, the exchange was being pressed daily to keep up with the growth in trading volume. Records were being set and broken too often to bother mentioning them. The automated DOT system, originally set up to expedite small retail orders, already was handling larger orders, many of them arising from the complex index arbitrage strategies of institutional investors. That arbitrage trading was rapidly tying the NYSE closer to the futures and options markets in Chicago.

Those new links were demanding attention on Wall Street. Earlier in the year, on the third Friday in March, the Dow had eked out a small gain during the day and then, suddenly, had fallen by a full percentage point in the last hour, on heavy trading. According to the traders on the floor, the dramatic end-of-day drop had occurred because several brokerage houses needed to unwind positions that exploited price differences between stocks and the options on those stocks that expired on the third Friday of the month. To do this, they had instituted automated selling programs to unload stocks in the last hour of trading. Similar last-minute nosedives had been occurring occasionally on these "third Fridays" going back at least a year.

As the third Friday in April approached, the *New York Times* sounded an early alert. "Superstitious or not, many stock investors have come to regard the last hour of trading on the third Friday of each month as the 'witching hour,' a time when the market seems to plunge for no apparent reason," the paper's commodity markets columnist noted. That was the expiration day for the Amex's Major Market Index option, known as the MMI, an option contract that closely tracked the Dow Jones index.

There was also an MMI futures contract traded on the Chicago Board of Trade. Days when stock index futures expired on the same day as stock index options were known as "double witching hours." However, four times a year (on the third Friday of March, June, September, and December), stock options for the company stocks included in various indexes also expired along with the index options and index futures, creating a "triple witching hour." That was what was in store for June.

"Whatever happens on April 19," one trader said, "we think June's witching hour will be most interesting."

———

THE STOCK MARKET'S witching hour in April was surprisingly benign; trading closed with barely a ripple, leaving the Dow essentially flat. Trading was relatively calm in May as well, though there were a few moments of sharp selling just before the closing bell.

But all eyes were on the third Friday in June, a "triple witching hour." In the final moments of trading, stock prices leapt higher, sending the Dow close to a new record and pushing trading volume to more than 125 million shares, a 50 percent jump over the previous day.

For most investors, an abrupt rally is always more pleasant than a sudden nosedive. Here, what was worrisome to professionals was the frenzy of the late trading. "Typically, expiration Friday is a psychotic day in the market," one analyst noted. But this day's outburst, which strained the NYSE's computer capacity, was crazy enough to be worrisome.

Clearly, the market's metabolism was changing. It was hard to see how these regular spasms up and down could be explained by "rational" changes in investor sentiment occurring in an "efficient" market.

IN THE SPRING of 1985, Leo Melamed saw an opportunity to expand the Chicago Merc's influence in Washington. President Reagan's chief trade negotiator, William Brock, had been named secretary of labor in mid-March, leaving an opening for a new U.S. trade representative. Melamed heard the news on the car radio as he headed toward his vacation home in Arizona. "The idea struck me like lightning: Clayton Yeutter," he recalled. Merc president Clayton Yeutter had held the same post in the Ford administration, and his return to Washington would add luster to the Merc's reputation.

In a masterful exercise of political power, Melamed worked the telephones for an entire weekend, calling three dozen chief executives to urge them to lobby for Yeutter. The effort paid off, and Yeutter was soon sworn in as the new U.S. trade representative.

Yeutter's move to Washington opened the door for William J. Brodsky to assume the presidency of the Chicago Mercantile Exchange. Bill Brodsky had joined the Merc from the American Stock Exchange, leaving roots that reached deep into the bedrock of the Manhattan markets. His father had worked on Wall Street for almost 60 years, and Brodsky had easily snagged summer jobs on the NYSE floor while he was in high school. At Syracuse University, he was president of his fraternity, and after finishing law school there, he went to work for the brokerage firm where his father was a partner.

With the bear market of 1973 bearing down on the firm, Brodsky's wife, Joan, encouraged him to pursue some research that might grow into a law review article to burnish his credentials. He chose to explore the Chicago Board Options Exchange, which was just opening its doors, and gained a solid legal grounding in the world of options. Meanwhile, he landed a job in the legal department of the American Stock Exchange, where he was soon overseeing the Amex's ambitious options trading operation. A few years later, he was appointed to the board of the Options Clearing Corporation, which acted as the central clearinghouse for settling all options trades, and he traveled regularly to Chicago for board meetings.

The trips had become a bit of a romance for the lifelong New Yorker. "I was smitten by the ingenuity and creativity and willingness to take risks that I found in Chicago," he later recalled. "There was an openness, a freshness, a lack of haughtiness in Chicago. The question here was 'are you smart?' not 'what's your pedigree?'"

So, when a recruiter called in the summer of 1982 about a spot as executive vice president at the Chicago Merc, Brodsky was tempted. He flew west to meet with Melamed and the exchange's executive committee. He saw the Merc's new home under construction and was astounded that the exchange was prosperous enough to finance the building largely from the recent sale of new memberships. He soon signed on and, over the next year, organized the management staff for the successful move into the new facility in the fall of 1983.

Despite his embrace of Chicago, Brodsky never burned his bridges to New York. He easily maintained cordial relationships with people that some of his Merc colleagues considered adversaries—exchange officials in New York and regulators in Washington and executives of the upstart Chicago Board Options Exchange. One of his close friends was Bob Birnbaum, the new president of the NYSE.

IN NEW YORK, witching hours continued to create uncertainty and unease. After the turbulence in June, the July expiration date was more orderly. A trading desk executive had an explanation for this. He said that the giant institutional investors "seemed interested in reducing the volatility, and therefore [they] spread the buying over several hours," instead of slamming into the closing bell.

There is no way of knowing whether money managers working for Gordon Binns at the General Motors pension fund were among the traders showing restraint. Binns had authorized trading in the S&P 500 futures contracts, after one of his senior staffers invited Leo Melamed and Bill Brodsky to visit Binns at the GM building.

Melamed had been delighted to make the trip, and Brodsky soon became an admirer of the warm, intellectually curious pension fund manager. They invited Binns to attend various conferences to talk about his use of futures contracts. They knew that the cachet of the GM pension fund, the largest in the corporate world, could only burnish the Merc's reputation.

Derivatives were not the only experiment Gordon Binns had undertaken. For nearly a year, he had watched the activities of the Council of Institutional Investors and was confirmed in his opinion that corporate pension funds would always be an awkward fit there. So, in the fall of 1985, he and several other corporate pension fund executives formed their own organization, the Committee on Investment of Employee Benefit Assets, or CIEBA.

The new organization was a way for Binns and his corporate counterparts to have a seat at the table when Congress investigated market developments important to these institutional investors. Program trading was one of those developments; Binns believed it was crucial to preserve program trading—and CIEBA was a way for another army of giant institutional investors to make that case to Congress.

IN NOVEMBER 1985, Jerry Corrigan learned firsthand that human panic wasn't the only way a crisis in one market could spread to another. In an increasingly automated market running at an accelerating pace, a computer malfunction would work just as effectively, with less warning.

At 8 a.m. on Thursday, November 21, a vice president at the Bank of New York called a New York Fed official to report a delay in the bank's computerized tally of the previous day's trading in Treasury securities. The Fed official was not alarmed; minor problems like this occurred frequently, and the Bank of New York was one of the busiest processing hubs in the government bond market.

The New York Fed and the Bank of New York were both part of a massive electronic network that could fairly be called the nation's financial circulatory system. Insiders called it "the payment system." It was the banking industry's modern equivalent of the "back offices" on which Wall Street once relied to send stock certificates to the right buyer and cash to the right seller. So-called "clearing banks" such as the Bank of New York served as the back office for legions of other financial firms and institutions engaged in Treasury trading and other complicated high-speed activity.

Unlike the old engraved stock certificates, however, Treasury securities existed only as distinct bookkeeping entries in a vast electronic ledger. Each had a unique identifying number so that it could be tracked through the system. Clearing banks such as the Bank of New York made sure that a Treasury bond that had been sold was removed from its seller's electronic ledger and entered into the electronic books of its buyer, and that the money the buyer paid was electronically subtracted from the buyer's bank account and added to the seller's.

Like the back offices of the late 1960s when the "paper crunch" hit, this was not glamorous work, but it was work that could bring the markets to a halt if it didn't get done. Normally it was carried out at blinding speed and in astonishing volume, as computers received information from other computers and automatically sent instructions on to still other computers, with the Fedwire (the New York Fed's electronic money-moving service) as the primary artery in the system.

Jerry Corrigan sometimes likened the financial payment system to the nation's interstate highway system. Instead of cars and trucks, there were electric impulses, which shuttled virtual securities and intangible cash between buyers and sellers. On a typical day, about $200 billion in transactions traveled smoothly from bank to bank, around the country and out into the wider world.

November 21, 1985, would not be a typical day.

At about 10:15 a.m., the Bank of New York alerted the New York Fed that the bank's customer data files, belatedly updated with Wednesday's transactions, had somehow been corrupted. For hours, programmers at the bank and its outside software consultants tried to find the flaw.

The rest of the market was up and running, the start of a busy Thursday. Securities were being electronically delivered to the Bank of New York for processing; the sellers expected cash, and the buyers expected to be credited with ownership and interest on the securities. With its computer system disabled, the bank was the equivalent of a drawbridge that had frozen in the open position. Government securities piled up on its books and had to be paid for with the bank's cash. The bank couldn't deliver the securities to, or collect cash from, the buyers on the other side of the broken bridge.

But there was some breathing room. The New York Fed, via the Fedwire, could take cash from the Bank of New York's account at the Fed and transfer it to the sellers of the securities, but with no cash flowing into the bank's account, it was soon overdrawn. And this was no garden-variety overdraft. By 11:30 a.m., the Bank of New York's account at the New York Fed was overdrawn by $12 billion.

Back at the bank's data processing center, as one team worked to find and fix the database flaw, another worked on a temporary patch to allow the bank to start clearing transactions before the Fedwire's daily closing time of 2:30 p.m. Around 2 p.m., the first patch was tested. It failed. Work was begun on a second one, and a third one; none was successful. A senior bank executive called the New York Fed to ask that the Fedwire be kept open past its normal closing time.

By 4 p.m., both Corrigan and J. Carter Bacot, the chairman and chief executive of the Bank of New York, had been alerted to the problem.

Corrigan agreed to keep the Fedwire open as late as possible on Thursday night, to give the bank additional time to fix its system and catch up on the mountainous logjam of unprocessed business. In a fortuitous decision, he also told his legal team to immediately prepare the paperwork for an emergency overnight loan to the bank, just in case.

As the afternoon slipped into the evening, the Bank of New York's overdraft at the Fed continued to grow. By 8 p.m., the bank was overdrawn by almost $32 billion. At that point, Corrigan sent an envoy to hand-deliver the special loan documents to the bank's headquarters; the bank's chief financial officer signed them, just in case. The documents called for the bank to pledge, as collateral for the loan, every penny of its domestic assets, a stack of collateral that totaled about $36 billion.

Finally, a patch held up and the bank was able to process enough business by 10 p.m. to reduce its overdraft by about $8 billion. But these transactions were moving slowly through the computer system, and people were getting tired.

Soon after midnight, Corrigan called Carter Bacot in his war room at the bank—they had talked countless times since 10 p.m.—and told him that 1 a.m. was positively the last Fedwire deadline for the bank. Almost as soon as Bacot hung up, he was told that the latest computer patch had failed and the computer had crashed again.

At 2:15 a.m. on Friday, November 22, the New York Fed officially made an historic $23.6 billion loan to the Bank of New York, the largest overnight loan it had ever made, a loan many times larger than the credit the Fed extended to Continental Illinois in its hours of crisis.

And there was still the rest of the Treasury market to worry about.

When the business day opened on Friday, the Bank of New York system was still not fully operational, and it once again began to overdraw its account. By 11:30 in the morning, with another $2 billion added to the bank's overdraft, Corrigan made another fateful—and almost disastrous—decision.

He ordered the Fed to stop accepting securities being delivered by other banks to the Bank of New York's account at the Fed, as the bank could not pay for them. He explained that he was trying "to see whether it was practical to prevent further increases in the overdraft without causing excessive disruption in the market."

By lunchtime on Friday, Corrigan had his answer—and it was "absolutely not." Within an hour of his decision the vast Treasury market had started to freeze up. Wary traders were suddenly unwilling to complete trades with one another. Some were trying to back out of deals they had already done with firms that relied on the Bank of New York for back-office processing. And the banks that could no longer complete transactions through the Bank of New York were suddenly incurring their own Fedwire overdraft problems, because they could not get paid.

Anyone in Jerry Corrigan's shoes might well have recurring nightmares about what would have happened on that nerve-racking Friday if the Bank of New York had not been able to repair its computer system as quickly as it did. Fortunately, by 1:30 p.m., the bank's processing system was more or less functional and Corrigan was able to lift the temporary and almost ruinous freeze on the bank's account at the Fed.

Weeks later, he tried to share the awesome warning delivered by this episode with the congressional committees that quizzed him about this unprecedented "bank bailout." As things now stood, Corrigan cautioned his critics, there was no other option. "It is unrealistic to think of 'disconnecting' a major participant except in circumstances which, in the end, might require closing the market as a whole." And closing any large market "as a whole" could create problems that would dwarf those the system had just survived.

Obviously, there was no such thing as a "minor computer problem" if fixing it meant more than a very brief shutdown of any part of the financial market's circulatory system. If a shutdown lasted longer, or had to be done in the middle of some other crisis—well, as Jerry Corrigan would say, "Katie, bar the door."

15

RATIONAL MARKETS?

On Tuesday, January 7, 1986, the stock market closed with the Dow at just under 1,566 points. By the closing bell on Wednesday, it had lost 40 points, more points than ever before, eclipsing a record set on the worst day of the crash in October 1929.

"There was pandemonium," an executive at one brokerage firm said.

Actually, the day's 2.5 percent loss was nowhere near as bad as the decline in 1929, which erased nearly 13 percent of the Dow's value at the time. Nevertheless, this historic 40-point decline was front-page news across the country.

In the aftermath, traders trotted out various theories about what had happened. Some cited fears that the Fed would curb takeover lending or would push up interest rates. But those fears had been baked into the day's news from the opening bell, and more than half the Dow's historic drop had come in the last hour of trading. That pattern was familiar on "witching hour" Fridays, but January 8 was not a witching hour. What on earth had happened?

Here's what happened: The price of stock index futures in Chicago, for some undiscernible reason, suddenly dropped, falling out of line with the current NYSE prices for the stocks in the index. It was an arbitrage opportunity for those who could move quickly. Giant institutional investors had swooped in, buying stock index futures and simultaneously selling the stocks that made up the indexes, using the NYSE's automated order delivery system. It was a classic case of buying the cheap widget and selling the expensive widget to reap an instant profit. It had happened before, of course—index arbitrage had been going on since mid-1982—but not on this scale, and never with this impact on the market.

"It was just unbelievable," said an institutional trader at Kidder Peabody. The head trader at E.F. Hutton said, "Panic may be a bit of an overstatement, but clearly there was a sense of urgency on the part of the professional trading community."

Further evidence for the role of arbitrage in the final hour's nosedive was the fact that stocks in an index tied to an option or futures contract, specifically the NYSE Composite index, the Standard & Poor's 500 index, and the Dow, suffered far more in the rout than other stocks did.

The entire ecosystem of investing was changing; events were becoming patterns, small tremors were becoming stronger, a fringe strategy was becoming a market force, a spasm in one market was felt instantly in another. Still, no one in Washington seemed to understand what was happening or how to respond.

Some regulators predicted that witching hours would become less disruptive as more investors got into the arbitrage game, which normally would reduce the profits available from that strategy. Rational and efficient markets would eventually erase these oddball opportunities for arbitrage, they said.

John Shad at the SEC saw the increased use of computer-driven arbitrage strategies as fostering a more liquid market that allowed "institutional investors to move large blocks of stock in a short time." He did not question that this was a good thing—or wonder how the markets would cope when those giant investors moved large blocks of stock or futures contracts in the same direction at the same time.

Already juggling the hot-potato issues of takeovers and insider trading, the SEC was caught between the ideology of Shad's latest chief economic adviser, a free-market purist named Gregg Jarrell, and the practical concerns of the agency's market regulation staff.

According to one account, "Jarrell was convinced that new trading regulations would merely benefit the old guard, the gray-haired Wall Street traders who were not keeping up." He strongly suspected that "the SEC staff didn't really understand what was going on as the markets in New York and Chicago became linked on the computer screens of high-powered traders."

Of course, it is not clear that Jarrell or the high-powered traders he admired understood what was going on, either. Some of their supposedly rational strategies were based on the far-fetched notion that there would always be investors who would take the other side of their trades, all the time, in every market, under any circumstances. Days such as January 8 showed how utterly unrealistic that assumption had become.

Even if regulators and lawmakers had grasped fully the new risks of these links among various markets, they still would have faced an uphill fight to do anything about them. Shad was wary of regulating what he saw as a healthy and probably inevitable consequence of computer technology. And without SEC support, it was unlikely anyone else could push such restrictions through Congress.

In any case, the SEC had announced in late 1985 that new rules for witching hours did not seem necessary. Perhaps it was coincidental, but the expiration day that fell nine days after the uproar on January 8 was a tame affair. Several traders did notice, though, that small investors were on the sidelines for much of that day.

John Phelan was growing increasingly worried that they would stay there. At a securities industry meeting in December in Boca Raton, Florida, he had reported on the NYSE's latest investor survey. Almost 60 percent of the trading volume on a typical day, much less a witching hour day, came from giant institutions and Wall Street firms trading for their own account.

The presence of pension funds in the stock market was growing exponentially. In 1975, they collectively held $113 billion worth of stocks. Five years later, in 1980, that had almost doubled, to $220 billion. By the end of 1985, it had doubled again, to almost $500 billion. Some of this vast sum of cash was in the hands of money managers who actively pursued a variety of strategies in the name of diversification, while some of it had flowed into passive index funds. The problem was these two styles of investing had sharply different effects on the market.

At any given moment, the active managers were scurrying around in different directions, like rabbits—some bought smaller stocks, some sought out international stocks, some specialized in one industry or another, some timed the market using various arcane theories, some relied on takeover speculation. Meanwhile, the index fund managers moved as one giant herd, all heading in one direction. On good days, they ambled there peaceably; on turbulent days, they galloped. A stampede was always a possibility.

The supposedly rational "quants" in academia and on Wall Street did not seem to fear that stampede. They apparently assumed that the mass movements of the giant herds would be offset by the trading done by the rabbits, the calm contrarians who did not follow the herd. But the power of wealthy contrarians was dwindling, while the herd of giant institutional investors was growing. The markets in both New York and Chicago were offering more evidence every month that there simply were not enough contrarian rabbits to buffer the effects of an institutional stampede.

Oddly, the little guys in the market could see quite clearly what was happening. "It's almost despair," a senior vice president at one large retail brokerage firm said. "Individuals don't want to get whipsawed in a market increasingly dominated by institutions."

BY FEBRUARY 24, 1986, the Federal Reserve Board had two new members, recent Reagan appointees who had replaced longtime Volcker allies. The days when Paul Volcker could easily command a unanimous vote, or even a majority vote, were over.

When the Federal Open Market Committee met that morning, the more recent appointees engineered a vote to cut interest rates, over Volcker's objections. The vote carried 4 to 3, to the chairman's shock.

He rose from his chair and looked down the long table at the committee's rebellious new members. "You can do what you want from now on," he told them, "but without me." According to an authorized biography, "he left the boardroom and slammed the door leading to his office, just in case anyone thought he might change his mind."

Volcker and Treasury secretary Jim Baker were scheduled to have lunch that day at Baker's office, joined by the Mexican finance minister. After the finance minister left, Volcker handed Baker "a handwritten resignation letter he had scribbled on a yellow pad" after his angry exit from the FOMC meeting.

Baker's memoirs are silent about the incident, but according to one Volcker biographer, Baker urged him not to make too much of that morning's vote, and to stay in office. Volcker said he would think it over, and returned to the Fed building. A bit later that afternoon, one of the morning's rebels visited Volcker's office and suggested a face-saving delay in the small interest rate cut.

News of the challenge to Volcker's leadership hit the Washington grapevine and spread north, where Wall Street's reaction was resoundingly negative. The White House and the Treasury Department immediately issued statements supportive of the Fed chairman. Unless he wanted to rattle the markets further by suggesting the White House had fired him, Volcker could not step down yet.

But the sun was clearly setting on his tenure. A first responder attuned to the way a panic-driven crisis could leap across the regulatory firewalls would soon be stepping down.

FOR ALL THE talk in Chicago about innovation and adapting to new market conditions, the futures markets were caught in the same romantic denial of reality that afflicted the "quants" advising institutional investors on Wall Street and the NYSE traders who opposed increased automation. They didn't truly believe their world needed to change in any dramatic way, and they resented anyone who suggested otherwise.

That was certainly true of the executives who gathered for an industry conference in Boca Raton in the first week of March 1986. For several days, they swapped gossip, enjoyed splendid food, and complained bitterly about their regulators.

Their gripes didn't have to travel far to reach the ears of Congress: there were four senators and a dozen congressmen attending the event, all giving short boilerplate speeches for handsome fees and enjoying the free food, lodging, and travel.

The futures industry had three big complaints.

One was that the CFTC wanted trading firms to carry a bigger cash cushion, to reflect the enormous growth in derivatives trading by giant institutional investors. The Chicago Board of Trade had formed a $1 million "defense fund" in November to fight these new capital rules at the CFTC, in Congress, or in court, if necessary. The Merc's Leo Melamed had complained that the new capital standards were "the result of inexperience or motivations beyond our comprehension."

Actually, the CFTC's motive was pretty easy to comprehend. A year earlier, in March 1985, Volume Investors, a significant clearing firm that stood behind trades on the New York Commodity Exchange, known as the COMEX, had been forced to close its doors abruptly after three of its customers lost $28 million almost overnight. The huge growth in institutional trading in an increasingly volatile market "heightens the potential for a default of far-reaching consequences," the CFTC warned in a subsequent report.

The giant institutions being welcomed into the futures markets were trading on a scale that dwarfed the capital held by many traders. But a number of smaller firms would have been winnowed out of the market by the new capital rules. Chicago was determined to prevent that.

The second prickly issue for the industry was the CFTC's most recent effort to get the biggest Chicago exchanges to time-stamp their trades to the closest minute. At the Merc and the Chicago Board of Trade, trades were stamped to the nearest half hour. For years, the CFTC had known that this was inadequate—it had found that up to 40 percent of the half-hour time stamps were wrong. Leo Melamed complained that the latest "audit trail" rule was "the foremost example of regulatory meddling in areas which the Commission inadequately comprehends."

The third issue inflaming Chicago was not what the CFTC was doing, but what it was not doing. It still wasn't taking effective action against swaps, the privately traded derivatives that were becoming enormously popular among giant institutional investors. The Chicago exchanges had argued for years that these new derivatives were futures contracts in disguise, and therefore illegal unless traded on an exchange. To Chicago, it was that simple.

It actually was not that simple. There were three species of off-exchange products that confronted the CFTC. Two of them, options on physical commodities and installment-purchase plans called "leverage contracts," were small pests that the commission had been battling from the day it first opened its doors. The third, the swap, was a massive creature that lived in the rarefied world of elite bankers, giant brokers, and corporate treasurers, and the CFTC clearly had no idea what to do about it. These were the risky derivatives that Jerry Corrigan was warning the banking community about—all the exotic bank-to-bank swap contracts or bank-to-broker swap deals that worked almost exactly like futures contracts but didn't show up on anyone's balance sheets and were not backstopped by anyone's clearinghouse.

Almost everyone outside the banking community agreed that these new products probably met the CFTC law's vague and elastic definition of a futures contract. As a federal judge in Chicago had once observed, what didn't? So, the Merc and the Board of Trade believed that swaps should trade on regulated exchanges and nowhere else.

It was not long before the CFTC backed off from enforcing its new audit trail standards against the Chicago Board of Trade and the Merc, and agreed to let the two exchanges come up with their own system for "reconstructing" trades, rather than automatically time-stamping them as they occurred. The debate over raising more capital would be more difficult to resolve, but the smart money was betting that Chicago would prevail on that issue as well.

Indeed, when CFTC chairman Susan Phillips next appeared before her overseers on the House Agriculture Committee, in mid-March 1986, their message for her was crystal clear: Don't ask the industry you regulate to do anything inconsistent with what it is already doing. If you do, we'll have to step in.

As for regulating swaps and similar "off-exchange" derivatives, Phillips was caught between Chicago's political power and the even more powerful defenders of a different status quo: Wall Street bankers, several of whom testified at the same hearing. Gary L. Seevers, a sharply dressed executive at Goldman Sachs—and a former CFTC official himself—joined with several other market professionals in testifying that they saw no reason to start regulating off-exchange derivatives, which were producing nice profits for Wall Street. "This off-exchange issue has been studied to death, and many articles have been written about it, many meetings have been held," he told the committee. "I would say that there is no one who has been in this room today who is really informed enough, or smart enough, to say if the CFTC should have more authority or less authority in the off-exchange area."

One skeptical Democrat on the committee, Congressman Dan Glickman of Kansas, saw the paradox: "You say it's been studied to death, and nobody knows enough about it?" he asked.

"Yes," Seevers persisted. "You're dealing with commercial reality here." The people using these new products were "sophisticated entities, dealing among themselves." His recommendation was "to do nothing."

This, too, was a remarkable suggestion: the CFTC and Congress weren't smart enough to regulate these new unlisted derivatives, so they should leave them alone.

Glickman looked at the other Wall Street professionals seated at the witness table and asked, "Does anyone have any contrary remarks to what Mr. Seevers has said on that issue?"

No one did.

"Okay, let me just ask one final question," Glickman said. He cited newspaper stories about the relationship between derivatives and stock market volatility. "I wonder if any of you might want to comment on that, as to whether that is an accurate characterization. I'm just curious."

Gary Seevers dismissed the issue as ignorant media finger-pointing, something that should not cause Congress any concern. "I'm not saying there's never been any effect in the 'third Friday phenomenon'—which we're going to have again in three more days," he noted. "It's a phenomenon that's been closely watched, and in general, any aberrations associated with that third Friday have been diminishing over the course of the last two or three years."

THE "THIRD FRIDAY phenomenon" that occurred three days later, on March 21, gave no evidence that the market's aberrations were diminishing.

The widely followed Dow Jones Industrial Average, which had closed just above 1,800 points the day before, lost 35.68 points, almost 2 percent of its value, most of that in the final minutes of trading. It was the fourth-worst point decline in market history.

A front-page story in the next day's *New York Times* blamed the day's "wild session" on a "late selloff linked to complex maneuvers by institutions." A second story, in the Business section, caught the mood in just four words: "'Triple Witching Hour' Havoc."

The prices of the Dow stocks, most of which traded on the NYSE, had risen faster than the prices of the expiring MMI options and MMI futures contracts linked to them. Index arbitrageurs grabbed a quick profit by buying the cheaper derivatives and selling the more expensive stocks on the Big Board—and selling them at the last possible second. The simultaneous expiration of stock options on those Dow stocks added to the "triple witching" uproar.

The evidence of these strategies was easy to find in the results of the day's trading. Of the 199.2 million shares traded, more than 45 million did so in the final minute. It took a half hour after the market closed before all the trades could be recorded. The number of very large orders, the hallmarks of the titan investors, was unprecedented.

This time, there really was no way to argue credibly that the day's results reflected an abrupt change in opinion among rational investors. Overall, more stocks rose in price than fell, and apart from the Dow, the other major market indexes lost only a few points. The American Stock Exchange index actually climbed almost four points, to a new record. Only the stocks tied to index arbitrage had been affected—but they had been affected so powerfully that they cost the market 2 percent of its value in just a few hours.

One senior institutional trader observed, "Moves like this used to take ten days to make. Now they take ten minutes. You can't get a handle on it. People trade stocks like they were a commodity."

For a growing portion of the market's population of institutional investors, that's exactly what stocks were becoming—a commodity, but one that traded on a stock exchange that had different regulators, different rhythms, and different rules.

———

JOHN PHELAN AND Bob Birnbaum looked skeptically over the luncheon china at John O'Brien, LOR's master salesman from California, while sitting in Phelan's private dining room a few months after the March debacle.

For O'Brien, the visit was a goodwill gesture of sorts. He had seen media reports blaming portfolio insurance for the increased turbulence on the NYSE trading floor. He wanted to explain why that didn't have to happen.

By nature, John Phelan and John O'Brien were not all that different. Both were smart, plainspoken, and entrepreneurial, but they had taken very different roads to this meeting. O'Brien had been an entrepreneur at the theoretical edges of finance, embracing disruptive ideas from scholars such as Mark Rubinstein and Hayne Leland and translating them for the single-minded investment giants on Wall Street. Phelan had been an entrepreneur within the deeply traditional culture of the Big Board, trying to apply practical technology and new rules without losing the human factors he saw as the glue that held his market together.

"Look at it this way," O'Brien said. When LOR sold stock as part of its hedging strategy, "it's really like we're having a sale—a bargain sale on stocks." His firm wasn't selling because it feared bad corporate news or some market downturn. It had no clue about the market's future direction or the value of the companies whose shares it was selling; it was simply *hedging.* So, for the rest of the market, LOR's hedges created bargains—as if someone had suddenly slapped "Marked Down for Quick Sale" stickers on a store full of full-price, first-class merchandise.

Traditional investors could pick up premium stocks at bargain prices by buying when LOR was selling. O'Brien's message to those investors, he told Phelan, was: "Come to our party!"

Phelan wasn't persuaded; the growing scale of portfolio insurance trades worried him. "If everybody's doing the same thing, what is going to prevent this from going down to nothing?" he asked.

O'Brien was confident that falling prices would always attract buyers, but Phelan wasn't so sure. When the market is hurtling downward in the last hour of trading, who is going to be brave enough to look for bargains?

Anyone who knows, in advance, that bargains will be sitting there waiting to be picked up, O'Brien answered. Anyone who knows that the only reason prices are falling is because of some academic hedging strategy. Anyone who knows that buying is the rational thing to do under those circumstances.

Like Phelan, Bob Birnbaum thought O'Brien was being naïve to think the market would adapt to portfolio insurance. "You know," said Birnbaum, "if I'm a regular guy and I get to my office some morning and see that the market has dropped by 3 or 4 percent, I don't think that picking up the phone to buy a bunch of stocks is going to be the first thing that crosses my mind." No, the first thing he would do would be to call someone who knew the market better, someone whose judgment he trusted, to find out what the heck was going on. If he couldn't get a reassuring explanation, or even if he could, he was probably just going to stay on the sidelines until things calmed down. That seemed to him to be the "rational" thing to do.

And if enough people did that, O'Brien's bargain-priced stocks would go begging—and the market, as Phelan feared, could drop "down to nothing."

O'Brien insisted that the modern market's institutional investors, professional traders, and quantitative analysts would not be frightened away by a sudden nosedive, the way Birnbaum's "regular guy" would. They would understand why all those shares were being sold; they would know that the selling didn't reflect any bearish sentiment at all and would calmly step in to buy at a bargain price.

There was no way these firm-minded men were going to resolve their disagreements about market psychology over lunch. Still, O'Brien thought, it had been an interesting theoretical discussion.

After the first week in July, it all seemed less theoretical. On July 1, the Dow hit a new record: 1,903.54 points, its fourth record since the beginning of the year. A week later, on July 7, the Dow, once again, lost more points in a single day than ever before, eclipsing the January decline and a larger drop in June. Once again, the new reality of the modern stock market was page-one news, and *rational* was not a word widely used to describe it.

———

IN AUGUST 1986, Continental Illinois—rescued from certain death two years earlier by the FDIC, which was still its majority shareholder—decided to buy First Options Inc., the largest clearing firm for traders on the nation's largest options exchange.

First Options started out processing transactions for options traders in the early 1970s, when the Chicago Board Options Exchange was young. Under the ownership of Spear, Leeds and Kellogg, a big specialist firm on the NYSE trading floor, First Options had accumulated enough capital to handle bigger trades for more clients. By 1986, its ambitions had grown bigger than its stock-trading parent in New York could finance, and it was looking for a new owner to underwrite its growth.

Continental Illinois was still trying to work its way out of its near-death experience. It needed profitable lines of business, and it needed to diversify. Buying First Options, which had long been a strong customer of the bank, satisfied both needs.

The acquisition upset some local bankers, who complained that the FDIC's backing gave Continental Illinois an unfair advantage in the marketplace. Despite spirited protests, though, the FDIC let the bank buy First Options.

As a result, a linchpin in the operation of the options markets left its former home with an NYSE specialist firm and moved in with the commercial bank that the FDIC and its fellow regulators had moved heaven and earth to save two years earlier.

Given all the mergers and takeovers making headlines that summer, Continental Illinois's friendly purchase of First Options did not seem even slightly important to Wall Street.

Wall Street was wrong about that.

16

PANDORA'S PORTFOLIOS

In three turbulent days in September 1986, John Shad began a sad and surreal pivot toward the end of his career at the SEC.

His enforcement division had been waging a long, rocky fight against insider trading, which was spreading like a bad cold through Wall Street. A number of notable midlevel executives had been arrested and sued; some had pleaded guilty in criminal cases and paid substantial fines to settle lawsuits filed by the SEC. Nothing seemed to help.

Then, in May, federal agents arrested Dennis Levine, an investment banker with Drexel Burnham Lambert. One of the people listed in Levine's address book was the arbitrageur Ivan Boesky, a veteran of the battle for Phillips Petroleum and the leading takeover speculator on Wall Street.

Boesky had not loomed large during John Shad's years on Wall Street, but at the SEC, Shad had come to respect Boesky's aggressive intellect. Just three months earlier, in February, Shad had welcomed Boesky to an SEC roundtable in Washington on how to curb the takeover rumors on Wall Street, a session that John Phelan had also attended. With Phelan sitting at the same big round table, Shad and Boesky made the case that it was unwise for Phelan to permit trading halts when takeover rumors swept the floor of the NYSE.

With Dennis Levine's arrest, the SEC's insider trading investigation was boosted into a new orbit. Levine pointed fingers at others in his ring of conspirators, including Boesky, who, he claimed, had been buying tips from him for more than a year. All through the summer, the SEC enforcement staff circled Boesky. By August they had him, and it was not long before his defense lawyer, the former SEC general counsel Harvey Pitt, secretly offered a deal: in exchange for leniency, Boesky would lead them to some of the biggest figures in the takeover game. Long days and nights later, a deal was struck—a single criminal charge, up to five years in prison, and a $100 million payment, covering both fines and restitution of his illegal profits.

On Wednesday, September 10, the SEC was scheduled to hold a public meeting to vote on a staff plan for calming down witching hour Fridays. The proposal asked that brokers send orders seeking the day's closing price, so-called market-on-close orders, to the trading floor a half hour before the closing bell, so any order imbalances could be publicized. That was as far as John Shad was willing to go in meddling with the new quantitative trading strategies.

Before that public session, however, Shad convened a "super-executive session," a meeting open only to the commissioners and a few key members of the enforcement staff. According to one account, this meeting was the first update on the Boesky case given to Shad or any other commissioner since earlier that summer. "They seemed stunned by the scope of the revelations, and the prospect of the reactions they were likely to trigger," that account noted.

The plea bargain with Boesky was unprecedented—at one stroke, he would be paying a penalty almost equal to the SEC's entire annual budget. And Boesky's recital of his corrupt dealings with some of the royalty of Wall Street was staggering, especially for John Shad, who had come to the SEC deeply convinced of the fundamental honesty of the world where he had spent his entire working life.

THURSDAY, SEPTEMBER 11, was shaping up as a steamy late summer day when John Phelan arrived at his desk at the New York Stock Exchange. It had been a dreary week for most investors; the previous day, the market had edged down for its fourth straight losing session.

Some market pundits blamed the downturn on money managers trying to dump their losers and dress up their portfolios in the final weeks of the third quarter. Others pointed out that the market had climbed more than 24 percent since the first of the year and some profit taking was to be expected. Still others said that investors were worried about interest rates going up, which would reduce demand for stocks. Who really knew? As J. P. Morgan had once famously said, markets fluctuate.

Phelan was not happy about John Shad's latest response to the wild fluctuations of witching hour trading, approved the day before. He didn't think the half-hour advance notice for market-on-close trades went nearly far enough, and he didn't hesitate to say so. He wanted the expiration value of Chicago's stock index futures to be based on the opening prices on the NYSE on those third Fridays, not the closing prices. Phelan believed, from his decades on the floor, that it was much easier to detect and deal with big order imbalances at the opening bell than it was in the frantic, last-minute trading at the end of the day.

Given the rivalry and paralysis built into the regulatory system, the SEC could not give Phelan what he wanted. Only the CFTC could do that. But Phelan's proposal was opposed by the Chicago exchanges, and the CFTC had not overruled them.

When the computer monitors on the credenza behind Phelan's desk came to life that Thursday morning, it initially looked like another dispiriting trading day. It soon turned into a disastrous one.

By noon, the Dow's decline matched the historic drop in early July. After a short-lived lunchtime rally, prices turned and dropped sharply for the rest of the day. By the time the closing bell rang at 4 p.m., traders were profoundly agitated, a record 237.6 million shares had been traded, and the Dow was down 86.61 points, more than 4.6 percent, the largest point loss ever and the largest daily percentage loss since May 1962.

One brokerage firm executive said, "I've never seen anything like this. I think money managers panicked."

Market analysts searched for rational reasons for the massive decline. One Wall Street executive even pointed a finger at John Shad, citing the SEC's vote the previous day on witching hour procedures and claiming there was "a lot of uncertainty, with the SEC putting in new ways to handle" the witching hour that was a week away.

A far more plausible explanation was tied to index arbitrage.

For the entire month of August and early September, the stock index futures contracts had been more expensive than the underlying stocks, and arbitrage traders had sold futures contracts and bought stocks—no doubt contributing to the market's new record high on September 4. Indeed, arbitrage trading had been credited with record-setting daily gains earlier in the year.

On September 11, for some reason, the arbitrage opportunity turned upside down. In the first minutes of trading in Chicago, the price of stock index futures dropped sharply and inexplicably, creating a ripe opportunity for index arbitrage traders. They started selling stocks and buying the cheaper futures contracts.

In theory, the arbitrage traders' sudden demand for the spooz contracts should have driven up their price, bringing the Chicago market back into line with New York. Mysteriously, that didn't happen—there simply wasn't enough buying by the arbitrageurs to offset the heavy selling that was hitting the spooz pit that day. Subsequent investigation showed that the S&P 500 futures contract sold at a discount "virtually throughout the day."

This wasn't the whole story about Thursday's historic decline. There had been a lot of other traders in the marketplace that day, selling stocks for reasons unrelated to the markets in Chicago. But it was a large part of the story.

When the closing bell rang, the spooz was still trading at an unusually deep discount to the stocks on the Big Board. Unless that changed, Friday was going to be another very bad day, as more arbitrageurs sold stocks and bought futures.

It did not change—it got worse.

The nosedive continued in the foreign markets that opened for Friday trading while New York was asleep. Tokyo had its steepest one-day plunge in history, and London experienced a record-setting drop before recovering late in the day.

Shortly after the opening bell in Chicago on Friday, S&P 500 futures plummeted, creating a gap between the futures contract and the prices of the underlying stocks that exceeded anything the market had ever seen. Spooz traders simply did not trust the prices they saw on their screens. They later told investigators that they did not try to lock in this extraordinary arbitrage profit because they did not believe they would actually be able to sell the underlying stocks on the Big Board at the prices reflected in the index.

It is no wonder they were wary. In New York that morning, the stock market fell almost straight down from the opening bell until around 10:30 a.m., when it rallied enough to recover almost all its losses before noon. Then it pivoted again and ground out another losing day, a decline of 34.17 points, almost 2 percent, with the trading volume at just over 240 million shares, breaking the previous day's record.

For Phelan and Birnbaum, the one silver lining in all this was that the Big Board's processing systems were able to cope with the surge in trading volume. "In the last five years, we've invested $150 million in systems and communications to handle all this," Phelan said after the closing bell on Friday. "We're anticipating peak volume of 300 million shares a day and sustained volume of 200 million shares a day, and if we could do it with the same lack of problems we had today, we'd be very pleased." He added, with a nod to the humans on his trading floor: "It's computers *and* people."

By the weekend, people were inevitably making comparisons with the worst two days of 1929, when the Dow lost more than 24 percent of its value, the steepest two-day drop in history. The comparisons were overwrought; in percentage terms, the 6.5 percent decline on September 11 and 12 was barely a quarter of the 1929 loss. Still, it was a shock, one that lingered even after the market eked out small gains on tepid volume early the following week and then lost about half those gains during an unremarkable "triple witching" Friday.

John Shad's team at the SEC began investigating the two-day crash. To do so, it would have to rely on the help of the CFTC and the trading records from the Chicago pits. The former could be counted on, thanks to the genial leadership of Susan Phillips. The latter was a crap shoot, given the unreliable audit trail maintained by the two giant Chicago exchanges.

It was clear to the largest players in the stock market, if not to Shad, that the answers to what was happening in New York could be found only in Chicago. The Chicago-based chief investment officer at Kemper Financial Services put it this way: "The price of a share of stock is, more often than not, now set in Chicago [rather] than on the floor of the New York Stock Exchange." Institutions "dominate the game," he continued, but arbitrage-related program trading was starting to dominate "what we perceive to be normal institutional activity, which is buying or selling based on value."

The market's public nosedive and the still-secret Boesky case affirmed that both the morality and the machinery of the marketplace were changing in profound and troubling ways. Little about this new world resembled what John Shad thought of as "normal."

IN BERKELEY, MARK Rubinstein watched the markets on those turbulent September days with a heavy heart.

He and his partners, Hayne Leland and John O'Brien, had prospered enormously from the portfolio insurance mania that was sweeping the pension fund industry. LOR was overseeing an extraordinary amount of money, almost $5 billion, most of it through the use of S&P 500 futures contracts. The partners had licensed their software to other firms, including two of the largest institutional money managers, Aetna Life Insurance and Wells Fargo Investment Advisors. Between their own clients and their licensees, their portfolio insurance concept covered more than $50 billion in assets—and by some estimates, copycat competitors were "insuring" an equal amount. This was a staggering number, especially when compared to the $150 million they had managed when *Fortune* magazine featured them so favorably in the spring of 1982.

LOR, like all portfolio insurers, had been a major seller in the S&P 500 futures pits in Chicago on Thursday and Friday, as it adjusted its hedges to reflect the losses in the market over the prior week. The firm sold not because Leland and Rubinstein were pessimistic about the economy or worried about rising interest rates, but simply because their portfolio insurance hedging strategy required them to sell.

The scale of what portfolio insurers were doing had begun to deeply worry Rubinstein. Leland, while temperamentally a calmer person, was also starting to become concerned, specifically about a possible "feedback effect," the chance that their trades would trigger a chain reaction that would destabilize the stock market.

"From the very first day I thought of portfolio insurance I said, 'Well, what if everyone tried to do it?' I didn't like the answer I came up with," Leland later told an academic researcher. It was not a fear he had ever shared with LOR's clients, but that hardly seemed necessary back when they had so few of them.

Rubinstein said he sometimes felt as if he and his partners had opened Pandora's box or freed some mischievous genie. "We had one client come to us who had a huge pension plan," Rubinstein recalled. "We wanted to tell that client that was too much money for us to handle. We were just too worried about the impact that the trading would have on the market." But like his partners, he also understood that if LOR turned prospective clients away, they would just go to one of its rivals. Indeed, even if LOR shut down completely, the genie couldn't be put back into the bottle.

Rubinstein was glad to hear that the SEC was going to investigate the two-day turbulence in the market, but he suspected the agency would not get to the heart of what was going on. "When I saw what happened in September," he said later, "I thought, that's us. That is *us*."

IN EARLY OCTOBER, Congress passed the Government Securities Act of 1986. The new law was supposed to address the hazards exposed four years earlier, when a default in the unregulated Treasury bond market leapt over regulatory fences and threatened brokerage firms, thrift institutions, and banks.

Ever since the silver crisis of 1980, reality had been saying, loud and clear, "It is all one market now." Time and again, a crisis in one market had quickly spread beyond the reach of that market's regulators. Given this indisputable reality, the new law was a monument to regulatory inertia and legislative myopia. It gave the secretary of the Treasury some temporary power to write rules for the government bond market; those rules would be enforced by the SEC or by whichever agency already regulated the outfit that violated them. Any government bond dealers not already supervised by somebody had to register with the SEC, but a firm could request an exemption from the Treasury secretary. The law entirely ignored Treasury futures and options. And the whole statute would expire in five years unless Congress renewed it. As an example of how Congress and Washington regulators responded to an increase in fundamental market risk, it was an ominous joke.

At the SEC, John Shad had opposed extensive regulation of the Treasury market, but he accepted this weak law. Paul Volcker had been equally uneasy about any new regulatory regime, but he was also content with this flimsy arrangement.

Those two men had a more urgent issue to discuss when Shad called Volcker on Thursday, November 13, 1986.

The issue was Ivan Boesky. Shad informed Volcker that the SEC and the U.S. attorney's office in New York would hold simultaneous press conferences after the market closed on Friday, November 14, to announce that Boesky had been arrested, had agreed to pay $100 million to settle SEC charges of insider trading, would plead guilty to a single criminal charge, and was cooperating with the government's continuing criminal investigation.

For several months, Boesky had been secretly recording his conversations with various Wall Street figures, including Drexel's powerful financier Michael Milken. So far, the clandestine tapes had not produced all that prosecutors had hoped for, but it wasn't possible to keep Boesky's undercover work a secret any longer. One of Boesky's investment entities was publicly traded, and the next day, under SEC rules, it had to release its quarterly report—which, of course, would have to disclose the small detail of its CEO's arrest. The news was still secret, but Shad wanted to alert Volcker in case there were aftershocks in the banking system.

The call did not reflect any greater grasp of the dangerous linkages among markets; it simply underscored how deeply Paul Volcker was trusted by his fellow regulators—especially by Shad, who did not share his blockbuster news with anyone else in the regulatory loop until the next day, when he notified the chairmen of the SEC oversight committees in Congress, just hours before the press conference.

At 2:45 p.m. on Friday, Shad alerted Jim Baker and Donald Regan to the news that Boesky, a major Republican donor, had fallen. It was clearly a jolt: within days, the two men would be conferring about whether the White House should develop some policy initiatives for the "arbitrage/junk bond arena."

Shad waited until 3:30 p.m. to notify the CFTC, which had not been privy to the investigation, even though Boesky had routinely hedged his enormous stock portfolio in the spooz pit. Shad then reached out to John Phelan, whose floor traders would have to deal with any selling panic the news might trigger on Monday.

As it happened, Phelan was traveling in China, and the call went to Bob Birnbaum, who knew that Boesky's timely trades in takeover stocks had frequently been flagged by the NYSE's surveillance team.

At 4:30 p.m., as federal prosecutors stepped to a podium in New York, John Shad and his enforcement chief took their seats in front of a bank of microphones at a table in an SEC conference room in Washington. Shad read his brief remarks from a single sheet of paper.

The settlement with Boesky, which called for the return of $50 million in illegal profits and an additional $50 million fine, "is by far the largest settlement the commission has obtained in an insider trading case," Shad said. Boesky's various investment partnerships currently held about $2 billion in securities, Shad continued, and "for a short period of time, he will be permitted to be associated with these entities in order to preserve the assets and avoid defaults on bank and other loans."

AFTER THE PRESS conferences, "three rumors—all of which turned out to be true—made the rounds on Wall Street," one account noted. One rumor was that Boesky had been wearing a wire for months, another was that he might implicate Michael Milken and Drexel, and the third— "the one that seemed the most incredible, almost impossible to fathom or accept"—was that Boesky had been allowed to secretly sell hundreds of millions of dollars of stock before the announcement of his arrest.

Yes, the SEC had let Boesky start liquidating his holdings in early November. It was a remarkably ill-considered decision—not Shad's first public relations blunder, but surely his worst. The only plausible excuse was that Shad thought the step would help ensure that Boesky retained enough wealth to pay the $100 million settlement.

As expected, the post-Boesky trading was hectic when the New York Stock Exchange opened on Monday, November 17. Takeover stocks bore the worst of the selling pressure, of course. With weekend headlines about government subpoenas being served at firms all along the Street, stock prices started falling in Europe even before New York's opening bell and continued to decline through the afternoon.

It wasn't the rout that John Shad had feared, but that was scant comfort. By Friday, the angry rumors on the Street about Boesky's pre-indictment selling had surfaced, and the news rapidly spread across the country.

The criticism was fed by ill-founded speculation that Boesky had hoodwinked regulators because his firm's profits were much larger than the penalty he paid to the SEC. Boesky's investors had reaped most of those profits, of course; by one credible account, Boesky actually paid fully half his entire net worth to settle the SEC case. Unfortunately, Shad could not shake the unfair accusation that he had let Boesky off easy.

It later emerged that Boesky had been actively trading S&P 500 futures contracts, as well as stocks, in the weeks before his arrest was announced. But thanks to legal loopholes Shad had not been able to close, insider trading wasn't illegal in the derivatives markets!

What should have been Shad's sweetest hour, his vindication after years of congressional taunts about flabby enforcement work, had almost instantly curdled into public recrimination and private exasperation. Shad and his senior staff "could not understand why the Boesky case had turned against them," one account noted. "They could not understand how so much could have gone wrong so quickly."

SHAD'S CONGRESSIONAL CRITICS initially were just as harsh as those on Wall Street and in the media—bashing Wall Street crime had proved to be a successful election issue for the Democrats. However, by December, attention on Capitol Hill had shifted and was firmly riveted on the jaw-dropping details of what was quickly dubbed the "Iran-Contra" scandal, in which President Reagan had authorized the secret sale of weapons to Iran in an effort to win Iranian help in freeing American hostages held in Lebanon; then, members of his staff had steered the profits from those arms sales to the Contras, the rebel forces challenging the leftist Sandinista government in Nicaragua, in defiance of a specific congressional ban on military aid to that group.

The scandal would ultimately lead to several clouded departures from Reagan's inner circle, but it almost immediately began to undermine the position of White House chief of staff Donald Regan.

Regan, for all his faults, had been a financially savvy cog in Washington's political machinery, perceptive enough to have sought out Wall Street opinions about the new arbitrage strategies linking the stock market and the futures market. He understood the "growing concern that too much more of this would badly shake the confidence of individual investors and many institutional investors in the whole equity market process."

He had not always agreed with Paul Volcker about the fragility of the banking system—his role in the Penn Square Bank crisis and his last-minute obstruction of the FDIC's rescue of Continental Illinois were cases in point—but he did understand the stock market. Soon after the Boesky scandal broke, in fact, Regan was considering ways the president could publicly show his support for John Shad's beleaguered enforcement staff—an insightful gesture that certainly would have been welcome at the SEC in those demoralizing weeks.

But as the Iran-Contra scandal eclipsed the continuing coverage of the Boesky investigation, Regan's days in the White House were numbered.

Volcker, too, was facing an uncertain climb into 1987. The Federal Reserve voted in December 1986 to liberalize its interpretation of the Glass-Steagall Act, allowing national banks to expand into certain precincts of the securities business. Whatever Volcker's misgivings, the Fed's new majority apparently planned to continue chopping holes in the Glass-Steagall fence until Congress either shored up the barrier between the banks and Wall Street or tore it down entirely.

For John Shad, the public and congressional reaction to the Boesky case may have been the final straw. Years before, in a private diatribe that he scribbled out in longhand and later incorporated into some private speeches to friendly audiences, Shad opened a window into his personal ambivalence about the price he'd paid during his tenure in Washington.

He titled the piece "Trials and Tribulations." It began: "If you're tempted to serve in Washington, you'll take a big cut in pay but you will have a part-time car, and get to read a lot of critical articles about yourself. It's a humbling experience. The politically motivated criticism comes from Democratic Congressmen . . . Their letters are delivered to the press. Before you receive a copy, the reporters call. The standard response is no comment, but the liberal press makes the most of such stories. The volume of accusations picks up in the even numbered years—election years."

He continued: "Some of my friends thought I was nuts to accept the job. One called me up and said, 'Tell me again—slowly—why are you doing this.'" While Shad wasn't ready to leave public service entirely, he let the White House know he had no appetite for another term at the SEC.

17

JANUARY OMENS, JULY ALARMS

It should have been a miserable week in New York.

On Sunday, January 18, 1987, the Long Island Rail Road had gone on strike. The rest of the weekend news had been ugly, a mix of local racial unrest and Washington scandals. The weather on Monday was a disgusting mix of snow, wind, and rain, with a blizzard predicted for later in the week.

None of that—or anything else, it seemed—could dampen the extraordinary exuberance in the stock market.

On Monday, January 19, the Dow extended a New Year's rally that had begun with the opening bell on January 2 and had now continued for a dozen consecutive sessions, tying a record set in 1970. The Dow had gained an astonishing 5 percent in the first five trading days of 1987, and had closed above the 2,000-point level for the first time ever.

Trading on Tuesday extended the rally to a record-setting length: thirteen straight gains. On this day, however, the Dow managed only a tiny advance, and other market barometers were down slightly.

Moreover, the prices of both the S&P 500 futures on the Merc and the Major Market Index futures on the Chicago Board of Trade dropped sharply in late trading. That last-minute nosedive in the futures pits was a "flashing red light" that could signal a sell-off by big institutions, one trader told the *New York Times*. If that happened, the New Year's string of consecutive gains would probably be broken.

And it was. At the closing bell on Wednesday, the Dow had dropped about 10 points. Traditional market reporters looked for the traditional reasons, but none of their explanations looked plausible the next day. On Thursday, the stock market defied a blizzard that blanketed the Northeast and rose to new record-setting levels. The Dow's climb marked its largest one-day gain in history, 51.60 points, and it closed at a new high of 2,145.67 points.

It seemed increasingly obvious that the engine driving the day's trading was the complex interplay between the futures markets and the stock exchange—and the program trading that professional investors used to exploit those connections. Other explanations were starting to look a little absurd.

Clearly, in less than five years, financial futures had fundamentally changed the way the traditional stock market worked.

BY JANUARY 1987, Leo Melamed was becoming increasingly worried that the witching hour gyrations in the markets would lead to a political witch hunt in Washington.

The triple witching hour on December 19, 1986, had been a case in point. The voluntary reports filed by brokers at 3:30 p.m. showed "a heavy imbalance of orders to sell stock at the closing bell," according to the *New York Times*. However, instead of falling, Big Board prices shot almost straight up, as they had in December 1985. There were reports that, in those final moments, Salomon Brothers had purchased a staggering $2 billion worth of stock. The SEC's only public response was to complain that those last-minute orders had not been disclosed in advance, as it had requested.

Regulators might be wary of trying to tame the witching hours, but Leo Melamed and John Phelan weren't. Even their rivalry had to bow before the threatening chaos of these expiration days.

Phelan's proposed cure—pegging the spooz's expiration value to the day's opening prices on the NYSE, not the closing prices—had been viewed with suspicion by Melamed simply because it was a New York proposal. To his credit, the Merc studied the idea and concluded that it actually made sense.

So, in mid-December, the Merc applied to the CFTC for permission to settle the S&P 500 contract based on opening prices, effective in June 1987. John Phelan applauded the step, but in Chicago, the reaction was more grudging. The Chicago Board of Trade would say only that it was "studying" the idea for its volatile MMI futures contract, and the Chicago Board Options Exchange flatly said it would not follow the Merc's initiative for its popular S&P 100 option contract. Still, the Merc's decision to accommodate Phelan in the spooz pit gave Melamed a little moral high ground, even if it didn't resolve all the potential witching hour problems.

FRIDAY, JANUARY 23, was the last trading day of a week that had already seen the end of a historic thirteen-day rally, record trading volume, and the largest one-day gain ever, which lifted the Dow to a new high. By the closing bell that day, those milestones would be forgotten footnotes.

The day's trading began normally enough. The market opened strong and then steadied itself. Around noon, traders recognized the hallmarks of program trading in the wave of buy orders coming in. Prices started to roar upward. By 1:39 p.m., the Dow had gained more than 3 percent, climbing over the 2,200 mark for the first time.

Then, in seventy-one shattering minutes, the Dow plunged 5.5 percent—an unprecedented drop of 115 points.

Index option prices began to fall within minutes of a newswire report on some comments Paul Volcker made about bank deregulation, although the link seemed tenuous. Index futures followed the options down; index arbitrage kicked in. On the NYSE, prices "suddenly were sucked into a free fall," the *New York Times* reported, a nosedive that "strained every system, electronic and human, in the world's largest capital market."

Just as abruptly, the free fall stopped—but the craziness continued. Prices careened up again, gaining 2.8 percent. Then there was another inexplicable pivot and the Dow plunged again, falling 2.3 percent from its peak just moments earlier. Seasoned NYSE specialists were caught repeatedly out on a limb as prices zigzagged. Terrified institutional investors had started to sell and move to the sidelines, as the Dow closed in on a 44-point loss. At the bell, the Dow had fallen 2 percent, to 2,101.52 points, a record 302.4 million shares had been traded, and even market veterans were stunned.

An experienced senior trader at First Boston reported, "There are no words to describe what we were going through. People were paralyzed." A strategist at a retail brokerage house said, "I thought my stock quotation machine would start to smoke." A retail broker admitted, "Frankly, I have great difficulty explaining to people what is going on." The head of trading at Morgan Stanley said, "I've been in the business for 18 years and I have never seen anything like it before. It's berserk. It's total confusion. No one knows what the heck is going on."

Well, they knew *what* had happened. In four hours, with no explanation, the market had soared up, plunged down, gone up again, then plunged steadily down until the closing bell, with more shares traded than ever before. What they didn't know was *why* all that had happened.

John Phelan was fit to be tied. With no small degree of professional courage, he let his public relations staffers know he was ready to talk even more forcefully about program trading and what he thought it was doing to the nation's premier stock market. Just find him the right venue, and he would let loose with both barrels.

One result was a cover story in the March 2, 1987, issue of *Investment Dealers' Digest*, which was widely read in the hard-core financial community Phelan wanted to reach. The headline said it all: "John Phelan vs. Program Trading."

It noted that Phelan had recently "been warning top officials in the securities industry of a program trading scenario—which he calls 'financial meltdown'—that could drive the market down hundreds of points. 'At some point, you're going to have a first-class catastrophe,' Phelan says."

Rather than allow that, he said, he was considering a plan to halt trading in as many as a hundred Big Board stocks if the market fell by somewhere around 25 percent.

For as long as anyone could remember, trading halts were the stock market's traditional safety valve when there were lopsided orders for specific stocks. Now Phelan publicly proposed using them on a widespread basis, as a buffer against an avalanche of computer-driven orders all falling on one side of the table and overwhelming his specialists. His emergency plan, which would inevitably disrupt the spooze pit in Chicago, was a tacit admission that the new forces in the market could make it impossible for the Big Board to keep trading during an onslaught of high-speed selling.

The article cited Phelan's dilemma: Many of his member firms profited hugely from program trading. It quoted the outspoken CEO of Bear, Stearns and Company, Alan "Ace" Greenberg, who called Phelan's concerns about a meltdown "totally ridiculous" and added, "Don't fix things that aren't broken."

Phelan acknowledged that, "theoretically, we ought to keep quiet about it," but he believed that "public needs and the needs of the market have got to transcend the needs of the individual."

EVEN BEFORE THE chaos of January 23, Leo Melamed thought the stock market had gone completely nuts. Prices had climbed too high, too fast; a downturn was inevitable, possibly a sharp one. "What worried me," he later said, "was that on the day of reckoning, our S&P contract would be the first to signal the bad news to the world. And I knew what people did to messengers with bad news."

He would have been wiser to worry that the Merc's S&P 500 futures contract would *not* be first with the bad news.

Trading in the spooz pit on January 23 had bordered on total chaos. Orders were not filled, or were filled late or incorrectly, and trade disputes accumulated throughout the day. The March contract sustained the biggest one-day price swing in its history. "The hectic day was enough to push Shearson Lehman to advise its clients to switch to stock index options on the Chicago Board Options Exchange," according to one account. "Tempers turned sour and snappish."

Melamed was atypically undiplomatic, telling the *Chicago Tribune*, "Traders bitch about a lot of things. When they lose money, they feel a lot better if they can say it's someone else's fault."

In fact, complaints about the S&P 500 pit had been building even before the breathtaking disorder on January 23.

Trading volume on the Merc had increased at the rate of 25 percent a year, and the spooz pit had experienced growing pains on an epic scale. "Traders were falling out of the pit due to the congestion[,] and quotations were running as far as 50 points behind actual real-time prices," a critical account in *Futures* magazine noted. Even a top Merc executive conceded that the recent volume and volatility had "stretched the pit to its absolute capacity." Trading desks at major Wall Street brokerage houses were starting to complain that it was difficult to get spooz orders filled on volatile days. "Brokers and traders began hurling manifold accusations at one another—on the floor and in the press," a Merc historian noted.

The complaints ranged from poor service to poor ethics. Customer orders sometimes took a backseat to a broker's personal trades; indeed, those personal trades were sometimes timed to exploit the customer's orders. One trader might pay off a debt to another by filling a customer order at a price that benefitted his creditor at the customer's expense. In the chaotic pit, "prices move so quickly it's often difficult for customers to prove they were cheated," the *Chicago Tribune* noted. Errors, which traders had to cover out of their own pockets, were becoming more common and expensive, tempting more traders to cheat to raise extra cash. A reliable audit trail would help with all these problems, of course, but thanks to the CFTC's leniency, the Merc still didn't have one.

On February 22, the *Tribune* detailed a shocking litany of abuses in the spooz pit, noting that "there is even an array of jargon to describe the cheating. Traders typically refer to 'sleazing' or 'burning' customer orders; floor buddies who received preferential treatment are known as 'bagmen.'"

The Merc board was already trying to respond. By late February, several committees were looking at trading practices and order processing systems, which were straining to deal with the growing institutional demand. Melamed was able to head off a rebellious referendum, signed by several hundred traders, demanding that all S&P 500 options and futures traders be barred from filling orders for their own account while handling customer orders. Melamed promised reforms, as soon as the board's research was complete.

THESE MARKET GYRATIONS had also become deeply worrisome to the LOR partners selling portfolio insurance.

John O'Brien had been cheerfully facing down critics of portfolio insurance for more than a year. He insisted that investors looking for bargains would always be ready to buy when portfolio insurers needed to sell. It was a familiar refrain: if stock prices fell to irrational levels, rational investors would buy them, forestalling a meltdown.

O'Brien sounded pleasantly confident in public, but in private he and his partners were growing concerned that the scale of portfolio insurance would soon exceed the market's capacity to absorb it.

They weren't alone. One knowledgeable market figure worried publicly that once the amount of money subject to portfolio insurance reached $50 billion, "the strategy could destruct under its own weight and lead to a market free-fall." Another asset manager set his threshold of alarm at $100 billion, but added that he was concerned that "the assets of the arbitrageurs and other money managers are not keeping pace" with the portfolio insurers whose trades they normally would offset. These comments were made in a magazine article that estimated that there was about $27 billion in portfolio insurance activity.

But of course, the LOR partners and their licensees alone were already doing almost $50 billion worth of business by the first months of 1987, as the rising but jumpy stock market made their product even more attractive. They were sure copycat products from other firms were growing at least as fast. They conservatively estimated that a minimum of $80 billion already was covered by portfolio insurance, a level that a number of sensible people had identified as a step too far for both the stock market and the futures pits.

There were other sources of uneasiness. Hayne Leland had been severely jolted by the way the markets had behaved during the tremor in mid-September 1986. Why had the S&P 500 index futures traded so far out of line with the underlying stocks on the NYSE, and for so long? The explanation Leland got from a senior executive at one big bank was that there was a temporary imbalance between the amount of money pursuing portfolio insurance and the amount of money doing the index arbitrage that was needed to keep the two markets in line. He was assured that more money was moving into index arbitrage, and that it was highly unlikely such an odd event would occur again.

After January, Leland wasn't comforted. The huge price swings on January 23, regardless of what had caused them, were just a few steps shy of the kind of market disruptions that could derail portfolio insurance.

As early as 1981, Leland had woven a key assumption into his academic papers about his hedging strategy: "that continuous trading is possible." That was how academic theories worked; you made assumptions and tested your theories on the basis of those assumptions. It certainly had not seemed to be a stretch back then to assume that the deep, liquid U.S. financial markets generally would allow for "continuous trading," barring a brief reaction to some abrupt crisis "like the Russians invading Iran," as Leland put it. Now, he began to worry whether that assumption was still valid.

During a sales trip to London in the second week of February 1987, John O'Brien and Steve Wunsch discussed their concerns about LOR's signature strategy. From Kidder's financial futures desk, Wunsch had his own window into the scale and reach of portfolio insurance. At least half his customers had developed competing products of their own to sell.

O'Brien expressed skepticism about John Phelan's widely publicized meltdown scenario. Could that really happen?

"Yeah," Wunsch replied. "It could happen. There are a lot of reasons to be nervous about it, at least."

Wunsch pointed to the circular problem of cause and effect that portfolio insurers faced. "If you are the cause of the volatility that you're reacting to, then the strategy isn't viable," he observed. Attempting to escape volatility that is being caused by your own attempt to escape volatility would be like trying to jog your way out of quicksand.

A few months later, in mid-June, O'Brien was in his office in Los

Angeles when he picked up a market report from Wunsch and saw this warning at the top, in boldface type: If the market did not find better ways to handle the so-called "information-less" orders from portfolio insurers and index arbitrageurs, Wunsch wrote, it could face disruptions that "could shake the market apart with uncontrollable volatility."

O'Brien promptly called his friend in New York: "Okay, Cassandra," he said, "come on out here."

He summoned Rubinstein and Leland from Berkeley as well. On the day of Wunsch's visit, the LOR partners and a few staffers gathered around a table in a conference room to listen to the young derivatives expert's warnings. Then they tossed around ideas for making portfolio insurance less disruptive to the overall market.

One approach would be to hedge with stock index *options*, chiefly the S&P 500 option on the CBOE, instead of using the S&P 500 futures on the Merc. It would work better if there were options that were more heavily traded and that ran longer than three months, and the exchange would have to agree to let them build up bigger positions than the rules currently allowed. Still, it was an idea the Berkeley partners thought worth pursuing.

As they talked, the men around the conference table came to feel that the heart of the market's reaction to portfolio insurance was fear. When traders saw a surge of sell orders coming in, they didn't know if it was a few portfolio insurers fine-tuning their hedges or the front edge of a vast wave of orders driven by negative news. They didn't know why the orders had suddenly poured in, so it was understandable that they might overreact.

But what if they did know? What if portfolio insurers such as LOR simply announced before the opening bell that they would be placing certain buy or sell orders that day as part of their hedging strategy? That would allow the traders to summon the buyers or sellers to the market in an orderly way. Trading by portfolio insurers would emerge from the shadows of fearful speculation and into the light of day. As they tossed the idea around, Wunsch observed that he already called this approach "sunshine trading."

Wunsch ran the "sunshine trading" idea past important figures in the market. Leo Melamed at the Merc was willing to consider it. Wunsch also had friends at the New York Futures Exchange, where futures on the NYSE Composite index were traded. He pitched the notion to them.

"They bought the idea!" he reported back to his Berkeley friends. The NYFE started the paperwork to put the concept to the CFTC. It looked possible that sunshine trading could be a reality by the summer of 1987.

"We can advertise our orders on the Goodyear blimp!" Wunsch joked.

AROUND THIS SAME time, Paul Volcker decided to step down as chairman of the Federal Reserve when his second term ended in August 1987. He handed in his resignation to President Reagan on the first day of June, and the news was announced the next day.

He would be part of a wholesale shift change in the pilot houses of regulatory Washington. In March, after months of rumors, the White House nominated John Shad to be the U.S. ambassador to the Netherlands, giving him a graceful way out of a job that no longer appealed to him. The ambassadorship was also a reward for having run the SEC for a longer time than any of his predecessors.

Susan Phillips, who had taken over the gavel at the CFTC when Phil Johnson left in 1983, was in the process of lining up a job at the University of Iowa, and planned to leave the commission by late summer.

There had been changes at the Treasury and the FDIC as well. Comptroller of the Currency Todd Conover and FDIC chairman Bill Isaac, veterans of some of the most harrowing financial cliff-hangers of the Reagan years, had both stepped down in mid-1985. And Donald Regan had left his post as White House chief of staff under the cloud of the continuing Iran-Contra investigations. He was replaced by former senator Howard Baker, a genial and politically astute Tennessee Republican whose financial experience was negligible.

And now Paul Volcker was exiting the stage as well.

The next financial crisis, whenever it hit, would find key spots in Washington occupied by novice regulators, unfamiliar with their jobs and with one another.

ONE OF THEM would be David S. Ruder, the Chicago legal scholar who had helped raise the alarm about the Reagan administration's early transition report on the SEC in 1981. Ruder had been a bystander to most of the subsequent financial crises, although he had had a somewhat closer view of the Continental Illinois rescue, given his tenure since 1977 as the dean of the Northwestern University School of Law in Chicago.

His conference and committee work had kept him in touch with the legal issues that preoccupied John Shad, and Ruder was similarly tolerant of corporate takeovers and opposed to insider trading. He was not vociferous about deregulation, but he was alert for areas where he felt the SEC was reaching beyond its legal jurisdiction.

On a weekday morning in the third week of May 1987, Ruder was in Washington, attending a meeting of the American Law Institute, when a lawyer he knew tapped him on the shoulder.

She leaned over and whispered, "They want to see you at the White House." He would find a message waiting for him when he got back to his hotel, she added.

When he telephoned a White House aide a short time later, he learned he was being considered as John Shad's replacement. He was invited to the White House mess for lunch the next day. Over lunch, two senior aides quizzed him a bit—there were the inevitable questions about his view on takeovers—and then they asked if he was a Republican. He was, he told them, but not an active one.

After lunch, Ruder was escorted to Howard Baker's office. In the course of their conversation about the SEC chairmanship, Ruder finally asked, "Why am *I* here?" After all, he said, he wasn't politically prominent and he'd never been a big party donor, as Shad had been.

Baker explained that Ruder's name had been put forward by a number of people, but it was clear to Ruder he wasn't the administration's first choice. The realization stung a little, but he was still intrigued by the opportunity.

He returned to his hotel and then flew home to Chicago, uncertain what the next step would be. He waited to hear from the president or his chief of staff, but in fact, it was John Shad who called, in mid-June, to tell him that he had gotten the job and to suggest that they meet before Shad left for his new post in the Netherlands.

Ruder flew to New York and took a cab through the light Sunday traffic to Shad's airy duplex apartment on Park Avenue. Shad told Ruder of the headaches ahead—"The administrative stuff! The budget! The commissioners!" Shad made the job sound almost tedious, but Ruder didn't let his predecessor's weariness discourage him.

Shad's former office would be dusty by the time Ruder finally moved in on August 7, 1987. To his surprise, his appointment was opposed by three powerful senators unhappy about his benign view of takeovers and his lack of enforcement credentials. It took the Senate almost two months to confirm his nomination, with seventeen votes against him.

At the Federal Reserve, Paul Volcker's successor was the Manhattan-based economic consultant Alan Greenspan, a former chairman of the Council of Economic Advisers and a prominent but pragmatic subscriber to the laissez-faire economic theories of his close friend and mentor, the philosopher Ayn Rand. In 1981, President Reagan had tapped him as chairman of a new bipartisan Social Security commission, whose well-received prescriptions for strengthening the retirement system were enacted in 1983. After an initial delay attributed to the complexity of his financial statements, Greenspan was confirmed easily—a single confirmation hearing on July 21 and a final Senate vote on August 3. On August 11, 1987, Greenspan was sworn into his dream job, chairman of the Federal Reserve.

TWO DAYS AFTER Greenspan's confirmation hearing, a House commerce subcommittee opened a hearing of its own, on program trading, chaired by Congressman Ed Markey, a Massachusetts Democrat. The subcommittee heard a remarkable litany of warnings about the fundamental changes reshaping the financial marketplace—warnings that would be totally ignored.

With David Ruder not yet confirmed and John Shad already in the Netherlands, the SEC was represented by its acting chairman, Charles C.

Cox. He and the CFTC's Susan Phillips assured the panel that no legislative action was needed to deal with program trading.

In her written testimony, however, Phillips made an ominous disclosure about the crazy trading on January 23 that she did not mention in her oral remarks: "There was no consensus among the traders concerning what did cause the sharp drop in prices," she wrote. "Several traders commented that some of the stock price volatility that day was due to the inability of the [NYSE] stock specialists to maintain an orderly market during periods of heavy volume and the lack of sufficient liquidity in the futures market to absorb the large, widespread selling that suddenly developed."

It was an observation that raised fundamental questions about how well both the Big Board and the Merc had coped with the avalanche of orders on that chaotic day, and how well they would cope if, or rather, when it happened again.

None of the subcommittee members questioned Phillips, or any of the day's other witnesses, about her revelation.

Another witness, Bill Brodsky of the Chicago Merc, argued that portfolio insurance was just "a twist on an old strategy" called a "stop-loss" order, which allowed an investor to order in advance that his shares be sold if their prices fell to a certain level—to "stop the losses" on those stocks. That, too, should have been at least a little worrisome: stop-loss orders had been in wide use before the 1929 crash, and several historians felt they had contributed to the selling pressure during the early hours of that market debacle.

Brodsky acknowledged that portfolio insurers had been selling heavily in the futures pits during the steep market decline on September 11, 1986, but he noted that investors had eventually "stepped in" to find bargains. Clearly, the markets could handle portfolio insurance selling, even when prices were falling, he said.

"We believe there are investors out there who will not panic or act in an irresponsible fashion," he said. "There are very sophisticated institutions out there who are paid to be rational investors—and I think some of those people may speak on the panel that follows me today."

That panel, the day's third and most instructive one, was nothing less than a tutorial on the most arcane new program trading strategies, led by some of the best-known figures in the business.

Hayne Leland had flown in from Berkeley, summoned to explain how portfolio insurance worked. Steve Wunsch of Kidder Peabody, LOR's ally in "sunshine trading," was there, too. So was Gordon Binns, whose huge General Motors pension fund was a major user of many of the strategies being discussed, including portfolio insurance.

They were joined by two other Wall Street insiders who were experts on program trading: R. Sheldon Johnson, a Wharton School graduate now with Morgan Stanley; and Thomas Loeb, the president of Mellon Capital, which had hired many of the trailblazing "quants" who had previously worked at Wells Fargo Investment Advisors in San Francisco.

Johnson was the first to testify. He acknowledged that program trading was used for index arbitrage, and that arbitrage traders would occasionally be selling stocks in a declining market. This was unlikely to lead to a meltdown, he explained, because "extremely hectic market environments do not permit arbitrage transactions to be executed economically."

That should have rung another loud warning bell with both the lawmakers and the other witnesses. Arbitrage trading was what kept the price of the stock index futures and the prices of the underlying stocks in alignment. If arbitrageurs stepped to the sidelines in "extremely hectic" trading, an imbalance could persist until the two markets were hopelessly out of whack.

No one questioned Johnson about his alarming observation.

Gordon Binns was next, and he candidly conceded that it was possible portfolio insurance could trigger "a downward cascading of prices." Remarkably, given his stature, no one on the subcommittee followed up on his admission. He was also worried that falling prices would bankrupt small players in the futures markets and lead to a domino chain of defaults. "Some changes to current practices might be useful in this area," he said blandly.

He was not asked what those changes should be.

Then it was Hayne Leland's turn. First, he explained that LOR didn't actually do any program trading, if that was defined to mean index arbitrage trading. He conceded that, for portfolio insurance to work, "the futures must closely track actual stock index levels" and this required the process of index arbitrage, which required program trading.

He also said that his firm was working on ways to reduce the impact of portfolio insurance on the market. Sunshine trading was one way to do that, he said, but it was still awaiting regulatory approval. Another buffer, he continued, would be for LOR to hedge with index options, which had less effect on other markets. Limits on the size of individual positions in the options markets made that difficult—so he urged regulators to raise those limits.

After Tom Loeb of Mellon Capital gave a brief history of index funds and index arbitrage—he said there was currently $250 billion in index funds, which should have been a sobering figure for the subcommittee—it was Steve Wunsch's turn.

Wunsch seconded Leland's call for rule changes to permit a greater use of index options and sunshine trading. In his written testimony, however, Wunsch laid out an intriguing theory of what might have happened in the market on January 23, one that supported his case for sunshine trading but raised other questions he did not address.

Imagine, he wrote, that on some quiet day in the market, there were two buyers, each needing to buy $500 million worth of stock, and two sellers, each needing to sell $500 million worth of stock. Imagine, too, that a trade of $500 million would move the Dow up or down by 60 points. Finally, assume that none of the four investors is aware of the trading plans of the others.

"Let's say Buyer #1 decides to do his buying at 10:00 a.m.," he continued. That would send the Dow up by 60 points. "Seller #1 does his selling at noon [and] Seller #2 does his selling at 2:00 p.m.," and together they push the Dow down by 120 points. Then, "Buyer #2 buys at the close," sending the Dow up by 60 points. "If such a scenario were to occur, I am sure that the papers on the following day would blame program trading." In fact, the price swings on this hypothetical day would have been caused by the "discontinuous arrival" of giant buy and sell orders at various points during the day.

If the $1 billion in sales could have been paired off at some point with the $1 billion in purchases, there would have been no effect on the market at all, he wrote.

Of course, if all four investors wanted to sell and decided independently to sell at the same time, the Dow would have suddenly plummeted by 240 points on a quiet day with no market-moving news. For Steve Wunsch, his hypothetical day was an argument for using computers to match buyers and sellers before they could whipsaw the market. In hindsight, it was also a powerful warning about the potential impact of like-minded trades by titan investors.

Nobody raised any questions about that, either. After some desultory discussion, the hearing was adjourned.

PART FOUR

RECKONING

18

THE WORST WEEKS EVER

Alan Greenspan settled quickly into his new berth at the Federal Reserve, getting to know the staff and other members of the board of governors.

While waiting to be confirmed, he had spent time in New York with Jerry Corrigan, no doubt hearing Corrigan fret aloud about the mismatch between the nation's financial reality and its regulatory structure. The two men quickly came to respect each other and to trust each other's judgment, even if they did not kindle the same rapport Corrigan had enjoyed with Volcker.

Though not visibly alarmed about the increasingly unsteady bull market, Greenspan was clearly uneasy. Soon after he took office, perhaps with Corrigan's warnings in mind, he agreed to set up an informal team of senior aides from the Fed, the Treasury, the SEC, and the CFTC to develop plans for responding to a crisis, and he had the Fed staff put together an internal report on "how the Fed could best respond to various exigencies, including a sharp market correction."

On Tuesday, August 18, 1987, Greenspan presided over his first meeting of the Federal Open Market Committee. Around the big conference table, worries were expressed about higher oil prices if tensions increased in the Persian Gulf, and comments were made about the dollar's strength in currency markets. There was the ritual round-robin of regional economic assessments. As the clock approached noon, it was finally the new chairman's turn.

"I'd like to make just a few observations," Greenspan said. "We spent all morning, and no one even mentioned the stock market, which I find quite interesting in itself."

Indeed, it was. The stock market had shaken off the jitters of January and was up about 40 percent for the year. Exactly a week after the FOMC meeting, on Tuesday, August 25, the Dow closed at another new high, 2,722.42 points. After five years, this remarkable bull market stood almost 1,950 points higher than in August 1982, a gain of 250 percent.

After his first two weeks on the job, Greenspan quietly negotiated with his fellow Fed governors for a small increase in short-term interest rates to tame what he later called the "speculative froth" in the financial economy—and, perhaps, to show that he would protect Volcker's gains against inflation.

In a departure from custom, he let the news go out just as the markets opened on Friday, September 4, rather than after the closing bell. He then nervously watched the computer monitor on his desk, tracing the impact of the rate hike in the stock market, the bond market, and the foreign currency market.

The Fed's news landed at the end of a dispiriting pre–Labor Day week in which the Dow had dropped every single day. The decline continued after the Fed's news hit that Friday, pulling the Dow almost 6 percent below its peak on August 25.

The short week after Labor Day had a few bright moments, but the rest of September was increasingly erratic: an occasional oversize rally, followed by days of grinding losses. By the end of a seesaw session on September 30, the Dow had rallied to 2,596.28 points, still about 4.6 percent off the market's high of five weeks earlier.

Of course, after five years without a bear market, no one was surprised that the Dow's losing days had become more frequent. No bull market lasted forever.

As October arrived, Greenspan seemed confident the Fed was taming any excessive financial speculation. Perhaps now the stock market would finally settle into a long-overdue correction, with stock prices drifting down to a stable and more reasonable level.

Meanwhile, at the SEC, David Ruder faced a rockier introduction to life as a financial regulator. He was immediately confronted by an urgent management crisis in the SEC's New York office. Not only was New York the agency's biggest and most important outpost, it was also the commission's closest contact with the stock exchanges and brokerage houses on Wall Street.

In the fall of 1986, John Shad—perhaps distracted by the unfolding Boesky case—had appointed a new regional director for New York, a longtime corporate lawyer with the Mobil Corporation. It had been a spectacularly poor fit. Within months, the New York staff began to complain that the new boss was undermining the office's enforcement effort, but Shad did not intervene.

In Ruder's first week on the job, the simmering unrest boiled over. The veteran enforcement chief in New York resigned, and three other senior staffers threatened to follow her out the door. The office uprising made headlines, provoking congressional concern and questions.

Ruder asked his senior aides to assess the situation and received a damning report about morale problems "so bad it would've taken a miracle to change them." He firmly demanded the regional administrator's resignation.

He could not summon a new regional administrator out of thin air— or, more accurately, out of the SEC's thin budgetary rations. In late September he asked two senior Washington staffers to do double duty, one as a part-time administrator for New York and the other as a part-time enforcement chief there, in addition to their existing responsibilities. The arrangement was far from ideal, but at least Ruder prevented a larger exodus of experienced staffers from his most critical outpost.

ON MONDAY, OCTOBER 5, after a modest month-opening rally, the Dow stood at 2,640 points. But the rally fell apart the following day, in a grimly familiar way. The Dow dropped sharply at the opening bell, bounced mostly downward until late afternoon, and then fell off a cliff in the final half hour. By the closing bell, the Dow was down almost 3.5 percent—a record-setting 91.55-point loss.

In the absence of any notable economic news, there was a lot of theorizing about what had caused Tuesday's epic decline. But what was clearly true was that index arbitrage trading had surged at the end of the day, most of it tied to offsetting trades in the S&P 500 futures pit at the Chicago Merc. Portfolio insurance trades had been sparse on Tuesday, but with the market's recent declines, those hedges would likely need to be adjusted soon. That would mean heavy selling in Chicago. Moreover, some aggressive speculators on Wall Street had started to trade ahead of the portfolio insurers, to profit from their anticipated sales. That copycat short selling could add extra weight to whatever the portfolio insurers did.

For most investors, the rest of the week was truly awful. By Friday, October 9, the Dow had fallen to 2,482 points, which was almost 159 points and 6 percent below its level the previous Friday. Measured in points, it was the worst one-week decline in Wall Street history. Those who had grimly expected a stock market correction for months must have gone home feeling vindicated, if battered. The market was almost 9 percent below its August summit. The worst, surely, was over.

MONDAY, OCTOBER 12, was the Columbus Day holiday. Banks and government offices were closed, and trading was light on the Big Board as the Dow sustained a modest loss of about 10 points.

Stocks involved in the continuing takeover frenzy had been weak for days, as a House committee considered reducing the tax breaks for certain kinds of takeovers. Takeover speculators may have been selling down their portfolios, but that was not an exceptional source of selling pressure—no more than the prior week, really. If the market's blue-chip stocks stayed steady, the takeover selling pressure wouldn't be a problem.

Then Tuesday brought a welcome rally, with the Dow up by about 1.5 percent, to 2,508 points. With their spirits lifting, several traders said they were watching for the next day's announcement of the nation's August trade deficit. Market analysts had become obsessed with this monthly statistic, watching it for clues to future currency and interest rate movements. Traders hoped that a shrinking trade gap would reduce the odds that the Fed would try to cool the economy by raising interest rates again.

When the August trade deficit was reported at 8:30 a.m. on Wednesday, it had indeed gone down, but nowhere near as much as analysts had expected. The news hit the markets like a dart hitting a balloon.

Foreign currency traders immediately began to sell dollars, leaving the U.S. currency weaker against the German mark and the Japanese yen. Fearful that a weaker dollar would force the Fed to raise interest rates, which would depress Treasury bond prices, traders promptly phoned London to start selling Treasury bonds there, before the market opened in New York. When the New York market did open, they kept selling. The sell-off pushed up the interest rate on long-term Treasury bonds to just over 10 percent, a two-year high.

After some historically awful days in the stock market, a 10 percent interest rate on something as secure as a U.S. Treasury bond was something any uneasy investor would have to consider. If you could earn 10 percent on your money without any risk that you would not get that money back, why would you invest in stocks, whose prices had been falling for weeks?

Not long after the trade deficit headlines, the news broke that Democrats on the House Ways and Means Committee were filing bills to curb takeover tax breaks. It was barely news—such actions had been rumored for weeks, and some kind of legislative assault on hostile takeovers had been threatened for months, if not years. And it was hardly a "done deal"—the influential SEC was leery of the idea, the Senate was in Republican hands, and President Reagan would surely veto any bill that made it as far as his desk. No one could have rationally assumed, based solely on that report, that takeover tax breaks were doomed.

Psychologically, though, this news may have dented investors' confidence, especially those professionals speculating in takeover stocks. By some accounts, these speculators began to sell stocks from their portfolios as soon as the opening bell rang at the NYSE on Wednesday morning.

By itself, that selling might not have been significant, but in Chicago, other newly pessimistic traders, and a number of indifferent portfolio insurers who were adjusting their hedging positions, were selling an enormous number of S&P 500 futures contracts. That drove the spooz price down until it was even cheaper than the slumping stocks in the index—a familiar invitation to the index arbitrageurs to go into action. So the relatively modest selling of takeover stocks on the NYSE merged into the much heavier selling by index arbitrage traders, who sent their huge trades directly to the specialists on the trading floor via the NYSE's automated DOT system.

In its first thirty minutes of trading, the Dow's fall was almost vertical. By 1:15 p.m., the index was down 89 points, or 3.5 percent. This nosedive was a textbook example of Phelan's "cascade" theory: The price of the S&P 500 futures on the Merc fell first, driven down by portfolio insurers who were selling in response to previous declines. Then index arbitrage traders stepped in to buy the cheaper futures contract in Chicago and sell the more expensive stocks in New York, transmitting the price decline from the Merc to the NYSE. These concentrated index arbitrage trades were a stormy force, accounting for about a quarter of all the trading during this turbulent hour.

This wasn't Main Street suddenly dumping stocks in a panic. Seventy-five percent of the selling on this day was coming from giant institutions and big brokerage houses trading for their own profit.

That was the story for the final hours of trading on the NYSE—heavy selling by index arbitrage traders concentrated within short windows of time, with similarly concentrated but not as abundant buying in the futures pits in Chicago.

As had happened before, however, the buying done by arbitrageurs in Chicago was never potent enough to push the futures prices into line with the cash prices on the NYSE. Briefly, just before 3:30 p.m., it looked like that would happen, but it didn't last. After a few moments, spooz prices began to fall again, as portfolio insurers continued to sell while index arbitrageurs struggled to feed a smaller stack of buy orders into the unruly scrum of traders. By the end of the day, the NYSE had handled $1.4 billion worth of index arbitrage trades, twice the normal level and 17 percent of the entire day's trading volume. But the flip side of those trades in Chicago had still not been enough to bring the two markets back into balance.

In New York, it was the worst one-day point loss in market history—95.46 points. At the closing bell on Wednesday, the Dow stood at 2,485.15 points, a one-day drop of 3.8 percent, the third largest ever.

THE NEW YORK Fed, led by Jerry Corrigan, had tried to calm the bond market's fears that the dollar's recent weakness would cause interest rates to climb and bond prices to fall. He let it be known early Thursday that the New York Fed was injecting cash into the system by purchasing Treasuries, which would help stabilize bond prices. In normal times, that would have eased such interest rate fears, but that didn't seem to be working.

Trading on the Big Board on Thursday, October 15, began badly and ended worse, punctuated by tantalizing rallies that dissipated the faint whiff of panic the market had smelled on Wednesday. Volume was extremely heavy, though, and almost two-thirds of the first half hour's volume was in the form of giant orders of 10,000 shares or more—additional evidence, if any was needed, that this was an institutional stampede. Portfolio insurers were among the big sellers in the Chicago futures pits as the day opened.

Fortunately, there was enough appetite for stocks to absorb the selling, and the Dow had recovered by late afternoon. At 3:30 p.m., it was down just four points.

Then, in the final half hour, the Dow fell an astonishing 53 points, or 2.2 percent.

While this should have been a grimly familiar pattern by now, one official report nevertheless concluded that "this sharp decline on heavy volume so late in the day bewildered investors." Remarkably, in this enormous market, just seven "aggressive" institutions accounted for 9 percent of the entire day's trading volume. By the end of Thursday, the Dow stood more than 13.5 percent below its August peak, a decline of almost 370 points.

Traders and analysts were calling it the "October Massacre." A few told reporters this could be the advent of an official bear market, meaning a decline of 20 percent or more within two months of a market peak. If so, it would be the first in more than five years.

There was evidence of free-floating anguish in every market—bonds, currencies, precious metals. The stubborn lack of progress in tackling the federal budget deficit, hardly a new development, suddenly seemed intolerable. The heated diplomacy over foreign exchange rates, a fixture of financial life since at least the beginning of the year, suddenly looked more perilous. Bad news that the market had shrugged off all summer suddenly seemed to be all anyone could think about.

That evening, having done all he could in the bond market, Jerry Corrigan boarded a jet bound for Caracas, Venezuela. He would change planes there for the short hop to Maracaibo, on the nation's far western coast, where he would be giving a speech on Friday, October 16. After the speech, he would return to Caracas to consult on Monday with Venezuela's president. He planned to fly back to New York on Monday afternoon.

On the sixth floor of the NYSE, exchange president Bob Birnbaum was holding down the fort for the vacationing John Phelan, who was calling in frequently for updates. Volume had been heavy, but that wasn't the problem. The problem was the way the volume was hitting the floor. What mattered to the DOT system was how many separate orders it had to deal with at any one time. One order for ninety thousand shares was a lot easier to handle than a hundred orders, each for nine hundred shares, especially if those orders all slammed into the market at once— as was more frequently the case.

This pattern was an unintended side effect of the NYSE's decision to open its electronic order-processing system to larger and larger orders. Index arbitrageurs and other program traders wanted to use the DOT system, but even the higher DOT cap was too low to accommodate their vastly larger orders. Consequently, they would deliberately break large trades into many separate orders, each of which came in just under the DOT limit, adding to the number of orders the system had to handle.

It was not a sustainable situation.

THE MORNING NEWS on Friday, October 16, was upsetting. In the Persian Gulf, tensions simmering for months had suddenly boiled over with an

Iranian attack on an oil tanker flying the American flag. From Washington, there were reports that Treasury secretary Jim Baker was annoyed about Germany's recent interest rate hikes, which worried the currency and credit markets. At least the major foreign stock markets were not in turmoil: Tokyo's market had declined just a bit, while London's trading had been shut down by a freak gale that knocked out power across much of the region.

The calendar was still a threat: Friday was a witching hour day for the options markets, and it would be hard to imagine a less welcome one. Stock index options—notably the S&P 100 options on the Chicago Board Options Exchange and the Major Market Index options on the American Stock Exchange—were set to expire at the closing bell. Since the options markets had resisted the move to "morning-after" prices, which had helped calm expiration days in the futures markets, this witching hour was alive and unpredictable.

The Chicago Merc was in for a heavy day, too—again, thanks to developments in the options markets. There simply weren't enough index option contracts available at prices that reflected the week's sharply lower stock values. With nowhere else to turn, options traders were using the futures markets to hedge their own positions, linking those two derivatives markets more closely than usual.

Despite the morning's worrisome headlines, the stock market opened firmly, and promptly rose 12 points. Then, in familiar fashion, it bounced down a lot and rallied a little, over and over, like a Slinky falling down a steep flight of steps—a very long flight of steps. The market dropped to new lows, then dropped further.

The institutional selling pressure was coming from all sides now—from big brokerage houses selling short, betting on further price declines; from endowments, pension funds, and hedge funds that had grown suddenly pessimistic; and even from a few mutual funds that were getting calls all day Friday from nervous investors who suddenly wanted to cash out. Those demands were running $750 million ahead of the selling that mutual funds were doing on this crazy day.

Before Friday's trading was done, just four giant institutional investors had sold at least $500 million worth of stock from their portfolios. "To put this in perspective," one official account noted, "an investor transacting $10 million [in trades] on a normal day would be considered an active trader."

A momentary rally just before 2:30 p.m. jerked the Dow back to within 30 points of its noontime level, but then the dizzy index arbitrage dance began again. Arbitrage selling accounted for almost 20 percent of the trading volume over the next hour.

By 3:30 p.m., the Dow was 3.4 percent below the Thursday close, a drop of about 81 points. In the next twenty minutes, it plunged another 50 points. The gathering loss was astounding—a 5.5 percent nosedive.

Index arbitrageurs and portfolio insurance traders together sold more than $730 million worth of stock, accounting for more than 43 percent of the trading volume during this short white-knuckle period. Some traders later said it felt as if the floor had simply given way—"free fall" had become a threadbare phrase during the previous two months, but this time, they said, it really did feel as if the market were falling through thin air.

Ten minutes before the closing bell, the witching hour for stock index options struck—but, miraculously, its spell was benign and produced enough buying demand to move the Dow up 22 points. The rally was quick; prices plateaued for a moment, then started to slip—but with the Dow at just under 2,247 points, the closing bell rang. The last-minute rally, according to one account, produced "the odd spectacle of a market full of people relieved that the Dow is only down 108 points."

In the context of the time, Friday's 4.6 percent drop was a shocking, unprecedented loss. It was the largest one-day point loss in history, breaking a record set just two days earlier. It was also the first time the Dow had ever closed down more than 100 points. The week's 235-point loss wiped out the previous week's dismal record. This, now, was the worst week in Wall Street history. Unlike in the prior week, however, no one felt any confidence that the worst was finally behind them.

IN CHICAGO, THE torrent of trading in the stock index futures and options pits had mirrored the deluge in New York.

The options market had been under intense pressure. Some firms were racking up enormous losses. First Options, the Continental Bank subsidiary that was the largest clearing firm in the options market, was a special concern of the Options Clearing Corporation, the market's central clearinghouse. First Options essentially backstopped all the trades of its twelve hundred client firms; and the clearinghouse back-stopped First Options.

By the close of trading on Friday, nine First Options clients, all firmly in the black on Wednesday night, were in serious trouble. Only three of them had not run up big losses, and one of those was near the edge. First Options was on the hook for those accounts, no matter how big the losses got.

The Merc had made some progress in addressing problems in the S&P 500 pits, but it was still crowded, chaotic, and loud. Despite that, Leo Melamed had been making money like crazy there almost all week. Bearish about the market, he'd been piling up futures contracts that would rise in value if the market fell.

And boy, had the market fallen! It had been such a profitable run that Melamed almost decided to roll his positions into the next week. He shook off the temptation: "After a week like that, you get out, take your profits, and go home." So, he closed out his bets, planning to head into Monday with a clean slate.

AROUND 4 P.M. on Friday afternoon, SEC chairman David Ruder left his sixth-floor office and went down to the division of market regulation, one floor below, to check the market's status on the computers there. He learned that there likely had been heavy index arbitrage trading that day, and he told his staff to stay in close touch with John Phelan's team at the New York Stock Exchange.

On Friday evening, the SEC office was busy as five dozen staffers called contacts on Wall Street and at the exchanges to get a sense of where things stood after the day's historic debacle. Over the weekend, Ruder would confer with his chief of market regulation, Rick Ketchum, to review what they'd learned and to plan for Monday. Ketchum told Ruder that he was booked to serve on a conference panel in New York early Monday morning, but his deputy would be in the office.

Ruder, too, was scheduled to give a speech on Monday, but thankfully it was just across town, at a Washington hotel.

THE WHITE HOUSE was in an uneasy holding pattern. First Lady Nancy Reagan had recently had a mammogram that required further investigation. She would have a biopsy and, if necessary, breast surgery over the weekend at the Bethesda Naval Hospital. The president was understandably worried and distracted.

For weeks, Beryl Sprinkel, an outspoken bank economist who was chairman of the Council of Economic Advisers, had been urging chief of staff Howard Baker to let him caution the president about the Fed's unwise interest rate hikes and the Treasury's clumsy diplomacy over the dollar's exchange rate.

So, on Friday afternoon, Alan Greenspan was summoned to a meeting with the president in the family quarters at the White House. When Reagan arrived, he was met by Greenspan, Sprinkel, Howard Baker, and Jim Baker. No one seemed to have thought to invite David Ruder of the SEC, despite the historic events in the stock market that week, and indeed, on that very day. Nor did they invite the CFTC's new acting chairman, a genial Kansas rancher named Kalo Hineman; they apparently did not think the futures market was relevant to their discussion.

There are slightly differing versions of what happened at this meeting, but the consensus is that first Jim Baker and then Alan Greenspan, under polite questioning by Howard Baker, assured the president that their current policies were sound and there was no reason to be overly concerned about the turbulent financial landscape. Then Sprinkel forcefully disagreed with them both, urging Greenspan to ease up on interest rates to reassure the markets and telling Jim Baker to leave the currency markets alone. In any case, "after considerable bickering, the meeting broke with nothing resolved," according to one careful account.

Greenspan was scheduled to fly to Dallas on Monday to address the American Bankers Association. Jim Baker would appear on *Meet the Press* on Sunday morning; then he planned to fly to Stockholm for a hunting trip with the king of Sweden. Howard Baker would be left to man the White House into the next week, as the president focused on his wife's anxieties, and his own.

ON SATURDAY EVENING, October 17, Hayne Leland and his wife were holding a dinner party in the high-ceilinged dining room at their home in Berkeley. The guest of honor was the economist Gérard Debreu, who had joined the Berkeley faculty in 1962 and won the Nobel Memorial Prize in Economics in 1983.

The conversation around the table turned quickly to the historic events in the market that week, and Debreu noticed how upset his normally urbane host was. The night before, Leland had learned that LOR's chief (and only) trader in Los Angeles had not been able to sell enough futures contracts on Friday afternoon to fully hedge LOR's client accounts. It had been too chaotic in the spooz pit in Chicago, and the trader hadn't been able to get all the orders filled.

John O'Brien hadn't seemed all that alarmed, but Leland could not shake the sense that something was going profoundly wrong with the markets. On Sunday morning, Mark Rubinstein answered the phone at his Marin County home and was shocked at Leland's tone—he could not remember his campus colleague ever sounding so upset. Leland explained his concern, and said he was determined to catch a 6:30 a.m. flight to Los Angeles on Monday. He would be taking off just as the NYSE was opening.

Rubinstein decided that he would take a later flight and meet up with Leland at LOR's offices in the First Interstate Tower. He thought his colleague was overreacting but trusted his instincts.

THE LARGELY INSTITUTIONAL rout of the previous week was rapidly becoming a public panic. Call centers at some major mutual fund houses and discount brokerage offices were ominously busy all weekend. At the scattered branch offices of Charles Schwab, a household name thanks to its national advertising, customers were getting incessant busy signals all through Saturday. The "phones were melting down," one account noted, "but 99 percent of the calls that did go through were orders to sell."

On Sunday, October 18, when Jim Baker arrived at NBC's Washington studio for his *Meet the Press* appearance, he learned he would be appearing after a segment with Henry Kaufman, a prominent economist at Salomon Brothers. The journalists repeatedly pressed Kaufman for a market forecast, but he remained soothing and noncommittal. "Friday already had investors on edge and I had no intentions of adding to the turmoil," he said later.

After Kaufman left the set, he watched on the studio monitor as Baker was quizzed about the apparent rancor between the United States and its allies over monetary policy. "We will not sit back in this country and watch the [trade] surplus countries jack up their interest rates and squeeze growth worldwide on the expectation that the United States . . . somehow will follow by raising its interest rates," Baker said.

Kaufman cringed; he didn't think the markets were going to hear the comments in the spirit Baker intended. They were going to hear sabers rattling and would worry even more about a currency crisis, a declining dollar, and an exodus of foreign investors. He said as much, politely, to Baker after the program. The treasury secretary replied firmly, "Henry, some things need to be said."

IN EVERY MARKET, there was a foreboding sense that Monday would be difficult. These rumors felt different in Chicago than they did in New York because the two markets lived on different timetables. The investors who bought or sold during Friday's frantic trading session on the NYSE didn't have to come up with the stock or the cash until the following Friday—stock trades officially "settled" in five business days. Futures and options traders had to settle up their accounts overnight, or they couldn't trade the next day.

The Merc's clearinghouse, like all its counterparts across the markets, was the "other side" of every trade—it bought from every seller, sold to every buyer, and thereby ensured that traders could do business without fear of a default. Implicit in that arrangement was the expectation that the clearinghouse had the resources to cover any losses. The clearinghouse had to know everyone's financial exposure before it could calculate its own.

On Sunday evening at his suburban home north of Chicago, Merc president Bill Brodsky picked up word about sharp price declines in the Asian markets, where it was already Monday. He called his head of market surveillance, the man who would have to monitor the financial stability of the firms doing business on the Merc, and asked him to be at his desk as early as possible the next morning.

BY FRIDAY'S CLOSING bell, the Dow had fallen almost 10 percent just since the previous Friday; since its August peak, it had fallen 17.5 percent, more than 475 points.

The short rally just before Friday's closing bell didn't comfort anyone but rank amateurs. The professionals knew the day "could have been—should have been—far worse." All over the Street, people were whispering about the pent-up reservoir of selling waiting to engulf the market on Monday. The estimates were terrifying: by one calculation, portfolio insurers, who sold the futures market equivalent of $2.1 billion in stock on Friday, still had the equivalent of $8 billion more to sell.

It was frighteningly easy to see who would be coming back into the market to sell on Monday. Who would come back to buy?

19

508 POINTS

Sometime before 8:30 a.m. on Monday, October 19, 1987, John Phelan asked a secretary to track down Leo Melamed at the Chicago Merc. Phelan, who had cut his vacation short and flown home on Saturday, could see how the day was shaping up, and it made even the worst fears of Friday night look optimistic.

Tokyo had fallen sharply overnight, as traders reacted to Friday's epic decline in New York. The Hong Kong markets had plunged so far and so fast that officials there decided to close their doors completely, to forestall total panic and widespread defaults. London was already down 10 percent, in part because of $90 million worth of sell orders from the trading desk at Fidelity Investments in Boston. Fidelity's $9 billion Magellan Fund was the largest stock mutual fund in the country; it was chilling to think how much it would try to sell when the Big Board opened. Traders were predicting the Dow could drop that morning by at least 9 percent, a staggering percentage figure that was twice the record-setting 108-point loss on Friday and almost within reach of the historic daily losses in October 1929.

The New York Stock Exchange's DOT system was being swamped with orders, many of them apparently from index arbitrageurs. Specialists downstairs were struggling to find a price at which they could open trading in their blue-chip stocks, a task that suddenly had become as difficult as dealing with a deluge of closing-bell orders, Phelan connected with Melamed and briefed him on the viciously lopsided orders piling up in the DOT system. "We're seeing 'sell' orders like never before," Phelan said, adding, "It looks like a very bad market." And then, he said, "Everyone loves a free market, but we need to slow volatility on the down side. If no action is taken, the industry stands to lose something it wants."

It's not clear what Phelan thought Melamed could do about the market's wild swings. The portfolio insurers were going to sell, no matter what the local traders did in the spooz pit. And if such selling made the futures cheaper than the cash market on the NYSE, the index arbitrageurs would keep dumping stocks and buying futures. Neither Melamed nor Phelan could prevent that from happening so long as these two linked markets were open.

Then Phelan checked his calendar: a young White House aide was scheduled to visit that day, and Phelan planned to show him around; he expected to be back in his office around noon.

MANY OF THE other men who would have to cope with the day's developments, some of them still new to their regulatory duties, were scattered from Sweden to Venezuela.

Fed chairman Alan Greenspan was at his Washington office on Monday, but was packed for a midday flight to Dallas. SEC chairman David Ruder also was in his Washington office, but he had been in it for barely ten weeks, and his more experienced aide, Rick Ketchum, had taken a 6:45 a.m. shuttle to New York. Treasury secretary Jim Baker was on a flight to Stockholm, by way of Frankfurt. White House chief of staff Howard Baker had never before dealt with a financial crisis from the Oval Office. And New York Fed president Jerry Corrigan was in Caracas.

IN A FOGGY rain, John O'Brien followed the curves of Route 18 out of the mountains north of San Bernardino. It was around 7 a.m., Pacific time, on Monday, October 19. He had spent the weekend helping his wife unpack at their new home at Lake Arrowhead.

About halfway down the mountain, he turned on the car radio for the news. The stock market had opened sharply lower, and was still falling. Feeling a jolt of concern, he pulled up to a roadside restaurant and called the office from its pay phone. He recalled later being told the market was off 200 points; there were lots of calls from worried clients. He got back in the car, speeding south and west toward Los Angeles, still an hour away.

The market had not yet opened in New York when Berkeley professor Hayne Leland boarded a 6:30 a.m. flight to Los Angeles. Before the plane took off, a flight attendant announced that the market was down 60 points—"serious, but less than catastrophic," Leland thought. When he landed, he got in a cab and asked the driver to turn the radio to the stock report. The market was down hundreds of points by then. "Oh God," Leland said. The taxi wove through the growing traffic to the First Interstate Tower.

Up north in Marin County, Mark Rubinstein called a taxi when the market decline hit 200 points, and headed for the airport. He got to the LOR offices in Los Angeles around 10 a.m. (1 p.m. in New York), just as the stock market was chewing up the last of a fragile hour-long rally.

Leland was already there, hovering anxiously around the firm's harried trader, who had telephone receivers in both hands and a computer monitor in front of him showing the growing disaster. In Chicago, he and other portfolio insurers had been selling for the last hour in larger volumes than they had all morning.

Around 11 a.m. (2 p.m. in New York), the trader looked up at Hayne Leland.

"I'm getting behind," he said. He still needed to sell even more heavily in Chicago to carry out the hedging strategy, he added, "but I think the market would go to zero if I did that."

Shocked, Leland instantly replied, "No! Don't do that!"

ALERTED BY HIS staff to the morning's sell-off, Jerry Corrigan immediately booked a seat on an earlier flight home from Caracas, and spent the time before he left for the airport making calls to New York and Washington from an office in the presidential palace, where he had been scheduled to have breakfast.

IN CHICAGO, THE S&P 500 futures pit had opened on time, and the tension was fierce. The subdued crowd in the normally seething pit was smaller than usual. Melamed waited for the opening bell and saw the opening price. At first, he couldn't believe it. The spooz had dropped 7 percent on the first trade, a staggering decline.

"There were blank stares. No one could believe it was happening. Some people began to leave the pit," a senior Merc trader later recalled. Portfolio insurers sold more than three thousand spooz contracts in the first thirty minutes, and the futures price seemed to be falling more steeply than the S&P index itself.

This was an illusion. When Chicago opened at 8:30 a.m. (9:30 a.m. in New York), many of the S&P 500 stocks had not yet actually started trading on the floor of the NYSE because there were no buyers. In that interval, the S&P 500 index was being calculated with stale prices from Friday, making the stocks seem far more expensive than the futures contracts—far more expensive, in fact, than they actually were.

Nevertheless, index arbitrageurs began their familiar dance, with a slight but devastating variation. As usual, they sold stocks heavily in New York, and in the first ninety minutes, the Dow dropped 208 points, more than 9 percent, the loss predicted for the entire day. However, instead of immediately buying the S&P 500 futures, a number of index arbitrageurs held back, waiting for even lower prices in Chicago. And by not buying, of course, they helped guarantee that prices in Chicago would continue to fall.

By 11 a.m. in New York, most of the stocks on the Big Board were open for trading, and there was a brief rally. After forty minutes, though, it was snuffed out. With the S&P 500 futures still dropping in Chicago, the Dow now sank under wave after wave of sell orders from all kinds of professional investors—mutual fund managers, index arbitrageurs, and Wall Street's own proprietary trading desks.

BY THEN, SEC chairman David Ruder had returned to his office from the Mayflower Hotel after giving a half-hour speech at a conference there sponsored by the American Stock Exchange.

Needless to say, it had been an uneasy audience; people were slipping out to the pay phones in the hall to check on the market. The SEC chairman had been surrounded by a scrum of journalists the minute he stepped from the podium. They pressed him to know if any steps had been taken to close the plunging market—perhaps because, two weeks earlier, Ruder had given a speech saying that a brief trading halt might be wise during a disorderly market collapse. With professorial caution, he told them that no discussions had been held but "anything is possible . . . There is some point, and I don't know what that point is, that I would be interested in talking to the NYSE about a temporary, very temporary halt in trading."

Trading halts in individual stocks were the cornerstone of John Phelan's last-gasp plan to preserve the exchange. He had mentioned the plan in a call with Ruder that morning, and described it months earlier in a magazine article. At that point, however, Phelan himself had not suggested closing the exchange as a whole. A more experienced regulator than Ruder likely would have been more cautious about even mentioning the issue in public at such a stressful moment. After fifteen minutes of questions, Ruder hurried out to his waiting car.

Upon returning to his office, he almost immediately got a call from Rick Ketchum. Ketchum had raced downtown to the NYSE following his early panel in Midtown Manhattan and had met with Phelan moments after the Big Board chairman wrapped up a meeting with the CEOs of the biggest Wall Street firms.

Ketchum said Phelan had told him that the executives "didn't seem to have any inkling of how bad the situation really was."

THE COMPUTER MONITORS on the credenza behind Gordon Binns's desk on the twenty-fifth floor of the General Motors Building in Manhattan were as bleak as anything he had ever seen—it was already a market crash on a par with 1929.

Binns may have thought back to his childhood in Richmond, to a powerful story his mother had told him about finding a little slip of paper in their basement, on which their worried housekeeper had carefully itemized every penny of her tiny $12 budget. His mother, already pinched by the gathering Depression, had sat on the basement steps and wept at her housekeeper's far more desperate plight. She resolved that the family would do everything they could to avoid letting the woman go in the hard times ahead. Binns, a public-spirited man, had been raised to think of others. He never talked about the decisions he made that dark Monday afternoon, but the facts are intriguing.

On his fund's behalf, Wells Fargo Investment Advisors had been sending enormous sell orders to the Big Board's DOT system all morning, every hour on the hour. Instead of selling futures contracts in the disorderly spooz pits, the firm had started selling the actual stocks out of GM's vast $33 billion portfolio, in thirteen separate transactions of 2 million shares each, for a total of almost $1.1 billion.

Specialists on the NYSE trading floor would never forget that relentless bombardment. One regulator recalled how a specialist had described it to him: "Boom, another sell order, then boom, another sell order, like it would never stop."

At 2 p.m., for some reason, it stopped.

The portfolio insurance specialists at Wells Fargo never conceded any concern; top executives at that firm would argue for decades that portfolio insurance was an innocent scapegoat in this crisis. It is unlikely that the hedging sales required for GM's portfolio had been completed by 2 p.m., with no need for further selling. Indeed, by one account, Wells Fargo had another 27 million shares to sell for GM before the closing bell.

Nevertheless, at 2 p.m. in New York—the same hour that LOR's chief trader in Los Angeles was worrying that the markets would "go to zero"—this specific barrage of sell orders hitting the NYSE just . . . stopped.

A LITTLE AFTER 1 o'clock, a newswire sent out a story reporting David Ruder's comments about a "very temporary" trading halt. In the next hour, the Dow fell 112 points. The SEC quickly denied discussing any closure of the exchange, but the uncertainty was enough. Index arbitrageurs stopped buying in Chicago, afraid they would not be able to execute the other side of their trades if the Big Board closed. As a consequence, the gap between the cash index and the futures price now widened to unprecedented—indeed, unthinkable—levels. Panic was flickering in the eyes of traders in New York and Chicago. The alarmed gossip hurtling between the two trading floors was becoming as dangerous as the investment strategies tying them together. No trading halt could unplug this lightning-fast rumor mill. Both markets dropped further and further, under selling from all quarters. By 2:30 p.m., the Dow's loss, about 13 percent, had eclipsed the worst day of the 1929 crash. The market was falling into history now, and no one knew where the new bottom would be.

ROLAND MACHOLD HAD $6 billion worth of South Africa–related stocks that he was obligated to sell before the middle of 1988, under New Jersey's anti-apartheid divestment law. His staff had regularly been selling between $100 million and $200 million worth of stock a day. "Our noses were to the South African grindstone," he later recalled. But Machold had grown increasingly wary of the market and had put the cash from these sales into safer investments.

Sometime after 2 p.m. on Monday, October 19, one of his colleagues came into his office and told him what was happening at the NYSE. He hurried to the room that served as the fund's trading desk. In one corner was a small Knight Ridder newswire printer, perched on a flimsy tripod, spewing out four-inch-wide strips of newsprint with barely an eye blink between updates.

The market was down almost 300 points.

Machold looked at the individual stock prices spooling out of the machine. He instantly asked, "How much cash do we have?"

His team found about $200 million that could be quickly deployed, and they started trying to get through to brokers to buy some of the dirt-cheap blue chips going begging. Working against the clock, they put the whole $200 million to work, plucking up bargains as fast as they could.

They were the bargain hunters the professors in Berkeley had been counting on, but with no way of knowing that the avalanche of sell orders was coming, they had limited time and limited cash, compared to the giant institutions lining up to sell at any price. "Nothing would slow that market," Machold said.

As the clock's hand moved toward 4 o'clock, the market dropped like a bouncing boulder, smashing through the 300-point loss line, plunging past the 400-point loss line. A strange hilarity seized Machold and his staff. They began to perversely applaud each new negative milestone, even though it meant their own stock portfolio's value was shrinking.

When the index was down 492 points, it bounced back up a bit—and the little squad in the trading room groaned. Then, in a final rush, the Dow broke the 500 level and finished down a staggering 508 points. "We all cheered," Machold said. "What else could we do?"

WHEN JOHN PHELAN saw his Washington visitor out the door and returned to his desk in the early afternoon, the Dow was already down a historic 200 points. Then, as he watched, the market simply "melted away." At the close, the Dow stood at 1,738.74 points; it had fallen 22.6 percent since the opening bell. That was twice as bad as the worst day of the fearsome 1929 crash, and the point loss was almost five times worse than Friday's epic decline. In its speed and scale—an unprecedented 604 million shares had been traded, twice as many as on Friday—it was the most apocalyptic one-day crash the market had ever seen. Monday, October 19, 1987, would thereafter be known as Black Monday.

Phelan, outwardly calm but grim, summoned his staff at the closing bell: "I want to know what went wrong, not right. Bad news first."

Then he headed down the hall to the stately boardroom, where he and his top aides sat in front of a small wooden table crowded with microphones and faced the biggest assemblage of reporters, television cameras, and photographers Phelan had ever seen.

After a poised and reassuring press conference, he called David Ruder with a far more alarming update. He had seen "no hint of any buying interest" at the close, he said, but the "combined judgment" at the exchange was to open for business on Tuesday morning.

The trading floor had been bombarded by selling. Specialists were carrying approximately $1.3 billion in inventory—stocks for which they had been the only buyers, stocks they would have to pay for with borrowed money. The DOT system had been overwhelmed, printers had faltered, systems had malfunctioned, and orders for more than 1 million shares had not been executed.

The wreckage stretched far beyond the Big Board—indeed, the only rallies in sight had been in gold and Treasury securities, as panicked investors sought safety. In Chicago, the S&P 500 futures contract had fallen a historic 28.6 percent. The American Stock Exchange was down 12.6 percent, a loss on a par with 1929. The Nasdaq market had been frozen much of the day, and was down 11 percent—a number no one believed because some dealers had just stopped trading. The options market was a disaster, able to handle barely a third as much trading as on Friday, as prices gyrated wildly. The dollar had tumbled in foreign currency markets. Stock markets from London to Tokyo were battered. Even the futures prices for farm commodities such as wheat and pork bellies, sensitive to the fears of worried pit traders, had plummeted.

JERRY CORRIGAN, WHO had gone directly to his New York office from the airport, listened patiently during a long conference call that Alan Greenspan conducted from his hotel room in Dallas. The Fed culture called for consensus. At some point, one Fed governor suggested, "Maybe we're overreacting. Why not wait a few days and see what happens?"

Greenspan, normally diplomatic, snapped back: "We don't need to wait to see what happens. We *know* what's going to happen."

Fear, simple irrational fear fed by this historic and almost incomprehensible crash, was going to infect every senior banker in the country. Credit was going to dry up like a summer puddle, just when the markets needed it most. Unable to borrow, the markets would be unable to function. The daily transactions that lubricated the economy—selling commercial paper, extending credit through overnight loans, hedging a big purchase made in some foreign country—would all stop.

For Greenspan, it was clear that the Fed had to inject not only cash but confidence into the financial system, and it had to do so before the markets opened on Tuesday.

AT ABOUT 2 a.m. on Tuesday, October 20, John Phelan woke up. He got out of bed and walked to the window of the Manhattan apartment where he spent weeknights. The market had fallen almost 33 percent in three trading days. Phelan wondered: What would that mean to those people out there? How would it hit the rest of the country? What if the whole system came unhinged on Tuesday?

The NYSE was the tip of the spear, in Marine Corps parlance. It would take the brunt of the day, and it had to get through it.

"WILL YOU OPEN in the morning?"

Alan Greenspan's question, delivered in a calm midnight phone call from Dallas, echoed in Leo Melamed's mind in the predawn hours of Tuesday, October 20, when he heard the stunning figure from the head of the Merc's clearinghouse: $2.53 billion. That was how much the losing futures traders owed their luckier trading partners after Monday's debacle.

Like all futures markets, the Merc was a "pay-as-you-go" operation. The previous day's trades had to be settled (double-checked, tallied, and paid for) before the market could open for a new day of trading. On a typical morning, that meant somewhere around $120 million changed hands. Melamed was aghast at the scale of the settlement challenge.

The Merc's foreign currency traders, attuned to Europe's trading day, were supposed to start testing the day's bids and offers at 7:20 a.m., Chicago time, on Tuesday morning. The Merc had to be open and ready for business by then.

The NYSE had been battered on Monday, and the entire world knew it. While the general public didn't follow news about the Merc, it would still be calamitous if it failed to open on Tuesday. Professional investors would instantly realize that the losers on Monday had been unable to fully pay their debts to the winners, who then might not be able to meet their own obligations. Doubts would tumble through the market like dominoes—dominoes made of dynamite.

While some traditionalists might cheer to see the innovative trouble-makers in Chicago brought low, it would be a body blow to the financial system. That system was held together by invisible strands of trust—the confidence that debts would be paid, trades would be settled, institutions would function, money would circulate. Shred that web of trust, and the system would not hold together. The Merc simply had to open on time on Tuesday; the world had to see that it and its trading firms could be trusted.

These were not Chicago pit gypsies whose credit was on the line. The Merc was owed roughly $1 billion by Morgan Stanley; in turn, it was obligated to pay $670 million to Goldman Sachs and $917 million to Kidder Peabody.

There already was sand in the machine, the kind of computer trouble that Jerry Corrigan had confronted nearly two years before at the Bank of New York—the kind of blindsiding mechanical malfunction that can erupt in any high-speed crisis. Because of a software flaw, the reports sent out by the Merc clearing system after the close on Monday had failed to reflect a margin call collected earlier in the day, making it appear that the Merc was calling for an additional $2.5 billion, not a total of $2.5 billion. That had thoroughly spooked a number of already nervous banks, and credit had tightened sharply.

Nerves in the banking industry were further rattled when the Fedwire, the critical electronic highway that moved cash from bank to bank, broke down entirely on Monday between 11 a.m. and 1:30 p.m., New York time, overwhelmed by the unprecedented volume of traffic it had to handle. Thus, Chicago banks had to pay clearinghouses before New York banks could deliver the cash to cover those payments. That took a lot of faith, and faith was in short supply.

The markets in Chicago had already dodged a potentially ruinous crisis late Monday night, thanks in part to the Merc's exhausted president, Bill Brodsky. A major trading firm had incurred big losses on the Merc, but had made a big profit on the Chicago Board Options Exchange. Unfortunately, it had to pay the Merc before it collected its money from the CBOE. If the two exchanges didn't agree to net out the firm's position, a default was inevitable. Before that happened, Brodsky worked out an ad hoc payment deal with a longtime friend who ran the options market's central clearinghouse. It was done virtually on a handshake. "There was no writing, no lawyers," Brodsky said. "It was the middle of the night." The deal had forestalled a devastating chain of defaults that could have crippled both markets.

Now the Merc was facing another default threat.

By 7 a.m., Chicago time, Morgan Stanley still had not fully settled its account. Bill Brodsky had checked repeatedly that morning with Wilma Smelcer, the chief financial officer at Continental Illinois, where the Merc had its clearinghouse account. As the minutes ticked away, Leo Melamed stood at a wall phone in a conference room upstairs from the trading floor, waiting for the latest update from the bank.

You're still short some $400 million, Smelcer reported.

"You mean we're down to $400 million from $2.5 billion? That's pretty damned good," Melamed said.

"Yes, Leo, but not good enough."

Melamed grew increasingly upset, insisting that Continental could advance the $400 million to the Merc as a short-term loan; they knew the loan would be repaid within hours, if not minutes.

"Leo, my hands are tied." The loan was too large for her to authorize. She sounded close to tears, Melamed thought.

Then Smelcer spotted the bank's new CEO, Tom Theobald, outside her office and hurried to consult him. As Melamed and his Merc colleagues again waited on hold, he noticed the clock. He recalled later that it had ticked toward 7:17 a.m. before Smelcer got back on the line and said, in a triumphant tone, "Leo, we're okay. Tom said to go ahead. You've got your money."

Three minutes later, the Merc opened for business.

THERE WOULD BE plenty of money for loans like that, Alan Greenspan assured the nation's bankers less than a half hour later.

At 8:41 a.m., New York time, the Fed released a succinct message whose wording Greenspan and Corrigan had labored over on Monday evening: "The Federal Reserve, consistent with its responsibilities as the nation's central bank, affirmed today its readiness to serve as a source of liquidity to support the economic and financial system."

Of course, it would do no good for the Fed to put money into bankers' hands if they hoarded it like frightened gnomes. They needed to lend it out—immediately—to the financial institutions that held the market together. Corrigan was growing increasingly worried that they would not.

He was right to worry. During those frightened hours, the president of Merrill Lynch was outraged when one of that firm's bankers "called me and said, 'You need X number of dollars to cover your positions and we need it here in ten minutes—or else.' I'll never forget that. I said, 'Hey, you son of a bitch, calm down. Relax. This is Merrill Lynch. You'll get your money.'"

In his cavernous wood-paneled office in New York, Corrigan worked the phones, cajoling the chairmen of all the major banks, one by one. He assured them that the Fed understood their plight, and was standing by to help. Of course, he couldn't order them to make the loans that Wall Street needed, but he wanted them to consider "the big picture, the well-being of the financial system"—in short, the mounting danger of total financial gridlock—in the crucial hours and days ahead.

THE FEDERAL RESERVE Bank of Chicago was making similar calls to local bank CEOs, but Continental's Tom Theobald didn't need encouragement to lend. He was lending like crazy to try to save his subsidiary, First Options, which was facing an old-fashioned run. Traders, hearing rumors that the giant clearing firm was in trouble, were pulling out surreal amounts of cash.

It wasn't hard to imagine what would happen if the firm that handled nearly half the trading accounts on the Chicago Board Options Exchange, the nation's largest options market, suddenly was shut down. Its clients stood little chance of finding a new clearing firm in this storm; they would have no choice but to stop trading. Liquidity would drain away, and the central clearinghouse, which served every options exchange in the country, would take a body blow that might trigger panic elsewhere.

Continental Illinois had already defused a crisis at the Chicago Merc. Now it was imperative that it rescue its First Options subsidiary, if it possibly could.

SHORTLY BEFORE THE NYSE opened at 9:30 a.m. on Tuesday, Phelan asked member firms not to use the DOT system for program trades, to keep it free for small investors' orders. However well intentioned, this fateful step essentially unplugged the index arbitrage machine. Phelan may have hoped to stanch the arbitrage sell orders in New York, but the step would also curb the arbitrage buy orders in Chicago, where they were desperately needed to offset the selling being done by portfolio insurers.

Despite this sea of worry, Tuesday opened with a rally. The Dow climbed a record-setting 11.5 percent (or 200 points) above Monday's close, though still far from its closing price on Friday. Nimble specialists were able to shed some of the shares they had been holding overnight, but within a half hour, the selling pressure returned in greater force than anyone had ever seen. All the gains in the morning rally were wiped out, and the market kept falling. By 12:30 p.m., the Dow was hovering just above 1,700 points, 38 points below Black Monday's nadir.

The shortage of index arbitrage buyers in Chicago and the inevitable whispers about a crisis at the Merc clearinghouse put the S&P 500 index futures into free fall. Between 9 and 11:15 a.m. (that is, between 10 a.m. and 12:15 p.m. in New York), the spooz price fell almost 27 percent, reaching a level that implied that the Dow's value was actually 1,400 points.

The spooz traders began to step out of the pit—some because of sheer panic or an instinct for self-preservation, some because their clearing firms had insisted on cutting their losses. The liquidity that Melamed had boasted about for years was drying up before his eyes.

The yawning gap between the futures price in Chicago and the apparent cash price in New York became "a billboard" to professional investors, warning that stock prices were likely to drop even further. Blue-chip buyers held back, waiting for bigger bargains, so the demand to buy NYSE stocks was vastly unequal to the pressure to sell them.

By midday on Tuesday, both John Phelan and Leo Melamed must have feared they were watching the destruction of the world they had known all their lives.

AT 11 A.M. IN New York, with the Dow off about 100 points, Phelan had left his office and gone down to the trading floor. The floor was crowded but eerily quiet, like the eye of a hurricane. For lack of bids, trading had been halted in IBM, Kodak, and ten other stocks that accounted for 54 percent of the value of the Dow Jones index. In the unnatural stillness, Phelan mustered the four senior floor officials and led them behind a canvas flap screening some construction work at the edge of the trading floor.

"Get them open," he told them. "Let's get these stocks up and trading and get on with it. We've got to trade out of this." He added, "We're not going to close this place down, but we'll continue to shut down stocks."

More than eighty or ninety stocks were already shut down or soon would be, Phelan was told. In the next few minutes, specialists would manage to open all but fifteen of them, but as the selling pressure increased, those and sixty others would stop trading.

Phelan returned to his office. He took a few calls, possibly one from Leo Melamed, and then strode out to the reception area and told his secretary to place calls to "Baker, Ruder, Corrigan." It was 12:05 p.m.

ACCORDING TO NOTES David Ruder made during his brief noontime conversation with Phelan, the NYSE chairman said that there were "no bids" and he was "really worried about liquidity." The next phrase reads: "*thinking*—about closing for a short time." Phelan also reportedly said, surprisingly, that "the Chicago Mercantile Exchange was interested in stopping trading." It is unclear how or when he had gotten that impression.

Phelan told Ruder that "he had been in contact with the White House, and would call the White House again to seek support for a trading halt." Message slips and phone logs from the Oval Office show that Howard Baker spoke with Phelan at 12:15 p.m., and again at 12:22 p.m.

Decades later, Phelan insisted he had assembled his staff in his office sometime between noon and 12:30 p.m. and told them that "come hell or high water, we were going to stay open." His backup plan was to keep shutting down individual stocks, without actually closing the exchange. There were more than 1,500 stocks listed on the Big Board. "They could not all be under intense pressure at once," he thought.

According to Ruder, however, Phelan told him that he "thought he needed 10 minutes to get more support, but he expected to issue a press release in 10 minutes announcing that they were halting." On the strength of that comment, the SEC quickly alerted the other exchanges and the CFTC that the NYSE might close.

Phelan later said he had been misunderstood. "When I mentioned a backup plan to the SEC and the White House, they seemed to interpret this as if I were about to shut the market down. This, of course, was not true." He said everyone in his office heard the call on a speakerphone and knew that "I was determined to keep the market open."

In Washington and Chicago, people who talked with Phelan by phone in these ghastly minutes clearly got the impression that the Big Board was most likely going to be forced to close, at least for a short time. Their certainty was such that they acted on that impression without seeking further clarification or confirmation. That, more than anything, is a measure of how terrible the situation was that confronted John Phelan at that noontime hour on Tuesday.

IN CHICAGO, THE Chicago Board Options Exchange, dependent on current NYSE stock prices that were not available, had halted trading. The American Stock Exchange's options market and other regional futures markets were closing. Now, Leo Melamed's regulators told him the NYSE was "considering closing." He was rattled. "If the NYSE closed, uncontrollable panic would follow. In such a case, if the Merc was left open, the world would dump on us."

According to Melamed, he called Phelan at around 11 a.m. (noon in

New York), using a speakerphone in Bill Brodsky's office. He asked Phelan if it was true that the NYSE was going to close.

"Phelan's voice sounded like death warmed over," Melamed later reported. Phelan's reply, according to Melamed, was: "It's getting close to that . . . There are no buyers . . . We are going into a meeting to decide. We may very well close." The Merc executives in Brodsky's office looked at one another. "There was virtual certainty that the NYSE was about to close," Melamed would recall.

The Merc officials decided they had to close the S&P 500 pit first, before news about an NYSE shutdown leaked out. Had Melamed somehow conveyed that desperate intention to Phelan? Was that the germ of the comment Phelan made to Ruder? It's possible, but not documented.

Sometime after his first call to Ruder—it's not certain how long after—Phelan called back and told the SEC chairman the NYSE "was not going to close; the market had turned up and it would try to stay open." Corrective calls were quickly made to everyone that Ruder's office had called just minutes earlier.

This obviously raises the question of why Phelan made this call at all, if his prior call had been to announce that the exchange *wouldn't* close.

In Chicago, at 11:15 a.m. (12:15 p.m. New York time), Leo Melamed and several other Merc executives left the phones and went down to the floor to announce that the spooz pit was closing immediately, pending a clear answer about what the NYSE would do.

The Chicago Board of Trade, characteristically, would have nothing to do with a Merc-led trading halt. Its MMI pit, thinly populated and wildly volatile, continued to trade. And thank God for that, thought Blair Hull, a well-known trader on the Chicago Board Options Exchange and the only member of his small trading firm who also had a seat on the Chicago Board of Trade.

Hull needed to meet a margin call. With the CBOE closed, he hurried to the Board of Trade's trading floor, stepped into the MMI pit, and began buying to cover a short position that was costing him a lot of money. Sellers swarmed him, and he quickly bought what he needed.

And on the strength of his buying, the MMI futures contract suddenly rallied, spurting up beyond any sensible level, as it regularly did. On trading desks everywhere, where computer monitors flashed red for downticks and green for upticks, there was a sudden, unexpected spark of green.

THE GREEN FLASH showed up on the trading desk at Salomon Brothers in Manhattan. By then, the desk was a hive of activity. Sometime around noon on that frightening Tuesday, Stanley Shopkorn, the legendary head of the firm's equity trading desk, finished a phone call and bustled out of his glass-walled office. He told his legion of traders to start making bids to buy, and they went to work.

Shopkorn had just spoken with Robert Mnuchin, his counterpart at Goldman Sachs, and they had decided they would both step in as big buyers of the major stocks that had been halted on the NYSE. They wanted to make a profit, obviously, but they also had to consider "the good of the system."

An enormous number of stocks had been halted—more than 160 at one point. The normal routine at the NYSE was that trading halts were promptly reported to the newswires. Today, for some reason, they weren't. So, when certain stock prices appeared to have stabilized, it wasn't immediately clear that they simply were not trading. Indeed, in what was later called a mistake, an NYSE staffer publicly denied reports of specific Dow stocks having been halted.

As the clock crept toward 12:30 p.m., with the Dow trading 38 points below its disastrous close on Black Monday, Phelan and several senior staffers simply stared at the big computer monitor on the credenza behind his desk. "The market *had* to rally," he thought.

They saw the MMI futures flash green. They saw the number of Dow stocks that were open for trading begin to bubble up a bit. A number of big corporations had announced they were buying back their own shares—David Ruder had waived certain SEC rules to speed that process up—so perhaps that was finally kicking in.

To Phelan's sixth sense, the market felt stronger. Without the grim "billboard" effect of the futures prices in Chicago, and with many stock prices at a standstill, the market was perfectly poised to respond to the buy orders that had begun to trickle in, no matter where those orders came from. As it recovered, more people rushed to snap up bargains before this demented market came to its senses.

That was most likely the moment John Phelan picked up the phone to tell David Ruder that the NYSE was not going to close. "We're still hanging in," he said.

The NYSE stayed open, and a short time later the spooz pit reopened, after having been closed for forty-nine minutes. As the Amex and the Nasdaq markets continued to lose ground, the Dow climbed a record 200 points by 3:30 p.m., and then lost half that gain in the half hour before the closing bell. It ended the day at 1,841 points, up 102 points, or almost 6 percent.

Once upon a time, a few weeks earlier, a 102-point gain would have been historic, a cause for celebration. Today, it merely meant survival, for at least one more day.

DID THE NYSE deliberately mislead the market about how many stocks were actually open for trading during those grim hours on Tuesday? Did that allow it to hold out until titan buyers such as Salomon Brothers and Goldman Sachs stepped in? Or was there a bigger conspiracy, one in which all the stock index futures markets deliberately stopped trading except for the Chicago Board of Trade so that traders there could ram up the thinly traded Major Market Index futures contract until it was more expensive than its underlying Dow stocks, thereby sparking arbitrage-linked buying interest on the NYSE?

The Chicago Board of Trade and the CFTC investigated the allegations of MMI manipulation and concluded that the vague reports were unfounded. Beyond that, there are myriad commonsense reasons to doubt a larger conspiracy. It would have required lightning-fast coordination among natural enemies, including the rebelliously uncooperative Board of Trade, which would have been the spear tip market willing to keep trading while every other futures market closed. The Board of Trade might team up with the Merc to beat New York, but it seems unlikely it would link arms with the Merc, at substantial risk to itself, to save the NYSE. Blair Hull's trades were pure self-preservation, as he consistently said both at the time and decades later, when there was no need to preserve a cover-up. The MMI pit was notoriously illiquid, as its wild swings throughout Monday and Tuesday demonstrated, so no manipulation was needed to produce a sharp spike on the strength of a few purchases. Moreover, with the DOT system closed to program trading, many index arbitrage traders were on the sidelines that day, so it was far from certain that an MMI uptick would actually have produced any arbitrage buying in New York. There is even some dispute about whether, at the time, the Street, obsessively focused on the S&P 500 futures, would even have noticed the volatile MMI's uptick, or cared; if it hadn't, that alone would have doomed the plot to failure.

So, what caused the market's "miraculous" turnaround between noon and 1 p.m. on Tuesday, October 20? The power of the money that Salomon Brothers and Goldman Sachs started pumping into NYSE stocks (estimated by several sources at several hundred million dollars) would have been psychologically enhanced by the legendary status of both firms and their chief equity traders. If they were buying big, it would certainly have given heart to the NYSE specialists and to other shaky trading desks, as would have the proliferating announcements of corporate stock buybacks that day. And certainly, the MMI's spike after Blair Hull's buy orders would have helped stave off despair. If there was any "conspiracy," it was an opportunistic one centered on the concealment of how widespread the trading halts were on the Big Board.

The fact remains: While the market had *fallen* on Monday, it had almost *fallen apart* on Tuesday. All that had saved it was a makeshift web of trust, pluck, and improvisation—and perhaps a few bits of inspired subterfuge here and there.

Only misinformed hindsight sees that midday turning point as the "end" of the 1987 crash. For Phelan and Melamed, for Ruder and Corrigan and Greenspan, for the stunned portfolio insurers in California, it was simply a fragile rally that let the market stumble toward the blessed closing bell on Tuesday without shattering the world's confidence in America's financial system.

The bell on the balcony of the Big Board would ring again at 9:30 a.m. on Wednesday, and none of them knew how that day would end.

20

JUGGLING HAND GRENADES

Very early on Wednesday morning, October 21, 1987, Goldman Sachs was supposed to pay $700 million to the hard-pressed Continental Illinois bank to cover some trading debts, but it was holding back until it received money it was owed by others. "Then, Goldman thought better of it, and made the payment," Alan Greenspan later recounted. If it had not, he said, "it would have set off a cascade of defaults across the market."

It was going to be that kind of week, each day threatening to be worse than the dreadful day before.

A little before 9 o'clock that Wednesday morning, David Ruder sat at his desk, listening intently and taking notes as top staffers outlined the day's possible nightmares.

A floor below, staffers in the SEC's market regulation division were sweeping the Street for rumors of firms slipping into failure; some were true, some weren't—or, weren't yet. Still, the market situation could be severe, a key aide told Ruder, pointing out that the "total numbers are bad." The aide added that if any big firms were "screwed up, we're going to have problems."

The overarching worry was that a major firm would fail. In the wee hours of Wednesday morning, an NYSE specialist firm had been quietly merged with Merrill Lynch; three small trading firms and a Midwest broker had faltered, but few people had ever heard of them. While First Options in Chicago was a desperate worry—the firm had "gone to the wall" during Tuesday's trading, an aide reported—it was hardly a household name.

The same could not be said for Charles Schwab and Company. The aggressive discount brokerage firm, with 1.8 million customer accounts, had been advertising heavily for years and signing up tens of thousands of new customers every month. Schwab had embodied Main Street's growing obsession with the stock market during the long bull rally that began in August 1982.

In the spring of 1987, Chuck Schwab had bought his company back from Bank of America, and in mid-September he sold a stake in the firm to the public. The stock initially traded on the NYSE for $16.50 a share, and Schwab customers were among the most ardent buyers.

But by Wednesday morning, Schwab was in total disarray. Its telephone system had been disabled by the storm of weekend calls from nervous investors, and now callers were lucky if they even got a busy signal. Its stock price had fallen 30 percent from its initial value. Its computer system had finally crumpled, too, and some orders had not been executed, leaving Schwab on the hook for any subsequent drop in market prices.

Without its computer systems, the firm was struggling to calculate its own financial position. Even without those calculations, though, Schwab's top executives knew that the firm was in terrible trouble—indeed, with the Bank of America no longer there to bail it out, its very survival was in doubt—because of a $124 million margin debt run up by one brash speculator in Hong Kong.

If Schwab had to shut its doors in the aftermath of the crash, the psychological impact among individual investors would be horrendous.

Main Street was already complaining loudly about the breakdown of the Nasdaq market on Monday and Tuesday, complaints that were echoed by professional investors. By Wednesday morning, the Nasdaq, which had branded itself "the market of tomorrow," was still digging out from two days of bungled business, during which it had fallen almost 20 percent. The flow of price quote updates and inquiries through its electronic system had been twenty times the normal volume. Investors had trouble reaching their brokers by phone, trading desks could not cope with the crush of business, and the pace of orders moving through the system slowed from a few minutes to more than an hour. Rapid fluctuations in price quotes had left the electronic markets frozen for much of Black Monday. Nasdaq president Joseph Hardiman, in office for barely three weeks, was trying to address the rising level of complaints and rally his shell-shocked dealers.

As for the options markets, trading was still curtailed for hours at a time as traders struggled to establish opening prices. For two nights running, the automated pricing service relied on by clearing firms and the Options Clearing Corporation had failed, and prices had to be entered into the system manually. As a result, First Options had opened for business on Tuesday morning unsure of its actual financial status. Its parent, Continental Illinois, had been steadily lending it cash, and so far, a default had been averted. Everyone knew how much was hanging in the balance; Alan Greenspan noted later that "the Chicago options market nearly collapsed" under the weight of the First Options cash crunch.

To make matters worse, the First Options rescue operation had hit a surreal roadblock.

Continental Illinois's primary regulators in the Office of the Comptroller of the Currency had balked at the bank's effort to save its subsidiary. The comptroller's staff had complained on Tuesday, as the markets were teetering on the edge of chaos, that the bank's $130 million loan to First Options on Monday had exceeded limits set by the FDIC when it saved Continental Illinois back in 1984. Nevertheless, the resolute bank had lent another $138 million to its desperate subsidiary on Tuesday, preventing a default that would have torn a gaping wound in the options market on that terrible day.

Now the comptroller himself, the less experienced successor to the crisis-tested Todd Conover, was adamant that he would not waive the loan limits. The bank's support for First Options had to be hastily rerouted through the bank's holding company—the very holding company that Donald Regan had wanted to kill in 1984 as the price of saving the bank. If the comptroller's obstruction became public, it could fuel the options traders' panic and intensify the run on the clearing firm.

In New York, Jerry Corrigan must have been flabbergasted by the comptroller's unilateral action. If the largest options clearing firm in the country—moreover, a firm owned by a major bank—had failed, it undoubtedly would have damaged the options markets, frozen cash owed to other firms active in other markets, and further traumatized every trader in Chicago. It also could have alarmed Continental's depositors around the world, putting the bank's hard-won financial stability at risk.

And if all that happened because one regulator would not allow Continental Illinois to do what other regulators desperately wanted it to do? It was absurd. The failure of any linchpin financial firm in the coming days could be disastrous. Every financial crisis since Silver Thursday had made clear how quickly, and unpredictably, a financial crisis could spread beyond regulatory control.

After his morning briefing on Wednesday, Ruder called the other regulators to touch base. Then he reached out to his fellow commissioners at the SEC and got their approval for a request from John Phelan. The Big Board chairman wanted permission to close the exchange a few hours early for the next few days, so it and its member firms could catch up on processing the 1.5 billion shares that had changed hands since Friday morning. The market's unspoken fear was that the immense backlog of orders, scribbled or punched in during the most chaotic trading days in history, concealed errors that would spell financial ruin for the firms on the losing side of the mistakes. Until all those trades had been tallied and paid for, no one really knew which firms were in trouble, and how deep that trouble was.

BY WEDNESDAY MORNING, the task of getting Charles Schwab, and likely the entire market, out of a desperate situation was in the hands of an adventurous Schwab executive named Robert Rosseau, an argumentative Vietnam veteran dispatched from San Francisco to collect the unpaid debt that threatened the firm's survival from halfway around the world.

The debt was owed by Teh-huei "Teddy" Wang, the biggest customer of Schwab's small Hong Kong office.

Wang was a wealthy businessman with a somewhat lurid past. Six years earlier, he had been kidnapped and released after an $11 million ransom demand was calmly paid by his formidable wife, Nina, who had teenybopper pigtails and bear trap instincts. He traded stock index options on a huge scale—tens of thousands of contracts at a time, when a few hundred were typical. He had profited greatly in recent years by betting on a rising stock market, using money borrowed through his margin account at Schwab.

The market's relentless decline since August and the historic collapse the previous week had cost Teddy Wang a lot of money. By sunrise in Hong Kong the previous Saturday morning, Wang owed Charles Schwab $124 million, and if he didn't pay, Schwab would be on the hook for the full sum. In response to two margin calls from the firm, Wang paid $40 million. Then, with his margin debt at the still-fatal level of $84 million, he stopped returning Schwab's calls.

Wang's disappearance ratcheted up the pressure. As a publicly traded company, Schwab had ten days under U.S. securities law to disclose any material change in its financial condition; time would run out on Thursday, October 29.

Bob Rosseau flew to Hong Kong early on Black Monday. He found the entire financial community there in turmoil, with both the stock exchange and the futures market closed. His first request for a court-ordered freeze of Wang's assets was denied, and he hastily hired a new law firm to revise the request. Rosseau went into "special ops" mode—by one account, he taped paper over the windows of a rented office to deter telescopic snooping, swept his phones constantly for wiretaps, hired private detectives, and used unconventional methods to track down Wang's far-flung bank accounts.

The Schwab troubleshooter finally connected with the elusive options trader and arranged a meeting for Wednesday. Wang knew exactly where things stood. "Well, Mr. Rosseau," he said, "it appears that Schwab is worth $72 million and I owe the company $84 million." Then he stepped out, leaving the rest of the negotiating to Nina. This was not going to be easy.

ON THAT SAME Wednesday, October 21, the stock market barreled into a nervous rally that eased the financial stress on the NYSE floor, with the Dow gaining almost 187 points. But the rally vastly increased the financial stress for Hayne Leland, John O'Brien, and Mark Rubinstein.

The Berkeley professors had remained in Los Angeles following their hasty morning flights on Black Monday, struggling to maintain some part of the hedges they had put in place to protect their clients' portfolios. On Tuesday afternoon they had been able to establish some protection in the futures market, but Wednesday's rally meant they had to come up with more cash margin to maintain those positions. The only way to raise that cash in their clients' accounts was to sell stocks, but because of the different settlement schedules in the two markets, they would have to shell out additional cash in the futures market before they collected their cash in the stock market.

John O'Brien explained the situation carefully to the firm's clients: they would either have to come up with the cash from a different source, or they would have to sell stock for immediate payment, which meant they'd get a lower price.

As it was, Leland estimated that clients probably had been protected against only about 80 percent of the market's decline, and would have to bear the remaining 20 percent as a loss. It was better than no protection at all, he and his partners reasoned, but it was not what they had advertised and expected.

Rubinstein was angry over media reports singling out portfolio insurance as the single cause of the crash. He and Leland believed the blame should be shared with those who effectively banned or abandoned index arbitrage on Monday and Tuesday. As early as September 1986, they understood that they and other portfolio insurers sat on one end of the market seesaw, and index arbitrageurs sat on the other end. It wasn't just the selling by portfolio insurers that drove prices in the spooz pit so far below prices in the cash market; it was also the absence of buying by index arbitrageurs. Try explaining that to journalists, few of whom could grasp either strategy.

What was harder to explain was how Black Monday could have happened *at all* in an efficient market where prices instantly adjusted to changes in "rational expectations" about future stock values. That model of how markets operated, the "efficient market hypothesis," had become so deeply embedded in the traditional world of quantitative finance that experiencing Black Monday and Tuesday was like tossing a rock out a window—and watching it float up.

WHILE SCHWAB'S FATE was being decided in Hong Kong, the fate of four other linchpins of Wall Street was being haggled over in London, with the same weeklong fuse and the same enormous psychological risks to the market's fragile stability.

On the previous Thursday, October 15, a consortium of investment banks in London, New York, and Toronto had eagerly taken up the British government's proposal to sell off its stake in British Petroleum. The $12 billion underwriting was one of the largest stock offerings in history, with 2.1 billion shares scheduled for sale at a price established by the underwriters at roughly $5.45 a share. Then came the worst stock market crash in U.S. history, with collateral damage in markets around the world. The BP shares were certainly worth much less now than the investment banks had agreed to pay for them. If the British government did not cancel or amend the deal, the underwriters could be looking at a global loss of about $840 million—and roughly $500 million of that would be sucked out of New York at the worst possible moment.

Goldman Sachs and three other flagship firms on Wall Street, Salomon Brothers, Morgan Stanley, and Shearson Lehman Brothers, had been caught midstream in the deal. Goldman, a private partnership, would take the biggest hit, with a loss of up to $150 million; the other three firms, whose shares traded on the NYSE, would each face losses of around $120 million.

The London market had remained weak on Tuesday, partly because of worry about the BP deal. Bankers in Britain were lobbying for relief, but the Tory government was in a difficult spot. Under Prime Minister Margaret Thatcher, it had invoked free-market principles on issues that had cost working-class jobs, so how could it now abandon those principles to rescue a lot of rich bankers? The government insisted the deal would close on schedule on Friday, October 30, at the agreed-upon price.

On Wall Street, where brokerage industry stocks had already declined much further than the Dow that week, the shares of the three firms caught in the deal were starting to slip even further, and rumors began to brew. At the New York Fed, Jerry Corrigan knew how even a little doubt could quickly strip a brokerage firm of the overnight loans that financed its daily existence. He added his voice to those urging the British authorities to amend the deal.

ON THURSDAY MORNING, October 22, shortly before the opening bell, John Phelan and a trio of board members climbed up to the stone balcony overlooking the NYSE trading floor. Traders, specialists, and clerks listened appreciatively as Phelan read them a message from President Reagan complimenting the "calm and professional manner" in which they had done their jobs that week.

Then Phelan rang the opening bell, and the Big Board plunged into another dreadful day.

With sickening déjà vu, specialists looked at an opening avalanche of sell orders from giant institutions, with few buyers in sight. For some, it felt like the prelude to another meltdown like Monday's, and many no doubt knew their firms might not survive if that meltdown came. "When I can't trade IBM, I know I'm in big trouble," one trader told the New York Times.

On the crowded trading floor that morning, traders juggled their orders, and their fates. At its low point, the Dow fell to 1,837.86 points, more than 9 percent below Wednesday's close. Then the index recovered some of its morning loss and closed at 1,950.43 points, down 77.42 points, a drop of 3.8 percent. Not many weeks ago, this day's loss, like Tuesday's gain, would have looked epic; three days after Black Monday, it looked like a reprieve. As it was, both the broader NYSE Composite index and the S&P 500 index were hit harder in the sell-off than the Dow.

At a press conference after Thursday's closing bell, Phelan announced that the exchange would close early, at 2 p.m., beginning on Friday and continuing into the following week. The mood at the press conference was tense, but Phelan and his team hadn't lost their sense of humor. During that dismal day, staff members and floor traders were wearing orange buttons that read, "Don't Panic."

———

BY THURSDAY, THE big worry among regulators was why the historically large and stubbornly persistent price gap between the S&P 500 futures contract and the S&P 500 stocks hadn't gone away.

Regulators at the CFTC thought it was because John Phelan had told NYSE firms not to use his DOT system for program trading, which inhibited index arbitrage. At midmorning on Thursday, the CFTC's acting chairman, Kalo Hineman, spoke with David Ruder at the SEC about that.

Ruder understood Hineman's argument to be that a futures market cut off from the stock market would give investors the wrong impression about market values. But it would do far worse damage than that: it would prevent arbitrage from bringing the two markets back into alignment. Portfolio insurers were continuing to sell heavily in the S&P 500 pits, so there had to be buyers there, too. And those potential buyers included the index arbitrageurs, who relied on the DOT system to place their stock market trades. Without the DOT system, many of them were not trading in either market, and the futures price gap wasn't closing. As a result, potential stock buyers were holding back, seeing the discount in Chicago as evidence that prices on the NYSE would soon fall.

Hineman was right, of course. With the adoption of index arbitrage strategies by a number of giant institutional traders, the two markets had been shackled together and neither market's prices could remain in equilibrium without that arbitrage activity. And the ban on DOT-assisted program trading blocked a lot of that now-necessary trading.

But the spooz pit's prices had swung wildly out of line even when index arbitrage was unfettered, which may have cast doubt on Hineman's case. More important, Phelan wanted to reserve the DOT system for individual investors, who were the bedrock of the stock market Phelan believed in—and the market Ruder regulated. Ruder did not order the NYSE to reverse its ban on program trading.

So, the price gap persisted—providing additional evidence that however connected they were by investing strategies, New York and Chicago were still galaxies apart in their view of how markets worked and whom markets served.

There were other cross-border arguments. As the market made

its terrible plunge on Thursday, the SEC was wrestling with whether to ask the CFTC "to urge or even force" the futures markets to delay their daily stock index trading until the NYSE had been able to get all its stocks open for trading, to buffer the impact of the selling that hit at the instant of the opening bell in New York. There was a spirited discussion among the SEC commissioners on Thursday, but no agreement, and Chicago was firmly opposed to the change.

But Merc president Bill Brodsky, the tireless diplomat trying to find some common ground, had been able to help persuade the Merc, at least temporarily, to impose daily price limits on the S&P 500 index contract— the very step that Leo Melamed had been unable to sell eight months earlier. The Merc board of governors, meeting on Thursday night, approved the price limits as an "emergency action."

AT 8 P.M. on Thursday, after the day's market nosedive, President Reagan stepped to the podium in the East Room of the White House for his first news conference in seven months. "Well, it just seems like yesterday," he mused to some rueful laughter from reporters. His first words were about his wife, who had returned home after surgery. "It sure is good to have Nancy back home, and she's doing just fine," he said.

No one could have missed how distracted Reagan was by Nancy Reagan's medical crisis, or how uninformed he seemed about Wall Street's financial crisis. On Black Monday, he had fielded reporters' questions through the thumping din of the helicopter that would take him to visit his wife.

"What? Oh, the stock market," he said after figuring out what the shouted questions were about. "I think everyone is a little puzzled, and I don't know what meaning it might have, because all the business indices are up. There is nothing wrong with the economy." Aides cringed: it sounded too close to Herbert Hoover's optimistic pronouncements after the 1929 crash.

The next question was about panic. The president was blasé. "Maybe some people are seeing a chance to grab a profit, I don't know," he said. He almost visibly shrugged off the biggest market crash in history. Carrying a gaily wrapped present for Nancy, he climbed into the helicopter.

On Wednesday, with the market up more than 186 points, the president was asked if he thought the Wall Street crisis was over, again over helicopter noise.

"Well, it would appear to be," Reagan said, casually. "Certainly, when more than half of the loss has already been regained."

Thursday's steep market plunge once again shook everyone in the West Wing, and the president's evening news conference was an effort to deliver a more coherent message.

"While there were a couple of days of gains after several days of losses, we shouldn't assume that the stock market's excess volatility is over," Reagan said, looking earnestly into the television cameras. "So while there remains cause for concern, there is also cause for action. And tonight I plan to take the following steps to meet this challenge."

He said he would sit down with the leaders in Congress to discuss ways to reduce the budget deficit, and he would also urge Congress to reject any protectionist policies that could tip the country into a recession. Finally, he would set up a task force "that over the next 30 to 60 days will examine the stock market procedures and make recommendations on any necessary changes." The leader of this team would be Nicholas F. Brady, a former U.S. senator from New Jersey and a lifelong member of Wall Street's old guard.

BY THE TIME the NYSE opened for business on Friday morning, foreign markets had already shown dissatisfaction with President Reagan's response to the financial crisis. Hong Kong markets remained closed, but the Tokyo stock market opened just as Reagan's press conference began, and prices immediately plunged. Australia's market fell almost 7 percent; Singapore and Taiwan also piled up big losses. Europe was similarly unsettled—Switzerland's leading index set a new low for the year, and London fell sharply until stronger domestic trade numbers spurred a small midday rally that cut the day's losses in half.

In the first thirty minutes of trading in New York, prices fell sharply. From his office at the SEC, David Ruder spoke with a Goldman Sachs executive to get a sense of the market's mood and was told, "All is well." Indeed, the market did rally sharply over the next half hour, but prices gradually weakened through the shortened afternoon session.

Ruder decided to hold a press conference at the end of this tumultu-
ous week, and he used the occasion to disparage the notion that his off-
the-cuff comments about a possible trading halt on Black Monday had
precipitated that day's final disastrous plunge. "I would be amazed if I
had the power by a single comment of that kind to cause a major decline
in the stock market," he said.

Responding to questions, Ruder described his midday conversation
on Tuesday with John Phelan, asserting that Phelan had been "very close"
to shutting down the Big Board, and affirming that the SEC would have
backed him if he had taken that step. The NYSE immediately disputed
that account, with Phelan insisting, "We didn't come close to closing."
He added, "We let them trade out. By closing you almost exacerbate
something that is intolerable to begin with."

In Chicago, traders on the Merc were confronted for the first time
ever with limits on how much the prices of the spooz contract and its
related options could fluctuate during the day. Under the new rule, trading would close for the day if the futures or options rose or fell the equivalent of 30 points on the S&P 500 index. Bill Brodsky told reporters
that "price limits are anathema to a free market, but we're reacting to a
very extreme situation. It was the responsible thing to do." Other futures
exchanges had followed suit.

By Friday's closing bell on the NYSE, which rang two hours earlier
than on Thursday, the Dow stood at 1,950.76 points. That was almost 300
points below its level the previous Friday, but nearly flat with Thursday's
close. It was a remarkable anticlimax to a week that had opened with the
worst trading day in market history. For an exhausted John Phelan,
though, it was "the ideal script. The market needs time to breathe."

Outside the exchange, the sidewalks were a spectacle. By one account,
the scene featured "vendors, sidewalk preachers, artists, protestors and
spectators" mingling with television camera crews and workers from
Wall Street firms, who "poured out of their offices and onto the streets
for the exchange's final moments of trading."

One Wall Street worker said, "We're out here to see what's going on.
After all, this is history." Another observed, "Everybody talks about '29,
and this is going to be talked about as long as that was."

But anyone expecting an exodus of exhausted traders after the closing bell was disappointed. As one departing exchange worker explained, "Everybody's still in there, and they will be for a long time. Trading stopped. Work didn't."

The most pressing work was the final tally for the trades done during that grim and briefly historic session on Friday, October 16. Trades on the exchange had to be settled and closed out in five business days; for Black Monday's trades, that day of reckoning was just a weekend away.

LEO MELAMED WAS intensely worried about the political backlash from Black Monday. In a few days, Chicago's futures exchanges had been transformed from obscure markets of little interest to the general public into targets of international attention and Washington controversy.

Melamed was hardwired to play offense. David Ruder lived in Highland Park, a lakefront suburb north of Chicago, and Bill Brodsky suggested to Ruder, through an intermediary, that he and Melamed visit him when he was home from Washington for the weekend. At 3:30 p.m. on Saturday, October 24, they arrived at Ruder's home.

It had already been an eventful day for the SEC chairman. A few hours earlier, he'd gotten a call from President Reagan, asking a few questions about the backlog of orders and thanking Ruder and the SEC staff for "the tremendous job that you have done this week under very difficult circumstances." It had been gratifying, if a little stilted.

After welcoming his visitors and getting them settled, Ruder took out a legal pad and sat down to listen. For almost ninety minutes, Melamed and Brodsky reviewed the week from their perspective—explaining Tuesday's decision to temporarily stop trading, and insisting that the pressure on the NYSE would have been even greater if the futures market had not existed to absorb so much of the institutional selling.

Their point was that, for giant institutional investors, Chicago was becoming the market where prices for NYSE stocks were being "discovered," and there was no way to put the genie back in the bottle. Ruder listened, but he was skeptical. Stock markets had set stock prices for hundreds of years. Had that changed in the five short years since the S&P 500 index futures contract started trading in Chicago?

Brodsky, feeling the dialogue had been healthy and helpful, was determined to keep the lines of communication open. He and Melamed were scheduled to be in Washington the following Wednesday, October 28, to meet privately with the key committees on Capitol Hill and make the case that the Chicago markets were blameless in the Black Monday crash. Brodsky suggested that Ruder and Rick Ketchum join them for dinner the evening before. The invitation was accepted, and the Merc leaders left.

That afternoon visit was the opening volley in a tireless Merc campaign that would extend for months—indeed, for years. As the exchange's official history put it, "Like a frustrated teenager screaming at parents that 'you don't understand,' the Merc sought to explain itself."

David Ruder returned to Washington on Sunday night, knowing that the next day's back-office work, settling the transactions from Black Monday, would be the acid test for many Wall Street firms.

ONCE AGAIN, ON Monday morning, October 26, stock prices started plummeting in Asia, and the decline rolled west with the sun.

It was still Sunday night in Manhattan when Monday's trading opened in Hong Kong, the first trading session in ten days. The fall was stunning—stock prices there declined by more than 30 percent, which some cited as the largest one-day drop ever in any stock market in the world. The Hong Kong futures market fared even worse, falling 44 percent. In Tokyo, the Japanese stock market fell 4 percent, the third-worst decline ever, after the records set on two precipitous days the previous week. The German market dropped 6 percent. The stock market in Paris gyrated wildly, and ended down almost 8 percent.

So, when Monday morning trading opened in New York, John Phelan was braced for a disaster. He got one.

"Tough, again," one staffer would tell David Ruder that morning, after detailing the global tumult. "Worldwide panic selling," an economist told the New York Times that night. The Dow fell 8 percent (just under 157 points) to close at 1,793.93 points, which was within 56 points of its level at the closing bell on Black Monday.

Near the close, Phelan spoke with Ruder and gave him some comfort. The Black Monday trades had settled without any disastrous problems.

As for the market, "it's soupy but not panicky," Phelan said. "The market's doing its thing, we just have to trade it out, let it test its lows."

These global, east-to-west market nosedives were unsettling. Phelan knew there wasn't a single major firm in New York that didn't also have at least some business in Hong Kong—and in London and Tokyo and Europe, for that matter.

TUESDAY, OCTOBER 27, was still bleak for traders in London's stock market, but it brought a narrow and welcome rally to New York, with rising stocks slightly more numerous than declining ones. Wednesday, October 28, was rockier; the Dow managed to close up by an eyelash, but most other market barometers (and most foreign markets, including Hong Kong) declined.

Schwab's troubleshooter, Bob Rosseau, was still in Hong Kong on Wednesday, inches away from a deal with Teddy Wang. With Chuck Schwab himself due to announce the firm's financial results early Thursday morning, the firm's public relations staff had prepared two scripts, and by late Wednesday night, Schwab's founder still did not know which one he would be using.

One announced an awful $22 million loss, which would wipe out most of the firm's profits for the year and drive its stock price even lower than it already was—and that was the one that Chuck Schwab fervently hoped he would be able to read.

The other script announced a loss of $100 million, which would wipe out the firm's net capital, violate the terms of its bank loans, and force it to seek an emergency buyer or close its doors. That was the one that knowledgeable regulators feared would ignite a Main Street panic and shove Wall Street back into Black Monday territory again.

At 5 a.m. in San Francisco on Thursday morning, October 29, Chuck Schwab got a call from Rosseau, reporting that Wang had proposed settling his $84 million margin debt by paying 80 cents on the dollar—$67 million. Schwab swallowed hard and agreed. He picked up the script that announced the $22 million loss, most of it attributable to Teddy Wang, and headed to his 6 a.m. news conference.

"I am profoundly unhappy," he told reporters, who did not yet know that he was far less unhappy than he had feared he would be.

When the stock market opened in New York a few minutes later, there was an honest-to-goodness rally. The market opened strong and stayed strong all day, and even the battered Nasdaq stocks gained ground. By the closing bell at 2 p.m., the Dow was up more than 91 points, its third gain in a row—although Wednesday's had been barely visible to the naked eye. The Dow was still almost 30 percent below its August peak, and everyone was still skittish, but the daily and hourly threats of some new crisis seemed to have eased.

At 4 p.m. that day, John Phelan was in Washington, testifying at a closed-door session of the House Commerce Committee's finance panel. It was a remarkably prescient and earnest presentation.

In that secret session, Phelan acknowledged that if widespread trading halts in individual stocks hadn't worked on Black Monday and on Tuesday, "I suppose as a backup, we would've had to close the market down." He did not sugarcoat the fears he had confronted between 10:30 a.m. and 1 p.m. on Tuesday.

He also spoke about the lessons offered by the market's experience with portfolio insurance. "One is that when everybody wants to leave the room at the same time, it is not possible to get out," he said. The other was that insurance is only easy to get when you're healthy: "When the market is under extreme pressure, you just cannot get the kinds of insurance that they were hoping for."

Most insightfully, he warned about the new derivative products that, like a lever and fulcrum, allowed an investor to boost his profits or expand his losses beyond what they would have been if he had been using just cash.

"See, I don't see the root problem on the floor of the Chicago pit or [a] New York options exchange," Phelan said. "I see it with the customer up here who has $3 trillion they are managing, and that up until two years ago[,] when they bought equities, they put up a dollar and bought a dollar's worth of equities. Now, they can put up five cents and buy a dollar's worth of equities. You have gotten that incredible leverage into the institutional part of the market."

Somehow, he said, the crucially important issues of leverage and scale had to be addressed.

"We must decide, here in the next year to 18 months, what kind of equity market we want in this country," he said. The stock market was rapidly approaching a level of volatility and institutional dominance that had long been commonplace in the commodities markets, where high levels of leverage were built into the futures contracts by design. "If the volatility continues in this way," he warned, "we are going to drive out all [investors] but the professionals in the market, and I don't think that that is going to be very good for this country."

The congressional panel listened politely but showed no sign that it actually heard what this battle-scarred market veteran was saying. His warnings were almost a forecast of the future facing Wall Street, and the world.

BY THURSDAY AFTERNOON, David Ruder dropped his shoulders for the first time in what seemed like months. Schwab's stock had fallen a full point, to $6.50, after it announced its quarterly loss. That was about a third its value in September, but the firm—and, more important, the market—could survive that. First Options, too, would muddle through, no thanks to the comptroller of the currency. It was meeting all its required margin calls, its cash cushion had stabilized, and its parent, Continental Illinois, was quietly negotiating a settlement with the comptroller over the way the emergency rescue had been carried out.

And a deal was in the works to address the British Petroleum underwriting losses. At around 5 o'clock that afternoon, right at the deadline, word of a compromise finally came from London: the deal would not be postponed, but the Bank of England would buy back any unsold shares at a price that would reduce, but not eliminate, the losses the firms would face.

The stock market rallied again on Friday, October 30, gaining 55 points to close at 1,993.53; it had clawed back more than half the losses from Black Monday. It was the first four-day rally since before the crisis. It was not the end of the 1987 market crash, but it was perhaps the beginning of a new post-crash "normal."

The toll of the crash had been enormous. More than a trillion dollars in wealth had been lost since the market peak in August, half of that on Black Monday, along with a great deal of investor confidence. Layoffs at weakened Wall Street firms already threatened the economy of New York City and other financial centers, and a wider recession seemed a plausible threat.

As Wall Street closed the books on a disastrous October, few people except the regulators and market insiders knew that, as bad as it was, the damage from Black Monday came very close to being far, far worse.

Catastrophe had been averted, not through careful political oversight and astute regulatory foresight, but through sheer luck: an eleventh-hour deal with an options trader in Hong Kong; a belated willingness to compromise at the Bank of England; an extremely persuasive Irishman at the New York Fed; a pension fund manager who may have shown uncommon restraint; two momentarily cooperative stock-trading rivals in Manhattan; and, in Chicago, some time-tested friendships, a few bankers willing to defy their regulators and their own fears, a timely payment by Goldman Sachs, and one fortunately timed purchase in the Major Market Index pit at the Chicago Board of Trade.

Subtract even one of those elements, and the aftermath of Black Monday would have been cataclysmic for the nation's financial system.

THE REVISED TERMS for the British Petroleum deal, the final bit of luck the market needed to reach November, unfortunately meant that the official underwriting statements had to be revised as quickly as possible, so the brokerage firms could start to sell off their risky inventory.

On Friday evening, David Ruder's chief of corporation finance, Linda Quinn, stepped into his office and handed him the revised documentation. Surprised to see it so soon, Ruder took the document, looked for the new terms—and smiled.

In neat block letters, Quinn herself had written out, by hand, the lengthy new section disclosing the new terms of the deal.

Ruder approved the document, marveling that a market almost brought to its knees by high-technology trading was righting itself partly on the strength of a corporate document produced much as it would have been in the early days of the stock exchange.

21

PLACING BLAME, DODGING REALITY

A war of words had broken out in what was supposed to be a peace pipe breakfast in John Phelan's private dining room at the New York Stock Exchange on Thursday, November 5, 1987.

Phelan's dark Irish temper was a match for the redheaded fury of Tom Donovan, the president of the Chicago Board of Trade, and the two men were spitting insults at each other. Bill Brodsky, the Chicago Merc's president, and Bob Birnbaum, his counterpart at the NYSE and a longtime friend, were dismayed, and tried to defuse the escalating argument.

Donovan's scorn for the NYSE's performance during the crash was fierce and bitter: *What do you mean you stayed open? Maybe the air-conditioning was on! But you were not actually trading on that Tuesday! We were—we never closed! And the Merc closed only because you lied about being ready to shut down. Our guys did their jobs and your guys didn't!*

Leo Melamed respected John Phelan, and he would not have said all that to Phelan's face while sitting there eating Phelan's food. But he agreed with much of Donovan's complaint. Melamed had recently told a friendly lawmaker that "stockbrokers are looking for a scapegoat" for the failings of their own market. As the Chicago market leaders saw it,

Phelan's claim that all the NYSE specialists had performed heroically under fire simply wasn't true. And they were right; it wasn't.

Melamed's own mantra became "our markets performed flawlessly during the crash." Of course, that wasn't true, either.

The NYSE's frequent, prolonged trading halts in dozens of index-related stocks had certainly created excruciating problems in the S&P 500 pits and index options pits in Chicago. Some specialists, perhaps as many as 30 percent of them, had dumped stock when they should have been buying and had posted erratic opening prices. Various computer systems and order printers at the NYSE had been overwhelmed by the extraordinary volume. Phelan's ban on program trades via the DOT system had backfired in both markets.

As for Chicago, the Merc's eleventh-hour cash crisis on Tuesday morning had been exacerbated by software glitches and communication breakdowns, and rumors of its troubles certainly added to the spreading panic. The city's options market had been battered to a standstill, and its chief clearing firm had come within an inch of a calamitous failure. At least a quarter of the spooz pit traders had melted away during the crisis. And however the decision was rationalized later, the entire S&P 500 futures pit had been shut down for forty-nine minutes.

What is hard to understand is why anyone expected perfect performance during a period when dozens of gigantic investors were generating a tsunami of sell orders at a pace that bordered on wholesale panic and on a scale that dwarfed the capacity of any market to absorb them. Neither New York nor Chicago had been built to deal with an institutional selling stampede of that magnitude. Indeed, most people in both markets had persuaded themselves that it could never happen, that Phelan's warnings of a meltdown were groundless.

Still, the "flawless" performance of the Merc became as much an article of faith in the legends of the crash as John Phelan's steadfast refusal even to consider shutting down the Big Board.

As insults were hurled back and forth in public, the long-standing Chicago–New York rivalry had become an overheated reactor, and this breakfast was supposed to be a step toward cooling it down. It wasn't working out that way.

"Listen," said Karsten "Cash" Mahlmann, the Board of Trade's chairman, "it's in nobody's interest to be throwing hand grenades at each other. We're got to pull together."

Melamed agreed. This kind of public acrimony was "bad for the industry." It was time to dial back the rhetoric.

Despite the evident flaws in the stock market's performance, Phelan, with his genial, reassuring manner and top-notch public relations staff, was proving adept at shaping the post-crash headlines about the NYSE. And despite the shortcomings in the futures markets, the men from Chicago were articulate and aggressive; they had a lot of hearts and minds in their pocket, too, thanks to their generous political contributions and their powerful allies in the White House. It was the ideal recipe for a stalemate, which is what both sides, and the nation, would ultimately get.

To the relief of everyone at the breakfast, the meeting was portrayed in the press as "constructive in opening up a dialogue," despite getting "acrimonious at times." The officials had agreed at least to try to present "a more united front as debate about new market regulations commences."

AS A CONGRESSMAN had memorably observed after the Penn Square Bank collapse in 1982, regulators were supposed to be gifted with foresight, but congressional committees were in the hindsight business. And by November 1987, that business was booming.

Closed-door hearings were held at the end of October; public ones would be held for the next several months. Various "blue-ribbon" postmortem studies were under way: Leo Melamed had put four notable Chicago economists on his investigative team. David Ruder had put Rick Ketchum in charge of the SEC's mammoth investigation. The CFTC didn't wait for a full-dress study; it released its first preliminary report on the Monday after the raucous NYSE breakfast, insisting there was no evidence yet that futures market trading was responsible for the crash.

Of all the reports in the pipeline, the most prestigious, and potentially the most influential, would be the one from the Brady commission, appointed by President Reagan just days after Black Monday and led by a Republican who had spent his life on Wall Street.

Nicholas F. Brady was a man whose fourth-generation wealth and Ivy League pedigree had long enabled him to speak his mind without worrying too much about the consequences. He had been a success at the old-line firm of Dillon, Read and Company, and had overseen two earlier U.S. government commissions. A close friend of both Vice President George Bush and Secretary of the Treasury Jim Baker, he was an able and well-connected choice to lead the new commission.

To fill out the tribunal, Brady recruited two corporate executives and two institutional investors, but he needed a hands-on staff director who could help him meet the White House's tight sixty-day deadline.

One of Brady's partners at Dillon, Read mentioned Robert R. Glauber, a bespectacled young finance professor at the Harvard Business School who had once pitched an investment fund to the firm. The fund had been a flop, but Brady did remember its razor-sharp founder. He asked his secretary to find Bob Glauber.

Glauber was found and hired. He then recruited his Harvard Business School colleague David W. Mullins Jr. as his associate director, and quickly arranged his life so that he could spend the next two months working almost around the clock for Nick Brady. Early in November, his tiny team moved out of a modest office at Brady's firm and into a vast space on the eleventh floor of the New York Fed, offered to Brady by his friend Jerry Corrigan. Within four days, the Fed's operations staff had created temporary cubicles and installed phones, desks, chairs, and computers. Brady, Glauber, and Mullins mined their address books to recruit free labor from top Wall Street firms and elite university faculties.

Some of President Reagan's White House staffers were opposed to any kind of new market regulation in response to the crash; behind the scenes, they quietly ridiculed the commission as "the Brady Bunch," a reference to a lightweight television show from the early 1970s. Some suggested that the White House just ignore whatever recommendations the panel produced. "There are several other investigations going on," one aide noted. "If we don't draw too much attention to the Brady Commission it may just get lost in the shuffle."

The commission staff, which quickly grew to more than fifty people, cast a broad net. They interviewed Hayne Leland, visited Leo Melamed and his team at the Chicago Merc, and got a critical assessment of the NYSE's performance from Gordon Binns at GM's pension fund. They investigated index arbitrage. They interviewed NYSE specialists, other exchange officials, academic theorists, institutional investors, and regulators. They analyzed the global sweep of the crash. They demanded, and finally got, the cumbersome reels of computer tape that contained the NYSE's trading data for Black Monday and the day after. They then pulled strings to borrow the computing power needed to analyze them.

GIVEN THE PRESSURES on the futures markets, where post-crash trading volume had declined sharply, it is not surprising that the CFTC bowed at last to Chicago's persistent demand that it crack down on the swaps and other futures-like products that the big banks and Wall Street dealers were trading privately, instead of on futures exchanges. These private trades had long been draining away business that otherwise would have put money in Chicago's pocket and liquidity into Chicago's markets; memories of Black Monday made both those losses harder to swallow.

The commission acted on December 11, a week after the White House nominated a deregulatory advocate, Wendy Gramm, the wife of Senator Phil Gramm of Texas, to head the CFTC. Unfortunately, the proposed rules the agency published in the *Federal Register* were murky and confusing. The new rules might render a host of over-the-counter swaps illegal unless they were traded on a futures exchange, but it wasn't clear whether these derivatives would be banned outright, or simply had to get case-by-case exemptions.

The regulatory filing kicked off a storm within the community of bankers and brokers, who saw swaps as a huge source of profit—one they could not afford to lose in the wake of Black Monday. They complained fiercely to their regulators. At a time when Washington was paying lip service to the need for regulatory cooperation, a major schism was opening up under the CFTC.

FRIDAY, JANUARY 8, 1988, was hardly an ideal day for the Brady task force to deliver its report in person to the president of the United States.

A blizzard had swept into Washington, with snowdrifts of nearly a foot. More than 340,000 federal workers had been sent home early. The airline shuttles from Washington to New York were delayed, and then canceled.

Staff director Bob Glauber and his team had lived on pizza and Chinese food and worked through nights, weekends, and holidays—but they had met their deadline. When their report emerged from the Government Printing Office, it was an impressive 350-page volume bearing the presidential seal on a shiny blue cover. Squads of messengers, bundled against the bitter cold, delivered copies of it to largely deserted legislative offices on Capitol Hill, newspaper bureaus with early deadlines because of the weather, and television stations wholly preoccupied by the storm.

It scarcely mattered. The previous day's edition of the *Wall Street Journal* had carried a leaked and inaccurate account of the report's recommendations. That morning's edition of the *New York Times* had a front-page story in which unnamed administration sources detailed (and, in some cases, distorted) the report's findings and played down the task force's meeting with the president. "The approach at this point is simply going to be to thank the task force for its efforts and be careful not to seem like we are endorsing it," one administration source said.

A call to the White House produced two weather-worthy vehicles capable of getting the Brady team through the snowdrifts on Pennsylvania Avenue. At the White House, after a brief wait, they were ushered into the Oval Office, where President Reagan and Vice President Bush, along with Fed chairman Alan Greenspan and a handful of White House aides, awaited them.

The setting was a warm contrast to the wintry scene outside—and to the chilly reception the task force's report had already gotten in the press. A bright red flowering plant sat on the butler's tray table between two pale gold velvet sofas, and a cheery fire flickered behind the brass fender of the tall fireplace.

The president invited Brady to take one of the two white damask armchairs in front of the fire, and he settled into the other. The task force members and its two top staffers sat on the sofas, with Bush and the other officials in wooden side chairs near the president's desk. Reagan commended the task force's splendid work "under severe time constraints" and said the report was "a significant contribution to our understanding of the events of mid-October." Photographers came and went. Brady chatted with the president. Bush warmly shook hands all around. After less than twenty minutes, they all stood to go.

About 3:30 p.m., as most of the Brady team's members were returning to their hotel, prices on the New York Stock Exchange started to plummet sharply. By the closing bell, despite no explanatory news anyone could see, the Dow had shed 140.58 points, almost 7 percent of its value, with most of the decline coming in the final thirty minutes of trading. The decline was the second-largest point decline since Black Monday, which meant, of course, that it was the third-largest decline in history.

The arc of the day's decline was familiar to the Brady task force team, who saw it as further evidence of how the titans and their new trading toys were affecting the nation's markets. At least they had this comfort: the unflattering leaks about their report on Wednesday had spared them any accusations that they had caused Friday's nosedive.

The key conclusion of the task force, as Brady explained to reporters after his Oval Office visit, was that technology and financial innovation had welded once-separate markets into a single marketplace, but government, the financial industry, and academia had failed to see what had happened and adapt to it.

"To a large extent, the October break can be traced to the failure of different market segments to act as one," he said.

This unified market needed to figure out in advance how clearinghouse payments and margin issues would be handled, and how and when trading would be halted, he said. A single agency should be responsible for harmonizing those "critical regulatory issues," and the commission had nominated the Federal Reserve for this task, as it was the regulator with the broadest view of the overall financial system.

The achievement of the Brady task force cannot be overstated, even though its proposals were dead on arrival in that election year. Its report offered Washington and Main Street a chance, finally, to see the emerging financial markets the way Wall Street did: as one vast global structure with many rooms but no doors.

That structure housed a small family of giant investors: pension funds, endowments, aggressive speculators, mutual funds, hedge funds, and in-house traders at major brokerage firms and banks. Every hour of the day, these giants hurtled from room to room at breakneck speed. In one room, they traded stocks; in other rooms, they traded foreign currencies, government bonds, stock index futures, and index options. Their hectic trading was based on similar computer-guided strategies, and sometimes, a lot of them wanted to leave or enter the same room at the same moment.

If they did that—indeed, every time they did that—their stampede dramatically shook the market. If that tremor was sufficiently frightening to small investors and big lenders, as it had been in October 1987, it could create a crisis that could threaten the entire financial system.

While Washington insiders picked apart the Brady Report to see whose turf was threatened and who was being blamed, a few observers realized what was truly noteworthy in the report's findings: that a relatively small number of enormously large investors had played an extraordinarily significant role in driving the market's decline.

"The idea that less than 10 large financial institutions could bring the financial system to its knees ... is a terrifying prospect," noted one analysis. It was even more remarkable that the brilliant people guiding those giant institutions did not realize that the markets—no, this single market—simply could not function if they all decided, at roughly the same time, to do the same thing with hundreds of billions of dollars.

The Brady Report wasn't about market prices; it was about market power—unprecedented market power, capable of derailing the financial engines of the country, and of any country. All that was required was for a significant portion of the world's biggest and wealthiest investors to move in the same direction at the same time.

The challenge was to build a market structure that could deal with this new reality, to weave America's haphazard regulatory agencies into a single safety net and then somehow temper the power of the forces that could rip it apart. And that was going to require more respectful cooperation than Washington regulators were displaying.

ALAN GREENSPAN HAD zero interest in taking on the duties outlined in the Brady Report, and the White House had even less interest in pushing the report's reform proposals in Congress. But with the market still bucking and lurching in early 1988, it wasn't politically feasible to do nothing. In March, Reagan created the President's Working Group on Financial Markets, to be comprised of the Fed chairman, the CFTC chairman, the SEC chairman, and a top Treasury official. The panel's first task was to decide whether any reforms were actually needed in response to Black Monday—a graceless slap at the Brady task force—and if so, what they were. Its defenders did note that it could also provide the coordination that the Brady Report, and numerous other official studies, had recommended.

However, the President's Working Group was neither a happy family nor an effective market monitor. Greenspan, far more focused on his duties as a central banker, paid little attention to it. The new CFTC chairman, Wendy Gramm, was a far more ideological and determined deregulator than her predecessor. That tended to irritate SEC chairman David Ruder, who was growing increasingly convinced that markets needed more supervision, not less. Bank regulators at the Treasury, beset by the rapid deterioration of the savings and loan industry, had little time for wholesale market reform.

In early February 1988, Ruder had helped bring Leo Melamed and John Phelan together with CFTC officials to discuss ways they could coordinate "circuit breakers" to halt trading in both markets when prices had moved up or down to an extreme degree. A plan for coordinated trading halts would be put in place on the NYSE and the Chicago Merc later that summer, but no one was sure it would actually help.

This eggshell-thin collegiality among the working group's members nearly cracked over the CFTC's bid to regulate swaps and other over-the-counter derivatives, an effort that was more responsive to the Brady Report than anything the report itself proposed. The swaps market, valued at hundreds of billions of dollars, was the very definition of concentrated financial power reaching across regulatory borders. Unlike the futures exchanges and the options market, the swaps market had no central clearinghouse to reduce the risk of a domino chain of failures. If a major swaps player defaulted, the SEC and the bank regulators would have trouble even identifying who else was at risk.

In short, although swaps had not played a key role on Black Monday—

beyond the liquidity they had drained away from the futures pits—the overall financial system would be safer if swaps and other hybrid derivatives had to be traded on a regulated futures exchange. A titanic market force would be pulled out of the shadows and into the sunlight—as portfolio insurance might have been, in wiser times.

Wendy Gramm acknowledged that the "law is quite explicit that futures are to be sold on an exchange." Still, she hedged: "We know there is a certain amount of regulatory uncertainty, so we're trying to put some thoughts out on the table and get reaction."

The reaction to the CFTC's thoughts, due on April 11, was intensely negative. The harshest rebuttals came from Gramm's fellow regulators. A top Treasury aide, George D. Gould, the chairman of the President's Working Group, warned that the CFTC's swaps proposal would "seriously inhibit the efficient operation of financial markets." The comptroller of the currency complained that the proposal "amounts to an unnecessary interference with banking activities and their regulation" by his office.

The SEC's response was exceptionally fierce. It complained that the proposed rule would have a "chilling effect" on financial innovation, and it accused the CFTC of an "unjustified attempt to expand its jurisdiction."

These arguments echoed those being made by the nation's top bankers. This was not a retail market, they said, and professional investors could look out for themselves—a laughable assertion after Black Monday. They warned that the enormous swaps market could move offshore, and they complained about a "power grab" by the CFTC that would destroy that "much-needed" market. Privately, they whispered about the CFTC's minuscule budget and unimpressive track record during the crash.

Perhaps the most brazen argument from other regulators was that the CFTC had not consulted them before publishing its proposed swaps rule in December, "a departure from the regulatory doctrine developed in the wake of the market crash—a doctrine that holds that there must be coordination among various agencies in the market system." Unfortunately, the only thing the various agencies seemed capable of coordinating was the preservation of the dysfunctional status quo.

Ultimately, with its influence weakened by Black Monday and the regulatory squabbling that followed, the CFTC backed off from this effort, creating an exemption for hybrids that put virtually all of the swaps market beyond the reach of regulation. These unregulated derivatives would play a major role in several subsequent financial crises, most devastatingly in 2008, when hidden swaps losses threatened the survival of a major insurance giant and the investment banks to which it owed billions of dollars.

ON WEDNESDAY, MAY 4, 1988, Hayne Leland flew to Los Angeles, arriving late in the evening. He planned to meet up with John O'Brien in the lobby of the Biltmore Hotel.

Their consulting business had shrunk by 80 percent in the aftermath of the market crash—only $10 billion in assets were now covered by portfolio insurance, compared to $50 billion in August 1987. Some clients acknowledged that LOR's hedging strategy had mitigated their losses, but it had also pulled them out of the market before they could benefit from the subsequent erratic rallies.

The publicity, of course, had been dreadful. Portfolio insurance had become a media punching bag. O'Brien and Leland had gamely talked to reporters, with O'Brien calmly explaining that their strategy had always assumed markets would function normally—which they clearly had not done on Black Monday and the days following. You cannot hedge in markets where you cannot trade, he told the *Los Angeles Times*.

Mark Rubinstein was not part of those early conversations. After the crash, he experienced what he later regarded as "clinical depression." One account reported that "he could not rid himself of the fear that the weakening of the American markets could tempt the Soviet Union to [pose] a challenge to the United States akin to the one that had provoked the Cuban missile crisis, and nuclear war might ensue." He quickly shook off the worst of his irrational alarms, but there was no disputing how traumatic Black Monday had been for him, and for his partners.

Beyond the attacks in the media, he and Leland were facing friendly fire, too, as some prominent academics indicted portfolio insurance as a menace. No less a monument than Harry Markowitz, a legendary financial theorist, had said, "I believe that a significant cause—if not the prime cause—for the precipitous fall in prices on October 19 was portfolio insurance." Others in the academic community were still debating and studying the issue.

One of them was Leland himself. He was at work on a new paper that tested the hypothesis that the markets overreacted to portfolio insurance because they simply had not known what was coming. Was it possible that "sunshine trading" could have ameliorated the effect of portfolio insurance during the October crisis? Leland believed it was not only possible but likely.

Such thoughts may have been in his mind as he made his way to the Biltmore. But what he saw as he neared his destination drove every thought from his head. The First Interstate Tower was wearing a belt of fire.

Leland's taxi could not get near the scene, which was clogged with dozens of fire trucks and emergency vehicles, as sheets of glass and burning debris crashed into the surrounding streets. Flames were shooting from the shattered windows of the thirteenth floor, where LOR had its offices and kept its trading records.

It took until 2 a.m. for firefighters to extinguish the blaze, whose advance they finally halted on the sixteenth floor of the sixty-two-story building.

By the time Leland and O'Brien met at the hotel, O'Brien had confirmed that their staffers were all safe. Leland had always insisted that one of the firm's young computer analysts take the computer tapes home with him every night. The LOR partners were immensely relieved to learn that he had indeed done so that Wednesday night.

O'Brien soon found modest office space in a nearby building and leased a computer; the firm recovered sufficiently to resume its fight for survival. Even the First Interstate building would ultimately be repaired and reoccupied.

It would not be quite as easy to repair the intellectual foundations on which so many modern market theories and deregulatory initiatives had been built, but it would happen.

The "rational market hypothesis" had been attracting an increasing amount of academic skepticism, and Black Monday encouraged its critics. They "felt vindicated by the crash," according to one account. After all, if it had been rational to sell stocks so precipitously on October 16 and 19, how could it have been rational to buy them back on October 20 and 21, and then sell them almost down to the Black Monday levels on October 26? And what was the rational explanation for the crazy roller-coaster ride of January 23, 1987, or the last-minute nosedive on January 8, 1988?

Defenders of the hypothesis did not stand down so quickly, however. They found ways to explain Black Monday that did not violate their theories, with some even suggesting that the free fall that day simply proved how rapidly an efficient market processed new information—although there was a good bit of disagreement about what that new information had been. The theory that markets rationally, efficiently, and continuously weave new information into market prices would remain a touchstone in some academic and financial circles for years after the crash.

And the corollary concept, the notion that government regulators simply muck up that rational and efficient market, and should therefore leave it alone, lives on, hale and hearty, to this day.

IN THE SUMMER of 1988, SEC chairman David Ruder rebelled against the reluctant regulators on the President's Working Group and carried his own set of market reforms to Congress, but without success. In reality, his proposals did not address the big things that had gone wrong on Black Monday; it was impossible to forbid giant institutions from all selling at the same time.

Still, Ruder knew better than most how narrowly the financial system had escaped disaster. He considered the noontime hours of Tuesday, October 20, 1987, as the most memorable of his SEC tenure, a moment when "the nation's securities market came close to collapse, with potentially catastrophic consequences."

And some of those dangers arose because regulators were ill-informed about one another's turf and overly protective of their own. Quick communication had been difficult, and sometimes impossible. No one could see the whole market at once; no one could identify the worst fires and make sure they were put out. Some potential flash points, including the swaps markets, the options pricing services, the overseas traders, and the bankers making loan decisions that affected U.S. financial giants, could barely be seen at all.

These were complaints that Paul Volcker would have understood; they echoed arguments that Jim Stone had made a half-dozen years earlier. They were reflected in the Brady Report's account of the crash itself. And they would remain true for future financial crises, for decades to come.

However, 1988 was an election year. In August, Nick Brady was named by President Reagan as secretary of the treasury after Jim Baker resigned to run his friend George H. W. Bush's presidential campaign. Soon Brady would be knee-deep in the savings and loan crisis, which gave him little time for the reforms his own commission had recommended. As the stock market gradually and fitfully recovered, any sense of urgency in Congress evaporated.

In September 1988, David Ruder's enforcement staff filed a landmark civil complaint against Drexel Burnham and its star executive, Michael Milken. As Drexel negotiated a settlement with the SEC and the Justice Department, it turned to former SEC chairman John Shad, asking him to serve as the firm's new independent chairman as it desperately tried to rebuild its business.

CHICAGO WOULD NEED to rebuild, too.

In January 1989, Leo Melamed was determined to enjoy the five-day pageantry surrounding the inauguration of George H. W. Bush. Chicago had pumped hundreds of thousands of dollars into the successful Bush campaign, and many futures market executives were in Washington for the celebration.

On Wednesday evening, January 18, as the president-elect and his wife were lighting an Olympic-style flame at the Lincoln Memorial, FBI agents were fanning out across Chicago and its suburbs, delivering subpoenas to dozens of traders at the Merc and the Chicago Board of Trade. Soon after midnight, copies of the *Chicago Tribune* were being delivered; its front page was dominated by news of a sweeping federal investigation of corrupt trading practices in the commodity pits.

According to the *Tribune*, federal agents had gone undercover and allegedly had observed traders cutting side deals at the expense of customers, prearranging trades to benefit one another, and making a mockery of the audit trail the exchanges were supposed to maintain.

The Merc and the Board of Trade had their work cut out for them, and the job of mopping up after this corruption probe would take years.

The CFTC, too, would be damaged by the scandal. Initially, news accounts portrayed the agency as being "out of the loop" in the investigation. In fact, the CFTC had not been as out of touch as reported—its enforcement chief had cooperated with the FBI from the beginning, as had a key staffer in Chicago. But, according to the most complete account of the investigation, neither of Wendy Gramm's predecessors had known about the long-running investigation, and Gramm herself did not learn about it until a week before the subpoenas were served.

The CFTC's stature among its fellow regulators faded with each new revelation from Chicago.

Surprisingly, no one questioned whether the scandal's revelations about the flawed audit trail in Chicago cast doubt on the reliability of the trade data used in the various studies exonerating the futures markets after Black Monday. The crash seemed too distant to be relevant to the hot new scandal.

In reality, the carnage from the crash had still not been repaired by January 1989. The S&P 500 index would not regain its pre-crash peak until July 1989, fully six hundred days after Black Monday. If you bought stocks in August 1987, your portfolio did not move back into the black for almost two years. By every measure, the markets were still languishing a year after the crash. Despite those facts, though, the myth of a "crash without consequences" was already taking shape.

PRESIDENT GEORGE H. W. BUSH was cheerfully sworn in as president of the United States on Friday, January 20, 1989, and Ronald Reagan made his departure from the White House.

In his televised farewell to the nation a little over a week earlier, Reagan had urged Americans to cherish an understanding of their nation's history, to study it in detail and learn its lessons.

"If we forget what we did," the president said, "we won't know who we are."

EPILOGUE

Unfortunately, we cannot simply turn the page on the crash of 1987, because we are still living in the world revealed to us on Black Monday.

The people who confronted that crisis had not faced an apocalyptic market disaster since 1929. Today, anyone of working age in America has lived through a number of baffling market malfunctions, four extremely disruptive market crises, and one acute five-alarm meltdown: the devastating financial crisis that climaxed in September 2008 with the bankruptcy of Lehman Brothers. In the aftermath of that collapse, the nation endured the worst hard times since the Great Depression.

Two months after Lehman's fall, with markets still shaking, the chairman of the SEC told a congressional panel that "coordination among regulators, which is so important, is enormously difficult in the current Balkanized regulatory system." His warning was seconded by a former Treasury secretary, who said, "We have a fractured regulatory system, one in which no single regulator has a clear view, a 360-degree view, of the risks inherent in the system. We need to change that."

We didn't change that—indeed, neither man even mentioned that the Brady Commission had offered exactly the same diagnosis after the 1987 crash. Instead, all the major mutations that were central elements of the Black Monday crisis have become even more deeply embedded in Wall Street's genetic code:

- Computer-driven trading has accelerated, as the human middle-men of 1987 have been replaced by the circuitry of electronic markets.
- Armies of titan investors, whose scale and speed shocked regulators in 1987, have grown exponentially larger, faster, and more powerful, ultimately measuring the race to market in nanoseconds and wielding global portfolios worth trillions of dollars.
- Fragmented and feuding regulatory agencies continue to defend their political turf, aided by rigidly ideological lawmakers on the right and the left. As they squabble, the unregulated financial derivatives of the 1980s have mutated and spread around the world, and the arcane investing strategies that hastened the march to Black Monday have become even more obscure.

The crash of '87 proved beyond argument that pragmatism is the only ideology that can deal with a large-scale modern financial panic. The crisis should have produced a more flexible, better-coordinated regulatory framework, but it didn't—not even after its bitter lessons were reinforced by the 2008 meltdown. Even the most obvious policy lesson from 1987—that is, do not let a linchpin firm collapse in the middle of a panic—was ignored in 2008, when regulators allowed Lehman Brothers to fail, even though the markets were already nervous and on a hair trigger. Panic spread around the globe, essential markets froze up, and only extraordinarily creative intervention prevented the kind of fuse-blowing meltdown feared by the frantic regulators of 1987.

In response to the 2008 crisis, Congress actually has made it more difficult for regulators of the future to attempt a pragmatic, ad hoc rescue of the financial system. It has passed laws that greatly restrict the use of what were derisively called "bailouts," and it has added new agencies, with rigidly defined missions, to an already crowded and poorly coordinated lineup, burdening all of them with rules that defy reality and common sense.

THE FRONT-LINE VETERANS of the road to Black Monday followed their own paths and drew their own lessons.

Former SEC chairman John Shad, who watched the 1987 market crash from the U.S. embassy in the Netherlands, died in 1994, at the age of seventy-one. His legacy includes a $30 million gift he made in March 1987 to help support a program in ethics at the Harvard Business School.

John Phelan, the NYSE chairman, retired in 1990. When he died in 2012, at the age of eighty-one, his leadership on Black Monday was hailed as "his shining hour." His lieutenant during the crash, Robert J. Birnbaum, left the exchange in March 1988 and spent the rest of his career at a New York law firm.

Leo Melamed and Bill Brodsky remained pillars of the Chicago derivatives markets for decades. As of this writing, the eighty-four-year-old Melamed still occupied a handsome suite in the tower looming over the Merc trading floor. But that trading floor was largely deserted; the Merc had absorbed the Chicago Board of Trade in 2007, and both futures markets became almost entirely electronic. Brodsky left the Merc a decade after Black Monday to become chairman and chief executive of the Chicago Board Options Exchange. In 1997 he tapped his long-time friend Bob Birnbaum for the CBOE's board of directors.

After leaving the Fed, Paul Volcker worked for a time at the Wall Street investment firm Wolfensohn and Company but devoted most of his time to other forms of public service—notably as the head of a mul-tinational panel that mediated Holocaust-era claims on Swiss banks. In 2009 he returned to Washington as a special adviser to help President Barack Obama deal with the wreckage left by the 2008 crisis.

His former troubleshooter, Jerry Corrigan, worked tirelessly in the years after Black Monday to strengthen the global network of financial clearinghouses. In 1994 he joined Goldman Sachs, where he continued to press for greater transparency for potentially dangerous derivatives. He retired from the firm in 2016.

When David Ruder stepped down from the SEC chairmanship in 1989, he returned to the law faculty at Northwestern, where he continued to teach securities law, and serve on multiple regulatory task forces and market advisory committees, for more than twenty-five years.

As for the CFTC leaders: Phil Johnson continued to write and advise clients on derivatives law, eventually settling outside Jacksonville, Florida. Susan Phillips served from 1991 to 1998 as a member of the Federal Reserve Board and then returned to academia. Jim Stone returned to Boston and had a long career as an insurance executive. In 2016 he published a book titled *Five Easy Theses: Commonsense Solutions to America's Greatest Economic Challenges.* The dust jacket carries a complimentary quote from Paul Volcker.

After forty years at General Motors, pension manager Gordon Binns retired in July 1994; by then, his staff was overseeing $55 billion in investments. He returned to his native Richmond, where he served for four years as the chief investment adviser to Virginia's public pension fund. He died in 2002 at the age of seventy-two, leaving behind a trove of vintage travel guides that entirely filled the three-bedroom apartment he rented to house them. Roland Machold remained at the helm of the New Jersey Division of Investment until 1998; during his tenure, New Jersey's pension fund was routinely ranked as one of the top-performing state pension plans in the country.

In the aftermath of Black Monday, Hayne Leland, Mark Rubinstein, and John O'Brien tried to launch another new financial product: the "SuperTrust," a complicated forerunner to the now-popular exchange-traded funds. They enlisted a selling syndicate that included all the top Wall Street firms, but they met daunting and costly regulatory delays— perhaps because their idea was novel and complex, or perhaps because they were the people responsible for the "much-maligned" portfolio insurance. As the years passed and the legal obstacles piled up, other competitive products were developed and Wall Street's interest in the SuperTrust concept waned.

The little consulting firm waned with it, but the three LOR partners remained friends and allies for decades. John O'Brien became an adjunct professor at Berkeley, where Hayne Leland and Mark Rubinstein continued to teach, lead path-breaking research, and win awards. Leland retired in 2008, and Rubinstein followed his friend into retirement four years later.

Steve Wunsch, LOR's ally in the fight for sunshine trading, put his idea to work in 1990 by launching the Arizona Stock Exchange, a computer-driven "single-price" auction market that could match up big buyers and big sellers electronically, but it failed to attract enough institutional trading volume to survive.

Perhaps none of the first-line responders to the 1987 crash had more influence over the way financial markets have evolved than Alan Greenspan, who remained chairman of the Federal Reserve until January 2006 and was repeatedly credited with masterful management of the nation's economy. In 1998 he was described by *Time* magazine as belonging, along with Treasury secretary Robert Rubin and his deputy, Lawrence Summers, to "the most powerful economic triangle in Washington," in a cover story that dubbed the trio "The Committee to Save the World."

But during his tenure, the Fed also favored a more laissez-faire approach to financial regulation and failed to assert its power to curb predatory subprime lending, sowing the seeds for the reckless practices that helped trigger the 2008 crash. His confidence that Wall Street could be trusted to act prudently was an enormous mistake, he later acknowledged. He decided, on reflection, that the forecasting models on which he had long relied simply did not give enough weight to raw human nature—to "fear and euphoria," risk aversion, herd behavior, and a host of other market-moving emotions.

WHERE DOES THIS leave us today, thirty years after Black Monday? Exactly where we were then: in a storm-tossed lifeboat in which all the passengers are shackled together with the obnoxious crew members who carelessly steered our ship into the storm. Imagine, if you can, that the angry passengers vote to toss the crew members overboard to punish them for their folly. That's the current plan for dealing with a future crisis in the American financial system.

The excuse for this insanity is that keeping the reckless crew in the lifeboat would be an undeserved "bailout." This is a recipe for national and personal ruin—unless the shackles are first struck off. And no one has devised a remotely realistic plan for doing that, since it would involve a degree of federal intervention in private enterprise that seems politically unlikely—or a degree of market self-discipline that would be historically unprecedented.

When a market merely falls, it "recovers" by rising again to its previous price levels. And that certainly happened after 1987—though not nearly as quickly or as painlessly as Black Monday's mythology claims.

But when a market falls apart, because of dangerous levels of stress and unseen and unprecedented shocks, it should "recover" by rebuilding itself so that it can withstand those shocks and stresses in the future. And that certainly did not happen after 1987.

It still hasn't happened—and unless we finally learn the right lessons from Black Monday, it never will happen.

The crash of '87 revealed the iron link between market regulation and market structure. Policing a labyrinth at night is vastly harder than supervising an open field in the daylight. Allowing a market to become a dark and opaque maze ensures that it cannot be adequately supervised by anyone, even the giant investors who trade there.

Yet that is precisely what happened on a global scale after 1987. Left to shape its own future, Wall Street created profit-driven electronic markets catering to its richest and most powerful customers; today's corporate-owned exchanges barely even pay lip service to the notion that they serve anyone but their own shareholders. A host of "dark pools" (private "members-only" computer networks) now handle a substantial amount of the world's institutional trading activity. Individual investors have become not only irrelevant but virtually invisible in the regulatory conversation. In recent years, even the individual investors' surrogates, mutual funds and pension funds, are being drowned out by the demands of an immense army of high-speed traders and algorithm-wielding speculators, all trying to squeeze drops of profit from an increasingly volatile, robot-driven market.

At every step, the justification for this radical transformation has been that it has reduced trading costs—as if saving a fraction of a penny on a trade makes up for the immeasurable social damage done by structural instability on a global scale.

Those pennies, of course, came out of the pockets of the specialists at the New York Stock Exchange and the traders in the spooz pits in Chicago. Their personal battles to survive the catastrophe of 1987 were victories in a losing war. Today, the New York Stock Exchange has disappeared into a giant global conglomerate, taking with it the last memory of a deep and liquid central marketplace. Other stock exchanges, in the United States and abroad, have followed suit. Small wonder that today's fragmented public market is usually the last place any sensible entrepreneur would turn to raise capital for a new venture—which was once the fundamental reason for the market's existence.

The policy makers in Washington and the titan players on Wall Street thought the lesson of Black Monday was that the market's machinery was too slow, too small, too parochial, too hamstrung by antique rules and traditions. They set out to fix that, to repeal the technical and legal limitations on the markets.

But that is not the lesson of 1987. The actual lesson is that human beings do not cope well in a crisis when speed, complexity, secrecy, and fear all batter our emotions at the same time. We panic—or, most of us do. We are not the cool, rational investors postulated in academic theories, and we never will be.

There simply is no way to repeal the limits imposed on the market by human nature and all the messy emotional baggage that being human entails.

The road from Black Monday could have led to a different outcome, to broader, deeper, and more coherent markets operated for the public good, with technology applied in ways that foster stability, liquidity, and transparency. Instead, it led us here—to a global market that is a fragile machine with a million moving parts but few levers to govern its size or its speed.

Imagine a delicate but powerful sports car hurtling through a labyrinth in the dark. What could possibly go wrong?

NOTES

PROLOGUE

2   exceeded only during the historic crash of 1929: A few market history sources
     show that the Dow Jones Industrial Average declined 24.4 percent on Decem-
     ber 12, 1914, but that "crash" was a trick of backdated arithmetic and never
     actually happened. In October 1916, Dow Jones replaced its original 12-stock
     index with a new 20-stock index. Then Dow Jones statisticians revised the his-
     torical records to show how the new index would have performed going back
     to December 12, 1914. The new index's value on that date, if it had been in use,
     would have been 54 points. That was 24.4 percent lower than the previous day's
     reported value for the old Dow index, 71.42 points. (Some records show a
     20.5 percent drop on December 14, 1914, based on slightly different day-to-day
     comparisons.) In the real world, the Dow index actually in use in 1914 climbed
     4.4 percent on Saturday, December 12, and rose another 3 percent on Monday,
     December 14. See *The Dow Jones Averages 1885–1970* (New York: Dow Jones
     & Company, 1972). That is why the *New York Times* did not report an epic
     crash on either of those two dates in 1914, but instead noted on December 15,
     1914, that the stock market had rallied.

3   Black Monday and the 2008 crisis sound so much alike: This point was made,
     spontaneously, in interviews with numerous veterans of both crises, includ-
     ing E. Gerald Corrigan, former president of the Federal Reserve Bank of New
     York; Stanley Shopkorn, former head of equity trading for Solomon Brothers;
     Nicholas F. Brady, former secretary of the treasury and chairman of the
     Brady Commission, which examined the 1987 crash; Richard G. Ketchum,
     former director of market regulation at the SEC and chairman of the Finan-
     cial Industry Regulatory Agency (FINRA), the self-regulatory agency for Wall

Street; David S. Ruder, former chairman of the SEC, and several other high-placed Wall Street executives and regulators who spoke to the author in confidence.

1. SILVER THURSDAY

9   The Fed had almost no authority: The Federal Reserve did have the statutory responsibility for setting Wall Street margin levels, the percentage of stock holdings that could be financed on credit, but it had long delegated that chore to the SEC, as Wall Street's direct overseer.

9   a crisis in the silver market: *The Silver Crisis of 1980: A Report of the Staff of the U.S. Securities and Exchange Commission* (hereafter, *SEC Silver Report*), (Washington, DC: the U.S. Securities and Exchange Commission, October 1982), pp. 91–92. Henry Jacobs acknowledged to the SEC staff that his call was not entirely public-spirited: "I guess from a more parochial point of view we thought it would help put pressure on the COMEX," the Commodity Exchange in New York, which had refused Jacobs's demand that silver trading be halted because of an "extremely illiquid situation" developing in the market.

9   a pair of billionaire brothers in Texas: These and subsequent details about the silver crisis are drawn from *SEC Silver Report*, pp. 3–14; William Greider, *Secrets of the Temple: How the Federal Reserve Runs the Country* (New York: Touchstone, 1987), pp. 190–91; Stephen Fay, *Beyond Greed: How the Two Richest Families in the World, the Hunts of Texas and the House of Saud, Tried to Corner the Silver Market, How They Failed, Who Stopped Them, and Why It Could Happen Again* (New York: Viking Press, 1982), pp. 206–7, 209–10; and transcripts of various congressional hearings, especially "Silver Prices and the Adequacy of Federal Actions in the Marketplace, 1979–80" (hereafter "Rosenthal Hearings"), Hearings Before a Subcommittee of the Committee on Government Operations, 96th Congress, 2nd Sess., March 31, 1980.

10   the last thing Volcker needed: Interview with Paul A. Volcker, August 6, 2015, (hereafter "Volcker interview").

10   had reached out to Harold Williams: Harold M. Williams, a lawyer by training, headed up several major corporations in the 1960s before becoming dean of the UCLA Graduate School of Management in 1970; he was appointed to the SEC in 1977, and after stepping down in 1981, he ran the Getty Foundation in Los Angeles.

10   Williams then hurried back: Steve Lohr, "Silver's Plunge Jolts Hunts' Empire and Brings Turmoil to Wall Street," *New York Times*, March 28, 1980, p. 1.

10   Both headed for the Fed's headquarters: Rosenthal Hearings.

11   published as a prescient book: James M. Stone, *One Way for Wall Street: A View of the Future of the Securities Industry* (Boston: Little, Brown and Co., 1975). As he saw it (pp. 8–9): "The worst of Wall Street's long-term illnesses is technologically rooted. For over a century now, the New York Stock Exchange has conducted the auction process and generated paper work in an essentially unchanged manner. The entire system rests on the foundations of oral commands, physical paper flows, and good faith between participants . . . [With] the

back office nightmare . . . must eventually go the exchange floor, the specialist system, and half of the securities community employment roles."

11   at odds with his more laissez-faire CFTC colleagues: There were some anony-mous complaints in the press about his management style and "abrasive per-sonality," which are unintentionally revealing about the strangely casual agency culture he inherited from former chairman William Bagley. See Jerry W. Markham, *The History of Commodity Futures Trading and Its Regulation* (New York: Praeger, 1987), pp. 119, 267n8, 267n9, crediting nationally syndi-cated columnist Jack Anderson with reporting (in a column published in the *Oklahoma City Journal*, August 22, 1979) that Stone "made unannounced visits to various staff offices, then ordered that all posters, commercial calen-dars and pin-ups be taken down. He also dismantled the private bar that Bagley had installed in the Chairman's office." In the same notes, Markham attri-butes to journalist John Edwards ("Profile: James Stone: Chairman with a Sense of Stern Purpose," *London Financial Times*, January 16, 1981) a report that Stone "refused to have social contacts with the industry and required the CFTC staff to address him formally as "Commissioner" or "Dr. Stone." That courtesy was routine at other federal agencies.

11   dismissed him as a "little twerp": Chicago Board of Trade Archives, Part One, University of Illinois at Chicago Library (hereafter "CBOT Archives"); see III.1397.3, Folder 3/13, labeled "Executive Committee Meeting, November 6, 1980."

11   he could barely get support for approving the minutes: This is apparent from numerous reports filed by the Washington lawyers who monitored the CFTC's public meetings for the Chicago Board of Trade. For a memo in which the board's lawyers in Washington reported that Stone was "essentially isolated," see III.1397, Folder 12/13, "CFTC Meetings—Speculative Limits (May 13, 1980)," CBOT Archives.

11   Volcker got Stone on the phone: Rosenthal Hearings, pp. 10–11.

11   "I can't tell you that": Volcker interview, confirmed by other confidential inter-views.

11   he "did not react very well" to Stone's refusal: Ibid.

11   did not have the authority to comply: Ironically, the restrictions on releasing information were added to the law after the same Hunt brothers complained to Congress about a previous CFTC chairman, who had publicly disclosed the family's alarmingly large (and, in the CFTC's view, illegal) stake in the soybean market in 1977, in the course of disciplinary action against the Hunts. Volcker would have been even angrier if he'd been able to foresee that, at an emergency meeting early the next morning, the CFTC's majority would decide "that the CFTC should not reveal confidential information about market positions to the Treasury, the Federal Reserve, or the Securities and Exchange Commis-sion," according to Fay, *Beyond Greed*, p. 213. Fay notes: "It was a startling decision and the reasoning behind it was curious. 'They've exhibited great ignorance about the markets. We know the significance of the number of contracts in jeopardy, but I don't think they do,' said one commissioner."

11   the silver crisis was a danger to the financial system: Indeed, Stone was one of

the first Washington regulators to openly warn about what would later be called "systemic risk," the risk that a crisis in one market would spread and undermine the entire system. See his letter, dated September 30, 1981, to Representative Ed Jones [hereafter "Stone Letter to Jones"] on the silver crisis:

> No one can be sure what would have happened if the price of silver had continued to fall. Would a major brokerage firm have failed? Would a bank have followed it down? Would ever-accelerating margin calls from a variety of markets [have] taken on a momentum of their own? Could we have seen a dissolution of trust and credit or a full scale [sic] panic? There is no way to be sure. I am certain, however, that no automatic safety net exists to allow confidence that a similar event in the future would not have these impacts.

This excerpt is from "Joint Agency Reports on Silver Markets" (hereafter "Joint Silver Report Hearing"), Hearing Before the Subcommittee on Conservation, Credit, and Rural Development of the House Agriculture Committee, 97th Congress, 1st Sess., October 1, 1981, p. 132. It is difficult to credit today how lurid his warnings sounded to the commodity market and its insular regulators in 1980. See Markham, *The History of Commodity Futures Trading and Its Regulation*, p. 267: "The industry was particularly *incensed by his exaggerated charge* [emphasis added], which followed the events in the silver futures markets in 1980, that commodity futures speculation threatened the financial structure of the entire U.S. economy." Contrast that with the *SEC Silver Report*'s 1982 assessment, at pp. 3–4: "For six days late in March 1980 it appeared to government officials, Wall Street and the public at large that a default by a single family on its obligations in the plummeting silver market might seriously disrupt the U.S. financial system . . . Although financial catastrophe was ultimately averted, the silver crisis provides a valuable lesson in the fragility and interdependence of the financial structure, and challenges both the private sector and government to respond." A similar rejection of interconnected fault lines would emerge from some precincts of Chicago after Black Monday.

11   Aides shuttled in and out, working the telephones: Rosenthal Hearings, pp. 35–37.

11   the ad hoc group had finally established: Ibid.

12   At $20 an ounce: See Stone Letter to Jones, p. 120.

12   Through it all, the Hunts kept buying: *SEC Silver Report*, pp. 3–9.

12   After that date, prices dropped sharply: Inarguably, this sharp price decline was partly the result of higher margins imposed on trading in silver futures on the Chicago Board of Trade and the Commodity Exchange in New York, known as the COMEX, and partly the product of spreading rumors about the difficulties facing the Hunts.

12   their lenders were pressing for more collateral: *SEC Silver Report*, pp. 3–9.

12   they were unable to pay anything more: Ibid.

12   That figure, which turned out to be an understatement, was so staggering: Fay, *Beyond Greed*, p. 219.

12   the stock market had a wild day: Lohr, "Silver's Plunge Jolts Hunts' Empire";
        and Laszlo Birinyi Jr. and Jeffrey Rubin, *Market Cycles III: An Anecdotal
        History of Bull and Bear Markets, 1961–2000* (Westport, CT: Birinyi Associ-
        ates, 2004). SEC chairman Harold Williams would later say that the face-to-
        face communication on the exchange floor stemmed potential panic, which
        increased his confidence in the exchange. See Judith Miller, "Regulators View
        Silver Aftermath," *New York Times*, March 31, 1980, p. D1.

13   prices have to drop sharply before buyers will bid: If there were no bids from
        buyers at all, even after a reasonable decline in prices, the NYSE typically
        would halt trading until a price could be found at which shares could be traded
        again.

13   shares can be sold only at increasingly lower prices: An old adage holds that a
        stock market crash is like yelling "Fire!" in a crowded theater—except the
        audience cannot jump up and run for the exits until someone else agrees to
        buy their seats. It's not a perfect analogy, but it does underscore the duality of
        stock trading—there is a buyer for every seller, although perhaps at sharply
        higher or lower prices than prevailed just seconds earlier.

13   the frenzied response to President John F. Kennedy's assassination: Birinyi
        and Rubin, *Market Cycles III*, p. 198.

13   no one really knew where all the fault lines ran: Fay, *Beyond Greed*, p. 218.
        Only a remarkably silly accounting convention allowed the brokerage firms
        exposed to the Hunts, especially Bache, to keep operating through the crisis.
        With the acquiescence of regulators, firms routinely valued silver in any form
        at the price quoted for silver futures contracts, not the price set in the cash
        market where the silver bullion would have to be sold. The exchanges that
        traded silver futures contracts had imposed daily "limit-down" restrictions;
        once the price had fallen by a certain amount, trading was halted unless there
        was a higher bid. So, the latest silver futures price was often considerably
        higher than the cash market price. If firms had valued their collateral at the
        more realistic cash price, all but three of the Hunt brothers' ten trading
        accounts with major firms would have been in the red on Silver Thursday. See
        SEC Silver Report, pp. 10–11.

13   The Fed chairman looked at the widening cracks in the nation's financial foun-
        dation: These impressions are supported by the transcripts of the Federal
        Open Market Committee meetings and conference calls for the months
        between October 1979 and April 1980, available at: http://www.federalreserve
        .gov/monetarypolicy/fomchistorical1980.htm.

13   a new $1.1 billion loan for the Hunt brothers: Volcker interview; Greider,
        Secrets of the Temple, p. 190; *SEC Silver Report*, p. 14.

14   he was as angry as Volcker had been: Rosenthal Hearings, p. 1.

14   Rosenthal demanded to know if there had been sufficient coordination: Ibid., p. 4.

14   The worrisome response: Maybe not: Ibid., pp. 10–11, 42–43.

14   "to do that only upon subpoena": Ibid., p. 9, emphasis added.

15   "deal with that as a separate issue": Ibid.

15   "There are certainly differences in philosophy," Stone answered: Ibid., p. 32.

15   posed any threat to the nation's financial health: Ibid., pp. 164–65, 167–69.

Commissioner Reed Dunn testified that he personally had been very concerned about the silver situation, but acknowledged that the CFTC had not taken any action beyond prodding the exchanges. Commissioners Robert L. Martin and David G. Gartner testified to their firm belief that (contrary to the views of Stone, the Fed, the SEC, and the Treasury) the Hunts' mounting silver hoard and their failure to meet their massive margin calls had never posed a systemic risk to the nation's financial system. "No one other than large speculators and their unwary brokers got hurt . . . The market, in a very real sense, cured itself," Commissioner Gartner said. Commissioner Martin agreed, saying, "I think our conduct in this case was the responsible thing to have done."

16   they had long resented any meddling: See John V. Rainbolt II, "Regulating the Grain Gambler and His Successors: Symposium on Commodity Futures Regulation," *Hofstra Law Review* 6, no. 1 (Fall 1977), p. 15. "Historically, commodities exchanges have resisted federal regulation . . . most exchanges continued to view themselves as champions of self-regulation and free enterprise." Mr. Rainbolt was one of the founding commissioners of the CFTC.

16   how a wheat farmer could use futures: This example is drawn from the Commodity Futures Trading Commission's website, accessed August 2016: http://www.cftc.gov/consumerprotection/educationcenter/economicpurpose.

17   closing out his position at a profit: The cereal company's situation is a mirror image. The company locked in a price of $3.50 a bushel for wheat that, at harvest, it could buy for just $3.00 a bushel. The loss on the futures contract raises the company's cost to $3.50 per bushel, which is the price the company originally wanted to lock in. If prices had risen to $4.00 a bushel, the cereal company would have taken delivery of the wheat at a savings of 50 cents per bushel.

17   blessing hedgers but denouncing speculators: Rainbolt, "Regulating the Grain Gambler and His Successors," pp. 5–9.

19   "a futures contract for people who buy lottery tickets": III.1398, Folder 9/9, CBOT Archives. While the folder is labeled "CFTC Meetings April 1980," these quotes are from a memo dated March 25, 1980, to CBOT president Robert Wilmouth from Rebecca J. Reid, reporting on "the CFTC meeting." Attached to that memo is a copy of a commission agenda dated March 24, 1980. Similar memos in the archives were sent to the CBOT promptly after each CFTC meeting, so it seems reasonable to conclude that the memo, from which this exchange is drawn, is an account of the CFTC meeting on March 24.

19   without having to put up as much cash: The ability to control a large stake in any market with a small amount of your own cash is called "leverage," and stock index futures contracts gave speculators much more leverage than the stock market did. In the stock market, a speculator who wanted to control a 100,000-share stake in the stocks that make up the Dow Jones index could borrow no more than half the money required to buy those shares and had to pay cash for the rest, a payment called "margin." In the futures market, a stock index futures contract representing the same stock market stake cost much less, and a speculator could post a much smaller percentage of that price up front.

2. BRIGHT IDEAS

20   Reagan strode toward the exchange entrance: Matthew L. Wald, "Reagan Tour of City Draws Cheers, Some Boos and Forecast of Victory," *New York Times*, March 20, 1980, p. B13.

20   He had first met Reagan: David A. Vise and Steve Coll, *Eagle on the Street: Based on the Pulitzer Prize–Winning Account of the SEC's Battle with Wall Street* (New York: Charles Scribner's Sons, 1991), p. 22.

20   had recently lost a bitter battle: Leonard Stone, "John S. R. Shad Dies at 71: S.E.C. Chairman in the 80s," *New York Times*, July 9, 1994, p. 11.

20   had earned law degrees together: Vise and Coll, *Eagle on the Street*, pp. 23–26.

20   Shad agreed to head up his New York campaign: Ibid.

21   waiters who relished stock tips: Michael Walsh, "Insiders," *Life* (Collector's Edition), "The Big Board: An Inside Look at the New York Stock Exchange in Its Bicentennial Year," Spring 1992, p. 48.

21   mumbled the obligatory introduction: Vise and Coll, *Eagle on the Street*, p. 23.

21   Shad arranged for Reagan to meet: Ibid.

21   Shad could hope for some role: Ibid., p. 24.

21   Volcker's progress against inflation: The story of Volcker's inflation battle is told by David E. Lindsey, Athanasios Orphanides, and Robert H. Rasche, in "The Reform of October 1979: How It Happened and Why," Federal Reserve Board, Washington, DC, 2005, p. 10, and more fully in William L. Silber, *Volcker: The Triumph of Persistence* (New York: Bloomsbury Press, 2012), pp. 125–90. The following passage relies on both sources.

21   Volcker believed the corrosive effect of inflation: Volcker opened his inflation war with a blitzkrieg attack. On Saturday, October 6, 1979, ahead of Monday's Columbus Day market holiday, the Federal Reserve announced a radical shift in its approach to monetary policy. It would no longer attempt to control the price of money, the interest rate on loans. It would leave that task to the marketplace. Instead, it would focus on controlling the supply of money, by requiring banks to keep more cash locked up in their vaults in the form of capital reserves. The law of supply and demand did the rest, and interest rates began to rise toward historic levels.

21   The Fed let interest rates rise sharply: "Transcript of Press Conference with Paul A. Volcker, Chairman, Board of Governors of the Federal Reserve System," October 6, 1979, available on the Federal Reserve Bank of St. Louis online archive of Fed records at https://fraser.stlouisfed.org/scribd/?item_id =8201&filepath=/files/docs/historical/volcker/Volcker_19791006.pdf.

22   attacks on government bureaucracy: Although Carter had already initiated the process of deregulating the nation's airlines, its commercial trucking industry, and parts of its banking industry, Reagan was deeply committed to dismantling and defunding much more of the federal bureaucracy.

22   "a 'hit list' much like the FBI's": Letter to Mr. Douglas S. Winn, Liaison for Small Business, Republican National Committee, from Thomas F. Renk, August 14, 1980, Securities and Exchange Commission Historical Society

website (hereafter "SECHS website"), used with permission from www
.sechistorical.org, http://3197d6d14b5f19f2f440-5e13d29c4c016cf96cbbfd197c
579b45.r81.cf1.rackcdn.com/collection/papers/1980/1980_0814_HitList.pdf.

23   stumbled upon the Chicago Mercantile Exchange: David Greising and Laurie
        Morse, *Brokers, Bagmen, and Moles: Fraud and Corruption in the Chicago
        Futures Markets* (New York: John Wiley and Sons, 1991), p. 9.

23   Melamed was drawn to the vital energy: Leo Melamed with Bob Tamarkin,
        Escape to the Futures (New York: John Wiley and Sons, 1996), pp. 3–87, where
        details of Melamed's early life are also described.

23   when he began trading full-time: Greising and Morse, *Brokers, Bagmen, and
        Moles*, pp. 88–89.

23   futures on shrimp, turkeys, and apples: Hal Weitzman, "Chicago's Decade of
        Innovation: 1972–1982," *Focus* (World Federation of Exchanges), no. 218,
        April 2011, p. 3.

23   In 1972, Melamed led the Merc: Author's interviews with William J. Brodsky
        on June 3, 2015 (hereafter "First Brodsky interview"), and with Leo Melamed
        on January 15, 2015 (hereafter "First Melamed interview").

23   he first got the idea in the late 1960s: Melamed, *Escape to the Futures*, p. 170.

24   by the economist Milton Friedman, an expert on monetary policy: Milton
        Friedman and Rose D. Friedman, *Two Lucky People: A Memoir* (Chicago: Uni-
        versity of Chicago Press, 1991), p. 351.

24   developing futures contracts pegged to foreign currencies: Melamed, *Escape
        to the Futures*, pp. 171–72.

24   International Commercial Exchange (ICE): CFTC Industry Filings website, as
        of January 27, 2016. Founded by members of the New York Produce Exchange,
        this now-extinct exchange should not be confused with the Intercontinental
        Exchange, known as the ICE, a modern electronic trading conglomerate whose
        holdings include the New York Stock Exchange and a host of commodity
        exchanges.

24   had already developed foreign currency futures: "Exchange to Deal in Money
        Futures," *New York Times*, April 14, 1970, p. 71. See also Ellen Lambert, *The
        Futures: The Rise of the Speculator and the Origins of the World's Biggest Mar-
        kets* (New York: Basic Books, 2011), pp. 75–76, and Richard L. Sandor, *Good
        Derivatives: A Story of Financial and Environmental Innovation* (Hoboken, NJ:
        John Wiley and Sons, 2012), p. 162. The new product was the brainchild of an
        almost forgotten pioneer, ICE chairman Murray Borowitz, who also conceived
        but never launched the first stock index futures contract. Sandor and Lam-
        bert describe his role. Both authors credit details about Borowitz to William
        Faloon, *Market Maker: A Sesquicentennial Look at the Chicago Board of Trade*
        (Chicago: Board of Trade of the City of Chicago, 1998).

24   flew to New York to take a look: Bob Tamarkin, *The Merc: The Emergence of a
        Global Financial Powerhouse* (New York: HarperCollins, 1993), p. 183.

24   There was no trading," Melamed reported: Melamed, *Escape to the Futures*,
        p. 174.

24   too small to be of interest to large-scale hedgers: Melamed's insight was cor-

rect. The struggling ICE closed its doors soon after Murray Borowitz's quiet death in February 1973.

24   a contract that commercial hedgers and speculators could easily use: Melamed, *Escape to the Futures*, p. 175. A key member of Nixon's Treasury team in this historic transition was a thirty-four-year-old undersecretary named Paul Volcker, whose work explaining the initiative to European central bankers and politicians thrust him, for the first time, into the financial news spotlight. See Silber, *Volcker*, pp. 85–95.

24   it had no clear jurisdiction over the new contracts: The law governing the CEA gave it jurisdiction over futures trading on an itemized list of agricultural products. Obviously, foreign currencies weren't itemized in the statute, so the CEA had no jurisdiction over them.

24   "there were a bunch of free market folks": Melamed, *Escape to the Futures*, p. 195. Melamed also reported (at p. 236) that he consulted with Alan Greenspan, then the chairman of President Ford's Council of Economic Advisers, during a subsequent Washington visit to promote Treasury bill futures in 1975, and got an enthusiastic endorsement from the future Federal Reserve chairman. "This meeting made him a friend, which he has remained throughout the years," Melamed writes. "Our friendship was of particular importance at the time of the 1987 stock market crash."

24   new international currency regime: Silber, *Volcker*, pp. 102–3.

25   after earning a doctorate in economics: Sandor, *Good Derivatives*, p. 17–18.

25   such as the daily prices on America's stock markets: Ibid.

26   mathematical ideas to guide investment strategies: The evolution of quantitative analysis from an academic specialty to a force in the modern market is ably told by Justin Fox, *The Myth of the Rational Market: A History of Risk, Reward, and Delusion on Wall Street* (New York: Harper Business, 2011); Peter Bernstein, *Capital Ideas: The Improbable Origins of Modern Wall Street* (Hoboken, NJ: John Wiley and Sons, 2005); David Leinweber, *Nerds on Wall Street: Math, Machines and Wired Markets* (Hoboken, NJ: John Wiley and Sons, 2009); Richard Bookstaber, *A Demon of Our Own Design: Markets, Hedge Funds, and the Perils of Financial Innovation* (Hoboken, NJ: John Wiley and Sons, 2007); Jeff Madrick, *Seven Bad Ideas: How Mainstream Economists Have Damaged America and the World* (New York: Alfred A. Knopf, 2014); Scott Patterson, *The Quants: How a New Breed of Math Whizzes Conquered Wall Street and Nearly Destroyed It* (New York: Crown Publishers, 2010); and of course, Roger Lowenstein's superlative *When Genius Failed: The Rise and Fall of Long-Term Capital Management* (New York: Random House, 2000).

26   a fully computerized stock market: This was Mark B. Garman, "Trading Floor/1: A Prototype of an Automated Securities Exchange," Working Paper No. 7, Research Program in Finance, Institute of Business and Economic Research, University of California at Berkeley, July 1972. On replacing the traders on the New York Stock Exchange with computers, see Nils H. Hakansson, Avraham Beja, and Jivendra Kale, "On the Feasibility of Automated Market

Making by a Programmed Specialist," Working Paper No. 106, Research Program in Finance, Institute of Business and Economic Research, University of California at Berkeley, October 1980. See also an even earlier paper by Beja and Hakansson, "From Orders to Trades: Some Alternative Market Mechanisms," Working Paper No. 56, Research Program in Finance, Institute of Business and Economic Research, University of California at Berkeley, January 1977.

26   a fully automated futures market: As noted, this was Richard L. Sandor. See "West Coast Looks to the Futures," by A Special Correspondent, *Financial Times*, June 25, 1970, np.

26   a faculty celebrity named Barr Rosenberg: A colorful and creative economist, Rosenberg could easily support a chapter of his own. After doing postgraduate work at the London School of Economics, Rosenberg returned home and joined the business school faculty at Berkeley, where he had done his undergraduate study. He brought with him a grant that paid for the computer time he needed to pursue his passion: developing a computer formula to show how various economic forces affected stock prices. By the early 1970s he was entering his corporate data into a bulky computer in the basement of his Berkeley home and designing software programs that played an endless series of what-if games: What if oil prices dropped by $10 a barrel? Based on history, what would that do to General Motors stock? What would it mean for Texaco's stock? By the late 1970s, Rosenberg's "quantitative models," which Wall Street nicknamed "Barr's Bionic Betas," had made him a multimillionaire and put him on the cover of *Institutional Investor* magazine, which featured a cheeky article by Chris Welles headlined "Who Is Barr Rosenberg? And What the Hell Is He Talking About?" (In finance, *beta* is defined as the measure of a stock's sensitivity to the movements of the overall market.) See Bernstein, *Capital Ideas*, pp. 256–68, 275, 280–82; and Fox, *The Myth of the Rational Market*, pp. 127, 138–40, 151, 224, and 326–27. After a long and influential career, he stunned the quantitative world by running afoul of the SEC by allegedly failing to disclose a software glitch that arose in one of his fund management programs. On September 22, 2011, the SEC announced that Rosenberg, without admitting or denying its allegations, had agreed to be barred from the securities industry and to pay $2.5 million to settle the case. (See "In the Matter of Barr M. Rosenberg," SEC Administrative Proceeding File No. 3–14559, September 22, 2011.) The incident cannot diminish his influence on the melding of academic finance theories and Wall Street practice.

26   an idea that, in a few years, would radically transform: This notion is usually connected with Princeton Professor Burton Malkiel's classic, *A Random Walk Down Wall Street*, first published in 1973. It had invaded the academic literature as early as 1960. See Edward F. Renshaw and Paul J. Feldstein, "The Case for an Unmanaged Investment Company," *Financial Analysts Journal* 16, no. 1 (January–February 1960), pp. 43–46. See also Michael J. Clowes, *The Money Flood: How Pension Funds Revolutionized Investing* (Hoboken, NJ: John Wiley and Sons, 2000), pp. 84–92 and 198–200; Kate Ancell, "The Origin of the First Index Fund," University of Chicago Booth School of Business, 2012,

http://www.crsp.com/files/SpringMagazine_IndexFund.pdf; and Fox, *The Myth of the Rational Market*, pp. 137–41.

27   that has had a greater impact on American markets: Indeed, Madrick, *Seven Bad Ideas*, nominates it as one of his "Seven Bad Ideas."

27   this innovative team was road-testing index funds: Bernstein, *Capital Ideas*, pp. 234–35; and Fox, *The Myth of the Rational Market*, p. 127.

27   measuring pension fund performance: Interview with Kelly Haughton, July 8, 2015. Haughton, a notable financial engineer who worked at WFIA in the late 1970s, had even closer ties to the finance professors at Berkeley: his young wife was the department's secretary, he frequented campus social events with Hayne Leland and his faculty colleagues, and occasionally a friend who worked for Barr Rosenberg invited him over to brew beer in Professor Rosenberg's basement.

28   why would they bother to gather that knowledge in the first place: Fox, *The Myth of the Rational Market*, p. 182. Economists Joseph Stiglitz and Sanford Grossman, both at Stanford in the mid-1970s, were especially trenchant in posing this puzzle. As they saw it, if market prices perfectly reflected any new information available, "those who spent resources to obtain it would receive no compensation" and would soon stop gathering new knowledge. Ergo, markets were not perfectly efficient, as the Chicago school's adherents insisted. But, Justin Fox noted, other scholars largely shrugged off their argument. "The overwhelming majority of research in finance in those days was no longer concerned with the question of whether markets were efficient. One just assumed that they were, and proceeded from there." The market's inefficient inability to distinguish "information-less" trades by portfolio insurers from those motivated by knowledge of negative news proved critical in the years before Black Monday.

28   Were human beings really the cool, rational investors envisioned: An excellent account of the development of this new "behavioral economics" can be found in Fox, *The Myth of the Rational Market*, especially on pp. 186–300. For deeper insights, see Daniel Kahneman, *Thinking, Fast and Slow* (New York: Farrar, Straus and Giroux, 2011); and Michael Lewis, *The Undoing Project: A Friendship That Changed Our Minds* (New York: W.W. Norton and Co., 2016).

28   visionary idea for an electronic futures market: Sandor, *Good Derivatives*, pp. 40–46. See also "West Coast Looks to the Futures," *Financial Times*, June 25, 1970, np.

28   Berkeley business school's first course on futures trading: Sandor, *Good Derivatives*, p. 50.

29   soon devised the world's second major financial futures contract: Ibid., p. 90.

29   desperately looking for a way to hedge: Ibid., p. 51.

29   One executive heard him out: Ibid., pp. 95–96.

29   the Commodity Futures Trading Commission, which had just opened its doors in Washington: Its first chairman was an avuncular California politician named William Bagley, who knew almost nothing about the futures market. He and his four fellow commissioners were appointed by President Gerald Ford, who had come very close to vetoing the statute that created the

commission in 1974, and had been extremely slow to make appointments to the new agency. See "10/23/74 HR13113 Commodity Futures Trading Commission Act of 1974 (1)," Box 10, White House Records Office: Legislation Case Files at the Gerald R. Ford Presidential Library, Grand Rapids, MI, pp. 1–12.

3. CHICAGO VS. NEW YORK

30   the chairman of the SEC at the time: Author interview with Harvey Pitt, February 2, 2016 (hereafter "Pitt interview"). Pitt, a future SEC general counsel and chairman who served as SEC chairman Ray Garrett Jr.'s chief staff assistant at the time, said Garrett talked with him about the White House call proposing that the SEC oversee the futures markets. According to Pitt, Garrett told the White House, "No, thank you. We have enough on our plate."

30   under the supervision of the congressional agriculture committees: William Robbins, "Commodity Bill Voted by House," *New York Times*, April 12, 1974, p. 43; Associated Press, "Commodity Giant Seeks Regulation: Cargill Urges Bigger Agency with SEC-like Powers," *New York Times*, September 19, 1973, p. 71; H. J. Maidenberg, "Commodity Option Deals Coming Under Scrutiny," *New York Times*, May 21, 1973, p. 51; H. J. Maidenberg, "Futures Trading Is Defended: Uhlmann, Head of Chicago Board, Denies Responsibility for Food Prices Rise," *New York Times*, September 26, 1973, p. 53.

30   gave the new agency exclusive jurisdiction: Author interviews with Philip Johnson, June 23–24, 2015 (hereafter "Johnson interviews").

31   Wheat was on the list, for example: Sandor, *Good Derivatives*, p. 100, and Markham, *The History of Commodity Futures Trading and Its Regulation*, p. 61.

31   but he felt that would have been "a red flag" to the SEC: Johnson interviews.

31   jurisdiction over the futures exchanges: Sandor, *Good Derivatives*, pp. 98–99 and note 5.

31   those contracts could be based on: Ibid., emphasis added.

31   unless Congress explicitly took such jurisdiction away: At the insistence of the Treasury, a provision was inserted that exempted from the new law "transactions in foreign currency, security warrants, security rights, resales of installment loan contracts, repurchase options, government securities or mortgages and mortgage purchase commitments unless such transactions involve the sale thereof for future delivery conducted on a board of trade" (Markham, *The History of Commodity Futures Trading and Its Regulation*, p. 67). For years, this was interpreted to mean that banks and other commercial institutions could enter into customized arrangements involving those items without being subject to regulation. Hence, a bank could enter into a contract to buy Treasury bills at some point in the future without falling under the act, but a standardized futures contract based on Treasury bills and traded on an exchange would be subject to regulation. This murky exclusion, combined with CFTC neglect, would ultimately contribute to putting vast amounts of over-the-counter derivatives beyond any regulatory oversight.

31   it had to beg Congress every few years: This "sunset" provision was unusual, and possibly unique, among federal regulatory agencies in the mid-1970s.

Philip Johnson, Reagan's first CFTC chairman, said he believed the sunset provision had made the CFTC especially vulnerable to political pressure throughout its life (Johnson interviews).

32   Pitt's message was firm and clear: Johnson interviews, confirmed in Pitt interview, although Pitt disputes his explicitly threatening a lawsuit. "I would only have itemized our options, and obviously one of our options was litigation," he said. "I would have *mentioned* it, but not threatened it."

33   Congress asked the General Accounting Office: The agency is now known as the Government Accountability Office.

33   was beset by weak management and high staff turnover: The Comptroller General, "Regulation of Commodity Futures Markets—What Needs to Be Done," GAO 1978 report (hereafter "GAO 1978 Report"), May 17, 1978, pp. i–iii. What is not explicit in the report, but is proudly detailed in Melamed, *Escape to the Futures*, p. 223, is how relentlessly Melamed and his CBOT counterparts worked to *capture* the young CFTC and shape it to their needs. As just a few examples, Melamed boasted of recruiting the CFTC's first executive director to work for him at a substantially higher salary, just nine months into her tenure; making an early "ally" of Commissioner and later Acting Chairman Gary L. Seevers and, when he left office, adding him to the Merc's paid board; and "persuading" the CFTC to appoint Mark Powers, a Merc executive, as its chief economist. "This appointment not only served as a stepping stone in Mark's career, *it was an insurance policy to keep the CFTC on track.* And this was only the beginning of a pipeline that would deliver talent from the futures industry to government . . . It took many talented staff people at the CFTC to produce the positive results achieved and, equally important, *to protect the futures market turf from poachers* at the SEC and other competitive forums" (pp. 222–23; emphasis added).

33   "lacking in the ability to enforce": GAO 1978 Report, p. iv. The SEC was in the midst of its own battle with fraudulent securities options trading, and had imposed a moratorium on that market pending better enforcement strategies. Interview with Richard G. Ketchum—Part I, April 17, 2008, "Oral Histories," SECHS website, used with permission from www.sechistorical.org, http://3197d6d14b5f19f2f440-5e13d29c4c016cf96cbbfd197c579b45.r81.cf1 .rackcdn.com/collection/oral-histories/ketchum_Part1_041708Transcript .pdf.

33   Congress ought to shift authority: GAO 1978 Report, pp. i–iii.

34   to urge the CFTC to impose a moratorium: "March T-Bill Shortage Gained Attention of Fed/Treasury Study of Financial Futures," *Securities Week*, April 2, 1979. This incident was one of two cited more generally in "A Study of the Effects on the Economy of Trading in Futures Options," submitted to the House Committee on Agriculture and the House Committee on Energy and Commerce; and to the Senate Committee on Agriculture, Nutrition, and Forestry and on Banking, by the Board of Governors of the Federal Reserve System, the Commodity Futures Trading Commission, and the Securities and Exchange Commission pursuant to Section 23(a) of the Commodity Exchange Act, as amended (hereafter "Joint Impact Study 1984"), December 1984, pp. VII-5 and VII-6.

34   on any additional contracts of that sort: Karen W. Arenson, "Chicago Exchanges Defy U.S. Request," *New York Times*, July 8, 1980, p. D4.

34   Archival documents show that the Merc and the Board of Trade: Letter to the CBOT board from Mahlon Frankhauser, Kirkland and Ellis, dated August 1, 1980, II.1378, Folder 17, CBOT Archives. The letter attached a letter from Volcker to Senator William Proxmire on the Senate Banking Committee, dated July 18, 1980 (hereafter "Volcker July 1980 letter"), updating him on the Fed's continuing study of financial futures, expressing concern about the amount of leverage available in the futures market, and urging limits on the size of the positions that speculators could build up in financial futures.

34   voted unanimously to ignore the CFTC's order: Karen W. Arenson, "Commodity Regulators Challenged," *New York Times*, July 12, 1980, p. 25.

35   Volcker found the whole episode "troubling": Volcker July 1980 letter. Volcker cited "the recent chain of events in which certain exchanges introduced new contracts in Treasury securities," and wrote, "Both the Federal Reserve and the Treasury were opposed to the introduction of these contracts and the CFTC, for its part, has attempted to bar trading in these new contracts. While this matter is still under judicial review and the outcome is not clear, the episode is troublesome. Indeed, at the very least, it suggests to me that it might be appropriate to firmly fix in the law authority whereby the Federal Reserve or the Treasury would have veto power over the introduction of any new futures contracts in Treasury securities and perhaps in foreign exchange as well. Similar consideration should be given to the potential interests of the government—including the SEC—with respect to the emerging markets for futures on equities and indices comprised of equity securities."

35   the boisterous approval from the crowd: No byline, "Futures Board: Day One," *New York Times*, August 8, 1980, p. D4.

36   Phelan had deep roots: Peter Grant, "John Phelan vs. Program Trading," *Investment Dealers' Digest*, March 2, 1987, p. 23.

36   the junior Phelan once observed: Floyd Norris, Profile of John Phelan, Associated Press, June 30, 1980 (hereafter "Norris, AP").

36   The senior John J. Phelan had been a proud and generous Irish Catholic: Unsigned obituary, "John J. Phelan Sr. Is Dead at 61; Head of Stock Exchange Firm," *New York Times*, June 14, 1966.

37   trading in about fifty stocks: Grant, "John Phelan vs. Program Trading."

37   proof of its good reputation: Robert J. Cole, "Big Board Implements Plan to Reward Specialists on Basis of Professionalism," *New York Times*, June 28, 1976, p. 41. The Phelan firm was one of eight that "came to mind," according to Cole, "when stockbrokers speak of professionalism on the floor of the New York Stock Exchange, a concept that means orderly pricing for the small investor." After several mergers, the firm was known at the time as Phelan, Silver, Vesce, Barry and Company.

37   "must be a better way to make money": Laurence Arnold, "John Phelan, Who Led NYSE in 1987 Stock Crash, Dies at 81," *Bloomberg News*, August 6, 2012; and Megan McDonough, "John J. Phelan Jr., Ex-Chairman of New York Stock Exchange, Dies at 81," *Washington Post*, August 8, 2012.

37   went to work for the family firm: McDonough, "John J. Phelan Jr., Ex-Chairman of New York Stock Exchange, Dies at 81," crediting the quote to *Institutional Investor* magazine.

37   as an active but unpaid vice chairman of the NYSE: Sharon R. King, "William M. Batten, Ex-Chief of Stock Exchange, Dies at 89," *New York Times*, January 27, 1999, p. A23; and William M. Batten, "National Market System Developments—Change at the Exchange," speech delivered to the Financial Analysts Federation's Twelfth Annual Investment Workshop at Dartmouth College, July 26, 1979.

38   a pencil-and-paper operation: John Brooks, *The Go-Go Years: The Drama and Crashing Finale of Wall Street's Bullish 60s* (New York: Weybright and Talley, 1973), pp. 182–205.

38   lit by the market rally that began in 1949: Birinyi Associates, *Bull Markets 1945–1991* (New York: Birinyi Associates, 1991), p. 3.

38   records were set every few weeks: Terry Robards, "Wall St. Asks: Can Crisis Happen Again? Most of Industry's Leaders Believe the Worst Is Over," *New York Times*, December 23, 1970, p. 35.

38   As the number of trades rose: The continued reliance on physical stock certificates was a significant element of the crisis, which would generate pressure that would ultimately result in the "paperless" stock portfolio of today. But many small investors resisted the idea of relying on an entry in an electronic ledger at a Wall Street clearinghouse as proof of their stock ownership, and the transition took many years.

38   One visitor behind the scenes reported: Robards, "Wall St. Asks: Can Crisis Happen Again?"

38   Hundreds of member firms were in danger: Alec Benn, *The Unseen Wall Street of 1969–1965—and Its Significance for Today* (Westport, CT: Quorum Book imprint of Greenwood Publishing Co., 2000), p. 29. Benn attributes this data to a 1984 oral history by Robert M. Bishop, a vice president of the exchange in charge of member firms, provided to him by Bishop. According to Benn, a number of similar oral histories about the 1960s and '70s had been compiled in the 1980s but were withheld from the public by NYSE management in the 1990s. He obtained two of them, including Bishop's, and cautioned, "The information in them differs in many respects from that in press releases, booklets, and books distributed by the New York Stock Exchange—and from books and articles based on those sources" (p. xiii). The existence of such discrepancies is a forceful argument for the release of those oral histories to scholars.

38   brokerage firms shut down: Ibid., pp. 23–41. See also Robards, "Wall St. Asks: Can Crisis Happen Again?"

39   even big firms with iconic names: Goodbody and Co., rescued by a merger with Merrill Lynch, and F. I. DuPont, Glore Forgan, bailed out with capital invested by H. Ross Perot, were two of the four largest retail firms in the country. Hayden, Stone, and Company, one of the largest retail firms, was saved by a merger into Cogan, Berlind, Weill, and Levitt—the "Weill" was Sanford Weill, who went on to become the architect of Citicorp; the "Levitt" was Arthur Levitt Jr., who became the longest-serving SEC chairman in the agency's

history, serving from 1992 to 2001. In January of 1971 the NYSE reported that it had "intervened in the affairs" of nearly two hundred brokerage firms, more than half the retail brokerage firms in the country, at an expected cost of more than $68 million. Terry Robards, "Failing Firms Cost Big Board $68-Million," *New York Times*, January 8, 1971, p. 39.

39   with its resulting customer losses: There was no safety net at the time for brokerage customer accounts; indeed, this crisis was the primary impetus for the creation of the Securities Investors Protection Corporation, a fund financed by Wall Street assessments, which protects customer accounts in the event of a brokerage firm bankruptcy. President Nixon signed the law creating the corporation on December 30, 1970, just hours before the bill would have been doomed by the expiration of that congressional term. See Benn, *The Unseen Wall Street of 1969–1965*, pp. 39–41. However, its charter barred it from aiding any firm already insolvent at the time of the charter's passage. That left a handful of large firms in the hands of the NYSE.

39   One committee member later recalled: Terry Robards, "Healer: Stanching a Wall St. Crisis," *New York Times*, January 24, 1971, sec. 3, p. 1. The committee member quoted was Felix Rohatyn, an Austrian-born partner at Lazard Frères. Five years later, Rohatyn would play a pivotal role in New York City's fiscal crisis as chairman of the Municipal Assistance Corporation, a private bond–issuing authority set up in 1975 as part of a rescue plan that ultimately involved short-term federal loans of $2.3 billion.

39   Tens of millions of dollars: Benn, *The Unseen Wall Street of 1969–1965*, pp. 86–89, 98–99.

39   the public had no idea how close to destruction: Ibid., p. xi.

39   his colleagues begged him to stay on: Karen W. Arenson, "They Wouldn't Let Him Go," *New York Times*, June 3, 1979, p. F7.

39   Washington became increasingly determined: That year, on the same day the 1929 trading volume record was broken, the Justice Department sent a sixty-seven-page white paper to the SEC, condemning the fixed commission structure at the NYSE as "price fixing" in violation of the Sherman Antitrust Act. The action came after a 1963 ruling by the U.S. Supreme Court that the exchange was not exempt from antitrust laws, as it had long contended. The white paper was the first serious volley in the regulatory war that would end with the elimination of fixed commissions on May 1, 1975. See Chris Welles, *The Last Days of the Club* (New York: Dutton, 1975), pp. 86–89.

40   lawyers with the Justice Department: Ibid.

40   said populist lawmakers suspicious of Wall Street: One of the hottest new trading firms in this new market was Bernard L. Madoff Investment Securities, whose well-respected owner would be unmasked in 2008 as the architect of the largest Ponzi scheme in history. See Diana B. Henriques, *The Wizard of Lies: Bernie Madoff and the Death of Trust* (New York: Times Books/Henry Holt, 2011), pp. 49–50.

40   The Big Board found few friends in Washington: In 1972, NYSE president James Needham initially argued that Wall Street's finances were too precarious to permit a change in commission rates, then offered to end fixed commissions

if regulators shut down the trading in Big Board stocks away from the exchange. His approach infuriated his board and baffled Washington. See "The Way It Was: An Oral History of Finance 1967–1987," by the editors of *Institutional Investor* magazine (New York: William Morrow and Co., 1988), pp. 304–5.

41   "Nobody wants to change anything": Grant, "John Phelan vs. Program Trading."

41   He had no intention of idly waiting: Karen W. Arenson, "New York's New Financial Markets," *New York Times*, November 16, 1980, p. 1.

41   beautifully crafted wooden trading posts: One of these lovely old trading posts, Post 15, was donated to the Harvard Business School, where it was closely examined by the author.

41   Phelan replaced these traditional posts: The installation process was an amazing feat: Workers assembled the new trading posts one at a time on elevated platforms in the soaring space below the trading floor's seventy-two-foot ceiling. When a new post was finished, workers would wait until the closing bell on Friday afternoon and then disconnect and cart away the old post before lowering the new one into place. It would be wired into the electrical system before the opening bell the following Monday. After fourteen successive Fridays, the new space-age posts were all in place—without a single interruption in trading. See James E. Buck, ed., *The New York Stock Exchange: The First 200 Years* (Essex, CT: Greenwich Publishing Group, 1992), pp. 212–13.

42   the increasingly competitive Nasdaq market: The Nasdaq, contrary to common wisdom, was not the nation's first "automated" exchange. That title probably belongs to Instinet, which opened for business in 1969, two years before Nasdaq. Nor was Nasdaq, as of 1980, even a fully automated exchange. Its computer system only displayed and updated dealers' offers to buy and sell; actual trades still had to be done over the phone by human beings. In 1980 the Cincinnati Stock Exchange closed its trading floor and shifted all its trading to a computer that was programmed to match orders, but it never attracted sufficient trading volume to be viable.

42   Nasdaq proclaimed itself: Eric J. Weiner, *What Goes Up: The Uncensored History of Modern Wall Street* (New York: Back Bay Books/Little Brown, 2005), pp. 187–98.

42   Nasdaq's traders were certain their market: Ibid.

42   "how you all make money in this venture": "Futures Board: Day One."

4. SHIFTING GEARS

44   a few rumbles of thunder: All weather descriptions are based on the Weather Underground historic archives, unless otherwise credited.

44   He planned to watch the election returns: Confidential interviews.

44   Massachusetts had landed in the Republican column: Gil Troy, *Morning in America: How Ronald Reagan Invented the 1980s* (Princeton, NJ: Princeton University Press, 2005), pp. 48–49, among several sources. Reagan's budget policies would steadily deepen the federal deficit in the march toward 1987. His own firm belief in "supply-side economics," which argued that tax cuts would

stimulate more than enough economic growth to pay for themselves, would steadily deepen, but it was not uniformly held among even his closest financial and economic advisers. See Sean Wilentz, *The Age of Reagan: A History of 1974–2008* (New York: Harper Perennial, 2009), pp. 140–41.

44   pending before the commission that he cared deeply about: Stone had testified the previous February, before a Senate agriculture subcommittee, about the tangled jurisdictional issues surrounding stock index futures, warning that congressional action might be needed to resolve disputes involving the Federal Reserve, the Treasury, and the SEC. At that hearing, according to one account, Stone said he was sympathetic with the points raised by the SEC and the Fed, although he felt Congress had given jurisdiction over all futures contracts to the CFTC. See III.1379, Folder 23/23, "Stock Index Futures 1980," Commodity News Service, February 21, 1980, CBOT Archives.

45   trimmed the regulatory burdens on small businesses: Jeff Gerth, "SEC Chief Is Inclined to Stay On," *New York Times*, November 17, 1980, D1.

45   unlikely the new president would leave a Carter appointee: Interview with Harold Williams, January 19, 2006, "Oral Histories," SECHS website, pp. 21–22, used with permission from www.sechistorical.org, http://3197d6d14b5f19f2f440 -5e13d29c4c016cf96cbbfd197c579b45.r81.cf1.rackcdn.com/collection/oral -histories/williamsH011906Transcript.pdf.

45   the Merc and the Chicago Board of Trade: In III.1397, Folder 6/13, labeled "Executive Committee Meeting December 2, 1980," are handwritten notes of a lengthy discussion of the "CFTC slot." See also III.1397, Folder 3/13, labeled "Executive Committee Meeting November 6, 1980," CBOT Archives, which contains handwritten notes of a meeting at the Mid-America Club two days after the election. The notes quote one director as cheering that they could "get little twirp [*sic*]—Stone." They also discussed how the election would affect the congressional committees on finance and agriculture.

45   "under Reagan we stand a chance to get the pick": Ibid.

45   one of the most lucrative: Vise and Coll, *Eagle on the Street*, p. 23.

45   and he was one of the firm's largest shareholders: Clyde H. Farnsworth, "Washington Watch; Battles Over Ex-Im Cuts," *New York Times*, February 2, 1981, p. D2.

45   Hutton's stock had hit a new high: The stock tables of the *New York Times*, November 4, 1980.

46   the last time it would do so: Alexander Hammer, "Dow Soars by 14.91 to 1,244.15," *New York Times*, November 7, 1984, p. D1.

46   By the final bell, a new record had been set: No byline, "Reagan's Landslide Sets Off Surge," *New York Times*, November 6, 1980, p. D16.

46   The exchange was coping well, too: Ibid.

46   was mailed out every Saturday: Ann Crittenden, "Granville Promotes Market-Turn Flair," *New York Times*, January 8, 1981, p. D6.

46   When Granville spoke, his subscribers not only listened: Christopher Drew, "Joseph E. Granville, Stock Market Predictor, Dies at 90," *New York Times*, September 18, 2013.

46   it encouraged investors to buy: Granville had issued an equally dramatic weekend "buy" recommendation months earlier, in April 1980; when the mar-

ket opened for Monday trading, the Dow surged up 30 points on heavy trading. See Jerome Baesel, George Shows, and Edward Thorp, "Can Joe Granville Time the Market?" *Journal of Portfolio Management* (Spring 1982), p. 5.

46   worked into the night making telephone calls: Kristin McMurran, "When Joe Granville Speaks, Small Wonder That the Market Yo-Yos and Tickers Fibrillate," *People*, April 6, 1981.

47   His message to those elite followers: Granville was a middling stock picker over the long run, but he was fair at calling overall market turns. According to Mark Hulbert, who tracked investment newsletters as the editor of *The Hulbert Financial Digest*, his calls only slightly underperformed a buy-and-hold index fund from 1980 to 2005. See Drew, "Joseph E. Granville, Stock Market Predictor, Dies at 90"; and Baesel, Shows, and Thorp, "Can Joe Granville Time the Market?"

47   The Dow ended down almost 24 points: Alexander R. Hammer, "Stocks Decline Sharply as Trading Soars to Record," *New York Times*, January 8, 1981, p. 1. An equivalent decline in 2016 would be more than 460 points.

47   if the Granville cult had included giant institutional investors: Ibid. The Granville groupies got the last laugh: a bear market had silently crept in at the end of November, and it would last for twenty months, accompanied for most of that time by a sharp, severe recession that finally doused the inflationary fire that Fed chairman Volcker had been fighting since November 1979.

47   he announced that the fifty-two Americans held in Iran: President Carter worked to free the hostages into the last hours of his presidency—indeed, he had not slept for two days prior to Reagan's inauguration. Iran accepted the deal on the morning of Inauguration Day, but refused to release the Americans while Carter was in office, so Reagan officially announced the happy news.

47   carried through to the inaugural balls that evening: Ronald Reagan, "Remarks at the Inaugural Balls," January 20, 1981, American Presidency Project website, at http://www.presidency.ucsb.edu/ws/?pid=43524. Although it was widely reported that the Reagans attended eight balls, the actual count was ten; they are enumerated in these archived remarks. The details about the First Lady's gown, which was loaned to her by designer James Galanos and later donated to the Smithsonian, are from Albin Krebs and Robert McG. Thomas, "Notes on People; Nancy Reagan Dress Becomes a Museum Piece," *New York Times*, November 5, 1981, p. C24.

47   they included a secretary of transportation: Ernest Holsendolph, "Reagan Designee Says He Supports Reductions in Aid for Mass Transit," *New York Times*, January 8, 1981, p. B15.

47   a secretary of the interior: Wilentz, *The Age of Reagan*, p. 140.

47   and a secretary of energy: Robert D. Hershey Jr., "Energy: James Burrows Edwards," *New York Times*, December 23, 1980, p. 13.

47   The new secretary of the Treasury: Regan recounted his recruitment in his memoir, *For the Record: From Wall Street to Washington* (New York: Harcourt Brace Jovanovich, 1988), pp. 139–41.

48   some of whom would be at the conference: There are speeches from the conference in the archives of the SEC Historical Society and the New York Stock

Exchange, and Harvey Pitt confirmed many of the details about the conference, which he attended.

48   Soon after he arrived, he learned: Author interview with David S. Ruder, December 27, 2016 (hereafter "Ruder interview December 2016.")

48   came to share their concerns: Interview with David S. Ruder, January 18, 2016 (hereafter "Ruder interview January 2016.")

48   The SEC transition team was urging: SEC Transition Team, "Final Report," December 22, 1980, p. I-5, SECHS website, used with permission from www.sechistorical.org, where the URL for the first of five parts is http:// 3197d6d14b5f19f2f440-5e13d29c4c016cf96cbbfd197c579b45.r81.cf1 .rackcdn.com/collection/papers/1980/1980_1222_SECTransition_1.pdf.

48   "the mission of the agency was still to be fully implemented": Ibid., p. I-6.

48   however, that mission would be different: Ibid., pp. I-4–5.

48   The report did acknowledge: Ibid., pp. I-9–10.

49   urged that Harold Williams be replaced as chairman: Ibid., p. VII-5.

49   "changes in senior staff": Ibid., p. VII-6.

49   He was worried about: Ruder interview December 2016.

49   consternation had spread through the Del Coronado: Ruder interview January 2016; Pitt interview; and a confidential letter from A. A. Sommer Jr. to the Honorable Edwin Meese III, dated January 29, 1981 (hereafter "Sommer/ Meese letter"), SECHS website, used with permission from www.sechistorical.org, http://3197d6d14b5f19f2f440-5e13d29c4c016cf96cbbfd197c579b45.r81 .cf1.rackcdn.com/collection/papers/1980/1981_0129_SommerMeeseT.pdf.

49   a distinguished securities lawyer and former SEC commissioner: In 1977 he gave a widely reported speech condemning the SEC for its crackdown on foreign bribery by U.S. corporations, which he said exceeded its statutory powers. See Eric Pace, "A.A. Sommer Jr., 77, Commissioner on the SEC in the 70s," *New York Times*, January 19, 2002.

49   former SEC commissioners and senior staffers of all political stripes: Sommer/ Meese letter, p. 1.

50   "can only have a devastating effect": Another letter of protest was sent to the White House by Senator William Proxmire, a well-known Wisconsin Democrat on the Senate Banking Committee, which was one of the SEC's overseers in Congress. The report "strikes at the heart of the SEC" and would reduce it "to a toothless tiger," the lawmaker wrote. He would "oppose with every means at my disposal" any SEC nominee who intended to implement the report's recommendations, he said. Letter to the president from William Proxmire, January 28, 1981, SECHS website, used with permission from www.sechistorical .org, http://3197d6d14b5f19f2f440-5e13d29c4c016cf96cbbfd197c579b45.r81 .cf1.rackcdn.com/collection/papers/1980/1981_0128_ReaganProxmireT.pdf.

50   senior staffers would inquire of one another: Confidential interview with a former senior SEC staffer.

50   Williams had submitted his letter of resignation: Letter from Harold M. Williams to President-elect Ronald R. Reagan, December 31, 1980, SECHS website, used with permission from www.sechistorical.org, http://3197d6d14b5f19f2f440

-5e13d29c4c016cf96cbbfd197c579b45.r81.cf1.rackcdn.com/collection/papers
/1980/1980_1231_WilliamsReaganT.pdf.

50   the nation's premier marketplace for options trading: The CBOE was frequently misidentified in news accounts and congressional hearings as the "Chicago Board of Options Exchange," which displays ignorance about its origins. It originally was an options exchange created by the Chicago Board of Trade—hence, it was the Chicago Board's options exchange. It later was spun off as an independent entity but kept the name, although it was no longer the Chicago Board's exchange at all.

50   Like a futures contract, an options contract allows: An option to buy something is a "call option," while an option to sell something is a "put option." In the market, these are typically referred to simply as "puts and calls." It helps to think of a call option as giving you the right to *call something in* from the market, which must sell it to you, while a put option allows you to *put something out* into the market, which must buy it from you.

50   In exchange for taking on that risky duty: Futures contracts impose obligations on both sides of the trade: the party that agreed to sell the commodity and the party that agreed to buy it. Options impose an obligation only on the seller of the option, not the buyer. Thus, for buyers, options are far less risky than futures—but that doesn't mean the options market is less risky, overall, than the futures market. Options sellers ("writers") face the same risks inherent in a futures contract, but the upside is limited to the premiums they collect when they sell ("write") the options.

51   Substitute Ginnie Mae mortgage certificates: Die-hard futures advocates insist that, if the CFTC had existed in 1973, the CBOE would have been put under its jurisdiction because of the similarities between futures and options. Of course, those similarities were also cited as a reason to put financial futures under the jurisdiction of the SEC, which was already regulating one financial derivatives market.

51   to argue that the SEC's action was illegal: The CBOT also argued that not even a CFTC-regulated exchange could legally trade the proposed GNMA option at that moment because the CFTC had imposed a moratorium on "commodity options" in 1977, and as the CBOT saw it, the GNMA option was a "commodity option."

51   until the matter could be sorted out: See *Board of Trade of the City of Chicago v. the SEC and CBOE* (hereafter "*CBOT v. SEC* ruling"), U.S. Court of Appeals for the Seventh Circuit, 677 F.2d 1137, No. 81–1660, March 24, 1982.

52   John Shad was the president's choice: It was widely, but wrongly, reported that Shad was the first Wall Street executive to be tapped to lead the SEC since FDR chose Joseph P. Kennedy as the SEC's first chairman in 1934. However, Kennedy (the father of President John F. Kennedy) had never led a Wall Street firm; he had merely been active in the 1920s as a Wall Street speculator. In fact, Shad was the first investment banker to serve as SEC chairman since President Truman chose the spectacularly unqualified Harry McDonald, a dairy farmer turned investment banker, for the position in 1949. See Joel Seligman, *The*

Transformation of Wall Street: A History of the Securities and Exchange Commission and Modern Corporate Finance, 3rd ed. (New York: Aspen Publishers, 2003), p. 243.

52   its choice for the CFTC chairman's post: Philip Johnson was originally named Philip Frederick Johnson, and was nominated and confirmed by the Senate as "Philip F. Johnson." A few weeks after his confirmation, he married a successful attorney named Laurie McBride, who was not inclined to change her professional name. In the spirit of gender equality, Johnson urged that each adopt the other's surname as a middle name. Thus, by the time he arrived at his new office at the CFTC, and for the rest of his career, Johnson's official name was "Philip McBride Johnson" (Johnson interviews).

52   Melamed and his colleagues had gotten their wish: H. J. Maidenberg, "Difficult Task Faces Chairman of C.F.T.C.," *New York Times*, June 15, 1981, p. D1.

52   "political appointees who knew nothing": Melamed, *Escape to the Futures*, p. 292.

52   he would ignore the controversial Reagan transition report: Office of Public Affairs, U.S. Securities and Exchange Commission, "Press Coffee with Chairman John S. R. Shad" (hereafter "Shad press coffee"), July 13, 1981, p. 7, SECHS website, used with permission from www.sechistorical.org, http://3197d6d14b5f19f2f440-5e13d29c4c016cf96cbbfd197c579b45.r81.cf1.rackcdn.com/collection/papers/1980/1981_0713_PressShadT.pdf.

52   The topic barely came up at his confirmation hearing: "Nomination of John S. R. Shad," Hearing Before the Senate Committee on Banking, Housing, and Urban Affairs, 97th Congress, 1st Sess., April 6, 1981, p. 11.

52   His answer no doubt reassured the SEC's legal staff: Ibid.

53   who delayed the vote on confirming him: Johnson interviews.

53   not as severely as many other federal programs were: Wilentz, *The Age of Reagan*, p. 141.

5. A DEAL IN D.C.

54   to arrange to have lunch with his counterpart: Johnson interviews.

54   On an afternoon in the early summer of 1981: There is conflicting evidence about when this meeting occurred. In his first week on the job, Johnson told a *New York Times* reporter that he would have his first meeting with Shad the week of June 15, 1981. (See Maidenberg, "Difficult Task Faces Chairman of C.F.T.C.") At a news conference on July 13, 1981, Shad told reporters that "there has been a meeting between Phil Johnson and myself." (See Shad press coffee, p. 3.) However, Vise and Coll, who did prodigious research but unfortunately do not supply source notes, put the luncheon, in *Eagle on the Street*, sometime in August. Phil Johnson remembered the luncheon as described by Vise and Coll, but could not clear up the confusion about when it occurred (Johnson interviews).

54   Both agreed with President Reagan: Vise and Coll, *Eagle on the Street*, p. 25.

54   both knew that they needed to craft a peace treaty: Johnson interviews.

55   "it would be desirable if we could do this quietly": Shad press coffee, pp. 3–4.

There is no transcript of this conversation of course, but Phil Johnson recalls that these statements, which Shad later used at a press conference to describe their conversation, accurately reflected what Shad said to him, so they have been inserted here.

55   persuade Shad to accept other CFTC-approved derivatives: Johnson interviews.

55   What Shad wanted was something called "cash settlement": Bragging rights are murky on the issue of cash settlement, at least in the American market. Richard Sandor asserts (in *Good Derivatives*, p. 162) that cash-settled futures contracts were in use since the dawn of futures trading in medieval Japan; he identified the first modern cash-settled contract as the Chicago Board of Trade's contract for iced chicken broilers, introduced in 1972, although cash settlement was optional for that contract. Leo Melamed claims that the Chicago Merc's Eurodollar contract, approved on December 8, 1981, was the first mandatory cash-settled contract in the United States. (See Melamed, *Escape to the Futures*, p. 293.) Phil Johnson argued that cash settlement was meaningless in the Eurodollar example since physical settlement and cash settlement would have amounted to the same thing: the exchange of dollars. Therefore, he gives the Kansas City Board of Trade credit for introducing the nation's first mandatory cash-settled contract, since the Value Line contract *could* have been settled on terms other than cash (Johnson interviews). In any case, the Sydney Futures Exchange, now part of the Australian Securities Exchange, traded a mandatory cash-settled futures contract in 1980, two years before the Value Line index contract's debut.

56   "You take the red ones and I'll take the green": Vise and Coll, *Eagle on the Street*, p. 40.

56   Feldman took a seat at a small conference table: Interviews with David P. Feldman, February 12, 2016, and Amanda Binns Meller, February 29, 2016 (hereafter "Amanda Binns Meller interview"). Meller provided detailed descriptions of her father's office, which she frequently visited as a child and young teenager.

57   majored in economics and earned a Phi Beta Kappa key: No byline, "Gordon Binns Jr. Dies—Advised VRS," *Richmond Times-Dispatch*, April 5, 2002.

57   but he didn't linger in the South: No byline, "Grandson of Late W. H. Matheny Has High Scholastic Record," *Highland Recorder* (Monterey, VA), May 13, 1949, p. 3. Binns's mother was the former Virginia Matheny, the daughter of the *Highland Recorder*'s founding editor, W. H. Matheny. Details about his college activities are from the *Colonial Echo*, William and Mary's student yearbook, for 1949.

57   A cheerful teetotaler for the rest of his life: Amanda Binns Meller interview.

57   its performance had been anemic, to put it kindly: Mercedes M. Cardona and Michael J. Clowes, "Reed Takes Over GM Fund; Successor to Gordon Binns Shares Many of His Views," *Pensions & Investments*, May 30, 1994, p. 2.

57   dead last among nineteen comparable corporations: Ibid.

58   the hands-on manager of that state's employee pension fund: In 1982 the New Jersey Division of Investment actually managed 76 segregated funds, including

6 pension and annuity funds, by far its largest responsibility. For simplicity's sake, these funds, in the aggregate, are referred to as the "state pension fund." In addition, the division managed 166 other, smaller accounts for various state agencies and authorities. Money in those funds is not included in the totals for the "state pension fund" portfolio.

58   a product of Philadelphia society: Machold was named for his mother's father, Roland S. Morris, a lawyer who served as President Wilson's ambassador to Japan. His mother's mother was a Shippen, a notable Quaker family that first settled in Philadelphia in 1693, and was very distantly related to Margaret "Peggy" Shippen, the second wife of Revolutionary War traitor Benedict Arnold.

58   with no strong sense of what to do next: These biographical details are from an interview with Roland M. Machold on November 13, 2014 (hereafter "Machold interview"), and portions of his unpublished memoir, in the author's files (hereafter "Machold memoir").

59   exceeded a quarter of a trillion dollars: Clowes, *The Money Flood*, p. 6. Clowes reports that "during 1974–1980 private pension fund holdings of equities increased to $235 billion from $63.6 billion, a 19.7% compound rate on increase," and asserts that "pension funds had replaced individual investors as the drivers of the stock market" by the 1960s, but he acknowledges (at pp. ix–x) that "no one noticed how powerful pension funds had become until . . . the mid-1980s."

60   as opposed to institutional investors: The term *institutional investor* was already sufficiently familiar in financial circles in the 1960s that it was chosen in 1967 as the nameplate for a new magazine serving the investing giants that were reshaping the marketplace.

60   The emergence of these titans as stock market investors: Clowes, *The Money Flood*, pp. 1–2.

61   capable of handling 150 million shares a day: The basic Designated Order Turnaround (DOT) system, introduced in 1976, handled small retail orders, but over the years, its capacity had been expanded to accept orders of up to 2,099 shares of market or limit orders. Larger orders could be submitted for more liquid stocks, but execution was not guaranteed unless arrangements with the specialist had been made in advance. In addition, the NYSE had expanded the DOT system so that it could handle orders to buy or sell an entire list of securities. The DOT list order-processing feature was called simply the LIST system, and it could handle trades in up to five hundred different securities. See "The October 1987 Market Break" (hereafter "SEC Crash Report"), a report by the Division of Market Regulation, the U.S. Securities and Exchange Commission, February 1988, p. 1.6. In this account, the term *DOT system* will encompass all these features, as they became available over time.

61   known as "hedged funds," were attracting money: The name was eventually shortened to "hedge fund" because many of these private investment pools were not, in fact, hedged in the way the original funds were.

62   The CFTC would continue to regulate all futures contracts: It would also reg-
      ulate the tiny new field of options based on those futures contracts.

62   The SEC would continue to regulate stocks, single-stock options: Both agen-
      cies agreed to a moratorium on futures contracts tied to individual stocks or
      municipal bonds, and that ban would last for decades.

62   Johnson agreed that the SEC would be consulted: This provision applied only
      to new applications filed after the agreement. It did not apply to the pending
      stock index futures contract applications filed by the Kansas City Board of
      Trade, the Chicago Board of Trade, and the Chicago Merc.

63   or if you were betting that a declining stock would keep dropping: At the time,
      a short sale (the sale of borrowed stock made in the hope of profiting when the
      price declined) could be made only after an "uptick," that is, a price higher
      than the previous price. The uptick rule made it difficult to sell short in a fall-
      ing market, and acted as something of a brake on the decline.

64   offered a research job at the New York Fed: Interview with E. Gerald Corri-
      gan, May 26, 2015 (hereafter "Corrigan interview").

64   "all from Ivy League schools or Stanford or Berkeley. And then there was me":
      Ibid.

64   That is where Paul Volcker found him two years later: Ibid.

65   The older gentleman explained that the final cash-flow tally: Ibid.

65   "Pack your bags. You're going to be my special assistant": Ibid.

65   these were all becoming more deeply entwined: E. Gerald Corrigan and Eve-
      lyn F. Carroll, "Meeting the Challenges of a New Banking Era," Federal
      Reserve Bank of Minneapolis Annual Report 1981, January 1, 1982.

6. STOCK FUTURES, BOND FAILURES

66   Johnson graciously made note of Stone's presence: "Commodity Futures Trad-
      ing Commission Reauthorization" (hereafter "Senate CFTC Reauthorization
      1982"), Hearings Before the Subcommittee on Agricultural Research and Gen-
      eral Legislation of the Senate Committee on Agriculture, Nutrition, and
      Forestry, 97th Congress, 2nd Sess., February 26 and March 1, 2, 10, and 11,
      1982, p. 3.

66   the borders between securities and commodities: Ibid., pp. 45–62.

66   had a new futures exchange: Ibid., p. 47.

67   Volcker finally agreed not to openly oppose: Ibid., pp. 33–34. In an interview
      with the author in 2015, Johnson gave a different version of his dealings with
      Volcker on the issue of margins on stock index futures, a version also cited in
      Tamarkin, The Merc, pp. 272–73. In Tamarkin's version, Johnson was visited
      by the Kansas City Board of Trade president twenty-four hours before the
      debut of the Value Line index contract and told that Volcker "would not allow
      margins as low as 3 percent to 5 percent." Johnson supposedly called Volcker
      directly and, "without dredging up the fight between the Fed and the CFTC
      over who had margin authority," asked if 10 percent margins would be accept-
      able. Volcker agreed, and "after years of bickering over margin control, the

problem had been solved, as Johnson later put it, 'in a five-minute horse trade.'" While this stopgap compromise may have occurred, it seems wiser to rely on the sworn testimony Johnson gave a congressional committee within days of the relevant events. That testimony, and later developments, made it clear that Volcker still had significant concerns about margin levels on stock index futures contracts, issues that had not been squared away in Johnson's "five-minute horse trade."

67   "speculators on the stock market could hedge their bets": Ibid., p. 24.

68   "What we are authorizing is, in effect, legalized gambling": Ibid.

68   "It will tell me how the people feel about the future": Associated Press, "KC Board of Trade Hails Stock Futures' First Day," *Lawrence* (Kansas) *Journal-World*, February 25, 1982, p. 2.

68   reviewing fifty-seven applications: H. J. Maidenberg, "Commodities: Emerging Index Futures," *New York Times*, March 8, 1982, p. D8.

68   no one tried harder than Richard Sandor: By 1982, Sandor was working for a commodity trading firm and was no longer on the economics staff at the CBOT, but he remained chairman of the exchange board's "financial instruments committee," the panel that had done the spadework for the historic GNMA futures contract in 1975.

68   He had been working on a stock index futures contract: Sandor would later contend (in *Good Derivatives*, pp. 163–64) that the two Chicago exchanges had made the strategic decision to let the Kansas City Board of Trade, "a small exchange aligned with a powerful senator, Robert Dole," take the lead in the fight for CFTC approval. The record does not bear him out. First, Senator Dole did not represent Missouri, so it is not clear why he would have been "aligned with" that state's commodity exchange. Nor did Dole's comments at congressional hearings suggest he was an advocate for the KCBT's new product, which he likened to "legalized gambling." Most conclusively, the archives of the CBOT show that it began work on its own stock index product at least by December 17, 1979, when its membership authorized Sandor's proposal, and first submitted it to the CFTC on February 25, 1980—three days before the Merc's application and after Kansas City's initial application had failed to get CFTC approval. See III.1373, Folder 6/16, labeled "Economic Analysis and Planning 1980," CBOT Archives, for a memo dated March 14, 1980, about "Portfolio Futures—Presentation of Salient Features of the CFTC Submission."

68   the most widely published stock market barometer: This account of the Dow Jones dispute is drawn from the filed majority opinion in *Board of Trade of the City of Chicago v. Dow Jones & Company* (hereafter *CBOT v. Dow* 1982) Appellate Court of Illinois—1st District (2nd Division), 108 Ill. App. 3d 681 (1982) [Also cited as "439 N.E. 2d 526"], August 17, 1982.

68   between $1 million and $2 million a year for the use of its name: Sandor, *Good Derivatives*, p. 164.

69   that *Dow*, like *aspirin*, had become a generic term: Ibid.

69   dubbed the "spooz" (which rhymes with "booze"): The ticker symbol for the S&P 500 index itself was SPX. The final letter in the symbol for the futures

contracts based on that index showed when it expired. Thus, the SPU expired in September, while the SPZ expired in December. Decades later, the S&P 500 futures contracts would collectively be called the "spoo" contracts, but at this time, they were referred to as the "spooz." The spelling is obviously flexible; Tamarkin's authorized history of the Merc uses *spooz*, which seems a better fit phonetically, while Leo Melamed's memoir, *Escape to the Futures*, spells it s-p-u-z, which seemed a little confusing as it could be pronounced to rhyme with *ooze* or *fuzz*.

69   The first day's volume easily exceeded 10,000 contracts: Two years later the contract was renegotiated to be more generous to S&P. See Melamed, *Escape to the Futures*, p. 295.

70   The Board of Trade's legal theory: It may have been slightly embarrassing to the CFTC chairman that the dissenting judge in the ruling quoted liberally from Johnson's own legal treatise on commodities law to argue that the majority opinion was wrong. Thus Johnson was caught on both sides of the argument: supporting the CBOT in the commission's amicus brief and, with his prior legal scholarship, providing ammunition to the judge who wanted to reject the CBOT's claims.

70   "anything other than onions could become a 'commodity'": Decision in *CBOT v. SEC* ruling, 677 F.2d 1137. The court acknowledged that GNMA certificates themselves were indeed securities, but decided the GNMA options fell under the CFTC's exclusive jurisdiction. See John D. Benson, "Ending the Turf Wars: Support for a CFTC/SEC Consolidation," *Villanova Law Review* 36, no. 5 (1991), p. 1187.

71   the judges felt it was the job of Congress, not the courts: *CBOT v. SEC* ruling.

71   inflame the SEC's allies in Congress and undo all his careful diplomacy: For this and other political reasons, the reauthorization bill would not be signed into law until January 1983. A few months later, Johnson resigned from the CFTC.

71   the SEC did not have jurisdiction over the market: Treasury bills and notes, Treasury securities with shorter maturities, also trade in the Treasury market, also known as the government securities market. For simplicity, this account will use "Treasury bond market" to incorporate the market where all those related securities also trade.

72   And that's what Drysdale Securities did: "Death Notice: Benedict, Coleman H.," *New York Times*, April 22, 2005. Coleman H. Benedict was a grandson and namesake of the firm's founder.

72   a small New York brokerage house whose roots went back: In April 1982, Drysdale's image was polished a bit when it announced it was paying $3.5 million for the storied Chamber of Commerce Building, a Beaux Arts jewel box at 65 Liberty Street in Lower Manhattan. See an unbylined article, "Postings: Leaseback," *New York Times*, April 18, 1982, sec. 8, p. 1.

72   a separate unit controlled by the firm's star bond trader: Barrie A. Wigmore, *Securities Markets in the 1980s: The New Regime 1979–1984*, vol. 1 (New York: Oxford University Press, 1997), p. 236. See also Scott E. D. Skyrm, *Rogue Traders*

(New York: Brick Tower Press, 2014), chap. 1. According to Skyrm (at p. 39), Heuwetter died on August 4, 2012, at the age of seventy-one.

72   had recently used some peculiar features of Treasury market accounting: The firm failures of 1982 prompted Treasury traders and dealers to formalize their accounting and paperwork to end some of the practices exploited by the Drysdale trader. These deals actually were nominally structured as a sale of the securities with an agreement to repurchase them—hence the term *repurchase agreements*, or *repos*. But the entire market thought of them as loans—until another dealer, Lombard-Wall Money Markets, filed for bankruptcy later that summer. The bankruptcy court ruled that the bonds the dealer had pledged to its lenders could not be seized as collateral on its defaulted loans but had to be treated as part of the debtor's estate. The securities were tied up for months in the bankruptcy process, and investors fled the repo market in droves. At the industry's urgent request, Congress adopted amendments to the federal bankruptcy code to clarify that a repurchase agreement should be treated by the court as collateral if a trading firm collapsed.

72   to build up a risky trading position: This is the Treasury market's version of short-selling in the stock market, in which a speculator pays a fee to borrow shares of a supposedly overvalued stock and then sells them, betting that the stock price will fall and he will be able to buy it back, return the borrowed shares, and pocket a profit. Here, the bond trader was betting that rising interest rates would push down the price of the bonds he had borrowed and sold, and he would therefore be able to buy them back at a lower price and profit from the difference.

72   that was a pretty good bet: Skyrm, *Rogue Traders*, p. 25. The trader's strategy exploited the repo market's outdated habit of ignoring the value of the owed interest in calculating how much margin the trader would have to put up to borrow the bonds. Thus, the trader could borrow bonds by posting a margin that did *not* reflect the accrued interest and sell them at a price that *did* reflect the accrued interest, and trade with the cash he raised until it was time to return the borrowed bonds. "It was, at its core, a superb way to get an interest-free loan regardless of interest rates," Skyrm notes. And with interest rates in the high teens, the technique was a bonanza—if nothing went wrong.

72   "using a secret and sophisticated computer-based trading strategy": Ibid., p. 24.

72   either insulate itself from Heuwetter's adventures: In a criminal case, Heuwetter later pleaded guilty to wildly exaggerating the financial strength of the spin-off firm, which claimed to have $20.5 million in capital when in fact it was $150 million in the red. See *U.S. v. David J. Heuwetter*, 84-CR-188, U.S. District Court, the Southern District of New York; and *SEC News Digest*, April 9, 1984, p. 2.

72   The spin-off alone might have been enough to worry some: Skyrm asserts (see *Rogue Trader*, p. 18) that the New York Fed also had early warning about the size of Drysdale's positions in the Treasury bond market: "The Federal Reserve had received tips from several market participants who thought Drysdale was trading far in excess of the firm's capital base, and many dealers

had already refused to deal with the firm because of its renowned risk trading." The source for this assertion is not provided. Senate testimony about the scandal disclosed only that Drysdale had applied to the New York Fed for primary dealer status on April 23, 1982, three weeks before its default, and had been told its application was "premature." See "Disturbance in the U.S. Securities Market" (hereafter "Senate Drysdale Hearing"), Hearing Before the Subcommittee on Securities of the Senate Committee on Banking, Housing, and Urban Affairs, 97th Congress, 2nd Sess., May 25, 1982, pp. 39–40.

72   a lesser amount was handled by two smaller but still substantial institutions: According to the Senate Drysdale Hearing, they were Manufacturers Hanover (p. 26) and U.S. Trust Company (p. 28).

73   None of these feckless traditions: Michael Quint, "Financing Quirk at Drysdale Studied," *New York Times*, May 25, 1982, p. D5.

73   Chase declined to extend the loan: Skyrm, *Rogue Trader*, p. 27.

73   that $160 million would surely be missed: Today, the sum would be about $480 million.

74   A group of senior staffers there met with him: These details are drawn from an extensive chronology that New York Fed president Anthony Solomon prepared for the Senate Drysdale Hearing, at pp. 24–28.

74   Corrigan made plans to travel to New York: At some point in these tense hours, Corrigan left Washington for New York, but the timing is not reflected in the subsequent testimony or official chronology.

74   was not endorsing any plan that Chase might present: Senate Drysdale Hearing, p. 25.

75   thirty angry brokers and bankers crowded into the conference room: Skyrm, *Rogue Trader*, chap. 1.

75   "a decision to pay interest would have a calming effect": Senate Drysdale Hearing, p. 27.

75   "a rather abnormal development in the market, to say the least": Transcript of Meeting of the Federal Open Market Committee (hereafter "FOMC Meeting transcript"), May 18, 1982, p. 1, the Federal Reserve website, https://www.federalreserve.gov/monetarypolicy/files/FOMC19820518meeting.pdf.

76   "If all of the financing arrangements in the government securities market are disrupted": Ibid., p. 3. All the direct quotations from the FOMC meeting are drawn from the same transcript.

76   the two other banks involved in the Drysdale default: Senate Drysdale Hearing, p. 28.

7. A PLAGUE FROM OKLAHOMA

81   a banker sat in a conference room: All of these details are drawn from Testimony of John R. Lytle, "Penn Square Bank Failure," Hearings Before the Committee on Banking, Finance, and Urban Affairs, House of Representatives, 97th Congress, 2nd Sess., Part 2, September 29–30, 1982, p. 6.

82   "I'm sorry," his friend replied: Ibid.

82   foreign currency futures would serve no purpose: Tamarkin, *The Merc*, pp. 189–90.

83   cut from the same innovative cloth as its traders: Ibid., p. 191. As Tamarkin put it, "Many of the traders, brokers, and clearinghouse members were good customers of the banks, and the banks understood the need for hedging and futures."

83   they gave the venture worldwide credibility: Ibid., p. 192.

83   "one of the five best managed companies": Wigmore, *Securities Markets in the 1980s*, p. 43.

83   capped the amount of interest: In the early 1970s, during the Nixon administration, a government commission recommended that this interest rate cap be lifted, but the thrift industry itself opposed the move because lifting the cap would have reduced the industry's profits by raising the cost of acquiring deposits. The federal government backed down and allowed the cap to remain in place, setting the stage for enormous taxpayer losses.

83   Congress was ineffectively mulling over what it should do: Under pressure to liberalize the rules and foster financial competition, Congress had enacted a law in 1980, under President Carter, that set up a committee to oversee a gradual phase-out of interest rate caps. By early 1982, however, little progress had been made, despite pressure from the new administration. By statute, Volcker was a member of the new deregulatory committee, but his lack of enthusiasm for its work is evident in the transcripts of private meetings held at the Fed during late 1981 and early 1982. See Robert A. Bennett, "Banks Square Off Against the Fed," *New York Times*, June 14, 1981, sec. 3, p. 1.

83   The problems at Penn Square quickly became public: Phillip L. Zweig, "FDIC Said to Launch Review of Oklahoma's Penn Square Bank," *The American Banker*, July 2, 1982. Zweig recorded the saga of the bank's collapse in *Belly Up: The Collapse of the Penn Square Bank* (New York: Crown Publishers, 1985), as did Mark Singer, *Funny Money* (New York: Knopf, 1984).

84   whose loan portfolio was stuffed: Phillip L. Zweig, "Oklahoma's Penn Square Bank, Maverick Oil Patch Lender," *American Banker*, April 26, 1982.

84   On May 11 they sent a warning to Washington: Testimony of C. T. Conover, Comptroller of the Currency, "Federal Supervision and Failure of the Penn Square Bank, Oklahoma City, Okla." (hereafter "Penn Square Hearing"), Hearing Before a Subcommittee of the House Committee on Government Operations, 97th Congress, 2nd Sess., July 16, 1982, pp. 44–53; and "Chronology of OCC Supervision of Penn Square Bank N.A., January 1, 1980, to July 5, 1982," Penn Square Hearing, p. 54–57.

84   the official regulator of roughly twelve thousand nationally chartered banks: The Office of the Comptroller of the Currency has long financed itself by imposing examination fees and assessments on the banks under its supervision. Unlike the SEC and CFTC, the OCC is a "nonappropriated" agency of the federal government, which means it neither receives revenues from taxpayers nor contributes any of its income to the Treasury for general use.

85   the largest loss by bank depositors since the Great Depression: Penn Square

Hearing, p. 1, quoting New York Democratic congressman Benjamin S. Rosenthal.

85 unless the troubled bank could somehow find a new owner: Irvine H. Sprague, *Bailout: An Insider's Account of Bank Failures and Rescues* (Washington, DC: Beard Books, 2000), pp. 116–17.

85 get IOUs for the rest of their money: These are called "receiver's certificates." See Penn Square Hearing, p. 41.

85 Latin American debtor nations were looking shakier: FOMC Meeting transcript, June 30–July 1, 1982, p. 29.

85 credit concerns were still unsettling the Treasury markets: Paul Meek, "Notes for FOMC Meeting," appendix to FOMC Meeting transcript, June 30, 1982, p. 3.

86 the FDIC could not just take over the bank itself: Sprague, *Bailout*, p. 157.

86 to Isaac it looked like the only option: Ibid., p. 116.

86 on the verge of its own financial crisis: Silber, *Volcker*, pp. 219–21. Volcker had quietly helped Mexico spruce up its financial reports for April and June; he later told Silber he regretted this "window dressing" because it "disguised the full extent of the pressures on Mexico." He excused it to himself at the time, he said, as a way to give Mexico time to negotiate a bailout package from the International Monetary Fund.

86 The five largest banks in the country would lose: Ibid., pp. 220 and 398n20, which provides the private Fed documentation on which the assessment was based.

87 Over the July Fourth weekend: Greider and Sprague disagree about the timing of this meeting. Sprague, a direct participant, puts it on Sunday, July 4; Greider, who is relying on secondhand information, puts it on Monday, July 5, which seems less plausible because the bank's closure was announced that night.

87 he took a seat on the sofa and listened: Sprague, *Bailout*, p. 119.

87 not clear if Regan sided with Isaac: Greider, *Secrets of the Temple*, p. 500–501.

87 or if Conover thought he had: Sprague, *Bailout*, p. 119.

87 the order was given for the FDIC to begin a payoff: Ibid.

87 when it closed the books on the second quarter of 1982: Robert A. Bennett, "Continental Posts $60.9 Million Loss," *New York Times*, July 22, 1982, p. D7.

87 insisted they had no reason to doubt the overall soundness: Robert A. Bennett, "Continental Knew in '81 of Problem," *New York Times*, August 5, 1982, p. D4.

87 more than $400 million in poorly documented oil loans: Wigmore, *Securities Markets in the 1980s*, p. 46.

87 warned investors it would incur substantial losses: Special to the *New York Times*, "Seafirst Loan Loss Causes Layoff of 400," *New York Times*, July 16, 1982, p. D3.

88 soon reported its own embarrassing losses on Penn Square: No byline, "Two Officials Quit at Chase," *New York Times*, July 20, 1982, p. D16.

88 Michigan National Bank owned $190 million: Special to the *New York Times*, "'Assurances' on Penn Square Recalled by Michigan Banker," *New York Times*, September 30, 1982, p. D4.

88   and several more had been hurt badly: Jeff Gerth, "Banks' Collapse Is Said to Impair Thrift Units," *New York Times*, July 23, 1982, p. D1.

88   before they could fully recover their cash: Penn Square Hearing, p. 30.

88   "Many millions of dollars will be lost by depositors": Ibid., pp. 2–9.

89   it was impossible to arrange a merger: Ibid., pp. 41–42.

89   there might be a few other sinkholes like Penn Square: Ibid.

90   "will provide the impetus to move forward on these issues": Ibid., pp. 43–44.

90   What could you expect?: Maggie Mahar, *Bull: A History of the Boom and Bust, 1982-2004* (New York: Harper Business, 2004), pp. 46–47.

8. BULLS AND BANKS

91   was launching an uninvited takeover bid for Martin Marietta: Hope Lampert, *Till Death Do Us Part: Bendix vs. Martin Marietta* (New York: Harcourt Brace Jovanovich, 1983), pp. 1–4.

91   One of the wildest corporate battles: Martin Marietta countered the unwelcome offer *from* Bendix by making a hostile takeover bid *for* Bendix. Another defense industry giant, United Technologies, stepped into the fray and made its own bid for Martin Marietta, but was unsuccessful. The Allied Corporation rescued Bendix from Martin Marietta's hostile bid by making a friendly takeover offer, which was accepted.

91   the great railroad wars of the nineteenth century: See John Steele Gordon, *The Scarlet Woman of Wall Street: Jay Gould, Jim Fisk, Cornelius Vanderbilt, the Erie Railway Wars, and the Birth of Wall Street* (New York: Weidenfeld and Nicolson, 1988).

91   the smaller postwar corporate raids of the late 1950s: See Diana B. Henriques, *The White Sharks of Wall Street: Thomas Mellon Evans and the Original Corporate Raiders* (New York: Lisa Drew Books/Scribner, 2000).

91   the so-called conglomerate kings a decade later: See Isadore Barmash, *Welcome to Our Conglomerate—You're Fired!* (New York: Delacorte Press, 1971).

92   courteous deals that "were prudently financed": Vise and Coll, *Eagle on the Street*, p. 100.

92   the bigger you were, the more risks you could take: It was during the Bendix battle that a young Kidder Peabody investment banker named Martin Siegel, who led Martin Marietta's defense, earned a $150,000 cash "bonus" from stock trader Ivan Boesky, in exchange for advance tips on the deal. That crime would eventually lead to Boesky's arrest and the downfall of junk bond innovator Michael Milken at Drexel Burnham Lambert. See James B. Stewart, *Den of Thieves* (New York: Simon and Schuster, 1991), pp. 94–97.

93   The closing bell brought a roar that filled the cavernous space: Robert J. Cole, "Euphoric Day for Wall Street," *New York Times*, October 8, 1982, p. D1.

93   the lines in front of Merrill Lynch's stock price video screens: Ibid.

93   "We've built models and tested them up to about 300 million shares": Ibid.

93   to talk about financial deregulation: Remarks by E. Gerald Corrigan, president, the Federal Reserve Bank of Minneapolis at the American Bankers

Association Annual Convention, Atlanta, GA, October 19, 1982 (hereafter "Remarks by Corrigan at ABA").

93   In recent years, banks had persuaded Congress: These examples, while cited widely elsewhere, are collected from Rebecca A. Craft, "Avoiding the Glass-Steagall and Bank Holding Company Acts: An Option for Bank Product Expansion," *Indiana Law Journal* 59, no. 1 (Winter 1983), p. 89n3.

94   any bank "can choose the regulatory system": Ibid., p. 92.

94   to ask "hard questions about what banks are": Remarks by Corrigan at ABA, p. 2. The remaining quotes are from that speech.

95   raised "important questions about the bank's management": Greider, *Secrets of the Temple*, p. 523.

95   but a few weeks later he confidently announced: Ibid.

95   He argued with the directors that Anderson should be replaced: Greider, *Secrets of the Temple*, notes at p. 527, that the annual rotation of membership in 1983 put Roger Anderson onto the Federal Advisory Council, "the select group of twelve commercial bankers who met privately each quarter with the Federal Reserve Board," which Greider called "a final, galling insult."

95   It could have tried to force the bank to change course: Greider, *Secrets of the Temple*, p. 524.

96   and it sat atop an impressively long article: Mary Greenebaum, "A Strategy for Limiting Portfolio Losses," *Fortune*, June 14, 1982.

96   each time, he waited for follow-up calls that never came: Interview with Hayne E. Leland and John O'Brien, April 25, 2014 (hereafter "Leland–O'Brien interview 2014").

97   Selling research ideas: Ibid.

97   casual, California surfer looks belied a polished pedigree: The high points of Admiral Ellis's career were traced in numerous articles, including "New Navy Ordnance Head," *New York Times*, June 2, 1931, p. 27; and "Admiral in New Post," *New York Times*, October 26, 1940, p. 6. The social status of the Ellis family is supported by dozens of small society page items in the *New York Times* and the *Washington Post*, including "Dinners Precede Newport Concert," *New York Times*, July 24, 1936, p. 14; and "Lucia Long Ellis Engaged to Wed," *New York Times*, March 16, 1941, p. 46. Leland's own lineage is detailed in "Engagements—Leland-de Bresson," *New York Times*, July 16, 1964, p. 31; "Other Wedding Plans—Ellis-Leland," *New York Times*, June 5, 1932, p. 31; and "New Home Acquired by Secretary Stimson," *New York Times*, June 29, 1929, p. 7.

97   Leland was born in Boston in 1941: Andrew Kupfer, "Leland, O'Brien, and Rubinstein: The Guys Who Gave Us Portfolio Insurance," *Fortune*, January 4, 1988.

97   and was tapped for several elite clubs: "Engagements—Leland-de Bresson."

97   he married the debutante daughter of a titled French family: "Annie-May de Bresson Bride of Hayne E. Leland in Paris," *New York Times*, December 5, 1964.

97   where he earned his doctorate in economics: His doctoral dissertation was sufficiently impressive to be published in 1969 in the prestigious *Journal of*

Finance. See Hayne E. Leland, "Dynamic Portfolio Theory," *The Journal of Finance* 24, no. 3 (June 1969), p. 543.

97 academic politics precluded him from getting tenure: Interview with Hayne Leland, John O'Brien, and Mark Rubinstein, April 1, 2016 (hereafter "LOR interview 2016").

97 convinced he had found an idea that could be valuable: Ibid. It is an oft-told tale, also recounted at length in Bernstein, *Capital Ideas*, pp. 269–73; Fox, *The Myth of the Rational Market*, p. 151; and Kupfer, "Leland, O'Brien, and Rubinstein."

98 What sane insurance company would write policies: Unfortunately, that idea did not seem absurd during the late 1990s and early 2000s to firms, such as AIG, that sold vast numbers of credit default swaps. The swaps essentially were insurance policies protecting the buyers from losses from corporate defaults. Since corporate defaults were likely to be highly correlated with turbulent economic conditions, it was likely that all those "insurance policies" would produce big claims at the same time—which is precisely what happened in the crisis of 2008.

98 If one policyholder experienced big market losses: The idea is similarly expressed by Bernstein, *Capital Ideas*, at p. 271.

98 stock options, which allowed their owners to buy: What distinguishes options from futures contracts, like the ones traded in Chicago, is that an option does not require the transaction, but merely allows it. Thus, the holder of a futures contract would be obliged to buy or sell the underlying commodity on the date fixed by the futures contract, while an option holder would not be required to act.

98 Leland could see that he needed a way: Bernstein, *Capital Ideas*, p. 272.

99 the sudden inspiration that got him out of bed that night: He noted later that his idea was built on a body of other research, notably the work of Fischer Black and Myron Scholes, whose model for pricing options was the foundation of the emerging options markets. From an interview with Hayne Leland and John O'Brien, December 26, 2016 (hereafter "Leland–O'Brien interview 2016").

99 he needed Mark Rubinstein, his trusted friend: Ibid.

99 He got his high school education at the Lakeside School: Bernstein, *Capital Ideas*, p. 274.

99 an early passion for computer programming languages: Ibid., p. 277.

99 He lost money as a trader: Ibid., pp. 276–78.

99 chuckling and expressing surprise: Ibid.

99 In a flash, the penny dropped: LOR interview 2016.

100 testing their concept on a small scale: Ibid.

100 It was a great success: Clowes, *The Money Flood*, pp. 210–11.

100 to introduce their idea for "portfolio insurance" to the world: Later, the concept would be called "dynamic hedging" and "dynamic asset allocation," but the evidence that "portfolio insurance" was the original name is indisputable: the first paper about the concept that Leland published is "Who Should Buy Portfolio Insurance?" (Working Paper No. 95, Institute of Business and Economic Research, University of California at Berkeley, December 1979). Moreover, the term is used repeatedly in the article itself.

100   they did have an endorsement from Barr Rosenberg: Besides having studied
       together at the London School of Economics in the 1964/65 academic year,
       Rosenberg and Leland had both returned to earn doctorates at Harvard in
       1968. Leland recalled that Rosenberg, while already a wealthy man, remained
       accessible and helpful to his faculty colleagues.

100   had already had a remarkable career in finance: Details are taken from an
       online curriculum vitae for O'Brien and his Haas School biography, except as
       otherwise noted.

100   when he joined an obscure but venerable firm, Jas. H. Oliphant: By then, the
       firm focused on selling institutional research to other brokerage firms; O'Brien
       was director of its analytical services division. Oliphant was a 1975 casualty as
       Wall Street's revenues plunged with the end of fixed commissions.

100   helped Oliphant develop and sell so-called beta books: Clowes, *The Money
       Flood*, pp. 52–53; and John Ilkiw, "Missing Persons Found: Jenson Coined Beta
       and Alpha but Tito Cashed Out," *Canadian Investment Review* (Winter 2006),
       p. 7. These "beta books" were forerunners of the enhanced "beta" assessments
       that Barr Rosenberg at Berkeley would develop with such success a few years
       later.

100   O'Brien unwisely sold the business to a partner: Clowes, *The Money Flood*,
       p. 111. The partner was his former Oliphant employee Dennis Tito, whose
       previous employers included the NASA Jet Propulsion Laboratory. In 2001,
       Tito became the first private citizen to "buy a ticket" to outer space, paying
       $20 million to travel on a Russian spacecraft to the International Space Station.
       See online *Encyclopedia Britannica* entry for Dennis Tito.

101   he was routinely scouting for new ideas: Leland–O'Brien interview 2014.

101   Best of all, he was a gifted communicator: "Some people have said that he is
       the ultimate salesman," one observer noted. "But he is really a patient teacher.
       He is willing to go and spend literally hours to describe all of the details in
       plain English . . . without using complex math." See Hal Lux, "LOR's Big
       Gamble on SuperShares," *Investment Dealers' Digest*, November 30, 1992,
       p. 14, cited by Barbara Kyrillos in a Harvard case study included in *Cases in
       Financial Engineering: Applied Studies of Financial Innovation*, ed. Scott P.
       Mason, Robert C. Merton, Andre F. Perold, and Peter Tufano (Upper Saddle
       River, NJ: Prentice Hall, 1995), p. 767.

101   The new firm's address sounded impressive: The community took its name
       from its heritage: it was once the back lot of Twentieth Century–Fox, but had
       been developed in the 1960s as a dense and self-contained cluster of office tow-
       ers, hotels, shopping malls, and apartments.

101   the small tenth-floor suite housed O'Brien: Interview with Hayne Leland and
       John O'Brien, June 10, 2015 (hereafter "Leland–O'Brien interview 2015").

101   rang three times with three new clients: Leland–O'Brien interview 2014.

102   One manager agreed to try: Clowes, *The Money Flood*, p. 211.

102   an influential industry publication: In 1990, this publication changed its name
       to *Pensions & Investments*, the name under which it was first published in
       1973; during the 1980s, though, it was known as *Pensions & Investment Age*.

102   The ad explained that the firm's strategy: The advertisement is reproduced in

Bruce I. Jacobs, *Capital Ideas and Market Realities: Option Replication, Investor Behavior, and Stock Market Crashes* (Malden, MA: Blackwell Publishers, 1999), p. 37. Emphasis is in the original.

102   offered a blessedly simple explanation of the strategy: Clowes, *The Money Flood*, p. 210.

102   One such seminar was held in Manhattan in late 1982: Jacobs, *Capital Ideas and Market Realities*, p. 8. Jacobs is a little unclear on the timing of this seminar; a memorandum he said he wrote soon afterward for Prudential's clients and sales staff is dated January 17, 1983, and refers to the new hedging strategy as "portfolio insulation." It notes that Kidder Peabody and Wilshire were already offering their own versions, which would seem to place the seminar in late 1982.

102   had earned a doctorate in finance from the Wharton School: Ibid.

103   falling prices would trigger more selling: Ibid., p. 303.

103   In a truly efficient market, they would soon go broke: Investor Warren Buffett had a lot of fun with the "rational market hypothesis" in his 1985 shareholder letter to investors in his flagship Berkshire Hathaway. "In the 1970s . . . academics at prestigious business schools . . . were preaching a newly fashioned investment theory: the stock market was totally efficient, and therefore calculations of business value—and even thought itself—were of no importance in investment activities. We are enormously indebted to those academics. What could be more advantageous in an intellectual contest—whether it be bridge [which Buffett played competitively], chess or stock selection—than to have opponents who have been taught that thinking is a waste of energy?" Quoted in Leinweber, *Nerds on Wall Street*, p. 97. Leinweber also framed beautifully (at p. 96) the paradox that Sanford Grossman and Joseph Stiglitz spotted in the efficient market hypothesis beloved by the University of Chicago's economic believers. "*If markets are efficient*, they reflect all information, and there is no profit to be had from trading on information. If there is no profit to be had, traders with information won't trade, so markets won't reflect [that information], and *will not be efficient*."

9. CHICAGO RISING

105   Timothy E. Wirth of Colorado opened a hearing: "FDIC Securities Proposal and Related Issues," Hearings before the Telecommunications, Consumer Protection, and Finance Subcommittee of the House Committee on Energy and Commerce (hereafter "1983 FDIC Hearing"), 98th Congress, 1st Sess., June 16 and 28, 1983, p. 1.

106   Shad had submitted budgets in 1981 and 1982: Seligman, *The Transformation of Wall Street*, p. 576.

106   Shad's budget request in 1983: Anne M. Khademian, *The SEC and Capital Market Regulation: The Politics of Expertise* (Pittsburgh: University of Pittsburgh Press, 1992), pp. 172–73.

106   promptly released the exchange of letters to the media: Nancy L. Ross, "Four Members Urge Bigger Staff for SEC," *Washington Post*, March 22, 1983, p. C7.

106   none of those overseers had any jurisdiction: As noted, the Federal Reserve had

statutory authority to set margin limits for stock purchases, but generally deferred to the SEC and the stock exchanges on that topic.

107   for a big loss on its swap strategy: Similarly, a foreign exchange swap would allow a U.S. lender who was going to be repaid with Japanese yen to exchange those future payments for payments made with U.S. dollars, thereby avoiding the risk of the yen's declining in value against the dollar. In time, swaps would mutate to cover all sorts of variables, from shifting commodity prices to plummeting credit ratings. The latter would figure disastrously in the 2008 financial crisis.

108   a loophole big enough to accommodate the entire banking industry: 1983 FDIC Hearing, p. 15.

108   but only through similar separate entities: Oddly, Shad did not suggest that Congress simply close the loophole identified by the FDIC by amending the Glass-Steagall Act to cover all banks, as many in Congress and most of the public assumed it already did.

108   Bevis Longstreth agreed with Shad that radical shifts: 1983 FDIC Hearing, p. 69.

108   whether a few legislative fixes would help: Ibid., p. 70.

108   the unexpected links among institutions: Ibid., p. 123.

109   Regan conceded that the market favored Volcker: Silber, *Volcker*, p. 233.

109   Reagan did not respond then: Ibid., p. 232.

109   he told Wall Street and the world: Ibid., p. 233.

110   had a million square feet of office space: Tamarkin, *The Merc*, pp. 289–90.

110   on the south side of the gigantic rectangle of the trading complex: It had long been Leo Melamed's dream to move the Merc into a building that would reflect the Merc's new global stature—one that was, "at a minimum, of a stature equal to that of the CBOT's building." The CBOT's Art Deco skyscraper, with its silvery statue of Ceres framed by the long corridor of LaSalle Street, is one of the iconic images of Chicago. The CBOT's building "was a city landmark," Melamed said. "I would never be satisfied until the Merc had one of its own." See Melamed, *Escape to the Futures*, p. 302.

110   All but two of the remaining months of 1982: Tamarkin, *The Merc*, p. 273.

110   Melamed had told a reporter in August: Ibid., p. 274.

110   By June 1983, the Dow stood 50 percent higher: Birinyi and Rubin, *Market Cycles III*, p. 265.

111   "to play the stock market without owning a share": Tamarkin, *The Merc*, p. 273.

111   were using the futures market to hedge interest-rate risk: Tamarkin, *The Merc*, p. 295. This pension fund tally did not include funds, such as General Motors, that relied on external managers; adding the external managers who used futures contracts would certainly have pushed the total higher.

111   the spooz pit generated more than 20 percent: Tamarkin, *The Merc*, p. 295.

112   even if regulators grasped all the complexities and risks: These details and conclusions are drawn from the account that CFTC chairwoman Susan Phillips gave in the transcript "Review of the Commodity Futures Trading Commission" (hereafter "CFTC 1984 Review Hearing"), Hearing Before the House Agriculture Committee's Subcommittee on Conservation, Credit, and Rural Development, 98th Congress, 2nd Sess., February 8, 1984, p. 8.

10. ARBITRAGE AND ACCOMMODATION

113 His assessment of the CFTC had been equally glowing: "Ronald Reagan: Remarks at the Swearing-In Ceremony for Susan M. Phillips, Chairman of the Commodity Futures Trading Commission, November 17, 1983," American Presidency Project website, http://www.presidency.ucsb.edu/ws/index.php?pid=40785&st=&st1=.

114 John Shad's response was waiting for her: CFTC 1984 Review Hearing, p. 8.

114 Shad raised the same objections: Ibid.

114 no matter how many stocks were in that index: Ibid., p. 9.

115 bowed to the CFTC's philosophy: This assessment is supported by testimony at the hearing by both John Shad and Susan Phillips, and is evident in the announcement of the new guidelines, which are described in Phillips's formal statement. See CFTC 1984 Review Hearing, pp. 9, 93–96.

115 Wunsch was something of a legend among climbers: Leslie Wayne, "A Rock Climber's Reach for the Top of Wall St.," New York Times, January 24, 1991, p. D1.

115 during one of his early meetings with O'Brien: Leland–O'Brien interview 2014.

116 a comfortable spot to stay during their frequent visits: LOR interview 2016.

116 one ad for the product noted: The ad was reproduced in Jacobs, Capital Ideas and Market Realities, p. 38.

116 "It's too much trading!": Leland–O'Brien interview 2015.

116 "We don't trade the stocks, we use the futures": Ibid., confirmed in an interview with R. Steven Wunsch, June 25, 2015 (hereafter "Wunsch interview 2015").

117 a put option on a broad stock market index: Indeed, this whole notion had a whiff of déjà vu for Rubinstein. In the late 1970s, he had teamed up with executives of the Philadelphia Stock Exchange to propose a stock index option, but it had been squashed in a massive options trading scandal that prompted the SEC to suspend new options products in 1977—and Rubinstein moved on. See Donald MacKenzie, An Engine, Not a Camera: How Financial Models Shape Markets (Cambridge, MA: MIT Press, 2006), p. 176.

117 "as long as our clients are satisfied with general market protection": LOR interview 2016.

117 this streamlined version of portfolio insurance: Leland–O'Brien interview 2016.

118 sparking all sorts of ideas in his own mind: Interview with R. Steven Wunsch, November 28, 2016.

119 that would be a profitable arbitrage opportunity: Obviously, the price gap would have to be big enough to cover the cost of shipping gold across the Atlantic.

119 there might be a chance to profit from the opposite trade: Index arbitrage was also being conducted using other stock index futures, or even index options. A popular arbitrage strategy involved the 30 stocks in the Dow Jones index and the Chicago Board of Trade's Major Market Index futures, which was based on a roster of stocks that closely resembled the Dow. Some arbitrageurs shifted cash between the Standard & Poor's 100 Index and the OEX options traded on the Chicago Board Options Exchange.

120   Index arbitrage remained a mysterious market force: The record is not entirely
      clear about who first came up with the idea of index arbitrage, which would
      have an increasingly powerful influence on the NYSE and the Merc in the com-
      ing years and get spotlight attention after Black Monday. By one account, a
      small specialty firm in New York, Miller Tabak Hirsch and Co., started exploit-
      ing arbitrage opportunities provided by the Value Line index futures contract
      trading in Kansas City in mid-1982. See Jennifer Lin, "Programmed for Dis-
      pute," Philly.com, December 3, 1989. Others say it was born in the fertile
      brains of people at Wells Fargo Investment Advisors but didn't find its footing
      until three WFIA innovators found their way to Mellon Bank and, in August
      1983, set up Mellon Capital Management. The three were legendary "quants"
      William Fouse, Thomas Loeb, and Polly Shouse. See "The Way We Were: 1982–
      1989," *Pensions & Investments*, October 29, 1998, accessed on its website; and
      Testimony of Thomas Loeb, chairman of Mellon Capital Management Corp.,
      "Program Trading" (hereafter "1987 Program Trading Hearing"), Hearing
      Before the Telecommunications and Finance Subcommittee of the House Com-
      mittee on Energy and Commerce, 100th Congress, 1st Sess., July 23, 1987, p. 224.
121   the opening courtesies could not mask the tension: CFTC 1984 Review Hear-
      ing, p. 1.
121   "the two commissions were meeting in a back room": Ibid., p. 4.
122   "it was Congress that kept jurisdiction over those issues, and nobody else": Ibid.
122   "prepared to respond flexibly": Ibid., p. 9.
122   "it was preferable to use their joint expertise": Ibid.
122   "the protracted uncertainties of litigation": Ibid., p. 12. Shad went on to caution
      the subcommittee that both the SEC and the CFTC had been sued two days
      earlier by the feisty Chicago Board of Trade, which was opposed to the mere
      existence of the new industry index guidelines, no matter how lenient, on the
      grounds that the two agencies had no power to draft or enforce them. "I would
      be grateful for whatever forbearance the committee wishes to exercise in terms
      of not compromising the Commission's case until we have had an adequate
      opportunity to respond to the complaint," Shad said.
122   "We do not believe that we gave up anything": Ibid., p. 17.
122   "I agree with Chairman Phillips," Shad answered: Ibid.

11. BANKS ON THE BRINK

124   The day was Tuesday, May 8, 1984: These details, while repeated in Greider,
      Secrets of the Temple, p. 624, and Silber, *Volcker*, p. 242, were more fully reported
      in a riveting reconstruction of the Continental rescue by the bank's hometown
      newspaper. See R. C. Longworth and Bill Barnhart, "The Panic Followed the
      Sun," *Chicago Tribune*, May 27, 1984, p. 1.
125   Taylor had scrambled to replace the lost domestic deposits: Robert A. Bennett,
      "Chilling Specter at Continental," *New York Times*, May 20, 1984, sec. 3, p. 1.
125   Continental needed roughly $8 billion in fresh cash every day: "History of the
      Eighties—Lessons for the Future," Federal Deposit Insurance Corporation,
      p. 242, at https://www.fdic.gov/bank/historical/history/.

125   before he would even consider approving a dividend for shareholders: Written statement of C. Todd Conover, "An Inquiry into Continental Illinois Corp. and Continental Illinois National Bank" (hereafter "House CINB Hearing"), Subcommittee on Financial Institutions Supervision, Regulation and Insurance, House Committee on Banking, Finance, and Urban Affairs, 98th Congress, 2nd Sess., September 18 and 19 and October 4, 1984, p. 273.

125   Bottum urged him to fly back to Chicago: Longworth and Barnhart, "The Panic Followed the Sun."

125   Those close-knit traders, glued to their news wires: Ibid.

125   the Chicago Tribune later pieced together what had happened: Some of these details were also reported by Peter T. Kilborn, Winston Williams, and Robert A. Bennett in "The High-Stakes Scramble to Rescue Continental Bank," New York Times, May 21, 1984, p. 1. The Times identified a Jiji news story as one of the factors in the sudden crisis, but did not report the details behind its production and translation. There are some differences between the two accounts; where local details were involved, the Tribune report seemed more authoritative; where New York details were featured, the Times account was helpful.

126   When Wednesday, May 9, arrived in Chicago: This phrasing is similar to a quote attributed to a Continental executive by Kilborn, Williams, and Bennett, "The High-Stakes Scramble to Rescue Continental Bank."

126   They were picked up by alert ears at an affiliate: Kilborn, Williams, and Bennett reported (in "The High-Stakes Scramble to Rescue Continental Bank") that Continental "was irritated with its neighbor across the street at the Board of Trade . . . A plea went out to the clearing corporation, and part of the money was returned." To be accurate, the clearing corporation was separate from the Board of Trade.

126   "Can you stop whatever you're doing and come over": Longworth and Barnhart, "The Panic Followed the Sun."

127   but that had only heightened the alarm: Ibid.

127   A sudden exodus of cash from money market funds: Mark Carlson and Jonathan Rose, "Can a Bank Run Be Stopped? Government Guarantees and the Run on Continental Illinois," Finance and Economics Discussion Series 2016-003, Washington, Board of Governors of the Federal Reserve System, http://dx.doi.org/10.17016/FEDS.2016.0003, p. 1. The link between money market funds and the wider economy, which became clear in the 2008 crisis, is that the funds are a ready market for corporate commercial paper, the very short-term notes that top-rated businesses can sell to finance their cash flow needs. In 2008, a run on money market funds—triggered by the Lehman bankruptcy, which caused a giant money market fund to lose money on Lehman's commercial paper—nearly disabled the commercial paper market.

128   Several had already had to jack up the rates they paid: Robert A. Bennett, "$4.5 Billion Credit for Chicago Bank Set by 16 Others," New York Times, May 15, 1984, p. 1.

129   the mighty Federal Reserve also stood ready to lend: Carlson and Rose, "Can a Bank Run Be Stopped?" p. 3.

129   the worst bank runs that would occur in the aftermath of the 2008 financial crisis: Ibid., p. 1. Carlson and Rose note that "Washington Mutual lost 10 percent of its deposits and IndyMac lost about 8 percent, each in about two weeks. Thus, even in a more digital, seemingly faster moving era, these runs were less dramatic than the one on Continental, while still severe enough to lead to the seizure of both institutions by the FDIC."

129   Todd Conover and Bill Isaac returned to Paul Volcker's office: Silber, *Volcker*, p. 244.

129   the three regulators left for the Treasury Building to answer a summons: Kilborn, Williams, and Bennett, "The High-Stakes Scramble to Rescue Continental Bank."

129   suggested that the banks in the "safety net" consortium be asked to contribute: Silber, *Volcker*, p. 245.

129   All told, about three dozen people were at the secret meeting: Ibid.

129   "to demonstrate to the world at large that we [have] the ability to cope": Ibid., p. 245.

130   "Why would I want to help a competitor?": Ibid., and Volcker interview.

130   the foreign exchange markets grew utterly chaotic: No byline, "Fed Intervention Disclosed," *New York Times*, September 8, 1984, p. 40.

131   The only path toward permanent stability: Longworth and Barnhart, "The Panic Followed the Sun."

131   The bank was living on borrowed time: Ibid.

131   the deal was almost torn apart by yet another jurisdictional battle: Sprague, *Bailout*, pp. 190–91.

131   Regan belatedly, and publicly, balked: Kenneth B. Noble, "Continental Plan Set Despite Regan," *New York Times*, July 26, 1984, p. D1.

132   "to distance itself from the largest bank bailout in history": Sprague, *Bailout*, pp. 189–90.

132   their argument that bank holding companies would insulate banks: Ibid., p. 189.

132   "Different problems required different solutions": Ibid., p. 199.

132   "massage our prejudices by allowing the holding company to fail": Ibid., p. 190.

132   "They are the banking regulators": Noble, "Continental Plan Set Despite Regan."

132   Bill Isaac outlined the rescue package: House CINB Hearing, p. 414.

133   an "extraordinary intervention in the banking business": Robert A. Bennett, "U.S. Will Invest $4.5 Billion in Rescue of Chicago Bank, Vowing More Aid If Needed," *New York Times*, July 27, 1984, p. 1.

12. MERGERS AND MUTATIONS

138   Corrigan told Paul Volcker and his colleagues: FOMC Meeting transcript, May 21–22, 1984.

138   in a speech to bankers attending the International Monetary Conference:

E. Gerald Corrigan, "New Frontiers in Banking—1984 and On: Regulation and Deregulation," Remarks Before the International Monetary Conference, Philadelphia, PA, June 5, 1984, p. 3.

138   a landscape that would contain a daunting array of risks: Ibid., p. 12.

138   and a host of other contingent liabilities: Ibid., p. 14.

138   one of the hottest products on the financial scene: One of the best early legal assessments of the rise of the swaps market is by Henry T. C. Hu, "Swaps: The Modern Process of Financial Innovation and the Vulnerability of a Regulatory Paradigm," *University of Pennsylvania Law Review* 138, no. 2 (December 1989), p. 333. The article indicates that it "speaks as of October 1, 1989" unless otherwise noted.

138   "barriers are broken and records set": David Shirreff, "The Way to Any Market," *Euromoney*, November 1983, p. 60, cited in Hu, "Swaps," p. 336.

138   No one could be sure how big: As a result of regulators' failure to deal with swaps and similar "hybrid" derivatives during the 1980s, despite myriad warnings, these privately traded derivatives would figure in many frauds and financial crises in the decades that followed.

138   covered a total of roughly $70 billion in debt: Fred R. Bleakley, "Rate Swaps Draw Concerns," *New York Times*, February 7, 1985, p. D1.

139   insurers alone had done roughly $100 billion in swaps: H. J. Maidenberg, "Futures/Options: Insurers' Own Risks," *New York Times*, October 22, 1984, p. D5.

139   "'Hey, I just made a loan to finance a forklift'": Robert A. Bennett, "Risky Trend in Business Borrowing," *New York Times*, May 27, 1984 sec. 3, p. 1.

139   "the inherent risks involved in this unregulated market": Maidenberg, "Futures/Options: Insurers' Own Risks."

139   had asserted in advisory letters: Alton B. Harris, "The CFTC and Derivative Products: Purposeful Ambiguity and Jurisdictional Reach," *Chicago-Kent Law Review* 71, no. 4 (January 1996), pp. 1117–19.

139   The argument was far from over: Ibid.

139   something of a legislative plaything: Ibid., p. 1118.

140   the concern quickly spread to other financial markets: Robert A. Bennett, "A Growing Case of Market Jitters," *New York Times*, May 25, 1984, p. D1.

141   A savvy Paine Webber executive on the NYSE trading floor: Tim Metz, *Black Monday: The Stock Market Catastrophe of 1987 . . . and Beyond* (New York: William and Morrow, 1988), pp. 69–71. The trader was Arthur D. Cashin Jr., who was also an NYSE floor governor. Cashin called his booklet "A Layman's Guide to Program Trading" and boasted (according to Metz, on p. 70) that it became "the most copied document on Wall Street for four months" after he started circulating copies of it in December 1984.

142   a duty to protect corporate shareholders: Michael Blumstein, "The Big Board's New Leader," *New York Times*, May 25, 1984, p. D1.

143   some concern about a practice called "greenmail": John S. R. Shad, "The Leveraging of America," Address to the New York Financial Writers' Association, June 7, 1984, p. 8, John S. R. Shad Papers, Baker Library, Harvard Business School, Cambridge, MA.

143   "There must be a better way than sitting by and getting ripped off": Fred R. Bleakley, "Tough State Treasurer: Jesse Unruh; A Trustee Takes on the Green-mailers," *New York Times*, February 10, 1985, sec. 3, p. 6.

143   he was making plans to attend: Machold interview.

143   Binns apparently was not comfortable with Unruh's idea: Ibid.

144   takeovers and the insider trading conspiracies they were feeding: A defense of the zeitgeist of the takeover era, made famous (or infamous) in Oliver Stone's 1987 film *Wall Street*, was proffered in May 1986 by Ivan Boesky in a commencement address to the business school graduates at Berkeley. His exact phrase was "Greed is all right, by the way. I want you to know that. I think greed is healthy. You can be greedy and still feel good about yourself."

145   Senior bankers across the country heard the bad news first: Robert A. Bennett, "Loss Takes Industry by Surprise," *New York Times*, October 4, 1984, p. D5.

146   and the city's leading bank since the sudden eclipse of Continental: Ibid.

146   Shares of almost every major bank in the country: Ibid.

146   denunciation of the toothless regulators and reckless bankers: House CINB Hearing, p. 1.

146   The next day, he pounced on Todd Conover: Ibid., p. 88.

146   Before the hearing, he had emphatically assured reporters: Robert D. Hershey Jr., "No Danger to Chicago Bank Seen," *New York Times*, October 5, 1984, p. D5.

146   "and this stretches a pessimistic scenario pretty far": House CINB Hearing, p. 396.

147   "They know what we did. They know why we did it": Ibid., p. 470.

147   Isaac painted a vivid picture of what he believed would have happened: Ibid., pp. 478–79.

148   "and I frankly didn't have the courage to do it": Ibid., p. 479.

13. BERKELEY RISING, BANKS FALLING

150   For several years, John O'Brien had been talking: E-mails from John O'Brien, April 24 and 25, 2016 (hereafter "O'Brien 2016 e-mails").

150   more than was needed to cover its retirement obligations: Joel Chernoff, "Manville Forming Contingency Plan," *Pensions & Investment Age*, March 5, 1984, p. 45.

150   which might produce even more money for creditors: Kyrillos, *Cases in Financial Engineering*, p. 773.

151   several people around the table had planes to catch: O'Brien 2016 e-mails.

151   the SEC had agreed to let mutual funds use them: Joint Impact Study 1984, Appendix IV-A, pp. 18–19.

151   After O'Brien finished his presentation: Leland–O'Brien interview 2015.

152   was finally delivered to Congress: Leo Melamed, *Leo Melamed on the Markets* (New York: John Wiley and Sons, 1993), pp. 122, 130.

153   the primary conclusions could have been written by Melamed: Joint Impact Study 1984, p. I.2. It is not clear when the report was actually delivered to Congress. Melamed cites a transmittal letter from Paul Volcker to Senator Jesse Helms dated January 11, 1985 (*Leo Melamed on the Markets*, at p. 128).

153   and "have similar potential for causing harm": Ibid. The report contained a vivid example of what could go wrong: For most of the day on April 19, 1984, the last trading day before the expiration of an OEX option contract, it looked as if the option would expire worthless because it gave traders the right to buy the S&P 100 index for more money than the index was currently worth. During the afternoon, a number of OEX traders had done trades that would allow them to profit when the OEX expired worthless. But in the last fifteen minutes of trading, a slew of large buy orders for fully half the stocks in the S&P 100 index hit the NYSE floor, driving up the final value of the S&P 100 index. Suddenly, the OEX option that was expected to expire worthless in Chicago was no longer worthless. The options traders who had bet against that happening lost money; those who had bet against them had made money. There were immediate demands for an investigation, but no disciplinary action was ever taken. (See Winston Williams, "S.E.C. Studying Trades on the S&P 100 Index," *New York Times*, April 26, 1984, p. D1. Further details were drawn from Joint Impact Study 1984, pp. VIII.8 and VIII.9.)

153   there was no need for new legislation: Ibid., p. I.3.

154   Machold made his way from his home in Princeton: Machold memoir, p. 193.

154   A tall, beefy man, Unruh hated to travel: Bleakley, "Tough State Treasurer."

154   a daylong engagement with the key players in a takeover drama: These details are from Bruce Wasserstein, *Big Deal: The Battle for Control of America's Leading Corporations* (New York: Warner Books, 1998), pp. 195–96.

155   It was better than any Broadway show: Machold interview.

155   a congressional hearing on a broad range of takeover issues: "Corporate Takeovers (Part 1)," Hearings before the Subcommittee on Telecommunications, Consumer Protection, and Finance, of the House Committee on Energy and Commerce, 99th Congress, 1st Sess., February 27, March 12, April 23, and May 22, 1985, pp. 51–52.

156   In the Phillips case, their opposition: Wasserstein, *Big Deal*, p. 479.

156   the extraordinary gathering in Paul Volcker's lofty conference room: Monica Langley, "Bank Board Chairman's Cool Initial Response to Ohio Crisis Linked by Some to GOP Politics," *Wall Street Journal*, entered into the record (without a date or page noted), of "Ohio Savings and Loan Crisis and Collapse of ESM Government Securities" (hereafter "Ohio S&L Hearing"), Hearing Before a Subcommittee of the House Committee on Government Operations, 99th Congress, 1st Sess., April 3, 1985, p. 53.

156   The unlikely fuse that triggered this crisis: The description of these events is drawn from the Ohio S&L Hearing's testimony and supplemental material, pp. 56–58.

157   quickly made emergency loans to the thrift: Ibid., pp. 178–79.

158   as he reportedly told the thrift executives: Ibid.

158   but regulatory barriers at the state and federal level: Gary Klott, "Governor of Ohio Asks U.S. Coverage for Savings Units," *New York Times*, March 17, 1985, p. 1.

158   currency traders pointed directly to the Ohio thrift crisis: Associated Press, "Currency Markets: Dollar Drops Sharply over Banking Worries," *New York Times*, March 19, 1985, p. D18.

158   "there's a systemic risk in those states": Robert A. Bennett, "Ohio Crisis Has Others Worried," *New York Times*, March 18, 1985, p. D1. Another series of bank runs broke out at privately insured thrifts in Maryland a month later, in April 1985, deepening regulatory concern about the speed with which such crises could spread.

14. WITCHING HOURS

160   where Reagan would deliver his prepared remarks: Ronald Reagan, "Remarks to Brokers and Staff of the New York Stock Exchange in New York, New York," March 28, 1985, American Presidency Project website, at http://www .presidency.ucsb/ws/?pid=38402.

160   Then he was on his way: Bernard Weinraub, "President Urging an Economic Shift," *New York Times*, March 29, 1985, p. 1.

161   He was no-nonsense in his business dealings: Erik Ipsen, "The Long Shadow of Bob Birnbaum," *Institutional Investor*, July 1987, p. 188.

161   "of course you'd be looking at whoever was in my job": Interview with Robert J. Birnbaum, July 3, 2015 (hereafter "Birnbaum interview").

161   promptly squelched by the Amex's chairman, Arthur Levitt: In July 1993, Levitt was appointed SEC chairman by President Bill Clinton; when he stepped down in February 2001, he was the commission's longest-serving chairman, eclipsing John Shad's record.

162   In his heart, he believed that the existing rule: Phelan often expressed this view publicly, including at "Impact of Corporate Takeovers," Hearing Before the Securities Subcommittee of the Senate Committee on Banking, Housing, and Urban Affairs, 99th Congress, 1st Sess., April 3, 4, June 6 and 12, 1985, p. 1112.

163   they had instituted automated selling programs to unload stocks: No byline, "Drop in Final Hour Cuts Dow by 12.70, to 1,247.35," *New York Times*, March 16, 1985, p. 33.

163   the *New York Times* sounded an early alert: H. J. Maidenberg, "Futures/ Options: Witching Hours for Investors," *New York Times*, April 15, 1985, p. D4.

164   "we think June's witching hour will be most interesting": Ibid.

164   sending the Dow close to a new record: No byline, "Dow Soars by 24.75, to 1,324.48," *New York Times*, June 22, 1985, p. 35.

164   "Typically, expiration Friday is a psychotic day": Ibid.

164   Melamed saw an opportunity to expand the Merc's influence: Melamed, *Escape to the Futures*, pp. 322–25.

164   "The idea struck me like lightning": Ibid. p. 322.

164   Melamed worked the telephones for an entire weekend: Ibid., p. 323.

165   roots that reached deep into the bedrock: These biographical details are from First Brodsky interview and various corporate biographies he provided.

165   "The question here was 'are you smart?' not 'what's your pedigree?'": Ibid.

166   A trading desk executive had an explanation for this: No byline, "Dow Sets Record 3d Time in a Week," *New York Times*, July 20, 1985, p. 35.

166   Binns had authorized trading in the S&P 500 futures: Confidential interview with former GM fund executive.

166   corporate pension fund executives formed their own organization: Testimony of W. Gordon Binns Jr., "Pension Funds in the Capital Markets: The Impact on Corporate Governance, Trading Activity, and Beneficiaries" (hereafter "1986 Pension Hearing"), Hearing Before the Subcommittee on Telecommunications, Consumer Protection, and Finance of the House Committee on Energy and Commerce, 99th Congress, 2nd Sess., March 19, 1986, p. 5.

167   a vice president at the Bank of New York called a New York Fed official: These events are drawn from a chronology submitted to Congress by the Bank of New York. See "The Federal Reserve Bank of New York Discount Window Advance of $22.6 Billion Extended to the Bank of New York," Hearing Before the Subcommittee on Domestic Monetary Policy of the House Committee on Banking, Finance, and Urban Affairs, 99th Congress, 1st Sess., December 12, 1985, pp. 105–9.

167   Corrigan sometimes likened the financial payment system: Ibid., p. 43.

169   he was trying "to see whether it was practical": Ibid., p. 27.

170   Weeks later, he tried to share the awesome warning: Ibid., p. 47.

15. RATIONAL MARKETS?

171   "There was pandemonium," an executive at one brokerage firm said: John Crudele, "Dow Plunges 39.10 as Stocks Retreat in Heavy Trading," *New York Times*, January 9, 1986, p. 1.

171   was nowhere near as bad as the decline in 1929: Ibid.

171   for some undiscernible reason, suddenly dropped: Ibid.

172   "Panic may be a bit of an overstatement": Ibid.

172   no one in Washington seemed to understand: On October 16, 1985, the SEC sent letters to the options exchanges it regulated, proposing that they limit the size of the stakes that investors could hold or arrange for options to expire on staggered dates, rather than simultaneously—steps that further deterred portfolio insurers from shifting from the futures market to the options market, where their strategy would have been less destabilizing. At a public meeting with the SEC on November 14, officials of the options exchanges protested any change in current market rules. An arbitrage trader with Kidder Peabody was remarkably candid in his opposition to the SEC's initiative. "I love volatility because I'm a trader," he said. Arbitrage trades "compress market movements into shorter spans of time," he continued, "but it just makes them do what they would have done anyway." See James Sterngold, "Futures/Options: Arbitrage-Led Stock Volatility," *New York Times*, November 25, 1985, p. D5.

172   Shad at the SEC saw the increased use of computer-driven arbitrage: Vise and Coll, *Eagle on the Street*, p. 198.

172   new trading regulations would merely benefit the old guard: Ibid., p. 197.

173   a healthy and probably inevitable consequence of computer technology: Ibid., p. 198.

173   without SEC support, it was unlikely anyone else could push: See Khademian,

The SEC and Capital Market Regulation, pp. 12–13. At the end of the 1980s, one former SEC staffer told her, "I don't know of a single time when the SEC opposed something that got enacted. Too many people in Congress . . . feel they have to defer to [the greater expertise of] the SEC." Congressional deference eroded substantially in later years; it is no longer uncommon for the SEC to find itself implementing laws it had opposed as unwise. Khademian provides an especially insightful look at the role this deference to expertise played in the 1970s when the agency largely fended off demands by a Democratic Congress that it move faster and more forcefully to end fixed commissions on the NYSE and create an interconnected electronic market, called the "national market system." The result, especially the SEC's fitful and fragmented concept of a "national market system," influenced by default many of the epic changes in market structure that erupted after 1980.

173   Several traders did notice: John Crudele, "Stocks End Mixed; Dow Eases by 0.92," *New York Times*, December 21, 1985, p. 37.

173   John Phelan was growing increasingly worried: To be sure, the number of people with an indirect stake in the stock market through a mutual fund had grown by more than 30 percent in two years. However, the number of people who owned stocks directly—who had enough confidence in the market and their own judgment to be hands-on investors—had fallen 3 percent just since 1983. The only comfort was that the NYSE had held on to more individual investors than the other exchanges, who saw their population of individual customers drop 5 percent. See James Sterngold, "Investor Rise Tied to Mutual Funds," *New York Times*, December 5, 1985, p. D17.

173   By the end of 1985, it had doubled again: Jay O. Light and Andre F. Perold, "The Institutionalization of Wealth: Changing Patterns of Investment Decision Making," a chapter in *Wall Street and Regulation*, ed. Samuel L. Hayes III (Brighton, MA: Harvard Business School Press, 1987).

173   some of it had flowed into passive index funds: Ibid.

174   "Individuals don't want to get whipsawed in a market": Sterngold, "Investor Rise Tied to Mutual Funds."

174   The vote carried 4 to 3, to the chairman's shock: Silber, *Volcker*, pp. 255–56.

174   "in case anyone thought he might change his mind": Ibid., p. 255.

175   Volcker handed Baker "a handwritten resignation letter": Ibid., p. 256.

175   a face-saving delay in the small interest rate cut: Greider, *Secrets of the Temple*, p. 700.

175   gripes didn't have to travel far to reach the ears of Congress: James Sterngold, "Futures/Options: Role of the Floor Trader," *New York Times*, March 10, 1986, p. D4. This practice by members of Congress was prohibited by ethics legislation enacted in 1991.

176   had formed a $1 million "defense fund" in November: James Sterngold, "C.F.T.C., Exchanges Fight It Out," *New York Times*, November 21, 1985, p. D1.

176   "inexperience or motivations beyond our comprehension": Tamarkin, *The Merc*, p. 306.

176   Volume Investors, a significant clearing firm: To its embarrassment, the New York exchange had no mechanism for rescuing the clearing firm, whose

customers became tangled in the labyrinth of bankruptcy court, although it did eventually cover about half of the $14 million lost in the default. See Tamarkin, *The Merc*, p. 265; and Charles R. Geisst, *Wheels of Fortune: The History of Speculation from Scandal to Respectability* (Hoboken, NJ: John Wiley and Sons, 2002), pp. 257–58.

176   "heightens the potential for a default of far-reaching consequences": Tamarkin, *The Merc*, p. 265.

176   For years, the CFTC had known that this was inadequate: Testimony of Susan Phillips, "Reauthorization of the Commodity Futures Trading Commission" (hereafter "House CFTC Reauthorization 1986"), Hearings Before the Subcommittee on Conservation, Credit, and Rural Development of the House Committee on Agriculture, 99th Congress, 2nd Sess., March 18 and 19, 1986, pp. 12–15.

176   "the foremost example of regulatory meddling": Tamarkin, *The Merc*, p. 306.

177   were small pests that the commission had been battling: Dealers defended leverage contracts as tools that let small investors buy actual commodities (almost always gold or silver) on the installment plan, and argued that the contracts were outside the CFTC's reach, as it did not regulate the sale of physical commodities. Critics said leverage contracts were a throwback to the bucket shop days of old Chicago, since investors used them chiefly to speculate, not to accumulate gold or silver. The second perennial off-exchange pest, the commodity option, was another retail product that had long been generating complaints from consumers about deceptive sales pitches and sham sales firms. Here, too, the CFTC had spent a lot of time and money battling fraud and abuse, without much to show for it.

177   the CFTC backed off from enforcing its new audit trail standards: Sterngold, "Futures/Options: Role of the Floor Trader."

177   rather than automatically time-stamping them: This was called the "computerized trade reconstruction," or CTR, system. It used prenumbered sequential trading cards and other bits of paperwork to "impute the one minute time of execution." Its deficiencies would be widely exposed in a subsequent federal investigation. See Jerry W. Markham, "Prohibited Floor Trading Activities Under the Commodity Exchange Act," *Fordham Law Review* 58, no. 1 (1989), pp. 15–17.

177   their message for her was crystal clear: House CFTC Reauthorization 1986, pp. 13, 20–21.

177   Seevers, a sharply dressed executive at Goldman Sachs: Ibid., p. 111. Seevers had been an original member of the CFTC and served briefly as its acting chairman before Jim Stone's appointment in the late 1970s. At Goldman Sachs, he worked with institutional investors—"mutual funds, pension funds and so forth," he said—who were starting to use the futures markets as part of their investment strategies.

178   "who is really informed enough, or smart enough": Ibid., p. 111.

178   "aberrations associated with that third Friday have been diminishing": Ibid., p. 112.

179   A front-page story in the next day's *New York Times*: John Crudele, "Dow Falls By 35.68 in a Wild Session," *New York Times*, March 22, 1986, p. 1.

179   caught the mood in just four words: James Sterngold, " 'Triple Witching Hour' Havoc," *New York Times*, March 22, 1985, p. D1.

179   It took a half hour after the market closed: Ibid.

179   "People trade stocks like they were a commodity": Ibid.

180   looked skeptically over the luncheon china: Neither Birnbaum nor O'Brien can recall exactly when this event occurred, though both remember it in almost identical detail. John Phelan, in an interview published in 2005, recalled that it occurred "sometime in the summer of 1986," so I have relied on that account. See Weiner, *What Goes Up*, pp. 275–76.

180   "it's really like we're having a sale—a bargain sale on stocks": LOR interview 2016.

180   the growing scale of portfolio insurance trades worried him: Weiner, *What Goes Up*, p. 276.

181   naïve to think the market would adapt to portfolio insurance: Birnbaum interview.

181   he was probably just going to stay on the sidelines: Ibid.

182   decided to buy First Options Inc., the largest clearing firm: Jayne Jung, untitled profile of O'Connor and Associates, Risk.net website, September 1, 2007, on the occasion of the thirtieth anniversary of the firm's founding.

182   when the Chicago Board Options Exchange was young: Ibid.

182   By 1986, its ambitions had grown bigger: Leslie Wayne, "The Secret World of the O'Connors," *New York Times*, September 12, 1982, sec. 3, p. 1.

182   It needed profitable lines of business: Ibid.

16. PANDORA'S PORTFOLIOS

183   an investment banker with Drexel Burnham Lambert: Stewart, *Den of Thieves*, pp. 66–67.

183   With Phelan sitting at the same big round table: Vise and Coll, *Eagle on the Street*, pp. 300–302.

184   Levine pointed fingers at others: Ibid., p. 310.

184   Long days and nights later, a deal was struck: Stewart's *Den of Thieves* provides a vivid account of the tense secret negotiations that led to this settlement. See pp. 274–89.

184   That was as far as John Shad was willing to go: Nathaniel C. Nash, "S.E.C. Acts on 'Triple Witching,' " *New York Times*, September 11, 1986, D1.

184   a meeting open only to the commissioners and a few key members: Vise and Coll, *Eagle on the Street*, p. 321.

184   "seemed stunned by the scope of the revelations": Stewart, *Den of Thieves*, p. 283.

184   a penalty almost equal to the SEC's entire annual budget: Vise and Coll, *Eagle on the Street*, p. 323.

185   Phelan believed, from his decades on the floor: Nash, "S.E.C. Acts on 'Triple Witching.' "

185   "I think money managers panicked": John Crudele, "Stock Prices Fall by Record Amount in Busiest Session," *New York Times*, September 12, 1986, p. 1.

185   One Wall Street executive even pointed a finger at John Shad: Ibid.

186   Indeed, arbitrage trading had been credited: Jeffrey M. Laderman and John N. Frank, "How Chicago Zaps Wall Street," *BusinessWeek*, September 29, 1986.

186   In the first minutes of trading in Chicago: James Sterngold, "A Harrowing Day on Wall St.," *New York Times*, September 12, 1986, D1.

186   a ripe opportunity for index arbitrage: "The Role of Index-Related Trading in the Market Decline on September 11 and 12, 1986" (hereafter "SEC September 1986 Report"), a Report by the U.S. Securities and Exchange Commission Division of Market Regulation, March 1987, p. 9.

186   Subsequent investigation showed that the S&P 500 futures: Ibid., p. 8.

186   This wasn't the whole story about Thursday's historic decline: On September 2, 1986, analyst Robert Prechter, who published the influential *Elliott Wave Theorist* newsletter, had urged investors to take their profits in the stock market, but his followers probably would not have waited a full ten days to act on his advice. A four-day decline in the market can have its own discouraging effects, turning optimists into pessimists; no doubt, that was an additional factor in the decline.

186   The nosedive continued in the foreign markets: Vartanig G. Vartan, "Stocks Continue to Drop Sharply; Volume Climbs to a Record Level," *New York Times*, September 13, 1986, p. 1.

186   Tokyo had its steepest one-day plunge in history: Barnaby J. Feder, "Stocks Fall on Foreign Exchanges," *New York Times*, September 13, 1986, p. 36.

187   they did not believe they would actually be able to sell: SEC September 1986 Report, p. 8.

187   Phelan said after the closing bell on Friday: Sloane, "Computers Keep Up with Action."

188   arbitrage-related program trading was starting to dominate: Kenneth N. Gilpin, "Big Funds Caught by Surprise," *New York Times*, September 13, 1986, p. D1.

188   especially when compared to the $150 million they had managed: Kyrillos, *Cases in Financial Engineering*, p. 778.

188   had begun to deeply worry Rubinstein: MacKenzie, *An Engine, Not a Camera*, p. 176, confirmed in an e-mail from Mark Rubinstein dated April 11, 2016.

189   he sometimes felt as if he and his partners had opened Pandora's box: Ibid., p. 184.

189   if LOR shut down: Ibid., pp. 183–84.

189   "I thought, that's us. That is *us*": LOR interview 2016.

190   Those two men had a more urgent issue to discuss: Vise and Coll, *Eagle on the Street*, p. 324.

190   would have to disclose the small detail of its CEO's arrest: Stewart, *Den of Thieves*, p. 289.

190   it simply underscored how deeply Paul Volcker was trusted: Even at his own farewell dinner in June 1987, Shad opened his remarks with a tribute to Volcker: "The purpose of this evening was to permit me to say, 'Thank you,' but as is not unusual in this town, subsequent events have overshadowed this modest occasion. On Tuesday Paul Volcker announced his decision to retire from the

Fed. I would like to propose a toast to Paul Volcker, in appreciation of his mon-
umental contributions to the nation and the world over the past 8 years" (John
Shad, "6/4/87 Dinner [Speech] Speaking Copy," dated June 6, 1987, John S. R.
Shad Papers, Baker Library, Harvard Business School, Cambridge, MA).

191   Shad alerted Jim Baker and Donald Regan to the news: Vise and Coll, *Eagle on the Street*, p. 324.

191   within days, the two men would be conferring: Donald T. Regan, "Note for Al
Kingon," November 17, 1986, #440502, FI003, Ronald Reagan Presidential
Library and Museum Archives. After weekend headlines linking Boesky to
Michael Milken and Drexel, Regan wrote, "I spoke with Jim Baker this morning regarding the recent developments in the New York arbitrage/junk bond
arena. He recalled that last year the [Economic Policy Council] had considered
this area but had decided not to recommend any action. However, in view of
recent developments, he agreed that this subject should be re-examined." The
same day, Regan had lunch with Mitchell E. Daniels Jr., assistant to the president for political and intergovernmental affairs. (See "Memorandum for
Donald T. Regan from Mitchell E. Daniels," November 18, 1986, #448003,
FI003, Reagan Presidential Library Archives, hereafter "Daniels Memo.") The
next day, Daniels sent Regan a lengthy and revealing memo about how the
White House should respond to the Boesky/Drexel news, recommending "that
we take the offensive regarding insider trading and other abuses in the securities industry . . . There is no need for us to take a back seat on this issue; in
fact, it would be dangerous to do so. It sounds as though you are already well
along in this area, but for the record my suggestions are:

- Have the President meet with John Shad, or the entire Commission,
  or Shad's enforcement staff, or in some conspicuous fashion receive a
  briefing on the overall situation and deliver congratulations for effective
  service.
- Direct the production of legislative initiatives to strengthen SEC powers
  in this area and/or extend them to international dealings or other uncov-
  ered areas.
- Select a prestigious business or financial forum at which the President
  could deliver a strong speech condemning shady practices, pledging continued vigorous enforcement, and perhaps commenting on the possible
  harm to competitiveness of the merger/takeover binge."

191   Shad waited until 3:30 p.m. to notify the CFTC: "Oversight Hearing on the
Commodity Futures Trading Commission" (hereafter "CFTC Oversight
Hearing 1987"), Hearing Before the Senate Committee on Agriculture, Nutri-
tion, and Forestry, 100th Congress, 1st Sess., July 15, 1987, p. 90.

191   and the call went to Bob Birnbaum: Interview with Robert J. Birnbaum,
April 30, 2007, "Oral Histories," SECHS website, used with permission from
www.sechistorical.org, http://3197d6d14b5f19f2f440-5e13d29c4c016cf96cbbf
d197c579b45.r81.cf1.rackcdn.com/collection/oral-histories
/birnbaum043007Transcript.pdf.

191   Shad read his brief remarks from a single sheet of paper: John Shad, "11/14/86

4:30 PM Press Conference," John S. R. Shad Papers, Baker Library, Harvard Business School, Cambridge, MA.

191   "three rumors—all of which turned out to be true": Vise and Coll, *Eagle on the Street*, p. 330.

191   "the one that seemed the most incredible": Ibid., pp. 330–31.

191   not Shad's first public relations blunder: Ibid., p. 332.

192   The only plausible excuse was that Shad thought: See Stewart, *Den of Thieves*, p. 289: "Chairman Shad, in particular, remained concerned about safeguarding the SEC's $100 million, which in part depended on the value of Boesky's huge portfolio."

192   prices started falling in Europe even before New York's opening: John Crudele, "Takeover Stocks Fall Sharply," *New York Times*, November 18, 1986, p. D1.

192   and the news rapidly spread: Stewart, *Den of Thieves*, pp. 295–96.

192   Boesky actually paid fully half his entire net worth: Ibid., p. 297.

192   Boesky had been actively trading S&P 500 futures: Some critics thought Boesky hoped to profit from any market decline triggered by news of his arrest, but there is scant evidence for that, as he unwound those positions too early to reap his rewards. His entire trading record was detailed in CFTC Oversight Hearing 1987, pp. 3–4. See CFTC commissioner Walter Seale's testimony at pp. 107–8: "There is no indication that Mr. Boesky somehow wildly profiteered from this announcement . . . Certainly, if Mr. Boesky . . . wanted to somehow illegitimately profiteer from futures positions, he needs somebody to give him lessons, because he did not do it here."

192   "could not understand why the Boesky case had turned against them": Vise and Coll, *Eagle on the Street*, p. 330.

192   bashing Wall Street crime had proved to be a successful election issue: One White House aide noted in a memo written a few days after the Boesky announcement, "The takeover artists fit the stereotype, to which the news media is receptive, of an overly acquisitive elite with no sense of social responsibility. The Democratic Party is at its demagogic best when it purports to defend the country and its 'little guys' from rapacious villains like these." See Daniels Memo.

192   and was firmly riveted on the jaw-dropping details: Wilentz, *The Age of Reagan*, pp. 212–33. The scandal would drag on through 1987, with criminal prosecutions stretching into 1988. For a wonderfully comprehensive account of this convoluted scandal, see Understanding the Iran Contra Affairs [sic], a website created under the supervision of Professor Ross Cheit at Brown University: http://www.brown.edu/Research/Understanding_the_Iran_Contra_Affair/about.php.

193   had been a financially savvy cog in Washington's political machinery: "Memorandum for Donald T. Regan, from Alfred H. Kingon, Subject: Program Selling," October 23, 1986, #452965, FI003, Reagan Presidential Library Archives. Kingon, a former Wall Street investment banker, was secretary to the Cabinet and a close Regan aide in the White House. The lengthy memo, clearly part of an ongoing conversation, showed that both Regan and Kingon were worried about program trading. Kingon wrote, "I thought you would like

to hear the Wall Street comments from my survey regarding whether effective action has been taken against the computerized sell programs that key off market future/stock price arbitrage. *Like us, the thoughtful people who have considered the problem are torn"* (emphasis added). His contacts all "had a strong free market bias and did not want the government to interfere," but they were concerned that if program trades led to a widespread loss of investor confidence, "the consequences of that would be frightening," Kingon noted.

193   ways the president could publicly show his support: See Daniels Memo.

193   Regan's days in the White House were numbered: Although the scandal led indirectly to his angry resignation as chief of staff, Regan was never accused of any wrongdoing. In his memoir (*For the Record*), Regan denied any advance knowledge about the complex Iran-Contra transactions and largely blamed his ouster from the West Wing on strong differences of opinion with First Lady Nancy Reagan.

193   to liberalize its interpretation of the Glass-Steagall Act: Simon Kwan, "Cracking the Glass-Steagall Barriers," Economic Letters, March 21, 1997, Federal Reserve Bank of San Francisco website, at http://www.frbsf.org/economic -research/publications/economic-letter/1997/march/cracking-the-glass -steagall-barriers/. The Fed permitted bank holding companies to underwrite and deal in certain securities so long as no more than 5 percent of their revenues came from those activities.

193   Whatever Volcker's misgivings: The evidence is murky on Volcker's position on every step the Federal Reserve Board took to open loopholes in Glass-Steagall. But the Fed chairman clearly differed with the Reagan administration on several key deregulation issues. See Nathaniel C. Nash, "How the White House Lost Its Big Bank Battle," *New York Times*, July 12, 1987, sec. 3, p. 8.

194   He titled the piece "Trials and Tribulations": There are two versions of the document in the Shad papers in the Baker Library. One, dated April 2, 1984, is handwritten in pencil, densely crammed onto two sheets of yellow lined paper from a legal pad. The other, dated April 10, 1984, is a typed, heavily edited version that seems to be "page 11" of a speech or presentation made to a group of major GOP donors. They are not identical; the quotes used here are from the typed version, given the many abbreviations and sentence fragments in the handwritten version. John S. R. Shad Papers, Baker Library, Harvard Business School.

194   he had no appetite for another term at the SEC: Vise and Coll, *Eagle on the Street*, p. 339.

17. JANUARY OMENS, JULY ALARMS

195   the Long Island Rail Road had gone on strike: Richard Levine, "Strike on L.I.R.R. Stops All Service; New Talks Today; Bus Runs Planned," *New York Times*, January 19, 1987, p. 1.

195   a mix of local racial unrest and Washington scandals: The racial unrest was ignited by an attack by a group of white teenagers on three young black men

who had wandered into their Howard Beach neighborhood in mid-December. On January 19, 1987, as this week opened, New York City mayor Ed Koch had an op-ed essay published in the *New York Times* urging citizens, black and white, to turn away from "stereotyping, discrimination and violence." See "3 in Howard Beach Attack Are Guilty of Manslaughter; A Year of Tension and Waiting for the Verdict," *New York Times*, December 22, 1987, p. B10.

195   The Dow had gained an astonishing 5 percent: John Crudele, "Dow Tops 2,000 for the First Time as Wall St. Extends Latest Rally," *New York Times*, January 9, 1987, p. 1.

195   That last-minute nosedive in the futures pits: H. J. Maidenberg, "Dow Up 13th Time, Closing at 2,104.47," *New York Times*, January 21, 1987, p. D1. Maidenberg's source was identified as John M. Blin, "who heads a company bearing his name that designs trading programs." Blin speculated that institutions were, in effect, shorting the S&P 500 futures contract, hoping their profits on those short positions would offset any losses they incurred in the stock market.

196   its largest one-day gain in history, 51.60 points: H. J. Maidenberg, "51.60 Surge Puts Dow at 2,145.67," *New York Times*, January 23, 1987, p. D1. Maidenberg's coverage was, as usual, more alert to developments in the futures market than was typical in stock market stories in the mainstream press.

196   the complex interplay between the futures markets and the stock exchange: Ibid.

196   Leo Melamed was becoming increasingly worried: Melamed, *Escape to the Futures*, p. 347.

196   showed "a heavy imbalance of orders to sell": John Crudele, "Wall St.'s Memorable Minute," *New York Times*, December 20, 1986, p. D1.

196   in those final moments, Salomon Brothers: Ibid. Further inquiry revealed that the orders reflected a sudden shift in strategy by index arbitrageurs. While the market's focus was on the expiring December S&P 500 index futures contract, Merc traders had unexpectedly bid up the unexpired March spooz contract to a price that was considerably higher than the underlying stocks. So, the sharpest arbitrageurs simply sold the March contract on the Merc and bought stocks on the Big Board. Their massive stock purchases also drove up the underlying index, and consequently made their expiring December contract more valuable.

196   The SEC's only public response was to complain: No byline, "'Witching' Trade Inquiry," *New York Times*, December 24, 1986, p. D12. This very brief report said the SEC had merely "expressed dissatisfaction" with the last half hour of trading on December 19, and said the source of "the SEC's mild upset" was Salomon Brothers' failure to report its massive buy orders in advance.

196   simply because it was a New York proposal: Melamed, *Escape to the Futures*, p. 346.

197   the Chicago Board Options Exchange flatly said: The CBOE later explained that it feared legal consequences from changing the terms of the popular option; instead, it amended the terms of the far less popular S&P 500 option, which remained far less popular.

197   Prices started to roar upward: James Sterngold, "Wall St. Day: Torrid Start, Sudden Chill," *New York Times*, January 24, 1987, p. 1.

197   By 1:39 p.m., the Dow had gained more than 3 percent: SEC September 1986 Report, March 1987, p. 28.

197   an unprecedented drop of 115 points: Ibid. The SEC calculated the midday plunge at 115 points, not 114 points, the figure widely used in news coverage at the time.

197   a newswire report on some comments Paul Volcker had made: John Crudele, "The Dow Average Swings 114 Points; Closes Down by 44," *New York Times*, January 24, 1987, p. 1.

197   Index futures followed the options down: The final studies of the day's trading were still months away, and would be inconclusive when they were done, but traders at the time noted immediately that there had been a huge surge in the volume of trading in the Major Market Index futures contract on the Chicago Board of Trade, and in the twenty stocks in the MMI that were traded on the NYSE, suggesting heavy arbitrage trading. (Volume in the S&P 500 index futures on the Merc, by comparison, was not as skewed, although it became sharply cheaper than its underlying stocks late in the afternoon—just before the market reversed and drove back up.) See Kenneth N. Gilpin, "Program Trading Widens the Swings," *New York Times*, January 24, 1987, p. 37.

197   prices "suddenly were sucked into a free fall": Sterngold, "Wall St. Day: Torrid Start, Sudden Chill."

198   Terrified institutional investors had started to sell: Ibid.

198   "There are no words to describe what we were going through": Ibid.

198   A retail broker admitted, "Frankly, I have great difficulty explaining": Vartanig G. Vartan, "Plenty of Orders, Few Explanations," *New York Times*, January 24, 1987, p. 37.

198   "It's berserk. It's total confusion": Crudele, "The Dow Average Swings 114 Points; Closes Down by 44."

198   Well, they knew *what* had happened: In Dow points, on January 23, 1987, the Dow rose 64 points, fell 115 points, rose 60 points, and then fell 50 points in the final 50 minutes. As noted, a modern reader should add a zero to each of those numbers to get a sense of what this chaotic day would have felt like.

198   One result was a cover story: Grant, "John Phelan vs. Program Trading."

198   "a program trading scenario—which he calls 'financial meltdown'": Ibid. Phelan later said (see Weiner, *What Goes Up*, p. 276) that he coined the term to echo events at Chernobyl, the Soviet power plant in what is now Ukraine, in April 1986. It is possible this was the first application of the term to the financial markets; the *Oxford English Dictionary* cites only scientific uses of the term as late as 1975. If so, Phelan's use of the term, routine to modern readers, would have been far more shocking to his audience, which would have linked it only to horrific nuclear accidents.

199   The article cited Phelan's dilemma: Ibid.

199   "theoretically, we ought to keep quiet about it": Ibid.

199   thought the stock market had gone completely nuts: Melamed, *Escape to the Futures*, p. 340. Melamed did not publicly acknowledge at the time that the

heavy use of index-related hedging strategies by giant pension funds, along with the buy programs that were the flip side of sell programs, may well have helped push the market up to its lofty levels. The SEC also attributed the rising market to "investor perceptions," not artificial trading strategies.

199   the first to signal the bad news to the world. Ibid.

199   "The hectic day was enough to push Shearson Lehman": Laurie Cohen and Carol Jouzaitis, "S&P Futures Pit Giving Merc Black Eye," *Chicago Tribune*, February 22, 1987.

199   "Tempers turned sour and snappish": Tamarkin, *The Merc*, p. 317.

199   "Traders bitch about a lot of things": Ibid., p. 318.

200   experienced growing pains on an epic scale: Ibid. p. 317.

200   a critical account in *Futures* magazine noted: Ibid.

200   Even a top Merc executive conceded: Ibid.

200   "began hurling manifold accusations at one another": Ibid.

200   "often difficult for customers to prove they were cheated": Cohen and Jouzaitis, "S&P Futures Pit Giving Merc Black Eye."

200   "there is even an array of jargon to describe the cheating": Ibid.

200   Melamed was able to head off a rebellious referendum: Tamarkin, *The Merc*, p. 319.

201   as soon as the board's research was complete: Ibid. Within days of the traders' petition, the Merc board announced several serious (and arguably overdue) disciplinary actions against specific S&P 500 pit traders, two of whom were expelled and hit with heavy fines.

201   had been cheerfully facing down critics: At a conference in New York in June 1986, he squared off in a formal debate with Bruce I. Jacobs, the former Prudential executive now running his own asset management firm in New Jersey. (See Trudy Ring, "Portfolio Insurance's Merits Spur Debate," *Pensions & Investment Age*, July 7, 1986.) Jacobs was not the only critic. A senior investment consultant at Mercer-Meidinger, a major benefits consulting firm, publicly compared portfolio insurance to "pouring gasoline on the fire of a declining market." (See Daniel Forbes, "Hidden Risks in Portfolio Insurance," *Dun's Business Month*, September 1986, p. 34.) The consultant, William M. Morris, also cautioned that "the selling pressure of insurers trying to get out of the market could magnify the decline until we get a 150-point drop." In a January 1987 paper, an executive at Batterymarch Financial Management cautioned, as Leland had, that portfolio insurance would not protect a portfolio "when the market drops rapidly," citing a 10 percent drop in the Italian market over two days in May 1986 as "a situation that would have been a nightmare for the dynamic hedgers." (See William E. Jacques, "Portfolio Insurance or Job Insurance?" *Financial Analysts Journal* 43, no. 1 [January–February 1987]: 7.) Jacques conceded, however, that portfolio insurance as typically employed "works fairly well," except in calamitous markets. Less publicly, the former Wells Fargo Investment Advisors "quants" who moved to Mellon Capital had become quiet but influential critics of portfolio insurance. (See MacKenzie, *An Engine, Not a Camera*, p. 322n2.) MacKenzie credits William Fouse, who

had joined Mellon after being key to the glory days at WFIA, and his colleague Jeffrey P. Ricker as the most significant pre-crash critics of portfolio insurance.

201 He insisted that investors looking for bargains: Forbes, "Hidden Risks in Portfolio Insurance."

201 One knowledgeable market figure worried publicly: Ibid.

201 They conservatively estimated that a minimum of $80 billion: The Brady Commission would later conclude that there was as much as $90 billion involved in portfolio insurance by October 1987, and noted that the amount had grown sharply just since the beginning of the year. Report of the Presidential Task Force on Market Mechanisms (hereafter "Brady Report"), January 1988, p. 29.

202 The explanation Leland got from a senior executive: Leland–O'Brien interview 2014.

202 Leland had woven a key assumption into his academic papers: Leland, "Who Should Buy Portfolio Insurance?" In this short paper, Leland inserted a half dozen times the proviso about continuous trading. (See pp. 581, 586, 591, 593, and 594.)

202 barring a brief reaction to some abrupt crisis: MacKenzie, *An Engine, Not a Camera*, p. 182.

202 he began to worry whether that assumption: LOR interview 2016.

202 had developed competing products of their own: For example, see Richard Bookstaber, *A Demon of Our Own Design: Markets, Hedge Funds, and the Perils of Financial Innovation* (Hoboken, NJ: John Wiley and Sons, 2007), pp. 10–12, for an account of his work at Morgan Stanley to develop a competing product; within a year, the product "covered" $3 billion in assets.

202 "There are a lot of reasons to be nervous about it": Wunsch interview 2015.

203 disruptions that "could shake the market apart": R. Steven Wunsch, "Stock Index Futures," Commentary from the Financial Futures Department of Kidder Peabody and Co., June 9, 1987, in the author's files. Wunsch was arguing for publicly announcing portfolio insurance and index arbitrage orders in advance so they could be matched up and filled separately—what he called sunshine trading. Wunsch warned that although Phelan and other NYSE officials were wrong to blame portfolio insurance and other program trading for the "meltdown" risk, their warnings nevertheless "should be taken very seriously, because . . . they are in a very good position to recognize approaching danger, having built, maintained and operated the machine that may soon fail."

204 The NYFE started the paperwork to put the concept: Wunsch interview 2015.

204 He handed in his resignation to President Reagan: Silber, *Volcker*, p. 260.

204 a graceful way out of a job that no longer appealed to him: Robert D. Hershey Jr., "Shad Plans to Leave SEC Post," *New York Times*, March 21, 1987, p. 37.

204 had both stepped down in mid-1985: Conover had been replaced by Robert L. Clarke, a Texas banking attorney who in 1987 was trying to persuade a recalcitrant Congress that he needed more money and additional powers to deal with an increasingly dismal outlook for S&Ls and banks. Joining him in the argument was Bill Isaac's successor at the FDIC, William Seidman, a veteran Washington hand.

205   and then they asked if he was a Republican: Interview with David S. Ruder, January 13–14, 2015 (hereafter "Ruder interview January 2015").

205   he wasn't the administration's first choice: Ibid. At some point during that day, Ruder learned that Rudolph Giuliani, the tough-talking U.S. attorney in Manhattan, and John C. Whitehead, a former Goldman Sachs partner then serving as a deputy secretary of state, had both declined the SEC appointment.

205   The realization stung a little, but he was still intrigued: Nathaniel C. Nash, "Novice Regulator: David S. Ruder; Seeking Tighter Control over the Financial Markets," *New York Times*, January 17, 1988, sec. 3, p. 10.

206   Ruder flew to New York and took a cab: Ruder interview January 2015.

206   It took the Senate almost two months to confirm: Nathaniel C. Nash, "Business People: Ruder Is Approved as S.E.C. Chairman," *New York Times*, August 7, 1987, p. D2.

206   his close friend and mentor, the philosopher Ayn Rand: Soma Golden, "Why Greenspan Said 'Yes,'" *New York Times*, July 28, 1974, sec. 2, p. 1. Golden wrote, "It is difficult, perhaps impossible, to understand the President's new adviser without understanding his 20-year relationship" with Rand, who told Golden that she believed in "the morality and the desirability of complete laissez-faire capitalism and what she called 'rational selfishness.'" She said Greenspan shared that belief, but added, "Neither he nor I expect it overnight." Greenspan confirmed this, saying, "If I were starting from scratch, I know what I'd like to see in this country. But to go from here to there would be an enormously difficult matter of disentanglement, with great problems of equity and justice along the way."

206   prescriptions for strengthening the retirement system: Justin Martin, *Greenspan: The Man Behind the Money* (Cambridge, MA: Perseus Publishing, 2000), pp. 146–47.

206   After an initial delay attributed to the complexity of his financial statements: No byline, "Briefing: Waiting for Greenspan," *New York Times*, July 8, 1987, p. B6.

207   Phillips made an ominous disclosure about the crazy trading: 1987 Program Trading Hearing, p. 49.

207   argued that portfolio insurance was just "a twist on an old strategy": Ibid., p. 74.

207   That, too, should have been at least a little worrisome: See John Kenneth Galbraith, *The Great Crash 1929* (1954; repr. New York: Mariner Books/Houghton Mifflin Harcourt, 2009), p. 103. Galbraith's 1954 classic, a bestseller in 1955 and still in print in 1987 (indeed, never out of print to this day), described the "chain reaction" of stop-loss orders that hit the market on October 24, 1929, the prelude to the next week's crash: "Prices as they fell that morning kept crossing a large volume of stop-loss orders . . . Each of these stop-loss orders tripped more securities into the market and drove prices down farther. Each spasm of liquidation thus insured that another would follow." A similar description was offered by economist Robert T. Patterson, who also noted that stop-loss orders had "added to the pressure upon the market" during several

precipitous declines in the months leading up to the two-day crash on October 28 and 29, 1929. (See Robert T. Patterson, *The Great Boom and Panic, 1921–1929* [Chicago: Henry Regnery Press, 1965], pp. 62 and 71.) Once portfolio insurance had been perceived as a newfangled stop-loss order, its potential for triggering a downward cascade of prices arguably should have been recognized, based on the 1929 experience.

207   Clearly, the markets could handle portfolio insurance selling: 1987 Program Trading Hearing, p. 76.

208   This was unlikely to lead to a meltdown, he explained: Ibid., p. 126.

208   until the two markets were hopelessly out of whack: If the subcommittee had read and understood Johnson's written testimony (ibid., pp. 143–44) they would have been even less comforted. He explained that various arbitrage strategies that called for buying futures and selling stocks were being regularly pursued by index funds—whose assets, as noted, totaled a staggering *$250 billion*. When the stock index futures were cheaper than the stocks, index funds could then sell all their stocks, replicate the value of the portfolio with index futures at a much lower cost, and invest the extra cash in Treasury bills. As the interest rates on Treasury bills rose—and they had been rising for months—this kind of arbitrage became even more attractive to these mammoth funds.

208   "Some changes to current practices might be useful": Ibid., pp. 170–71.

208   He was not asked what those changes should be: Binns's written testimony was a candid litany of what could go wrong with portfolio insurance, although he, too, placed a great deal of faith in bargain hunters coming into the market to avert a meltdown (ibid., pp. 182–83).

208   this required the process of index arbitrage: Ibid., p. 201.

209   he said there was currently $250 billion in index funds: Ibid., p. 222.

209   to permit a greater use of index options and sunshine trading: Ibid., p. 226.

209   there would have been no effect on the market: Ibid., pp. 227–28. Wunsch urged the exchanges to find a way to pair up those buyers and sellers; when they didn't, he developed such an electronic marketplace himself, the Arizona Stock Exchange.

18. THE WORST WEEKS EVER

213   getting to know the staff and other members: Justin Martin, *Greenspan: The Man Behind the Money* (Cambridge, MA: Perseus Publishing, 2000), pp. 171–72.

213   hearing Corrigan fret aloud about the mismatch: Corrigan interview.

213   to develop plans for responding to a crisis: Steven K. Beckner, *Back from the Brink: The Greenspan Years* (New York: John Wiley and Sons, 1996), p. 35.

213   the Fed staff put together an internal report: Ibid., p. 36.

213   Greenspan presided over his first meeting: FOMC Meeting transcript, August 18, 1987, p. 1.

214   "no one even mentioned the stock market": Ibid., p. 23.

214   the Dow closed at another new high: Some subsequent accounts of this period

put the Dow's August 25 peak at 2746.65, its high during that day. This account, like most of the official postmortems, uses the Dow's close that day as the benchmark for the subsequent decline, since it is invariably being compared with other closing levels, not with the Dow's high or low during those days.

214   what he later called the "speculative froth": Alan Greenspan, *The Age of Turbulence: Adventures in a New World* (New York: Penguin Press, 2007), p. 102.

214   He then nervously watched the computer monitor: Bob Woodward, *Maestro: Greenspan's Fed and the American Boom* (New York: Simon and Schuster Paperbacks, 2005), p. 33.

215   Within months, the New York staff began to complain: No byline, "Top New York Official Resigns from S.E.C.," *New York Times*, September 30, 1987, p. D1. The Mobil Corporation lawyer had worked briefly at the SEC right after law school, but spent the next two decades in corporate practice. See "Paid Death Notice: Warwick, Kathleen Ann," *New York Times*, October 10, 2010.

215   provoking congressional concern and questions: Letter to SEC chairman David S. Ruder from Senator William Proxmire, August 13, 1987, SECHS website, used with permission from www.sechistorical.org, http://3197d6d14b5f19f2f440 -5e13d29c4c016cf96cbbfd197c579b45.r81.cf1.rackcdn.com/collection/papers /1980/1987_0813_RuderComplaint.pdf. "I hope that cleaning up the reported mess in the New York regional office will be your immediate highest priority," Senator Proxmire wrote.

215   He firmly demanded the regional administrator's resignation: "Top New York Official Resigns from S.E.C." The official wrote, "It is my sincere wish that any controversy or misunderstanding resulting from internal matters or press reports, however erroneous I believe them to have been, do not reflect in any way on the Securities and Exchange Commission as an agency."

215   The Dow dropped sharply at the opening bell: SEC Crash Report, p. 2.4.

216   By the closing bell, the Dow was down: Ibid.

216   index arbitrage trading had surged at the end of the day: SEC Crash Report, Appendix A, p. A.2. It noted: "While the DJIA declined throughout most of the day, the sharpest movements were at the opening and close, when over 66% of the decline and most of the arbitrage selling on the day occurred."

216   Portfolio insurance trades had been sparse: Lawrence J. De Maria, "Market Place: Stocks Face New Pressures," *New York Times*, October 8, 1987, p. D10.

216   had started to trade ahead of the portfolio insurers: Many large players on Wall Street had a pretty good idea of what portfolio insurers were doing, and many had rough calculations of how much selling portfolio insurers would do after the Dow dropped a certain amount. See Brady Report, p. v. The report noted, "Selling by these [portfolio insurance] investors, and the prospect of further selling by them, encouraged a number of aggressive trading-oriented institutions to sell in anticipation of further market declines." In other words, these "aggressive" traders sold short (which, in a falling market, is far easier for brokerage firms and large institutional traders than for individuals), expecting to profit when the portfolio insurers drove the market down further.

216   For most investors, the rest of the week was truly awful: It should be noted that short-sellers, who had suffered enormous losses during the long bull market

and, especially, the extreme summer rally, welcomed every market decline, including the debacle on Black Monday. They were a tiny minority in the market, however, and the overall financial impact of the market's moves in September and October was extremely negative for the vast majority of equity investors.

216   no more than the prior week, really: SEC Crash Report, pp. 2.11–2.12. The SEC conceded that "both press accounts and the Brady Report have cited selling by risk arbitrageurs," as takeover speculators were known, "as a significant factor in the week of October 12" (ibid., p. 2.11). The White House and the SEC's chief economist's office were quick to blame the Democrat-controlled House Ways and Means Committee for helping to trigger the crash by tinkering unwisely with the market. The SEC, which got its data from thirteen major firms active in risk arbitrage, found that the volume of selling by risk arbitrageurs the week of October 12 almost exactly matched the selling of the week before. The SEC Report stated categorically, "The volume of selling by risk arbitrageurs does not appear to have been sufficient to depress market prices other than those of specific takeover securities. Nor did selling by these entities appear significantly different in the weeks of October 5 and October 12" (ibid., p. 2.12).

216   the takeover selling pressure wouldn't be a problem: In further support of the SEC's conclusion, the amount of takeover-stock selling the week of October 5, which included the sale of 2.6 million shares on October 6 and 4.3 million shares on October 9, was not widely cited as especially significant in the coverage of that week's briefly historic decline.

217   Traders hoped that a shrinking trade gap: Lawrence J. De Maria, "Dow, Reversing Slide, Rises by 36.72," New York Times, October 14, 1987, p. D12. It is curious that the stock market coverage for Monday and Tuesday, October 12 and 13, ran inside the Business section in the Times.

217   but nowhere near as much as analysts had expected: Robert D. Hershey Jr., "Trade Gap Shrinks Less Than Hoped; Markets Plunge," New York Times, October 15, 1987, p. 1.

217   Fearful that a weaker dollar would force the Fed: Brady Report, p. 15. The rationale was that the Fed would raise rates to prevent a flight from the dollar by foreign investors, whose purchases had become increasingly important to the Treasury market and, to a lesser degree, to the stock market.

217   The sell-off pushed up the interest rate: Ibid.

217   this news may have dented investors' confidence: Ibid.

218   a familiar invitation to the index arbitrageurs: Brady Report, p. 17.

218   transmitting the price decline from the Merc: Metz, Black Monday, p. 89.

218   accounting for about a quarter of all the trading: Ibid.

218   the selling on this day was coming from giant institutions: SEC Crash Report, p. 2.8.

218   Briefly, just before 3:30 p.m.: Ibid., Appendix A, pp. A.8, 26.

218   the NYSE had handled $1.4 billion worth: Brady Report, p. 17.

219   that the New York Fed was injecting cash into the system: Metz, Black Monday, p. 89.

219   Portfolio insurers were among the big sellers: Brady Report, p. 21.

219   it was down just four points: Ibid.

219   "this sharp decline on heavy volume so late in the day": Ibid.

219   just seven "aggressive" institutions accounted for 9 percent: Ibid.

219   the advent of an official bear market: As of the closing bell on October 15, 1987, the market was fifty-one days out from its August 25 peak, and had declined 13 percent.

220   Jerry Corrigan boarded a jet bound for Caracas: Metz, *Black Monday*, pp. 37–39.

220   even the higher DOT cap was too low: At the time, the DOT system would accept market orders (orders to be filled at whatever the current market price might be) of up to 30,099 shares and limit orders (orders to be filled at a price equal to or better than the specified "limit") of up to 99,999 shares. See Brady Report, p. 47.

221   With nowhere else to turn, options traders were using the futures: Brady Report, p. III-12. The report explained that, on expiration days, options investors either had to buy new contracts for future months (called "rolling" their positions forward) or liquidate their positions by buying or selling the underlying securities prior to the closing bell. However, the week's sharp drop in stock prices meant that there were no options contracts for future months that reflected those new lower prices. Unable to hedge in the options markets, these traders set up hedges in the futures markets. Thus, investors who normally were not part of the trade flow in the futures pits suddenly became active there on this expiration day.

221   Those demands were running $750 million ahead: Ibid., p. 29.

221   "an investor transacting $10 million [in trades] on a normal day": Ibid., p. 25.

222   By 3:30 p.m., the Dow was 3.4 percent: Ibid., p. III-12.

222   accounting for more than 43 percent of the trading volume: Ibid., p. III-12.

222   as if the market were falling through thin air: Interview with Stanley Shopkorn on December 1, 2015 (hereafter "Shopkorn interview)"; and confidential interviews with two other senior traders at two large Wall Street firms.

222   "the odd spectacle of a market full of people relieved": Metz, *Black Monday*, p. 91.

223   Only three of them had not run up big losses: SEC Crash Report, pp. 5.39–5.42. The distressed firms were primarily market makers for S&P 100 options, the OEX, the most deeply traded option on the CBOE.

223   So, he closed out his bets, planning to head into Monday: Weiner, *What Goes Up*, p. 281. Melamed would later bless his caution: "In the aftermath of accusations and investigations, of analyses and review, it would not have served my interests to read stories about how the leader of the Merc was short the market . . . and made a lot of money on Black Monday" (Weiner, *What Goes Up*, p. 282).

223   told his staff to stay in close touch: Ruder interview January 2015.

223   Over the weekend, Ruder would confer: Confidential interviews with former SEC officials.

224   Beryl Sprinkel, an outspoken bank economist: Melamed, *Escape to the Futures*, pp. 351–52.

224 Alan Greenspan was summoned to a meeting: Beckner, *Back from the Brink*, p. 42. Both accounts of this meeting clearly relied on Sprinkel, but Melamed apparently assumed the meeting was held in the Oval Office, while Beckner specifically placed it in the family quarters, which seems more likely given the First Lady's situation.

224 "after considerable bickering, the meeting broke": Ibid., p. 43.

225 It had been too chaotic in the spooz pit: LOR interview 2016.

225 Rubinstein decided that he would take a later flight: Ibid.

225 "phones were melting down," one account noted: John Kador, *Charles Schwab: How One Company Beat Wall Street and Reinvented the Brokerage Industry* (Hoboken, NJ: John Wiley and Sons, 2002), pp. 150–51.

226 "Friday already had investors on edge": Weiner, *What Goes Up*, pp. 282–83. The on-air statement attributed to Baker by Kaufman has been edited slightly, based on transcripts of his comments.

226 "Henry, some things need to be said": Ibid.

227 He called his head of market surveillance: Carol Jouzaitis and Laurie Cohen, "The Crash and Chicago's Markets: How Markets Survived Crash," *Chicago Tribune*, January 3, 1988, p. 1.

227 the day "could have been—should have been—far worse": Metz, *Black Monday*, p. 91.

227 still had the equivalent of $8 billion more to sell: Brady Report, p. 29. The estimates were based on the formulas the portfolio insurers were known to be using.

19. 508 POINTS

228 John Phelan asked a secretary to track down Leo Melamed: The timing and content of this call are subject to some uncertainty, but by all accounts, it had occurred at least by 8:30 a.m. In his memoir, Melamed reported taking the call in his car at 6:30 a.m. (7:30 a.m. in New York) as he raced down an expressway on his way into the Merc that morning. (See *Escape to the Futures*, p. 348.) Elsewhere (Tamarkin, *The Merc*, p. 325), Melamed recalled the call coming in at 7 a.m. (8 a.m. in New York). Within two months of the crash, he told the *Chicago Tribune* he got the call at 7:30 a.m. (8:30 a.m. in New York), which is the freshest memory and therefore the author's preference. It also fits best with the timing at the NYSE, where the NYSE staff started tabulating the DOT orders at 7 a.m. New York time. It seems unlikely Phelan would have seen enough order flow in the first thirty minutes to make such a pessimistic assessment. As for the content, a confidential SEC memorandum shows that Phelan recounted the conversation to SEC chairman David Ruder within an hour of the call; that is the most contemporaneous account available, and it seems consistent with Phelan's views.

228 could see how the day was shaping up: In an account written two decades later, Phelan insisted "this morning was much like any other, and there was little or no reason for alarm." That must be dismissed as hazy hindsight, as it is at odds with so many other contemporary and subsequent accounts of the day. See John J. Phelan Jr., "October 1987: A Retrospective," 2007, SECHS website, used

with permission from www.sechistorical.org, http://3197d6d14b5f19f2f440-5e
13d29c4c016cf96cbbfd197c579b45.r81.cf1.rackcdn.com/collection/papers
/2000/2007_0802_Phelan1987.pdf.

228   sell orders from the trading desk at Fidelity Investments: Diana B. Henriques,
Fidelity's World: The Secret Life and Public Power of the Mutual Fund Giant
(New York: Scribner, 1995), pp. 283–84.

228   it was chilling to think how much it would try to sell: Brady Report, p. 30. One
or two other, much smaller funds sold on Black Monday, but Fidelity represented the bulk of the day's mutual fund sell orders.

228   DOT system was being swamped with orders: As noted, the number of shares
traded was less relevant to the capacity of the DOT system than the number of
orders submitted. See Brady Report, p. VI-32: "On October 19 and 20, 1987,
470,100 and 585,000 system orders were received, compared to a daily average
for January to September, 1987, of 143,000 system orders. Prior to October 19,
the record number of system orders received in a day was 270,000." Thus, the
number of orders on Black Monday was at least three times larger than normal; on Tuesday, the load was four times the normal level.

228   many of them apparently from index arbitrageurs: Metz, *Black Monday*,
pp. 42–43.

229   "We're seeing 'sell' orders like never before": Tamarkin, *The Merc*, p. 325; and
Jouzaitis and Cohen, "The Crash and Chicago's Markets."

229   "Everyone loves a free market": Memorandum to Richard Ketchum from
David S. Ruder, October 19, 1987, in the author's files. The confidential memo
was Ruder's account of Phelan's description of the earlier call to Melamed,
delivered shortly after that call. Melamed does not recall Phelan saying these
specific sentences during this call, but acknowledged that Phelan had probably
conveyed that message to him during other conversations in these turbulent
days. "That's certainly how [Phelan] felt," Melamed said, in an interview on
February 17, 2017.

229   Then Phelan checked his calendar: Phelan, "October 1987: A Retrospective,"
p. 4.

229   He had spent the weekend helping his wife unpack: LOR interview 2016.

230   a flight attendant announced that the market was down 60 points: MacKenzie,
An Engine, Not a Camera, p. 187, confirmed by Leland.

230   The market was down hundreds of points by then: Ibid., p. 188.

230   The taxi wove through the growing traffic to the First Interstate Tower: LOR
interview 2016.

230   Shocked, Leland instantly replied: Leland–O'Brien interview 2016.

230   Corrigan immediately booked a seat on an earlier flight home: Corrigan interview.

231   Melamed waited for the opening bell: Melamed, *Escape to the Futures*, pp. 353–54.

231   "There were blank stares. No one could believe it was happening": Tamarkin,
The Merc, p. 330, quoting Alan Ross, the head of floor operations for the Merc
clearing member firm of Rufenacht, Bromagen and Hertz.

231   As usual, they sold stocks heavily in New York: Brady Report, p. III-20.

231   a number of index arbitrageurs held back: Ibid.

232   two weeks earlier, Ruder had given a speech: David S. Ruder, "The Impact of Derivative Trading and the Securities Markets," Remarks to the Bond Club of Chicago, October 6, 1987, p. 15. Advance text available at https://www.sec.gov /news/speech/1987/100687ruder.pdf.

232   "about a temporary, very temporary halt in trading": Brady Report, p. III-20.

232   were the cornerstone of John Phelan's last-gasp plan: Metz, *Black Monday*, p. 98. Metz observed that the spooz traders "don't realize the NYSE foot drag-ging at the opening [on Black Monday] is so purposeful. They read the delays as a sign of the impossibility, rather than [the] inadvisability, of opening the stocks. Their misreading . . . will heighten the fear in Chicago." Metz asserted that the spooz traders were also unnerved by the "widespread knowledge" that NYSE specialists were selling futures contracts in Chicago, to hedge their growing inventory of stock, taking that as a sign of New York's growing alarm. As the Brady Commission would later observe, the flow of perception-shaping information between the two markets could not be halted, even temporarily, and soon became "self-reinforcing" (Brady Report, p. III-26).

232   had mentioned the plan in a call with Ruder that morning: David S. Ruder, "Partial Chronology of Chairman's Office Participation in the October Market Break," prepared by Chairman Ruder's staff at the SEC," p. 2, from Professor Ruder's personal archives.

232   the executives "didn't seem to have any inkling": Metz, *Black Monday*, p. 98.

232   to a powerful story his mother had told him: Amanda Binns Mellar interview. Ms. Mellar said her father told her this story to show the duty people bore to one another in society. Binns would not talk publicly about GM's role in the 1987 crash. It was widely reported, and never denied, that GM was the client for whom these sales were made. (See, for example, Glenn Kessler and David Henry, "The Power to Drive the Market Down," *Newsday*, January 17, 1988, p. 93; and an unsigned Q&A, "Interview: General Motors' W. Gordon Binns," *Intermarket* magazine 5, no. 10 [October 1988].) His views at the 1987 Program Trading Hearing, especially in his written testimony, show he was keenly aware of the thin capital cushion under most specialist and futures trading firms, the fact that portfolio insurance hadn't been tested in a declining mar-ket, and the fact that past models for how portfolio insurance would perform did not account for its widespread proliferation. A pragmatist rather than an absolutist, Binns clearly knew where the fault lines were, and by 2 p.m., the market was nearing the point of free fall as all those fault lines gave way. It is not difficult to imagine him intervening, but it cannot be confirmed that he did.

233   Binns, a public-spirited man, had been raised to think of others: The author has interviewed a half dozen people who knew Binns well, and their view of him, reflected here, was unanimous. The author has also read dozens of letters written to Binns on the occasion of his retirement from GM by people he had met around the world, and they bear out that image.

233   One regulator recalled how a specialist had described it: Interview with David S. Ruder, July 7, 2015 (hereafter "Ruder interview July 2015").

233   Wells Fargo never conceded any concern: Elaine S. Povich, "Market Crash

Brings Battle over Changes," *Chicago Tribune*, January; 4, 1988, p. 1. See also, Reuters, "Big Investors Defend Programmed Trading," *New York Times*, November 19, 1987, p. D8.

233   Wells Fargo had another 27 million shares to sell: Tamarkin, *The Merc*, p. 328.

234   Both markets dropped further and further: Melamed, *Escape to the Futures*, p. 357.

234   "Our noses were to the South African grindstone": Machold interview.

234   Machold had grown increasingly wary: Machold specifically remembered an early forecast of Elaine Garzarelli, at the time an influential strategist at Lehman Brothers. She later recalled, "I turned bearish in late September, and then a week before the crash I went on CNN and said there was going to be a collapse like '29" (Weiner, *What Goes Up*, p. 280).

235   They began to perversely applaud each new negative milestone: Their response, while odd, was not unique. Fischer Black, the genius who helped develop a Nobel Prize–winning options pricing theory, was working at Goldman Sachs during the crash. In one account, a trader rushed in to report that a sell order had never been filled because prices were falling so fast. "Clapping his hands with glee," Black reportedly responded, "Wow, really? This is history in the making!" See Patterson, *The Quants*, p. 51.

235   "We all cheered," Machold said. "What else could we do?": Machold memoir, p. 187; and Machold interview.

235   "I want to know what went wrong, not right": Phelan, "October 1987: A Retrospective," pp. 4–5.

235   the exchange was to open for business on Tuesday: Ruder, "Partial Chronology," p. 5.

236   Greenspan, normally diplomatic, snapped back: Greenspan, *The Age of Turbulence*, p. 106.

236   the Fed had to inject not only cash but confidence: Ibid.

237   He got out of bed and walked to the window: Phelan, "October 1987: A Retrospective," p. 7.

237   when he heard the stunning figure from the head of the Merc's clearinghouse: Melamed, *Escape to the Futures*, p. 360.

237   Melamed was aghast at the scale of the settlement challenge: Ibid., p. 359.

238   The Merc was owed roughly $1 billion by Morgan Stanley: Ibid., p. 361.

238   There already was sand in the machine: Peter Norman, *The Risk Controllers: Central Counterparty Clearing in Globalised Financial Markets* (Chichester, UK: John Wiley and Sons Ltd., 2011), p. 137. In this remarkably researched volume, Norman notes that this account, given to him by Merc clearinghouse executive Phupinder Gill in 2008, was confirmed in the CFTC's January 1990 response to a GAO report: "The problem was largely caused by the fact that settlement banks did not receive accurate instruction sheets at the usual hour because certain non-cash intra-day variation payments made on October 19, 1987, were not accommodated by existing software and therefore were not reflected in the October 20 variation calculations" (pp. 137, 12*ff*).

238   overwhelmed by the unprecedented volume of traffic: Brady Report, p. VI-71. The Fedwire had remained open later than normal on Black Monday, but the

Brady Commission was critical of the New York Fed's failure to announce in advance that it would remain open until all wire traffic had been processed. "As each anticipated closing time approached and wire traffic remained incomplete, the Fed announced that it would extend the closing time. Consequently, the settlement banks did not know from minute to minute whether their supposed intraday credit extensions would be covered by the close of business."

238   had already dodged a potentially ruinous crisis: Interview with William Brodsky, July 27, 2015 (hereafter "Second Brodsky interview").

238   A major trading firm: This rescue is described in detail in Tamarkin's *The Merc*, p. 335, and is mentioned in Norman, *The Risk Controllers*, p. 142, but neither account identifies the firm involved. Neither Brodsky nor the friend involved, clearinghouse chairman Wayne Luthringshausen, could clearly recall the name of the rescued firm.

239   an ad hoc payment deal with a longtime friend: The options clearing firm had been trading both stock index "put" options on the Chicago Board Options Exchange and S&P 500 futures contracts on the Merc. Its losses in the futures market were fully offset by big gains on the put options. This eleventh-hour "cross-margining" arrangement allowed profits in one market to be applied to losses in the other, through the clearinghouses. Within a few years, formal cross-margin arrangements would be set up between the two markets, much along the lines of this ad hoc deal crafted between two good friends on the night of Black Monday.

239   It was done virtually on a handshake: Norman, *The Risk Controllers*, pp. 141–42.

239   Morgan Stanley still had not fully settled its account: Tamarkin, *The Merc*, p. 334. This account relies both on accounts by Leo Melamed, in Melamed's memoir and First Melamed interview, and on Bob Tamarkin's authorized history of the Merc. According to Tamarkin, Bill Brodsky was on the phone with Wilma Smelcer that morning—but it is possible Melamed was on the same call, using the phone in the conference room, or that he conducted a separate phone call with her. Tamarkin also credits Merc chairman Jack Sandner with getting Morgan Stanley to pay up, with the following conversation attributed to him: "Let me tell you the facts. This is a no-debt system . . . Yours is the only firm that hasn't made its payment. If the money isn't forthcoming, the headlines in tomorrow's newspapers will say that your firm defaulted." The payment was resolved, Tamarkin reported, "within 45 minutes." Melamed has stuck by his account over the years, and others have not publicly disputed it. But fairness, and an appreciation for Melamed's dramatic flair, demand that Brodsky and Sandner get a share of the credit for rescuing the Merc that morning.

239   She sounded close to tears: Interview with Leo Melamed on July 29, 2015 (hereafter "Second Melamed interview").

239   the bank's new CEO, Tom Theobald: It had been Theobald, then a senior Citibank executive, who briefly balked at joining the "safety net" consortium that helped bail out Continental Illinois in the summer of 1984 by reportedly saying, "Why would I want to help a competitor?" (See Silber, *Volcker*, p. 245.)

The what-if's that surround the role of Continental Illinois during and immediately after Black Monday are profound, starting with "What if it had been allowed to fail in 1984?" Would any other bank have been as accommodating to the Merc?

239   Smelcer got back on the line: Second Melamed interview.

239   the Fed released a succinct message: SEC Crash Report, p. 5.27.

240   He was right to worry: Weiner, *What Goes Up*, p. 294.

240   he wanted them to consider "the big picture": Interview with E. Gerald Corrigan, June 16, 2015.

240   First Options, which was facing an old-fashioned run: Jouzaitis and Cohen, "The Crash and Chicago's Markets." According to the *Tribune*, traders pulled more than $300 million of their cash balances out of First Options in those two days. At the Harris Bank branch in the lobby of the CBOT, "traders lined up to take out money" on Monday and Tuesday. One trader was seen stuffing cash into a Marshall Fields shopping bag; others were reported to have rented safe-deposit boxes and stuffed them with cash. One, the *Tribune* said, brought an armored car to the bank to collect $300,000 in cash, obtained "after cashing a check from a clearing firm." The *Tribune* slightly overstated the case. The SEC found that the withdrawals totaled $364.5 million between October 14 and 30, 1987, with $242.8 million of that taken out the week of Black Monday. (SEC Crash Report, p. 5.43.) The larger point that there was a "run" on First Options is clearly supported by the numbers.

241   Now it was imperative that it rescue its First Options subsidiary: If First Options had still been in the hands of its former owner, the big NYSE specialist firm of Spear, Leeds and Kellogg, it may not have survived the run on Black Monday, given how strained all the specialist firms were at that moment. And if it had not survived, this grim Tuesday would have been much worse.

241   Nimble specialists were able to shed some of the shares: Brady Report, p. 36.

241   hovering just above 1,700 points: Ibid., p. 40.

241   put the S&P 500 index futures into free fall: Ibid. "Contributing greatly to this freefall was the lack of index arbitrage buying which would normally have been stimulated by the huge discount of futures to stock," the Brady Commission reported.

241   that implied that the Dow's value was actually 1,400 points: Ibid. If the Dow had indeed closed at that level on Tuesday, the two-day decline on October 19 and 20, 1987, would have been far worse than the two-day crash of October 1929. At 1,400 points, the Dow would have dropped almost 38 percent in two days; in 1929, the two-day decline was just under 24 percent.

241   The liquidity that Melamed had boasted about for years: Tamarkin, *The Merc*, p. 344.

241   Blue-chip buyers held back, waiting for bigger bargains: Brady Report, p. 40.

242   the destruction of the world they had known all their lives: Confidential notes from two days later show regulators worrying that "if the market had closed down 200 points on Tuesday, a large number of specialists might have been lost."

242 The floor was crowded but eerily quiet, like the eye of a hurricane: Weiner, *What Goes Up*, p. 295.

242 stocks that accounted for 54 percent of the value of the Dow: Metz, *Black Monday*, p. 194.

242 led them behind a canvas flap screening some construction work: Ibid.

242 "Get them open," he told them: Weiner, *What Goes Up*, p. 295.

242 "We've got to trade out of this": Metz, *Black Monday*, p. 193.

242 "We're not going to close this place down": As noted earlier (and as Metz, *Black Monday*, notes at p. 195), Phelan had a plan that called for trading to be halted "on as many as 100 stocks at once if program trading drove the market down more than about 25 percent." The trading halts would "give the market time to breathe," Phelan had said then. Specialists could put out word that the last sale had been at X and the closest bid was Y. "Rather than let it somersault down, we try to establish a new equilibrium by reaching out to all the buyers and sellers," he had explained. (See Grant, "John Phelan vs. Program Trading.")

242 and then strode out to the reception area and told his secretary: Metz, *Black Monday*, p. 209. Metz attributed the description of this scene to notes taken by *New York Times* reporter Robert J. Cole, who was waiting outside Phelan's office to resume an interview that had been interrupted earlier that morning.

242 It was 12:05 p.m.: Ten minutes later, Melamed would close the Merc's S&P 500 pit, a step he said he took after a conversation with Phelan sometime around noon, New York time. His chronology is a bit cloudy—starting with his assertion in his memoir that the S&P pit was closed for "about 35 minutes." Precise records existed showing the pit was closed for 49 minutes.

242 "*thinking*—about closing for a short time": David S. Ruder, "Notes: October 19, 1987, to October 30, 1987" (hereafter "Ruder, 'October 19–30 Notes' "), p. 31. In his private archive, Professor Ruder has 132 pages of his handwritten notes relating to market events during this period, which he generously allowed the author to examine for this research.

242 Phelan also reportedly said, surprisingly: Ibid.

243 Message slips and phone logs from the Oval Office: The log, from the Howard Baker archives at the University of Tennessee at Knoxville, also shows an early morning phone conversation with Phelan, at 8:20, followed within fifteen minutes by conversations with Greenspan and Ruder.

243 "They could not all be under intense pressure at once": Phelan, "October 1987: A Retrospective," p. 10.

243 the SEC quickly alerted the other exchanges: Ruder, "Partial Chronology," pp. 10–11, and Ruder interview December 2016.

243 "I was determined to keep the market open": Phelan, "October 1987: A Retrospective," p. 10.

243 "If the NYSE closed, uncontrollable panic would follow": Melamed, *Escape to the Futures*, p. 365.

244 "There was virtual certainty that the NYSE was about to close": Ibid., pp. 365–66.

244 the spooz pit was closing immediately: Ibid. Melamed reported that this action occurred at 11:30 a.m., Chicago time, but according to the Brady Report, it came

fifteen minutes sooner. Phelan called the SEC at noon; Melamed said word worked its way to Chicago via the CFTC, at which point he called Phelan before going down to the spooz pit. Yet that was all accomplished in just fifteen minutes. It is possible, of course; it is also possible Melamed spoke to Phelan before the latter's call to the SEC—he told the CFTC he had spoken to Phelan several times that morning, and not all the calls are described in his memoirs.

244   who also had a seat on the Chicago Board of Trade: Interview with Blair Hull, March 31, 2016.

245   would both step in as big buyers of the major stocks: Although none of the participants in this scene confirms it, it is likely that Salomon and Goldman also steered buy orders to the S&P 500 futures pit at the Merc when it reopened a little less than an hour later.

245   but they also had to consider "the good of the system": Shopkorn interview, and confidential interviews with retired senior executives at Goldman Sachs and Salomon Brothers. Former *New York Times* columnist Floyd Norris, at the time a columnist for *Barron's*, was just outside Shopkorn's office when this incident happened, and described it in detail in his *Economix* blog ("It Never Happened," *New York Times*, October 24, 2007). The URL for that column is https://economix.blogs.nytimes.com/2007/10/24/it-never-happened/?_r=0.

245   an NYSE staffer publicly denied reports: Metz, *Black Monday*, pp. 225–26. It is, indeed, the most inexplicable event on this turbulent day. The NYSE staffer's boss, Richard Torrenzano, later told Metz the staffer "doesn't know" why she put out the erroneous statement. One possibility, of course, is that if the trading halts were not being reported to the newswires, they were not being reported to the staff, either. Still, it would have been protocol to check the accuracy of the statement before making it. Asked about the incident in 2016, Torrenzano said the mistake was most likely just part of the collateral damage of a turbulent day.

245   "The market *had* to rally," he thought: Phelan, "October 1987: A Retrospective," p. 8.

245   the number of Dow stocks that were open for trading: Ibid.

245   so perhaps that was finally kicking in: Brady Report, p. III-26: "Another force affecting the stock market at this time was the growing list of U.S. corporations announcing that they were willing to buy their stock from investors. On Monday and Tuesday, corporations announced approximately $6.2 billion in stock buybacks." These purchases may not all have been made, but the announcements had a salutary effect, according to the Brady Commission, because they "may have led market participants to believe that the buybacks were going to maintain a solid floor price. Bargain hunters rushed in to buy[,] and sellers finally could unload large blocks of stock directly to corporate buyers."

246   the moment John Phelan picked up the phone to tell David Ruder: That exact comment was made in a follow-up call to Ruder around 3 p.m. that day, but reflects what participants can recall about Phelan's comments on the earlier call.

246   Or was there a bigger conspiracy: Tim Metz, a fine financial journalist, made the most detailed case for the "big conspiracy" theory in chapter 11 of his

excellent 1988 book, *Black Monday*. This author does not find it convincing, but others may.

247   would even have noticed the volatile MMI's uptick: Somewhat inconsistently, Metz, *Black Monday*, at p. 217, argues that "most investors—even the pros—won't even notice" the MMI's rally. Noted technical analyst Laszlo Birinyi, at the time at Salomon Brothers, disagreed, saying the index was part of the dashboard on every computer monitor on Wall Street trading desks, and its uptick would definitely have been influential—more influential, in fact, than the reports that his firm and Goldman had come in with big buy orders. That development, he thought, was important chiefly to the despairing NYSE specialists, giving them enough hope to soldier on until the Dow rallied.

20. JUGGLING HAND GRENADES

248   Alan Greenspan later recounted: Greenspan, *The Age of Turbulence*, p. 109. Greenspan cited this as one of "a half dozen near disasters, mostly involving the payment system," that occurred in the days after Black Monday. He added, alarmingly, that a "senior Goldman official" later confided to him that if the firm had anticipated the "difficulties of the ensuing weeks, it would not have paid. And in future such crises, he suspected, Goldman would have second thoughts about making such unrequited payments."

248   sweeping the Street for rumors of firms slipping into failure: E.F. Hutton, John Shad's former employer, was the first subject of these unfounded rumors, followed by Bear Stearns and Morgan Stanley. See an unbylined article, "Brokerage Stocks Fall; Large Losses Rumored," *New York Times*, October 21, 1987, p. D20.

248   The "total numbers are bad": Ruder, "October 19–30 Notes," p. 50.

248   The overarching worry was that a major firm would fail: The market shared those fears: even in the afternoon market rally on Tuesday, October 20, some brokerage stocks fell even further than on Black Monday. The worst hit was Hutton, which fell more than 27 percent on Tuesday, despite announcing higher earnings. Morgan Stanley dropped almost 14 percent, after dropping by almost a third on Black Monday. First Boston lost more than 11 percent of its value on Tuesday, and was trading for less than its net worth.

248   In the wee hours of Wednesday morning: The specialist firm was A.B. Tompane and Company, which closed its sale to Merrill Lynch at 4 a.m. on Wednesday, October 21, 1987. (See Metz, *Black Monday*, p. 150.) The Michigan retail broker was H.B. Shaine and Company of Grand Rapids; three other small trading firms were also suspended from the NYSE on Tuesday, October 20: William D. Mayer and Co., Metropolitan Securities, and AIG Inc., which was not related to the insurance company of the same name. (See SEC Crash Report, pp. 5.8–5.9.)

249   the firm had "gone to the wall" during Tuesday's trading: Ruder, "October 19–30 Notes," p. 50.

249   Schwab had embodied Main Street's growing obsession: Joe Nocera, *A Piece of the Action: How the Middle Class Joined the Money Class* (New York: Simon

and Schuster, 1994), pp. 359–62. His account was relied on and expanded slightly by Kador, *Charles Schwab*, at pp. 152, 157.

249   the firm was struggling to calculate its own financial position: Nocera, *A Piece of the Action*, p. 362.

249   debt run up by one brash speculator in Hong Kong: Kador, *Charles Schwab*, p. 163.

249   complaining loudly about the breakdown of the Nasdaq market: This assessment is drawn from National Association of Securities Dealers, *Report of the Special Committee of the Regulatory Review Task Force on the Quality of Markets* (Ann Arbor, MI: NASD, 1988); the Brady Report (pp. 48–50); and the SEC Crash Report, chap. 9, which notes (at p. 9.2) that "of all the major markets, the OTC market was singled out for the most severe criticism by the respondents to the Brady Task Force's questionnaire." Fully 76 percent of survey respondents rated Nasdaq's performance on October 19 and 20 as "very poor."

250   was trying to address the rising level of complaints and rally his shell-shocked dealers: SEC Crash Report, pp. 8.6–8.9.

250   the automated pricing service relied on by clearing firms: Ibid., p. 8.7. In fairness to the vendor, the task was made immeasurably harder because the exchanges posted tens of thousands of new options contracts for trading to reflect the new lower prices in the stock market. Software capacity at the pricing firm was not limitless, and some older options had to be dropped to accommodate the new ones.

250   Everyone knew how much was hanging in the balance: Greenspan, *The Age of Turbulence*, pp. 109–10.

250   exceeded limits set by the FDIC when it saved Continental: Congressional defenders of the Glass-Steagall Act would seize on the incident as proof that banks should not be allowed to engage in the securities business, and would fiercely criticize Continental Illinois for its rescue of First Options. See Steve Labaton, "Market Turmoil: Major Infusion of Cash Kept Key Options Clearinghouse Afloat," *New York Times*, October 25, 2987, p. A24.

250   preventing a default that would have torn a gaping wound: The Continental Illinois holding company ultimately would provide $312.5 million in capital to First Options during the month of October 1987, financing the infusion by selling bonds. See SEC Crash Report, p. 5.42.

250   the bank's support for First Options had to be hastily rerouted: Of the $312.5 million loaned to First Options by its parent, about $277 million of that was provided between October 14 and 21, 1987.

250   Jerry Corrigan must have been flabbergasted: Ruder, "October 19–30 Notes," pp. 69–71 and p. 85, for conference calls with Corrigan at 10:25 a.m. and again at 2:30 p.m. on October 22, 1987. While these notes clearly show that First Options was discussed during those calls, the attribution of specific remarks is not clear. The notes suggest that Corrigan was urged, or intended, to intervene with the comptroller, Robert Clarke, but neither Corrigan nor Ruder could confirm that. Nevertheless, Continental Illinois was sanctioned by the comptroller for making the initial loans via the bank rather than the hold-

ing company, a step that Clarke said showed "the system worked." After the fact, Corrigan publicly disagreed with that action by the comptroller during a Senate Banking Committee hearing on December 10, 1987. (See Robert Trigaux, "Corrigan Endorses Proxmire-Garn Bill; NY Fed Chief Says Glass-Steagall Repeal Is Just First Step," *American Banker*, December 11, 1987.) Calling for "regulatory flexibility," Corrigan asked, "Would it have been in the public interest, or in the interest of the [parent] company as a whole, to have allowed or, even worse, to have forced First Options into bankruptcy during the week of October 19 . . . ? From my perspective, neither the public interest nor the interest of the parent company and its bank or other subsidiaries would necessarily be well served by a legislative or regulatory framework that is so rigid that it forces a 'solution' that could be highly disruptive, even though other, more acceptable alternatives might be available."

251   Ruder called the other regulators to touch base: Records show that Ruder became a tireless ad hoc communication hub for the various exchanges, regulatory agencies, Wall Street firms, and members of Congress for weeks after Black Monday. See Tamarkin, *The Merc*, p. 346: "Throughout the crash and its aftermath, Ruder and the SEC were at the center of a communications web that reached every corner of the financial community."

251   the biggest customer of Schwab's small Hong Kong office: Details of Schwab's experience with Teddy Wang are drawn from Kador, *Charles Schwab*, pp. 160–68; and Nocera, *A Piece of the Action*, pp. 360–65. Kador relied on Nocera's account, which was based on interviews with Rosseau and nine other Schwab executives (see Nocera, p. 441).

251    $11 million ransom demand was calmly paid: Judgment from the High Court of the Hong Kong Special Administrative Region Court of Appeal, Criminal Appeal No. 233 of 2013 Between HKSAR and Chan Chun Chuen Before the Honorable Lunn SP, Poon and Pang JJA, October 30, 2015. The case, an appeal by one of the men convicted in the 1983 kidnapping, provides details of that original episode. Teddy Wang was kidnapped a second time in 1990; although Nina Wang paid $34 million for his release, he was never found, and was declared dead in 1999.

252   Schwab would be on the hook for the full sum: According to Kador, *Charles Schwab*, Schwab's stake in his newly public company was worth $100 million at the time of its initial public offering. See p. 146.

252   He found the entire financial community there in turmoil: Norman, *The Risk Controllers*, p. 144.

252   he hastily hired a new law firm to revise the request: Nocera, *A Piece of the Action*, pp. 363–64.

252   Rosseau went into "special ops" mode: Kador, *Charles Schwab*, p. 166.

252   Wang knew exactly where things stood: Ibid, p. 165.

252   the stock market barreled into a nervous rally: Lawrence J. De Maria, "Wall Street Rebound Widens with Gains for Most Stocks; Dow up 186 on Heavy Trading," *New York Times*, October 22, 1987, p. 1.

253   The only way to raise that cash in their clients' accounts: Kyrillos, *Cases in Financial Engineering*, p. 776, 20ff.

253   and would have to bear the remaining 20 percent as a loss: Ibid. Actually, later studies cited by MacKenzie (*An Engine, Not a Camera*, p. 190) suggested that the protection provided by LOR was better than Leland feared. It met its promised hedge protection for about 60 percent of its clients, while the rest saw their portfolio values fall between 5 and 7 percent below the minimum values LOR aimed to maintain. "It was better to have it [portfolio insurance] than to not have it," one client cited by MacKenzie said.

253   was how Black Monday could have happened *at all* in an efficient market: MacKenzie, *An Engine, Not a Camera*, p. 191. MacKenzie notes that "It is extremely hard to identify 'new news' over the previous weekend that would rationally justify such a huge, sudden reevaluation of stocks." The headlines and developments of the previous days and weeks "would already have been incorporated into Friday's prices," MacKenzie explained. So, only the events since Friday's close are candidates for justifying a "rational" 508-point decline on Monday. Some theorists argued that the very fact of Friday's historic decline was the "new news," alerting rational investors to a new degree of riskiness in the market; but that would not explain the historically large afternoon rebound on Tuesday, when insiders knew the market actually had become far riskier than it was on Monday.

254   would be sucked out of New York at the worst possible moment: Kurt Eichen-wald, "Many Wary on Impact of B.P. Offering Now," *New York Times*, October 26, 1987, p. D1.

254   Goldman Sachs and three other flagship firms: Ibid.

254   but the Tory government was in a difficult spot: Ibid.

255   Corrigan knew how even a little doubt could quickly strip a brokerage firm: Beckner, *Back from the Brink*, pp. 57–58.

255   Phelan read them a message from President Reagan: Lawrence De Maria, "Stocks Fall, but Avert Plunge; Reagan Says He'll 'Negotiate' with Congress on the Deficit," *New York Times*, October 23, 1987, p. 1.

255   "When I can't trade IBM, I know I'm in big trouble": Ibid.

255   At its low point, the Dow fell: Ibid.

255   staff members and floor traders wearing orange buttons that read, "Don't Panic": Robert J. Cole, "Market Turmoil: The Professionals' Day; Specialists Man the Ramparts," *New York Times*, October 22, 1987, p. D14. Cole said the buttons were being handed out "as a promotion" at various Federal Express locations in the neighborhood, and were showing up "all over the stock exchange."

256   Regulators at the CFTC thought it was because John Phelan: Hineman made that argument in congressional testimony a few weeks later. See "Review of Recent Volatility in the Stock Market and the Stock Index Futures Markets," Hearing Before the Subcommittee on Conservation, Credit, and Rural Development of the House Committee on Agriculture, 100th Congress, 1st Sess., November 4, 1987, p. 14.

256   spoke with David Ruder at the SEC about that: Ruder, "October 19–30 Notes," p. 67; and Ruder, "Partial Chronology," p. 17.

256   Ruder understood Hineman's argument to be that a futures market cut off: Ibid.

256   Portfolio insurers were continuing to sell heavily: LOR had sold more than 5,000 futures contracts on Tuesday, which made it the second-biggest portfolio insurance seller in the pits that day. Salomon Brothers, Aetna, Wells Fargo, and "GM pension" (the fund overseen by Gordon Binns) were also identified by the SEC as big portfolio insurance sellers in the spooz pits on both Monday and Tuesday. See Ruder, "October 19–30 Notes," p. 92. Others were selling heavily, too, of course—among them, titan speculator George Soros. See MacKenzie, *An Engine, Not a Camera*, p. 198.

257   the SEC was wrestling with whether to ask the CFTC: This account of the SEC meeting is based on Ruder, "Partial Chronology," pp. 21–22.

257   to impose daily price limits on the S&P 500 index contract: Julia M. Flynn, "Market Turmoil: Merc Puts Daily Limits on Stock Index Futures," *New York Times*, October 24, 1987, p. 42.

257   His first words were about his wife, who had returned home: Ronald Reagan, "The President's News Conference," October 22, 1987, American Presidency Project website, at http://www.presidency.ucsb.edu/ws/index.php?pid=33594&st=&st1=.

257   No one could have missed how distracted Reagan was: Ronald Reagan, "Statement by Assistant to the President for Press Relations [Marlin] Fitzwater on the Stock Market Decline," October 19, 1987, American Presidency Project website, at http://www.presidency.ucsb.edu/ws/index.php?pid=33582&st=&st1=.

257   On Black Monday, he had fielded reporters' questions: Ronald Reagan, "Informal Exchange with Reporters," October 19, 1987, American Presidency Project website, at http://www.presidency.ucsb.edu/ws/index.php?pid=33581&st=&st1=.

257   it sounded too close to Herbert Hoover's optimistic pronouncements: Memorandum from Gary L. Bauer to Howard H. Baker Jr., Subject: Stock Market, October 20, 1987: "It is not sufficient for the President to only say that this is not 1929 and that the economy is good. I have attached President Hoover's statement after the October crash. You note that is exactly what he said. We do not need to give the press and liberals another 'parallel' to draw between then and now. The Democrats are on the floor [of Congress] now making the Hoover-Reagan connection. We must move *quickly* before the connection gets settled in the mind of the average citizen" (FI003, FI004, FG006-07, 615488PD, Ronald Reagan Presidential Library Archives).

258   "Certainly, when more than half of the loss has already been regained": Ronald Reagan, "Informal Exchange with Reporters," October 21, 1987, American Presidency Project website, http://www.presidency.ucsb.edu/ws/index.php?pid=33591&st=&st1=.

258   an effort to deliver a more coherent message: Ronald Reagan, "The President's News Conference," October 22, 1987, American Presidency Project website at http://www.presidency.ucsb.edu/ws/index.php?pid=33594&st=&st1=.

258   foreign markets had already shown dissatisfaction: Associated Press, "Foreign Markets Remain Uneasy," *New York Times*, October 24, 1987, p. 46. The same perception—that markets were disappointed that stronger steps were not

announced to reduce the U.S. budget deficit—was reflected in a report from Japan: Clyde Haberman, "Japanese Stocks Show Slight Gains," *New York Times*, October 24, 1987, p. 46.

258   Ruder spoke with a Goldman Sachs executive: Ruder, "Partial Chronology," p. 22. The call was from Goldman Sachs executive Robert Mnuchin at 9:55 a.m. on October 23, 1987.

259   "I would be amazed if I had the power by a single comment": Nathaniel C. Nash, "Market Turmoil: S.E.C. Was Ready to Support a Halt," *New York Times*, October 14, 1987, p. 45.

259   the SEC would have backed him if he had taken that step: Ibid.

259   Under the new rule, trading would close for the day: Flynn, "Market Turmoil: Merc Puts Daily Limits on Stock Index Futures." The limits were calculated in terms of "index points," or the value of the S&P 500 index implied by the price of the spooz contract. Thus, the limits kicked in at whatever futures prices reflected a 30-point gain or loss in the value of the underlying index. The rule also held that, if trading hit the limit for two consecutive days, the limit would expand to allow fluctuations of up to 45 index points.

259   "price limits are anathema to a free market, but we're reacting": Ibid.

259   "The market needs time to breathe": Lawrence J. De Maria, "Market Is Steady and Tension Eases in Shorter Session," *New York Times*, October 24, 1987, p. 1.

259   Outside the exchange, the sidewalks were a spectacle: Kurt Eichenwald, "Market Turmoil: T.G.I.F. on Wall St.: Time to Recover," *New York Times*, October 24, 1987, p. 45.

259   "We're out here to see what's going on": Ibid.

260   As one departing exchange worker explained: Ibid.

260   into targets of international attention and Washington controversy: Tamarkin, *The Merc*, pp. 344–45.

260   Bill Brodsky suggested to Ruder, through an intermediary: Merc director Donald Jacobs, the dean of Northwestern's Kellogg School of Management and Ruder's friend and former campus colleague, was the Merc's go-between to set up the meeting, and also attended.

260   A few hours earlier, he'd gotten a call from President Reagan: A memorandum and attachment titled "Recommended Telephone Call for the President to: David Ruder, Chairman, Securities and Exchange Commission," No. 497960SS, Series IV, 3/12/87-2/1/88, Ronald Reagan Presidential Library Archives. The memo is dated October 23, 1987, but shows that the call was made on October 24, to Ruder's Chicago home number. The attachment, called "Talking Points," is actually a short script, with specific questions such as "David, I am calling to get your assessment of how the paperwork backlog is going."

260   For almost ninety minutes, Melamed and Brodsky reviewed the week: Tamarkin, *The Merc*, p. 346. Besides Melamed, Brodsky, and Jacobs, the Merc was represented by Rick Kilcollin, the senior vice president of research. Ruder had alerted Rick Ketchum to the meeting in advance and reported back on what happened.

260   Ruder listened, but he was skeptical: Ruder interview January 2015.

261   make the case that the Chicago markets were blameless: Bruce Ingersoll, "Chi-

cago Merc Says Futures Trading Didn't Cause Crash," *Wall Street Journal*, October. 30, 1987. The meetings with the members of the Senate Banking Committee's securities subcommittee and the House Commerce Committee's finance subcommittee were private, but Brodsky held a press conference at midday, at which he repeated the argument that index arbitrage had little effect on the markets on Black Monday, and that futures market selling prevented the Dow's drop from being even greater than it was.

261   "Like a frustrated teenager screaming at parents": Tamarkin, *The Merc*, p. 345.

261   which some cited as the largest one-day drop ever: Nicholas D. Kristof, "Market Turmoil: Hong Kong Suffers Wild Fluctuations," *New York Times*, October 27, 1987, p. D14.

261   In Tokyo, the Japanese stock market fell 4 percent: Lawrence J. De Maria, "Market Turmoil: Stocks Fall 156, Loss of 8%, After Big Sell Offs Abroad; Joint Talks on Deficit Begin," *New York Times*, October 27, 1987, p. 1.

261   "Tough, again," one staffer would tell David Ruder that morning: Ruder, "October 19–30 Notes," p. 109. The notes are from a conversation with Phelan at 1:20 p.m., October 26, 1987, forty minutes before the new, earlier closing bell.

261   "Worldwide panic selling," an economist told the *New York Times*: De Maria, "Market Turmoil."

262   "we just have to trade it out, let it test its lows": Ruder, "October 19–30 Notes," p. 110.

262   Phelan knew there wasn't a single major firm in New York: Transcript of testimony by John J. Phelan, "Briefing by New York Stock Exchange," Thursday, October 29, 1987, House of Representatives Committee on Banking [*sic*], Washington, DC (hereafter "Phelan Private Testimony"), p. 8. New York Stock Exchange Archives, Mahwah, NJ.

262   The other script announced a loss of $100 million: Kador, *Charles Schwab*, p. 162.

262   At 5 a.m. in San Francisco on Thursday morning, October 29: Ibid., p. 168.

262   "I am profoundly unhappy," he told reporters: Nocera, *A Piece of the Action*, p. 359.

263   In that secret session, Phelan acknowledged: Phelan Private Testimony, p. 5.

263   He did not sugarcoat the fears he had confronted: Ibid., p. 9.

263   what kind of equity market we want in this country: Ibid., pp. 28–29.

264   First Options, too, would muddle through: The First Options subsidiary never regained its pre-crash profitability, in large part because of the continued trading slump in the options markets. In 1991 it was repurchased by its previous owner, the NYSE specialist firm Spear, Leeds and Kellogg, for just $15 million.

264   The Bank of England would buy back any unsold shares: James Sterngold, "Market Turmoil: U.S. Underwriters Relieved by London Accord," *New York Times*, October 30, 1987, p. D9.

264   Layoffs at weakened Wall Street firms already threatened the economy: Mahar, *Bull*, p. 73. Mahar notes: "A year after the crash, securities transactions of all types were down 22 percent and some 15,000 Wall Streeters had lost their jobs."

265   A market almost brought to its knees by high-technology trading: Ruder interview July 2015.

21. PLACING BLAME, DODGING REALITY

266   A war of words had broken out: The tenor and content of this episode has been reconstructed and paraphrased from interviews with three of the participants: Second Melamed interview, Birnbaum interview, and an interview with William Brodsky on July 27, 2015. In a memoir, Melamed briefly described the breakfast (see *Escape to the Futures*, p. 382): "When Phelan invited me and other CME officials to sit down for talks with NYSE officials, at first he didn't mean the CBOT. But I held my ground and made certain the CBOT was invited. Ultimately, CBOT President Thomas Donovan and Chairman Karsten Mahlmann joined Brodsky, Sandner, and me in a meeting with Phelan at the New York Stock Exchange. Alas, the age-old animosities between the NYSE and the CBOT again came to the surface, resulting in a clash of egos, and little was accomplished."

266   *We were—we never closed!*: That, indeed, was the boast of a full-page ad the CBOT ran the next morning in the *New York Times*: "Minute by minute, second by second, we were there. During record volume and volatility, our markets performed without interruption."

266   *And the Merc closed only because you lied*: Several participants specifically recalled that each side was accusing the other of "making things up."

266   Leo Melamed respected John Phelan: First Melamed interview.

266   Melamed had recently told a friendly lawmaker: Scott McMurray and Bruce Ingersoll, "Post-Crash Damage Control at the Merc," *Wall Street Journal*, November 5, 1987.

267   all the NYSE specialists had performed heroically under fire: Brady Report, pp. 49–50. The report acknowledged that most specialists had leaned into the wind and bought heavily during the first ninety minutes on Black Monday "in the face of unprecedented selling pressure." But the specialists' performance from the final hours of Black Monday and through the trading day on Tuesday was far more uneven. According to the Brady Report, "a substantial number" of specialists had not met their obligation to be "a significant force in counterbalancing market trends." The report did concede that "[t]he limited nature of the specialists' contribution to price stability may have been due to the exhaustion of their purchasing power following attempts to stabilize markets" on the morning of Black Monday.

267   "our markets performed flawlessly during the crash": Melamed, *Escape to the Futures*, p. 373. Melamed actually called the phrase "the Merc's party line."

268   "it's in nobody's interest to be throwing hand grenades": James Sterngold, "Exchanges Seek Ways to Heal Split," *New York Times*, November 7, 1987, p. 37.

268   This kind of public acrimony was "bad for the industry": Second Melamed interview.

268   thanks to their generous political contributions: Steve Coll and David A. Vise, "Stock Futures Market Is Flexing Its Muscle," *Washington Post*, October 16, 1988, p. 1.

268   To the relief of everyone at the breakfast: Sterngold, "Exchanges Seek Ways to Heal Split."

268   the Brady Commission, appointed by President Reagan: The official name was the "Presidential Task Force on Market Mechanisms."

269   Brady was a man whose fourth-generation wealth: Brady's great-grandfather, an Irish immigrant, made the family's first fortune in the electrical utility industry; his grandfather founded an early automaker that later merged with Chrysler; and the family had a founding stake in the Purolator Company. See Susan F. Rasky, "Man in the News: Blue-Chip Leader for Task Force: Nicholas Frederick Brady," *New York Times*, October 23, 1987, p. D10.

269   To fill out the tribunal, Brady recruited: The commission was originally to have had three members, including Brady, but he told the White House he needed a five-member panel. The White House came up with a list of prospects that included former SEC chairmen John Shad and Harold Williams, former CFTC chairman Jim Stone, and GM pension fund manager Gordon Binns. But Brady made his own choices, recruiting James C. Cotting, the longtime CEO of Navistar International, based in Chicago; John R. Opel, the retired chairman of IBM and a source of technology expertise; Robert G. Kirby, the chairman of the Capital Guardian Trust Company in Los Angeles; and Howard M. Stein, the head of the Dreyfus family of mutual funds, based in New York.

269   who had once pitched an investment fund to the firm: Some years earlier, Glauber had persuaded Brady's firm to invest in a fund whose portfolio would be selected through computer-driven statistical analysis. The fund was ahead of its time, but unfortunately was also ahead of the available computing power and market data of its time, and was a short-lived failure.

269   but Brady did remember its razor-sharp founder: Interview with Nicholas F. Brady, September 25, 2014.

269   two months working almost around the clock for Nick Brady: Interviews with Robert R. Glauber, January 8 and 19, 2015 (hereafter Glauber interviews).

269   Early in November, his tiny team moved: William Glaberson, "A Task Force Plays Beat the Clock," *New York Times*, February 14, 1988, sec. 3, p. 4.

269   behind the scenes, they quietly ridiculed the commission: Christopher Ladd, "Agency File: The Brady Bunch," *Legal Times*, December 1, 1987, FG258-24, 548495CW, Ronald Reagan Presidential Library Archives. The article reported on comments that Bruce Bartlett, a former Heritage Foundation economist who joined the White House staff in August, had made at a conservative think-tank meeting that he "apparently thought . . . was off the record." Bartlett called Brady's Wall Street firm a "fuddy-duddy" investment house, and urged that the commission be ignored. In the Reagan archives, this article is attached to a memo from Arthur B. Culvahouse Jr., counsel to the president, to Howard Baker and three other senior White House aides. The memo called the article "a very disturbing report." A month earlier, Bartlett had warned his boss, Gary Bauer, that "Brady is a well-known opponent of virtually every financial innovation of the last ten years, including junk bonds, options, financial futures, mortgage-backed securities, etc. If he had his way we would turn the clock back to the 1950s." Bartlett reported that Christopher Cox, then a deputy counsel to Reagan and later SEC chairman under President George W. Bush, "is aware of the concerns I have and has tried to address

them." Memorandum for Gary Bauer from Bruce Bartlett, November 3, 1987, FG999/FI003, FG006-07, 54666480, Ronald Reagan Presidential Library Archives.

269   "it may just get lost in the shuffle": Memorandum for Gary Bauer from Bruce Bartlett, Subject: Brady Commission, October 29, 1987, FI003, No. 611055 PI, Ronald Reagan Presidential Library Archives.

269   The commission staff, which quickly grew: Anise C. Wallace, "Pension Fund Group Links Specialists to Stock Plunge," New York Times, December 8, 1987, p. D1. A month earlier, Binns attended a meeting of the CFTC's financial product advisory committee in Washington to defend program trading. (See Reuters, "Big Investors Defend Programmed Trading.") He had been joined at that meeting by Frederick Grauer, the president of Wells Fargo Investment Advisors. Grauer complained that Wall Street firms traded ahead of the sales by portfolio insurers to lock in a profit, thereby exacerbating the selling pressure in the futures market. This suspicion was, in fact, proven correct by the Brady Commission, which said that seven firms had sold short in immense volume on Friday, October 16, anticipating the sales that portfolio insurers would need to make on Monday. Remarkably, Grauer told the New York Times that he thought other money managers in the market should have waited for the portfolio insurers to trade first! (See Anise C. Wallace, "Portfolio Insurers Reject Blame," New York Times, January 13, 1988, p. D1.)

270   They demanded, and finally got, the cumbersome reels of computer tape: Nicholas F. Brady, A Way of Going, a privately published and undated memoir, p. 112. According to Brady, the NYSE had said it could not provide the computer records of the trade data, but he and Glauber discovered that the tapes were actually in the custody of the Depository Trust and Clearing Corporation, Wall Street's central clearinghouse. "We had our general counsel [Joel L. Cohen] call . . . and instruct its officers that if [the tapes] weren't delivered to our office by 10 a.m. that day, we would quietly tell the New York Times that the tapes were being withheld. Within two hours, ten boxes of computer tapes arrived at our door."

270   to borrow the computing power needed: Glaberson, "A Task Force Plays Beat the Clock." The assistance came from Brady commissioner John R. Opel's team from IBM, which also noticed that the commission had been equipped by the Treasury Department with "IBM clone" computers and arranged to replace them with IBM equipment.

270   a week after the White House nominated a deregulatory advocate: Robert D. Hershey Jr., "Business People: Deregulator Chosen for Commodity Post," New York Times, December 4, 1987, p. D2.

270   rules the agency published in the Federal Register were murky: Harris, "The CFTC and Derivative Products," p. 1125.

270   The new rules might render a host of over-the-counter swaps illegal: The CFTC's action was spurred by a proposal by Wells Fargo Bank in 1987 to issue certificates of deposit with the interest rate pegged to the price of gold. The CFTC sued the bank in the fall of 1987, claiming the new CD was an illegal futures contract. The bank dropped the product, but joined with the

nation's other giant banks to protest the CFTC's action. See Nathaniel C. Nash, "A Chill over the Hot New 'Hybrids,'" *New York Times*, April 10, 1988, sec. 3, p. 1.

270   who saw swaps as a huge source of profit: One reason these over-the-counter swaps were so profitable, of course, was precisely because they were not publicly traded. Buyers of a swap had no way of knowing what others were paying at that moment for similar arrangements, so it was a seller's market.

271   A blizzard had swept into Washington: Robert D. McFadden, "Storm Hits East Coast After Burying South in Snow," *New York Times*, January 9, 1988, p. 1.

271   That morning's edition of the *New York Times* had a front-page story: Nathaniel C. Nash, "Task Force Urges a Major Overhaul of Stock Trading," *New York Times*, January 8, 1988, p. 1. The article incorrectly reported, based on the hostile leaks, that the commission would call for limits on daily stock price movements, similar to the daily limits sometimes imposed in the futures pits. The next day's story, based on the actual report, explained that inaccuracy: "The commission, however, apparently backed away from a radical proposal to impose limits on the daily price movements of all stocks." See Nathaniel C. Nash, "Task Force Ties Market Collapse to Big Investors' Program Trades," *New York Times*, January 9, 1988, p. 1. (In fact, both Brady and Glauber said in interviews that stock market price limits had never been even a draft recommendation.) To their credit, the major papers did not give the actual release of the report lesser play as "second-day news," as the administration's leakers may have hoped.

271   A call to the White House produced two weather-worthy vehicles: Glaberson, "A Task Force Plays Beat the Clock."

271   after a brief wait, they were ushered into the Oval Office: Glauber interviews. No one seems to recall Greenspan's presence at this brief meeting, so one can assume he didn't play a large role, but Brady's photograph of the event clearly shows Greenspan on one of the two sofas, next to Glauber.

272   with most of the decline coming in the final thirty minutes: Kenneth N. Gilpin, "Dollar Falls as Stocks Plummet," *New York Times*, January 9, 1988, p. D1.

272   it was the third-largest decline in history: The second-ranking loss was the 156.83-point drop on October 26, 1987.

272   A single agency should be responsible for harmonizing: Nash, "Task Force Ties Market Collapse to Big Investors' Program Trades," p. 1.

272   Its report offered Washington and Main Street a chance: The report remained, thirty years later, the most prominent of all the studies on the 1987 crash and certainly the most accessible and engaging one for a general reader. In a letter to President Reagan dated February 2, 1988, Charles Schwab called the report "outstanding." (See White House Correspondence Tracking Worksheet, FI003, 544319, Ronald Reagan Presidential Library Archives, p. 2.) Brady himself proudly reported later that investor Warren Buffett had told him the report was "the finest piece of reporting of a financial event he'd ever seen." (See "Remembering Black Monday: Nicholas Brady," *Fortune*, online archive at http://archive.fortune.com/galleries/2007/fortune/0709/gallery.black _monday.fortune/10.html.)

273   "The idea that less than 10 large institutions": James Sterngold, "Panel's

Concern: Power, Not Panic," *New York Times*, January 9, 1988, p. 39. Stern-gold continued: "The fundamental fact that the report underscored is that these institutions do not act like individuals. Using computers and sophisti-cated trading strategies, they have the ability to scan several different mar-kets at once and operate in them simultaneously." He noted that Congress had studied the growing concentration of institutional wealth almost two decades earlier, but it had concluded that giant funds were not acting in tandem then, and therefore did not pose a threat. That clearly was no longer true.

274   the Brady Report, and numerous other official studies: A separate book could be written comparing the various studies of the 1987 crash. Except for the CFTC study, which denied that there was any correlation between the stock market's period of sharp declines and selling related to portfolio insurance, they generally agreed that portfolio insurance strategies played *some* role in accelerating the decline, but they disagreed about how large that role was or what to do about it. They all agreed that breakdowns in the computer and com-munications systems exacerbated the developing panic, but implicitly left the creation and maintenance of such systems to the exchanges and their member firms. They agreed that coordinating the clearing and settlement process would be a good thing, but also agreed that doing so posed daunting difficulties. None of them even tried to tackle the problem of protecting the financial sys-tem from the immense power wielded by the giant investors who dominated the marketplace. Instead, their focus was on pushing the marketplace to find ways to provide the scale and speed that these giant investors demanded.

274   far more focused on his duties as a central banker: It is telling that neither Greenspan's memoir of these years nor any of the biographies by those with close access to him includes the "President's Working Group" as an index entry.

274   Ruder, who was growing increasingly convinced: It probably did not help that Wendy Gramm's husband, Texas Republican senator Phil Gramm, was so con-temptuous of Ruder's requests for additional SEC funding. When Ruder pre-sented the SEC's immense report on Black Monday to the Senate Banking Committee on February 3, 1988, Senator Gramm was in rare form: "Anybody's that's got a staff that could write that [report] does not have too small a staff. In fact, I would argue that that would be a fertile area to look at staff reduction. Also, a 26-page executive summary? Maybe you need a *chief* executive sum-mary that summarizes the summary. [Laughter.]" (See "'Black Monday': The Stock Market Crash of October 19, 1987," Hearings Before the Senate Commit-tee on Banking, Housing, and Urban Affairs, 100th Congress, 2nd Sess., Febru-ary 2–5, 1988, p. 133.)

275   "we're trying to put some thoughts out on the table": Nash, "A Chill over the Hot New 'Hybrids.'"

275   The harshest rebuttals came from Gramm's fellow regulators: Harris, "The CFTC and Derivative Products," pp. 1126, 61*ff*.

275   The SEC's response was exceptionally fierce: Ibid.

275   those being made by the nation's top bankers: Nash, "A Chill over the Hot New 'Hybrids.'"

275   "there must be coordination among various agencies": Ibid.

276   the CFTC backed off from this effort, creating an exemption: See Wendy L. Gramm and Gerald D. Gay, "Scams, Scoundrels, and Scapegoats: A Taxonomy of CEA Regulation over Derivative Instruments," *Journal of Derivatives* (Spring 1994), pp. 6–24.

276   He planned to meet up with John O'Brien: LOR interview 2016.

276   LOR's hedging strategy had mitigated their losses: Kyrillos, *Cases in Financial Engineering*, p. 778.

276   but it had also pulled them out of the market: Of course, that was the very complaint Leland's brother had made about the fate of his clients in the 1970s—the complaint that put Leland on the path toward portfolio insurance.

276   You cannot hedge in markets where you cannot trade: Douglas Frantz, "Leland O'Brien's Image Marred in 'Meltdown': Pioneer Portfolio Insurers on the Defensive as Role in Market Skid Is Questioned," *Los Angeles Times*, November 2, 1987.

276   After the crash, he experienced what he later regarded: MacKenzie, *An Engine, Not a Camera*, p. 206. The author asked Rubinstein to review Mackenzie's manuscript, and he did not dispute this passage.

276   One account reported: Ibid.

277   No less a monument than Harry Markowitz: Bernard Saffran, "Recommendations for Further Reading," *Journal of Economic Perspectives* 3, no. 1 (Winter 1989), p. 185. Markowitz would win the Nobel Memorial Prize in Economics in 1990, along with Merton Miller, a fierce defender of portfolio insurance and derivative markets, and William Sharpe.

277   Was it possible that "sunshine trading" could have ameliorated: See Gerard Gennotte and Hayne Leland, "Market Liquidity, Hedging, and Crashes," *American Economic Review* 80, no. 5 (December 1990), pp. 999–1021. This paper suggests that "relatively small unobserved supply shocks [i.e., sudden waves of selling] can have pronounced effects—more than 100 times greater than the effects of observed supply shocks—on current market prices . . . as a consequence of investors inferring information from prices. A supply shock leads to lower prices, which in turn (since the shock is unobserved) leads uninformed investors to revise downwards their expectations. This limits these investors' willingness to absorb the extra supply and causes a magnified price response." The paper basically concedes that "unanticipated hedging plans can lead to a 'meltdown' scenario. A small information change can trigger lower prices, which because of hedging lead to greater excess supply and a further fall in prices." But it concludes that "some changes in market organization can radically reduce the likelihood of crashes . . . Pre-announcement of trading requirements can lessen the impact of such trades by a factor greater than 100."

277   Leland believed it was not only possible but likely: Mackenzie, *An Engine, Not a Camera*, p. 196. Leland told MacKenzie, "If everybody knows that we are uninformed traders, then people don't revise their expectations downward when the price falls. They just say things are on sale. Then they will take the

other side more willingly. If everyone thinks the price is falling because somebody has information, then they won't take the other side." This analysis does
not allow for the Wall Street firms that began to anticipate portfolio insurance
trading and took positions to profit from it.

277   Flames were shooting from the shattered windows: The fire, in which one
maintenance worker was killed and a number were injured, began on the floor
below LOR's suite, where First Interstate Bank had a large government bond
trading desk. The cause was never determined. See Robert Reinhold, "Survivors Recall Terror of Tower Fire," *New York Times*, May 7, 1988, p. 36.

277   whose advance they finally halted on the sixteenth floor: Robert Reinhold,
"Los Angeles High-Rise Fire Kills One; Officials Cite Lack of Sprinklers," *New
York Times*, May 6, 1988, p. A20.

277   The LOR partners were immensely relieved to learn: LOR interview 2016.

278   and Black Monday encouraged its critics: Fox, *The Myth of the Rational Market*, p. 232.

278   Ruder rebelled against the reluctant regulators: David S. Ruder, "An SEC
Chairman's Recollection," June 2, 2004, pp. 5–6, SECHS website, used with
permission from www.sechistorical.org, http://3197d6d14b5f19f2f440-5e13d2
9c4c016cf96cbbfd197c579b45.r81.cf1.rackcdn.com/collection/papers/2000
/2004_0602_SECHS_RT_Ch_Ruder.pdf.

278   the most memorable of his SEC tenure: Ibid., p. 4.

279   filed a landmark civil complaint against Drexel Burnham: SEC Litigation
Release No. 11859, September 7, 1988.

279   it turned to former SEC chairman John Shad: Kurt Eichenwald, "Drexel Talking to Shad on Chairman's Job," *New York Times*, January 12, 1988, p. D1.
According to Eichenwald, Drexel had initially tried to recruit White House
Chief of Staff Howard Baker for the job. Drexel would file for bankruptcy in
1990.

279   the five-day pageantry surrounding the inauguration: Michael Oreskes,
"Transition in Washington: Lights! Action! Inauguration Is Underway," *New
York Times*, January 19, 1989, p. 1.

279   many futures market executives were in Washington: Melamed, *Escape to the
Futures*, p. 390.

279   FBI agents were fanning out across Chicago: Greising and Morse, *Brokers,
Bagmen, and Moles*, pp. 19–20.

280   by news of a sweeping federal investigation: Ibid., p. 220.

280   federal agents had gone undercover: Ibid., p. 230.

280   the CFTC had not been as out of touch as reported: Ibid.

280   neither of Wendy Gramm's predecessors had known: Ibid., p. 231.

280   until a week before the subpoenas were served: Nathaniel C. Nash, "C.F.T.C.
Insists It Had Role All Along," *New York Times*, January 24, 1989, p. D11.
Gramm called a press conference, which Nash called "extraordinary," to
counter reports that the CFTC had not played a role in the case. She explained
that she was disclosing the agency's role in the investigation to buttress investor confidence in the CFTC's oversight of the futures markets.

280   fully six hundred days after Black Monday: Birinyi and Rubin, *Market Cycles III*, p. 304.

280   markets were still languishing: By November 1988, compared with September 1987, NYSE trading volume had dropped 24 percent, trading in the Merc's S&P 500 contracts was down 54 percent, trading in the CBOE's S&P 100 options contract had declined 48 percent, and the number of large block trades on the NYSE had fallen 20 percent. See Seligman, *The Transformation of Wall Street*, p. 591.

281   "If we forget what we did," the president said: R. W. Apple Jr., "Reagan, in Farewell, Warns Against Loss of Spirit," *New York Times*, January 12, 1989, p. 1. The poignancy of that farewell message became clearer when Reagan disclosed, in 1994, that he had been diagnosed with Alzheimer's disease, which steadily erased the memories he had collected in his years in the White House. He died on June 5, 2004; Nancy Reagan passed away in 2016.

EPILOGUE

282   a number of baffling market malfunctions: In August 2012 a malfunctioning computer at Knight Capital Group started spitting out a flood of inadvertent orders, costing the firm $440 million and roiling the rest of the market; in August 2013, Nasdaq was abruptly shut down for three hours when its electronic in-box was overwhelmed with erroneous messages from the automated NYSE market; and in July 2015, the NYSE was frozen for hours by a computer glitch—just to name a few of the technology failures in recent years. Each took a toll on investor confidence and most cost at least some investors money.

282   four extremely disruptive market crises: On Friday, October 13, 1989, the Dow suddenly fell almost 7 percent, thanks in part to heavy selling by Wall Street firms trying to hedge the risks they'd taken on by selling a new-fangled portfolio insurance based on options. (See Office of Technology Assessment of the U.S. Congress, "Electronic Bulls & Bears: U.S. Securities Markets & Information Technology," OTA-CIT-469 [Washington, DC: U.S. Government Printing Office, September 1990].) In September 1998 a giant hedge fund in Connecticut that owed billions of dollars to giant Wall Street firms had to be rescued from the brink of default after private derivatives that were supposed to insure its counterparties against market losses backfired. (See Bruce I. Jacobs, "Risk Avoidance and Market Fragility," *Financial Analysts Journal* 60, no. 1 [January/February 2004]," pp. 26–30. For details of the collapse of the fund Long Term Capital Management, see Diana B. Henriques, "Billions and Billions: Fault Lines of Risk Appear as Market Hero Stumbles," *New York Times*, September 27, 1998, p. 1.) On May 6, 2010, an estimated $1 trillion was lost during a mysterious twenty-minute "flash crash" that saw blue-chip stock prices dive down to pennies a share in just a few seconds, before rebounding. (See Testimony of SEC Chairman Mary L. Schapiro, "Examining the Causes and Lessons of the May 6th Market Plunge," Hearing Before the Securities, Insurance, and Investment Subcommittee of the House Committee on Banking,

Housing, and Urban Affairs, 111th Congress, 2nd Sess., May 20, 2010, pp. 3-5.) On October 15, 2014, a similar and unprecedented "flash crash" hit the supposedly deep and efficient Treasury market; analysts later cited the runaway role of algorithm-driven computerized trading by giant institutional traders. (See "Joint Staff Report: The U.S. Treasury Market on October 15, 2014," produced by the Treasury, the Federal Reserve, the Federal Reserve Bank of New York, the SEC and the CFTC, July 13, 2015.) And on August 24, 2015, the Dow index plunged a record 1,089 points at the opening bell, rebounded amid sharp gyrations, and then dropped right at the final bell to close down 6.6 percent, or 588 points; extreme volatility triggered market "circuit breakers" more than 1,200 times that day. (See Matt Egan, "After Historic 1,000-Point Plunge, Dow Dives 588 Points at Close," CNN Money website, August 25, 2015.)

282   "in the current Balkanized regulatory system": Testimony of Christopher Cox, Chairman, U.S. Securities and Exchange Commission, "The Financial Crisis and the Role of Federal Regulators" (hereafter "Waxman Hearing 2008"), Hearing Before the House Committee on Oversight and Government Reform, 110th Congress, 2nd Sess., October 23, 2008. The online version of these hearings is not paginated, but a searchable text file is available at https://www.gpo.gov/fdsys/pkg/CHRG-110hhrg55764/html/CHRG-110hhrg55764.htm. In that version, Cox's statement is on p. 12.

282   "no single regulator has a clear view, a 360-degree view": Testimony of former Treasury secretary John Snow, Waxman Hearing 2008, p. 15 of the text version.

284   His legacy includes a $30 million gift he made in March 1987: Alison Leigh Cowan, "Harvard to Get $30 Million Ethics Gift," New York Times, March 31, 1987, p. D1.

284   Black Monday was hailed as "his shining hour": William Alden, "Dealbook: John Phelan Jr., Ex-Head of Big Board, Dies at 81," New York Times, August 7, 2012.

284   But that trading floor was largely deserted: As of this writing, some options trading continued to take place in a part of the facility.

284   to become chairman and chief executive: In 2013, Brodsky stepped down as CEO but continued as chairman until his retirement in early 2017. He was the longest-serving chairman in CBOE history.

285   The dust jacket carries a complimentary quote from Paul Volcker: One of the challenges Stone cited was "reining in Wall Street."

285   died in 2002: No byline, "Gordon Binns Jr. dies—advised VRS." A copy is available in GenLookups.com's obituary online archive at http://www.genlookups.com/va/webbbs_config.pl/noframes/read/434.

285   as one of the top-performing: Interview with Roland M. Machold, February 11, 2017.

285   perhaps because their idea was novel and complex: Kyrillos, Cases in Financial Engineering, p. 804.

286   dubbed the trio "The Committee to Save the World": The cover was for the February 13, 1999, issue.

286   favored a more laissez-faire approach to market regulation: Testimony of Alan Greenspan, Waxman Hearing 2008, pp. 17–18 in the searchable text file.

286   His confidence that Wall Street could be trusted: Ibid.

286   simply did not give enough weight to raw human nature: Alan Greenspan, *The Map and the Territory 2.0: Risk, Human Nature, and the Future of Forecasting* (New York: Penguin Books, 2013/2014), pp. 8, 18–34.

ACKNOWLEDGMENTS

Once again, I find myself thanking my lucky stars for the four guardian angels who have helped me get another book across the finish line. My irrepressible agent, Fredrica S. Friedman, saw me through dead ends and detours, and gave me excellent advice along the way. My editor at Henry Holt, Paul Golob, not only performed his usual (but by no means ordinary!) magic with the manuscript but also helped shape the concept of this book from our very first "brainstorming" lunch in 2013. My assistant Barbara Oliver, surely the most relentless bloodhound in the world of archival and online research, once again applied her formidable skills to the task of unearthing treasures filed away thirty and forty years ago. And above all, with archangel status, my husband Larry Henriques sustained and supported this project—and all the projects of my career—with unflagging generosity, love, and patience.

An additional angel has joined the team—Jody Hotchkiss, who represented me brilliantly in marketing the film rights for *The Wizard of Lies* and who shared his inspired cinematic instincts as I struggled with this complex story. It was enhanced by his help, and I was frequently reenergized by his enthusiasm.

I am also enormously in debt to the people who populated the front lines during the "Crash of the Eighties" and opened their files and their memories to me. Some of them have asked to remain anonymous, but they know who they are—and I will never forget their help. Among those who are cited by name, a few stand out for special recognition.

At the top of that list is Dr. David S. Ruder, the William W. Gurley Memorial Professor of Law Emeritus at Northwestern University. Besides sharing his remarkable memories, Dr. Ruder also gave me access to his personal archives from his tenure as the twenty-third chairman of the U.S. Securities and Exchange Commission. His records are a precious historical resource, and I hope they someday find a home where scholars can mine them even more deeply than I could. I am also grateful for the help of his assistant, Maryanne Martinez.

Chicago is truly a city of financial giants, and I was fortunate to have had the assistance of some of its best and brightest. William J. Brodsky, who was president of the Chicago Mercantile Exchange during the crash, was enthusiastic, thoughtful, and very funny—and his assistant Tudy Gomez made my life easier in a half-dozen ways during journeys to Chicago. The extraordinary Leo Melamed, a towering presence in the financial world for more than a half century, provided both heat and light for this story, and I will never forget our conversations.

Nicholas F. Brady spent hours sharing his memories of a distinguished life on Wall Street and in Washington; his account was augmented by Dr. Robert R. Glauber, who led the Brady Commission staff in producing a document that makes an incalculable contribution to America's financial history. Paul Volcker and E. Gerald Corrigan, both giants in the realm of banking regulation, were helpful and wise. Roland Machold, who was my first call on financial issues when I was a young reporter at the *Trenton Times* in the late 1970s, continued in that generous tradition by sharing both his acute memories and his unpublished memoirs. Dean LeBaron, David P. Feldman, and Amanda Binns Meller helped me evoke the character of Amanda's father, the late W. Gordon Binns, a gentle presence in this story. Richard Torrenzano and Sharon Gamsin, who were at John Phelan's elbow at the New York Stock Exchange during most of the years described in this book, shared not only their memories but their scrapbooks and address books. Retired FINRA chief executive Richard Ketchum, whose career as a financial regulator spanned this story and much of its aftermath, was unfailingly helpful—as was Nancy Condon, his communications chief. Dr. James M. Stone, Dr. Richard L. Sandor, and Philip McBride Johnson were sources of great insight into the "preamble years" of the late 1970s and early '80s. And Terrence A. Duffy, the chairman and chief executive of the CME Group, generously made his corporation's archives available to me in the crucial early days of my research.

I also want to thank the formidable Tim Metz, the author of *Black Monday: The Catastrophe of October 19, 1987 . . . and Beyond*. His meticulous research, conducted in the weeks and months immediately after the October meltdown, was immensely helpful, particularly his careful reconstruction of events inside the NYSE on Black Monday and Tuesday.

An extra helping of gratitude is owed to Professors Hayne Leland, Mark Rubinstein, and John O'Brien at the University of California–Berkeley. All three had very good reasons to be wary of any project exploring their role in the epic changes that shaped the American marketplace in the 1980s. Nevertheless, they responded to my frequent queries with generosity, a scholarly care for accuracy, and unfailing patience as I climbed my steep "quantitative" learning curve. Their willingness to share their story, with its successes and its disappointments, enriched my research beyond measure.

And thank goodness for archivists and librarians!

Carla Rosati, the capable director of the SEC Historical Society until early 2017, was an invaluable resource, and I hope everyone who enjoys this book will make a tax-deductible gift to the society, as I have done. Ditto for the Museum of American Finance, a Smithsonian affiliate in Manhattan and an important repository for an essential facet of American history that too often gets sent to the corporate shredder or the Dumpster.

In alphabetical order—because choosing first place would be impossible among so many helpful souls!—my thanks also go out to interim director Linda Beninghove at the Samuel C. Williams Library at Stevens Institute of Technology; assistant professor Laura Kristina Bronstad at the Baker Center of the University of Tennessee at Knoxville; Megan Keller, project archivist for the CME Group Collection at the University of Illinois at Chicago; special collections librarian Laura Linard at the Harvard Business School's Baker Library; archivist Jennifer Mandel at the Ronald Reagan Presidential Library and Museum; librarian David May at the Commodity Futures Trading Commission; librarian Herb Somers at the Jacob Burns Law Library at the George Washington University Law School; librarian Scott Vanderlin at the Illinois Institute of Technology's Chicago-Kent Law School; and archivist Stephen Wheeler at the NYSE archives in Mahwah, New Jersey, now a unit of the Intercontinental Exchange's NYSE subsidiary.

My cherished friends in the world of financial journalism, and their significant others in some cases, both encouraged and informed my research. Special thanks go out to CNN veterans Susan Lisovicz and Mike Kandel; my former *New York Times* colleague Leslie Eaton and her husband, Professor Mark Vamos; and my former *Barron's* colleague Jaye Scholl and her husband, Charles E. Bohlen Jr., one of my first readers for this project. Other friends and family—especially my sister Peggy van der Swaagh and sisters-in-law Noel Brakenhoff and Teakie Welty—have been extraordinarily patient with my three-year obsession with the 1980s, and with all the distractions and demands of the book-writing process. Thank you, each and every one.

I owe a final word of gratitude—truly bottomless gratitude—to Floyd Norris, my colleague first at *Barron's* magazine and then, for nearly twenty-five years, at the *New York Times*. Floyd's contribution to financial journalism during his long career is a testament to his integrity, his indefatigable research, and his simple brilliance. For that, we should all be grateful. But my debt to him is more personal: When I arrived at *Barron's* in 1986, I was woefully unprepared for the intensity of financial research required by *Barron's* legendary editor Alan Abelson. I would not have lasted a month without Floyd's tireless tutorials. In 1989 he recommended me for an opening on the *New York Times*, and thereby shaped the rest of my professional career. His friendship enriched my personal life, too, and we have seen each other over a lot of rocky ground that had nothing to do with market crashes or accounting scandals. Add to that the errors he kept me from making in print, the accounting puzzles he helped me solve, and the laughter he brought to my years in the newsroom.

Floyd and I share a passion for financial history, and it is my honor to dedicate this book to him. It does not come close to repaying the debt I owe, but it is the least I can do.

INDEX

ABOUT THE AUTHOR

DIANA B. HENRIQUES is the author of the *New York Times* bestseller *The Wizard of Lies: Bernie Madoff and the Death of Trust*, which has been made into an HBO film starring Robert De Niro and Michelle Pfeiffer. A writer for *The New York Times* since 1989, she is a George Polk Award winner and a Pulitzer Prize finalist. Her work has also received Harvard's Goldsmith Prize for Investigative Reporting and the Worth Bingham Prize, among other honors. She lives in Hoboken, New Jersey.